Antony Beevor was educated at Winchester and Sandhurst. A regular officer in the 11th Hussars, he served in Germany and England until he resigned his commission after five years in the Army. His fourth novel, *The Enchantment of Christina von Retzen*, was published in 1991. His other works of non-fiction have been a history of the Spanish Civil War and *Crete – The Battle and the Resistance*.

'Antony Beevor's book is an impressive achievement. It brings together an enormous amount of material, clear and accessible, and is a fair and forthright analysis of an Army and a society faced by enormous change and not quite sure how to react'
Evening Standard

'The book is one for the connoisseur . . . It is obvious from the thoroughness of his work that he was given an almost total freedom in his search for a balanced approach'
New Statesman & Society

'Beevor is a perfect interpreter in a mysterious world. His sharp social anthropologist's eye and story-telling skills combine to make what he found in a two-year journey through the British Army compelling'
Christy Campbell, *Sunday Correspondent*

'This very readable anatomy provides a many-faceted answer, which paradoxically, is both encouraging and alarming'
General Sir William Jackson, *Country Life*

'Extraordinarily well researched and lucid . . . we are taken in exacting scrutiny from soldier to officer, through the Ministry of Defence and the Regimental system . . . I strongly recomr
Major General S   *Institute Journal*

'A very well-written book, daunting both in its scope and detail'
Colin Wallace, *Sunday Tribune*

'Essential reading for anyone who wants to understand how the Army really works'
Peter Tatchell, *Tribune*

'There are wonderful details of behaviour and attitudes from the humblest "Tom" private to the most ambitious general that are enough to purple the face of the caricature Colonel Retired'
Charles Laurence, *Sunday Telegraph*

'Beevor not only crams an enormous amount of interesting and relevant information about the contemporary army into a reasonably sized book, but also manages to be funny, at times moving, at appropriate moments'
Anthony Powell in 'Books of the Year', *Spectator*

INSIDE THE
BRITISH ARMY

Antony Beevor

CORGI BOOKS

INSIDE THE BRITISH ARMY
A CORGI BOOK 0 552 13818 5

Originally published in Great Britain by
Chatto & Windus Ltd

PRINTING HISTORY
Chatto & Windus edition published 1990
Corgi updated edition published 1991

A CIP catalogue record for this book is available
from the British Library

This book is set in 10/11pt Plantin by
Falcon Typographic Art Ltd., Edinburgh & London

Corgi Books are published by Transworld Publishers Ltd.,
61–63 Uxbridge Road, Ealing, London W5 5SA, in Australia
by Transworld Publishers (Australia) Pty. Ltd., 15–23 Helles
Avenue, Moorebank, NSW 2170, and in New Zealand
by Transworld Publishers (N.Z.) Ltd., Cnr. Moselle and
Waipareira Avenues, Henderson, Auckland.

Made and printed in Great Britain by
Cox & Wyman Ltd, Reading, Berkshire

For Eleanor

Contents

PART FIVE: CONCLUSION

APPENDICES

CHARTS

Foreword

Six months after the original edition of this book was published, the ground offensive in the Gulf began. The implications of that unprecedented conflict are far-reaching: at the height of the ground battle, a staff officer in the Ministry of Defence remarked: 'People are going to be writing reports after this that'll keep 'em going for years.'

The point of this new revised edition is not to analyse the conduct of the land/air battle or assess the equipment, but to give an impression of how the Army, suffering from a depressing range of handicaps, managed to cope with great success, and how it now faces a very changed future. The purpose is still to describe the Army as an institution – a unique society awaiting dramatic changes, including the death of many regiments, with very mixed feelings.

No serving soldier needs to be reminded of the ironies over the past couple of years. At the start of 1990, while the Warsaw Pact and the Iron Curtain collapsed in rusty fragments, 'the next fixture', as the Army called the threat of World War Three in Nato's central region, looked as if it had been indefinitely postponed, if not cancelled. A euphoric press began to predict that the Army was virtually out of a job. Politicians on all sides were delighted at the prospect of the peace dividend. The 'heavy army' in Germany, with its armour and artillery, was the first to be measured up for the axe. Everything looked so simple to most commentators. Only a new lean, light army was needed: an international fire-fighting force. But then, in the very first post-Cold-War conflict, the British ground force deployed was a reinforced armoured division from Germany; and that most endangered of species, cavalry mounted in Challenger tanks, charged across the television screens as if in a Hollywood remake of Pathé newsreels from the Western Desert.

Yet in spite of the most devastatingly successful campaign in history, the decision-making process on the future of the Army, begun in the 'Options for Change' proposals set out by Tom King shortly before the Gulf crisis, had to proceed rapidly. The Army, as Field Marshal Sir Nigel Bagnall argued, needed to know the 'really painful decisions' without delay. If its suffering was 'callously prolonged', he warned, the effect on morale, and thus on the Army's ability to retain its most able personnel, would be disastrous.[1]

Several years of false economies from the salami-slicing of budgets and the evasion or postponement of decisions had created an underlying lack of confidence in Whitehall management. But the Army, as its own senior officers acknowledge, does not make decision-making easy. Its tribal intricacies, based on regimental and arm loyalties, and the Byzantine rivalries in the Ministry of Defence between the Services turn the process into a three-dimensional game of noughts and crosses with the players trying to block each other to save themselves. According to the current joke (which also highlights the Army's curious relish for mixed metaphors), 'All the chickens have come home to roost, but there's no room to land because the field is full of sacred cows.'

The power of regimental lobbies, reaching to Buckingham Palace, the House of Lords and the back-benches of the House of Commons, should not be underestimated, especially after a spectacularly successful war. In the months following the war, all levels in the Army were wondering whether the Army Board dared axe a regiment which fought in the Gulf? What of the other regiments and battalions who provided large reinforcement teams, sometimes whole squadrons and companies to bring the others up to strength? Would it boil down to the old system of chopping the junior regiment or battalion

– thus taking a decision on the grounds of historic precedence rather than military efficacy? Or would a quasi-Darwinian system of selection be employed: cutting the most under-strength units?

No quarter was expected in the battle of the regiments. 'God helps those who help themselves,' said an infantry brigadier in the Ministry of Defence, dismissing any sympathy for understrength battalions. Perhaps a measure of one's pity should be reserved for those who had to come up with a solution. That they would be hated more than loved was virtually a certainty.

The underlying problems described in the hardback edition of this book, essentially the effect of major changes in society at large which the Army faced before the Gulf war, are still covered in some detail because their importance has not diminished. One of the most encouraging signs, on the other hand, is the shift in official attitudes towards Army families.

Some senior officers had been very reluctant to come to terms with the grievances of wives, mainly because their natural desire for stability, with jobs and homes of their own, put the traditional system at risk: the individual family was threatening the regimental family. The change of view which has taken place was not entirely altruistic: something had to be done because the dissatisfaction of wives was persuading so many of the Army's best officers and NCOs to leave. Yet a new mood of realism had already spread before Operation Granby started. Deployment to the Gulf made improvements gather speed, mainly because the Army is at its best in a crisis. A scale of effort and imagination seldom seen during the last two decades of service in Northern Ireland was devoted to helping wives while their husbands were away. It is too soon to tell whether this change is capable of maintaining momentum, or whether the *status quo ante bellum* – bogged down by lack of funds, by administrative inertia and by an inherent reluctance to tamper with the traditional way of doing things – will gradually return.

One of the surprises of the first post-Cold-War year, when the future for a military career looked at its bleakest, is that officer recruiting picked up. The exodus from the ranks, on the other hand, accelerated. If the strength of 135,600 soldiers and servicewomen at 1 January 1990 given in the Statement on Defence Estimates was correct, then the Army suffered a net loss of 8,800 men by the end of January 1991, when non-commissioned strength stood at 126,800. This amounted to an average net loss of 680 men per month – roughly equivalent to a battalion a month.

The result of this haemorrhage has been the 'patchwork' regiment, when battalions ordered to Northern Ireland have to make up numbers by borrowing platoons and even companies from other units before they can hope to carry out their duties. Regiments sent to the Gulf needed considerably more reinforcements to come up to war establishment. One under-strength battalion ended up with men from twenty different capbadges serving in its ranks.

Not surprisingly, there is a widespread feeling that a 'patchwork' regiment, even with the best will in the world, can never perform as well as one which has lived and trained together. Whatever the decisions made by Nato for the post-Cold War years, it was clear that if regiments were not reduced in number and reorganized then the regimental system itself was at risk.

The next couple of years, with the disbandment or amalgamation of many regiments and battalions, may be sad for the Army but they are unlikely to be boring. This begs the assumption, of course, that the political will is there to make the necessary decisions. The post-Gulf debate will indeed be intense and wide-ranging: the budgetary implications of the high-technology land/air battle; the drastic reduction and reorganization of Nato armies; the creation of a rapid reaction force; the role of the attack helicopter within an air mobile division; the future of the main battle tank – all these have huge implications beyond technology and tactics. Decisions will affect the whole infrastructure of the Army, its nature, its deployment, its ethos and, above all, the lives of those who serve in it.

Acknowledgements

This book and the subsequent revisions for the paperback edition following the Gulf war were possible only with the brave co-operation of the Ministry of Defence, which allowed me unlimited access to all but the most secret areas. I would particularly like to thank Major General Sam Cowan, and his successors, Major General Christopher Wallace and Brigadier Bryan Dutton.

I am very grateful to all the staff officers who arranged visits and organized meetings with the individuals I wanted to interview: Major Spencer Gammond, 5th Royal Inniskilling Dragoon Guards, Captain Joanna Barry WRAC, and her replacement at the Ministry of Defence, Captain Jill Turner WRAC; Major Peter Roberts, Army Air Corps, at the Directorate of Army Training; Dermod Hill, the Chief Public Relations Officer at HQ United Kingdom Land Forces; Major John Wilkinson, The King's Regiment, at Joint Headquarters British Forces Germany; Lieutenant Colonel Rob Stewart, Royal Artillery, at HQ 1st (British) Corps; Major Piers Drew-Wilkinson, Royal Scots, at HQ 1st Armoured Division; those at HQ Northern Ireland; Philip Simpson at HQ British Forces Falkland Islands; and all those officers within units and establishments who organized my programmes.

To give an idea of the scale of their task – and of my gratitude for their efforts – in the course of nine months I visited 11 major units, 9 minor units, 13 training establishments, 5 recruiting offices and selection establishments, 6 arms directorates, 8 theatre and formation headquarters, and 14 departments of the Ministry of Defence. During the course of these visits and on other occasions I talked with 10 generals, 13 brigadiers, 16 colonels, 40 lieutenant colonels, 65 majors, 54 captains, 24 lieutenants, 15 second lieutenants, 14 officer cadets, 13 warrant officers Class I, 23 warrant officers Class II, 7 staff sergeants, 31 sergeants, 22 corporals, 16 lance corporals, and 37 privates. My debt to all these necessarily nameless individuals – anonymity was the only way I could expect them to speak freely – is enormous for their time, trouble and frankness.

I would also like to thank the following, either for consenting to be interviewed, or for their help and advice in other ways: Rupert Allason MP; Anne Armstrong; Dr Anthony Clayton; Colonel Michael Gaffney; Rt Hon. Michael Heseltine PC, MP; Captain David Horne; Lady Huxtable and members of the Federation of Army Wives; Rt Hon. Sir John Nott PC, MP; David Shukman; Sir James Spooner; Marie Thomas; and Sir Peter Wilkinson.

One of my biggest debts is owed to the officers I asked to read and comment on particular chapters in manuscript. They came from various parts of the Army and ranged in rank from second lieutenant to major general, although most were majors and colonels. Some of them were already friends; others were individuals I had met on my travels and whose judgement I respected. In a number of instances they have saved me from committing both blunders and injustices. Any which remain are, of course, my responsibility entirely. My other saviour, in this case from the more incomprehensible and awkward paragraphs, was my editor, Jeremy Lewis, who also helped enormously from the beginning with his suggestions on structure.

My greatest gratitude, as always, is owed to my wife, Artemis. With remarkable good humour she put up with my desertions and unsocial hours, and interrupted work on her own book to read passages and advise. Her apparent fascination with my descriptions of military life gave me much-needed encouragement at crucial moments, and her comments on the manuscript have been an incalculable help.

Introduction

My last major exercise took place south of Hanover in October 1968. In those days I commanded four Chieftain tanks in the form of 2 Troop, C Squadron, the 11th Hussars. During the long waits, of which there were many, I used to play chess with Trooper Dean, the loader/operator on my tank. We played with our heads and shoulders out of the top of the turret and the board laid out between our hatches. One of us studied the horizon through large binoculars while the other pondered his move. Meanwhile, deep inside the turret, the back of his head level with my shins, Trooper Valsler, the gunner, who could see the outside world only through the calibrated magnification of the sight, used to read one lurid-jacketed paperback after another. His hands were so impregnated with oil and dirt that the pages soon resembled fingerprint files – as did the white bread of the fried egg 'banjos' which Trooper Farmer, the driver, cheerfully handed out for breakfast. We were all filthy, and we were all constipated from compo rations and sitting around. But, just as it was supposed to be over, Exercise Eternal Triangle produced a rush of exhilaration. Our commanding officer, Lieutenant Colonel Peter Hamer, ordered the last charge of the 11th Hussars, a thoroughly untactical and unchoreographed attack in which two squadrons of Chieftains thundered in line abreast towards an astounded 2nd Panzergrenadier Brigade in a final, self-awarded encore before the regiment was amalgamated.

Twenty years and two weeks later, I found myself driving round the same patch of countryside in the dark, searching for the concealed headquarters of the 16th/5th Lancers, an armoured reconnaissance regiment. In the end, I found it more easily than the staff officer who had given me the grid reference expected, so I felt rather pleased with my map-reading, never exactly my forte. The 16th/5th was commanded by Lieutenant Colonel Mark Radford, an old friend from Sandhurst with whom I had lost touch after our paths divided, or rather my path diverged. Meeting fellow officers from those days provoked a strange mixture of feelings. At the back lay the inevitable question: what would life have been like if I had stayed in?

I arrived to find he had been delayed at the brigade orders group. His officers welcomed me in a freezing little barn, rigged up as the mess-cum-briefing-room with temporary lighting and collapsible tables. We chatted about mutual acquaintances and the Army in general. We dined on hot, solid English food and drank red wine from tumblers. Then there was a sudden scraping of chairs pushed back as everyone stood up saying 'Good evening, Colonel' in a ragged volley. I rose too. My first reaction on seeing people again after all those years was one of mild surprise at how little they had changed. The faces of many regimental officers on the verge of middle age had a curious weather-beaten innocence.

After the mess waiter had brought the plate he had been keeping warm, we caught up on each other's news, discussed what had happened to our contemporaries, and talked about how the Army had changed. An hour or so later, officers clutching maps, with sub-machine-guns slung over their shoulders, began to arrive from the squadrons. It was time for the commanding officer's orders group.

I watched him do what we had both been trained to do all those years before. He was explaining what the squadron's objectives would be after they had moved out of their hides just before dawn. So little had changed, and yet so much. He spoke well, confidently and competently and with a relaxed humour. The timing and tone of the jokes were the same as ever, almost a ritual, but many of the acronyms were new.

After the orders group we had time only for a short chat, walking up and down in the farmyard: he clearly needed to get some sleep. The night was silent apart from the hum of generators which came from the armoured command vehicles under the camouflage netting, and the occasional disembodied voice on the radio followed by a noise like the gush of a soda syphon run dry. He spoke of his next appointment, and of his wife's delight to be going home. Inevitably, we returned to the subject of how things had changed. It was not hard to see that this was the end of an era: the British Army would soon be withdrawing from Germany. On the other hand, neither of us imagined that the 16th/5th, commanded by Philip Scott, another contemporary of ours, would be acting in the not too distant future as 1st Armoured Division's reconnaissance screen in the Iraqi desert.

The idea for this book was put to me not long after the controversy over the television play *Tumbledown*. Above all else, the dispute had served to highlight the chasm that separates the civilian from the military. A true study of the Army could be written only by someone who had served in it and knew the language and the life, yet was far enough away to see it afresh. An outsider could never fully understand such a different existence, with all its tribal loyalties.

Although I thought the idea a good one, my first reaction was one of reluctance. I was preparing another book and did not want to change subjects, but, more to the point, any thought of returning to that now distant world prompted a slight if indefinable dread.

I also wondered whether comparisons with my own experiences might not be more risky than useful. I was very lucky to have been in the 11th Hussars. It was an unusual regiment with a relaxed and undogmatic approach. Shouting and stamping were virtually unknown. Relations between officers and soldiers were so informal that outsiders were often shocked. The danger of idealizing a distant past, particularly a central chunk of lost youth, was self-evident. Yet there had been bad times too. They came outside the regiment when, on its amalgamation with the 10th Hussars, I was sent as an instructor to an all-arms training establishment, long since disbanded in one of the Army's wisest decisions. This unit – may it rest in oblivion – embodied the worst examples of the military mind at its most suffocatingly petty. But the frustrations of the place proved an unexpected blessing. In my room each night I worked on my first novel. Needless to say it was about a frustrated young officer leaving the Army, and although mercifully it was never published it served its purpose in clarifying my feelings. It made me re-examine my original motives for becoming a career soldier, and I found them less glorious than I had thought. Much as I had enjoyed life with the regiment, and much as I knew I would miss it in many ways, the time had come to cut myself adrift with the requisite letter of short, stilted formulation: 'Sir, I have the honour to request leave to resign my commission.'

When I was trying to make up my mind about this book, friends persuaded me that the combination of distance and closeness was precisely what was needed – an inside and an outside view at the same time. Although I felt uncertain about my ability to bring off such a complex feat, the idea clarified my underlying purpose. Although it would be an anatomy, the book should not just be a mechanistic study of the British Army. To be of any interest it had to go behind the disciplined exterior and convey the hopes and fears and beliefs of its members.

During our initial discussions, Major General Cowan agreed with the idea of a broad reflection and said that a serious attempt to hold up a mirror to the whole Army could be both interesting and useful. He accepted from the start that he could hardly expect a book without criticisms. Clearly, it was up to me to present as honest and objective an account as I could.

Objectivity, that most relative of notions, was helped in an unexpected way. Virtually all the theories I set out with quickly proved unreliable, if not fundamentally mistaken. One major error was to assume that service in Northern Ireland must have created something of a psychological split in an army training for conventional warfare. And yet virtually everyone – officers, NCOs and soldiers alike – enthused at how good it was for both the individual and the regiment.

I had forgotten many things: how deep emotions run; how even the moments of self-parody are a very British way to disguise strength of feeling. I had also failed to envisage the impact which the last decade of social change might have had on an institution rooted in traditional values. That contradiction in terms, a military yuppie, would have been unthinkable in the past, and at first I tended to discount the appalled comments from generals about 'Thatcher's children' as one of those standard complaints against the younger generation, but after hearing relentlessly similar accounts from officers all the way down to captain, including many who were far from stuffy, I accepted that a significant change had taken place.

The Army survived the revolutionary, anti-militarist 1960s curiously untouched. (My favourite ludicrous image from 1968 is of dinner-jacketed officers in the disco at a regimental dance crooning against their partner's ear: 'When you go/ to San Francisco/ be sure to wear/ some flowers in your hair.') The 1980s brought about the most dramatic and devastating social change within a single generation.

As I knew from my own experience, sergeants and sergeant majors had never had a very high regard for subalterns, but now I found that their worries about the future dwarfed any previous grumbles. The Army, they felt, had become thoroughly contaminated by careerism: all too often nowadays officers treat the regiment as little more than a ladder for their own advancement. In this light, part of Mrs Thatcher's closing speech to the 1988 Conservative Party Conference acquired a particularly ironic ring. She had attacked those who 'accuse us of encouraging selfishness and greed'. She went on to praise ambition, saying that 'a parent's success is shared by his family, a pupil's by his school, a soldier's by his regiment'. Yet ambition is, quite simply, incompatible with regimental values, because it creates distrust. The Army is by nature essentially collectivist. It has to be. 'It's a cultural thing in the Army,' said a senior civil servant, still slightly bemused and fascinated by the organization with which he worked. 'They're a band of brothers, and if you haven't made the rapport you have great difficulty getting your point across.' This book turned out to be far more the portrait of a society within a society than I imagined at the outset. The intriguing part is that, since the first version of the book was finished, something of a shift back towards traditional values has occurred with the end of the 'Thatcher era'.

Sergeants were also dismayed at the change in the recruits they had been getting since about 1987. (Right across the Army almost everyone puts their finger on that year, although nobody can give a satisfactory explanation.) Not only was there a significant decline in the quality of recruits, but their attitudes were completely different. They're not necessarily insubordinate, one sergeant explained, but they just don't understand what authority or rank means. Like many instructors, he felt that they had little grasp of reality and that their expectations of the Army were based on film fantasies. How this generation would cope with the stress of battle was one of the great unspoken questions at the beginning of 1991 as the Gulf crisis turned to war.

Although my journey was eased by abandoning previously held theories, this did not mean that everything suddenly became clear or that the dangers of distortion vanished. As so many officers and NCOs remarked, the Army is a constant battle between perception and reality, and perception often gains the upper hand. A single mirror cannot reconcile the very dissimilar images and self-images held by various arms of the service, and by soldiers and officers of every rank. A particular issue may be described in slightly different ways at each step up the chain of command – so much so that the range of opinions between private and general covers every shade of the spectrum. On a few occasions accounts conflicted to such an extent that I wondered whether they were describing the same institution.

My task was to assess a vast quantity of often disparate views, and reconstruct a mirror in mosaic form. Two forms of imbalance threatened the reliability of the overall reflection. The first was common to almost any kind of reportage: problems are always of more interest and require more space to explain than perfection. The other was more complex. On my tours round the Army, I frequently found myself the only audience available for a large, and at times alarming, degree of pent-up resentment and frustration. However much I warned myself against the dangers of being overinfluenced, the risk remained. The thanks recorded in the Acknowledgements to my anonymous helpers are not merely a polite formula. Their criticisms, guidance and reassurance on particular chapters – in all cases admirably unselfserving – were vital. I was also extremely lucky to be able to check my impressions and the opinions of those who spoke to me against the results of the Army's own very thorough research programmes.

Part One begins in the only appropriate way – with the raw material of the ordinary recruit – and follows the private soldier from basic training to his regiment. It then shows what his life is like – daily routine, nights on the town, discipline, girlfriends, marriage, money problems and promotion, eventually to the sergeants' mess. Part Two follows a similar path, only for young officer candidates: how they are picked, their time at Sandhurst, their attitudes, aspirations and way of life, and then the career paths, with staff appointments, the vital step of commanding a regiment, the unforgiving line between success and failure, with the 'flyers' going on to become generals. Part Three, Command and Control, explains the organization and rivalries within the Ministry of Defence, and then describes the different theatres: the Gulf, the Rhine Army, United Kingdom Land Forces and the way 'out-of-area operations' are mounted, Northern Ireland and the last outposts – Hong Kong, Cyprus, Belize and the Falklands. Part Four is devoted to an examination of the Army's various tribes in the regimental system and the corps. Part Five looks at the Army and politics and, most difficult of all, the Army and the future.

For the uninitiated reader, there is a reference section at the beginning with a list of regiments and an explanation of the Army's rank structure and command organization. There is also an alphabetical guide to some key words or phrases to be referred to in case the exact meaning of a particular term is forgotten. There should not be many, and the reader has been spared the usual rapid fire of acronyms. There is also a glossary of Army slang at the end of the book, which might appeal to those with a taste for inventive language and dark, sometimes tasteless, humour.

For the sake of accuracy and linguistic flavour, I have tried to write the book using military terms while keeping the prose readily accessible to the outsider. At times, the right balance is hard to achieve (Nato-speak is not exactly poetic) but my wife and my editor, both of whom were entirely innocent of military knowledge until hit by a huge typescript, have helped make a slightly foreign country comprehensible to the civilian. For the professional soldier, who seldom gets such a chance to visit the very different parts and levels of his own world, this panoramic reflection might provide another sort of interest.

A Basic Guide to Regiments, Army Organization, Ranks and Terms

The Regiments and Corps of the Regular Army

COMBAT ARMS

Armour

Life Guards (LG) } Household Cavalry. Part of Household Division,
Blues and Royals (RHG/D) } not of the Royal Armoured Corps.
1st The Queen's Dragoon Guards (QDG)
Royal Scots Dragoon Guards (SCOTS DG)
4th/7th Royal Dragoon Guards (4/7 DG)
5th Royal Inniskilling Dragoon Guards (5 INNIS DG)
Queen's Own Hussars (QOH)
Queen's Royal Irish Hussars (QRIH)
9th/12th Royal Lancers (9/12 L)
Royal Hussars (RH)
13th/18th Royal Hussars (13/18 H)

	14th/20th King's Hussars (14/20 H) 15th/19th King's Royal Hussars (15/19 H) 16th/5th Queen's Royal Lancers (16/5 L) 17th/21st Lancers (17/21 L) 1st, 2nd, 3rd and 4th Royal Tank Regiment (RTR)
Artillery	Royal Regiment of Artillery (RA). In all 23 regiments: 12 field, 3 heavy, 1 missile, 1 locating, 4 air defence, 1 commando, and 1 para. (These include the three regiments of Royal Horse Artillery (RHA), two of which are field regiments, and the third, 7 RHA, is the regiment of parachute brigade gunners.)
Engineers	Corps of Royal Engineers (RE). 10 Engineer Regiments, 1 Armoured Engineer Regiment, 1 Amphibious Engineer Regiment. (Queen's Gurkha Engineers under Brigade of Gurkhas.)
Signals	Royal Corps of Signals (R SIGNALS)

Infantry

Guards Division
Grenadier Guards, 1st and 2nd Battalions (GREN GDS)
Coldstream Guards, 1st and 2nd Battalions (COLDM GDS)
Scots Guards, 1st and 2nd Battalions (SG)
Irish Guards (IG)
Welsh Guards (WG)

Scottish Division
Royal Scots (RS)
Royal Highland Fusiliers (RHF)
King's Own Scottish Borderers (KOSB)
Black Watch (BW)
Queen's Own Highlanders (QO HLDRS)
Gordon Highlanders (GORDONS)
Argyll and Sutherland Highlanders (A and SH)

Queen's Division
Queen's Regiment, 1st, 2nd and 3rd Battalions (QUEENS)
Royal Regiment of Fusiliers, 1st, 2nd and 3rd Battalions (RRF)
Royal Anglian Regiment, 1st, 2nd and 3rd Battalions (R ANGLIAN)

King's Division
King's Own Royal Border Regiment (KINGS OWN BORDER)
King's Regiment (KINGS)
Prince of Wales's Own Regiment of Yorkshire (PWO)
Green Howards (GREEN HOWARDS)
Royal Irish Rangers, 1st and 2nd Battalions (R IRISH)
Queen's Lancashire Regiment (QLR)

Duke of Wellington's Regiment (DWR)

Prince of Wales's
Division
Devonshire and Dorset Regiment (D and D)
Cheshire Regiment (CHESHIRE)
Royal Welch Fusiliers (RWF)
Royal Regiment of Wales (RRW)
Gloucestershire Regiment (GLOSTERS)
Worcestershire and Sherwood Foresters Regiment (WFR)
Royal Hampshire Regiment (R HAMPS)
Staffordshire Regiment (STAFFORDS)
Duke of Edinburgh's Royal Regiment (DERR)

Light Division
Light Infantry, 1st, 2nd and 3rd Battalions (LI)
Royal Green Jackets, 1st, 2nd and 3rd Battalions (RGJ)

Airborne Forces
Parachute Regiment, 1st, 2nd and 3rd Battalions (PARA)

Brigade of Gurkhas
2nd King Edward VII Own Gurkha Rifles, 1st and 2nd Battalions (2 GR)
6th Queen Elizabeth's Own Gurkha Rifles (6 GR)
7th Duke of Edinburgh's Own Gurkha Rifles (7 GR)
10th Princess Mary's Own Gurkha Rifles (10 GR)
Queen's Gurkha Engineers (QGE)
Queen's Gurkha Signals (QG SIGNALS)
Queen's Gurkha Transport Regiment (GTR)

Special Forces	Special Air Service Regiment (22 SAS)

Aviation	Army Air Corps (AAC)

Intelligence	Intelligence Corps (INT CORPS)

SERVICES

Royal Corps of Transport (RCT)
Royal Army Ordnance Corps (RAOC)
Royal Electrical and Mechanical Engineers (REME)
Royal Army Chaplain's Department (RAChD)
Royal Army Medical Corps (RAMC)

Royal Army Pay Corps (RAPC)
Royal Army Veterinary Corps (RAVC)
Royal Army Educational Corps (RAEC)
Army Legal Corps (ALC)

Royal Military Police (RMP)
Royal Pioneer Corps (RPC)
Army Catering Corps (ACC)
Royal Army Dental Corps (RADC)
Queen Alexandra's Royal Army
  Nursing Corps (QARANC)
Small Arms School Corps (SASC)
Military Provost Staff Corps (MPSC)
Army Physical Training Corps (APTC)
Women's Royal Army Corps (WRAC)

(For the sake of simplicity and space, corps are not necessarily placed in order of precedence, and full titles have not been used. Their official abbreviations are shown in brackets.)

Organization in the Field Army
[Headquarter and support elements not included]

Infantry	Armour	Artillery	Rank
Sub-Units			
Fire-team (4 men)			Lance Corporal
Section (2 fire-teams)	Tank (4 men)	(Gun)	Corporal
Platoon (3 sections)	Troop (3 tanks)	Section (2 guns)	Lieutenant
Company (3 platoons)	Squadron (4 troops)	Battery (8 guns)	Major
Units			
Battalion (3 rifle companies) (approx. 600–750 men)	Regiment (4 sabre squadrons) (approx. 500 men)	Regiment (3 field batteries) (approx. 600 men)	Lieutenant Colonel
Formations			
Brigade	Usually three units of infantry and armour mixed.		
Division	At least two brigades plus divisional artillery of three regiments.		

Theatre Headquarters

The two principal theatres in which each commander-in-chief is a four-star general are: the British Army of the Rhine with its headquarters at Rheindahlen, and United Kingdom Land Forces with its headquarters at Wilton near Salisbury. Troops in Northern Ireland come under United Kingdom Land Forces only for administrative purposes. Operational command is exercised by the General Officer Commanding, a three-star lieutenant general, with his headquarters at Lisburn. He answers to the Secretary of State for Northern Ireland and the Ministry of Defence, and works with the Chief Constable of the Royal Ulster Constabulary.

In Hong Kong, Cyprus, the Falklands and Belize, the Commander British Forces is a tri-service appointment, and the incumbent receives his instructions from the tri-service Defence Staff in the Ministry of Defence. The Chief of the Defence Staff is the only serving five-star officer in the armed forces. He may be an admiral of the fleet, field marshal or marshal of the RAF. The three service chiefs – First Sea Lord, Chief of the General Staff and Chief of the Air Staff – report to him on operational matters. On administrative and policy questions they report to the Minister for the Armed Forces and the Secretary of State for Defence.

Strength

The total strength of the Regular Army on 31 January 1991, officers, soldiers and servicewomen, including those under training, was 144,003 (17,245 officers and 126,758 soldiers). The Brigade of Gurkhas accounted for another 7,439 men. In addition to regular forces, the Ulster Defence Regiment was some 6,000 strong. There were also approximately 180,000 reservists and 80,000 members of the Territorial Army and Home Service Force.

About 55,000 members of the Regular Army were in north-west Europe and 70,000 in the United Kingdom. There were just over 11,000 in Northern Ireland, but many of them are there on six-month tours from the UK and the Rhine Army. There were also about 3,000 in Cyprus (some of whom are also on short tours). Most of the 8,000 men still in Hong Kong and Brunei are Gurkhas.

The theoretical profile for the Army's manpower is: 27 per cent infantry, 10 per cent REME (the largest single 'capbadge'), 9.7 per cent engineers, 9 per cent artillery, 8.5 per cent signals, 7.3 per cent armour, 6.9 per cent transport, 5.4 per cent ordnance, 3.1 per cent catering corps, 2.6 per cent medical corps, 1.5 per cent military police, and 1.2 per cent aviation.

Ranks in the British Army

Infantry	Armour	Artillery
Soldiers		
Private	Trooper	Gunner
Lance Corporal	Lance Corporal	Lance Bombardier
Corporal	Corporal	Bombardier

[An infantry private depending on his regiment might be called Guardsman, Fusilier, Ranger or Rifleman Smith. He would be Sapper Smith in the Royal Engineers, Signalman in the Royal Signals, Trooper in the SAS, Air Trooper in the Army Air Corps, Driver in the Royal Corps of Transport, and Craftsman in the REME.]

Senior NCOs

Sergeant		Staff Sergeant
Colour Sergeant	Staff Sergeant	Battery Sergeant Major
Company Sergeant Major (Warrant Officer Class II)	Squadron Sergeant Major	
Regimental Sergeant Major (Warrant Officer Class I)		

[The Household Division's variations and complexities are bewildering to the outsider – one might almost suspect deliberately so. Foot Guards corporals are called lance sergeants and Household Cavalry sergeants are called corporals of horse and their sergeant majors are corporal majors. A second lieutenant in the Blues and Royals is a cornet.]

Regimental Officers	*Example of Appointment*
Second Lieutenant	
Lieutenant	platoon or troop commander

[Both second lieutenants and lieutenants are known as subalterns.]

Captain	second in command of a company/squadron or battery, or adjutant
Major	company commander, squadron commander, battery commander
Lieutenant Colonel	commanding officer of a battalion or regiment

Staff and Formation Commanders

Colonel	senior staff officer
Brigadier	brigade commander
Major General	divisional commander
Lieutenant General	corps commander
General	Chief of the General Staff, Adjutant General or a commander-in-chief
Field Marshal	Chief of the Defence Staff

Imitating the American system, generals are differentiated by the number of stars displayed on their staff car. A brigadier is thus a one-star general, a major general a two-star general, a lieutenant general a three-star, a general a four-star, and a field marshal a five-star.

Some Acronyms, Initials, and Common Terms

ACE   Allied Command Europe. Main Nato command, presided over by SACEUR, Supreme Allied Commander Europe.

ACE Mobile Force   Multinational mobile reserve, primarily intended to reinforce the flanks of Nato, i.e. Norway or Turkey. The British contribution is based on 1st Infantry Brigade at Tidworth.

Airborne   Parachute troops and other forces landed by fixed-wing aircraft.

Air Mobile   Helicopter forces, combining attack helicopters armed with missiles and support helicopters carrying infantry and anti-tank detachments.

All-arms   Armour, infantry, artillery, etc., operating or training together as opposed to on their own.

Arm or Combat Arm   A combat arm (as opposed to a service) is one 'whose role is to be in close contact with the enemy'. There are seven: infantry, armoured corps, artillery, engineers, signals, Army Air Corps and Intelligence Corps. A combat arm used to be called a teeth arm.

Armoured regiment   A regiment (either cavalry or Royal Tank Regiment) equipped with Chieftain or Challenger main battle tanks.

Armoured recce regiment   An armoured reconnaissance regiment (either Household Cavalry or line cavalry) provides the modern version of a light cavalry screen scouting in front of an army. They are now mounted in Scorpion and Scimitar tracked light armoured vehicles, which replaced armoured cars.

Arms plot The British Army mechanism of moving infantry and armoured regiments en bloc at the end of every tour. Engineers, signals, transport, in fact most of the rest of the Army, 'trickle-post' their personnel between regiments which generally stay put. This gives them a mobility of labour both of officers and soldiers. Artillery regiments, although part of the arms plot, move less frequently, and the size of the Royal Regiment of Artillery allows it to cross-post individuals quite easily.

Army Board The Executive Committee of the Army Board, which includes the Chief of the General Staff and the three main administrative commanders, the Adjutant General, the Quartermaster General and the Master General of the Ordnance, is responsible for executing the decisions of the Defence Council and the Chief of the Defence Staff, as well as formulating strictly Army policy.

ATO Ammunition Technical Officer or bomb disposal expert (basically Royal Army Ordnance Corps for terrorist devices and Royal Engineers for wartime bombs).

BAOR British Army of the Rhine. Otherwise known as the Rhine Army. Its main component is 1st (British) Corps. The Commander-in-Chief BAOR also commands the Nato formation, Northag (*see below*).

Battalion An infantry unit, officially between about six hundred and seven hundred men strong, commanded by a lieutenant colonel. An infantry regiment, for example the Royal Anglian Regiment, the Royal Regiment of Fusiliers or the Light Infantry, usually consist of three battalions. But the infantry regiment is an administrative 'capbadge', not an operational organization.

Battle Group A mixed force of tanks and infantry in armoured vehicles based on either a battalion or a regiment commanded by a lieutenant colonel and supported by a battery of field artillery.

'Black Hole' The shortage of officers in a particular age group, usually captains and majors.

'Capbadge' The most widely used, although unofficial, term to describe a regiment, arm or corps with a separate identity and loyalty represented by its capbadge.

Central Region The Nato command area which stretches from the River Elbe in the north to the Swiss frontier. Comes directly under ACE.

Colonel commandant The equivalent of a colonel of the regiment for a large, three-battalion regiment, or corps.

Colonel of the regiment An honorary appointment, in which a former officer of a regiment, either serving or retired, interviews officer applicants and presides as figurehead at regimental occasions.

Commanding officer The lieutenant colonel who actually commands the battalion or regiment.

Corps Apart from the operational term, meaning several divisions commanded by a lieutenant general, the word corps is most widely used as a reference to large and small 'capbadges' which are not regiments, such as the Corps of Royal Engineers, the Royal Corps of Signals, the Army Catering Corps, etc.

Dry training Tactical training without live ammunition, as opposed to 'live firing'.

Fantasians An exercise euphemism for Warsaw Pact forces. (*See also* Orange Force.)

Field army A term designating regular units and formations deployed operationally, as opposed to 'the training army' or staff.

Formation commander A senior officer who commands a brigade, division, corps or army group.

Green army An informal term to designate conventional troops in uniform, as opposed to special forces and others operating out of uniform, particularly in Northern Ireland.

'Heavy army' The phrase 'heavy army', meaning the heavily armoured forces in Germany, in fact is more of a reference to the mentality of conventional warfare, as opposed to the 'light' role of peacekeeping, counter-revolutionary warfare and jungle warfare. The term the 'light army' can be safely applied only to parachute troops, commando forces and Gurkhas, i.e. those devoted mainly to out-of-area operations.

'Jointery' A slang term which has established itself to describe the practice of an integrated joint-service command and administration. (*See also* 'Purple'.)

Land/Air Battle The tactical doctrine of combining land forces, close air support and air-mobile (helicopter-borne) forces.

Line infantry/cavalry Infantry or cavalry of the line, an archaic expression, basically denotes all those outside the Household Division of Foot Guards and Household Cavalry.

Logistic corps A corps which supports the field army. The three largest are the Royal Corps of Transport, the Ordnance Corps and REME. Known as 'loggies' by the combat arms.

Military Secretary The Military Secretary's Department is responsible for managing officers' careers and handling the confidential reports made upon them.

NCO Non-Commissioned Officer. Any rank from lance corporal to RSM.

Officers' Mess The building where officers congregate off duty and where unmarried officers live and eat. The phrase is often used to describe regimental officers collectively.

Orange Force An exercise term to denote the enemy, which is a euphemism for Red Force or Warsaw Pact troops. (*See also* Fantasians.)

Out-of-Area Operations Out-of-area operations or responsibilities refer to anything outside the British Army's Nato sphere, such as the Falklands or Belize.

'Purple' An informal term to decribe joint-service appointments which usually alternate between the three services. Purple is a reference to the colour you allegedly get if you mix navy blue, khaki and air force blue together.

Regiment The administrative and operational unit of all arms and services except the infantry, whose operational entity is the battalion.

REME Royal Electrical and Mechanical Engineers.

Roulement The system of moving units and sub-units on six-month unaccompanied (i.e. without their families) tours, mostly to Northern Ireland, but also to Cyprus, Belize and the Falklands.

RSM Regimental Sergeant Major.

Sangar A small defended position, originally with stones. In Northern Ireland it refers to concrete sentry posts, often raised above the ground. A super-sangar is the most sophisticated version.

Selection Board The selection boards ranging from No. 5 right up to No. 1 are called together at particular times to select officers for promotion and, in the case of No. 2 and No. 1 Boards, for important appointments. Their work is organized by the Military Secretary's department.

Single service Royal Navy, Army or RAF, as opposed to tri-service or joint-service.

Sergeants' Mess The building where sergeants, staff sergeants and sergeant majors (warrant officers) congregate off duty. The phrase is often used to describe senior NCOs collectively, particularly in terms of general opinions and morale.

Service A service, as opposed to a combat arm, is a corps whose main role is logistic, medical, technical or training support. The word is of course also used to denote the three armed forces: Royal Navy, Army, Royal Air Force.

Special-to-arm The training which a recruit or newly commissioned officer undergoes after basic training to learn about the equipment, tactics and practices special to his arm.

Staff The Staff consists mainly of those departments in the Ministry of Defence and Headquarters responsible for the direction and administration of the Army. The staff officer is traditionally considered a very different animal from the regimental officer, but virtually all officers from the rank of captain serve both on the Staff and in the field army.

'Tied'   A 'tied' appointment is one reserved for personnel from a particular capbadge or service.

Trickle-post   System of posting soldiers and officers individually between units. (*See* Arms plot.)

UK Land Forces   United Kingdom Land Forces, with a commander-in-chief of equal rank to his counterpart in Germany, is very roughly the home-based equivalent of BAOR. Its headquarters is at Wilton, near Salisbury, and is responsible for home defence (UK Field Army – roughly the home equivalent of the corps in Germany), out-of-area operations, training and administering the home base.

Warrant Officer   Essentially a sergeant major. A company sergeant major or his equivalent is a Warrant Officer Class II and an RSM is a Warrant Officer Class I.

Part One

GOING FOR A SOLDIER

CHAPTER 1

Joining Up

At a quick glance, an Army careers office might easily be confused with a building society or a travel agent. The main Birmingham recruiting office, for example, is in the Palisades shopping centre, a huge concrete hive overlooking the Bullring. Most passers-by do not give the shopfront a second glance, but occasionally a pedestrian weighed down with carrier-bags stops for a moment, staring in with blank surprise. The reception area, manned by one of the recruiting sergeants, has the slightly forlorn air of a consulate in a foreign country.

The anonymous decoration – white melamine surfaces and grey walls – increases the impression of temporary accommodation. The only colours to stand out are board-mounted photographs of infantrymen on patrol, tanks at dawn, or artificers at work on a huge engine. Behind lies a warren of shoebox offices, sparsely furnished.

A teenager will have a mixture of reasons for coming in off the street. The more mature and gifted applicant usually wants to learn a trade and develop his potential in an exciting environment. The priorities of an immature or unintelligent recruit are reversed. He is fascinated by weapons and the idea of action; the opportunity to learn a trade merely provides a rationalization for his yearning. When asked his reasons for joining, he is the one most likely to reply 'to serve my country' in a tone of gruff stolidity. As the Gulf crisis developed, there was a surge in recruiting prompted by images on television of tanks and infantry fighting vehicles in the desert. To the majority of enquirers, the longer-term implications of disarmament in Europe meant little.

A large number, particularly from inner cities and

industrial ghost towns in the north, see the Army as an escape to a better and more exciting life. 'Boredom at work is our best recruiter,' said one officer, but many may also be fleeing the dole queue or life on a vandalized housing estate.

The Army's regimental tribalism has a strong appeal, even for a generation which cares little for history: the capbadge provides a favourite motif for a tattoo or T-shirt. This group identity promises a substitute family to the large minority who have been pushed out by mothers or by their mothers' boyfriends. 'It's a generation without fathers,' another colonel observed. Some applicants are trying to put behind them disturbing memories of home, from neglect to violence and even sexual abuse. Becoming a soldier seems the obvious way to build confidence. The saddest cases seldom make it through basic training, yet the Army often still finds itself acting as foster-parent to some of the nation's waifs and strays. Those who make it state their gratitude with conviction. The Army gave them a chance which they probably would not have found anywhere else.

At the other end of the scale, the Army attracts some impressive characters, both bright and self-assured, who will clearly have successful careers. They may well become a sergeant major by the time they are thirty, then a 'late entry' captain or even major. About eighty a year will be picked out early on to be sent to Sandhurst as 'Army entrants' for officer training. The confidence and patent competence of this new class of NCO has begun to make a number of the traditional barriers within the Army appear increasingly irrelevant.

Whatever the prevailing mood in the civilian world, there will always be boys who have dreamed from childhood of becoming a soldier. These devotees are known as the army-barmy. Far more common is the restless adolescent whose interest has been aroused at a later stage, probably between ten and fifteen, after a specific contact with the

Army, or sometimes simply through an image on television. On the other hand, the 'army brats' from service families and members of the Army Cadet Force should certainly have a more realistic idea of the life ahead than those whose impressions have been formed by films.

When a school-leaver or young man comes into one of the 180-odd recruiting offices around the country, the sergeant at the desk will sit him down, ask a few questions about his schooling, current employment and reason for interest in the Army, and then tell him something about the work and life. He will also check that he has Commonwealth or Republic of Ireland citizenship and no serious crimes to his name – a precondition which disqualifies a considerable number in inner-city areas, particularly Glasgow and Liverpool. The old practice of the sergeant visiting the boy's home to get an idea of family circumstances has had to be abandoned in case of an IRA trap. In 1990 there were 5 attacks on recruiting offices, 4 bombs and 1 shooting in which a colour sergeant was seriously wounded.

If the enquiry becomes a firm application, the boy will be given a date on which to return for a series of very basic education tests. A civilian doctor will also examine him, along with the rest of the current batch. The efficacy of these medicals comes in for strong criticism from training units, all of which have their horror stories of boys arriving with deformities such as curvature of the spine. One junior leaders' regiment even claimed to have been sent a recruit who lacked a vertebra. Asthma is now the most common problem. The increase in asthma cases is worrying, especially since it is seldom diagnosed until basic training, when recruits are taken on runs. The fitness test of sit-ups and heaves to the bar, which each applicant undergoes in an office at the back, remains a rather improvised affair. It is often a painful sight. About one candidate in ten fails the minimal standard of three heaves to the bar, and many cannot manage even one. The Army Personnel Research Establishment at Farnborough is currently developing new machinery to test fitness. The most useful would be a static bicycle to check aerobic function, but the risk of a chronically unfit applicant collapsing rules that out, now that the Army can be sued.

A battery of intelligence tests provides an indication of the jobs and therefore 'capbadges' open to the applicant. The overall intelligence level defined by these psychometric tests is known as the SSG, or Sum Selection Grading. This defines the recruit's suitability for an arm or corps. It extends from SSG 1, which indicates roughly a capacity to pass A Levels, all the way down to SSG 5, a warning that the candidate is virtually illiterate and will find even the simplest training very difficult to absorb. Those with the very top grades are pointed towards the corps most in need of their potential. The military police, for example, need a high standard of literacy for report writing. REME (the Royal Electrical and Mechanical Engineers) and the Army Air Corps, in which an air trooper might eventually become a helicopter pilot, also need high-quality candidates. An SSG 5 cannot really hope for anything better than the infantry.

The applicant will then be shown a video in another office about the arm or corps for which he appears most suited. If he has a strong reason for choosing a particular infantry or cavalry regiment, the Army does its best to answer it. A direct family connection, such as a father or brother in the regiment, is treated as almost sacred.

Occasionally, a recruiting sergeant with more regimental zeal than respect for the rules may try to persuade suitable applicants to join his own regiment. Guards NCOs appear to be the most shameless poachers, one or two even telling boys that they are too tall for such-and-such an arm or corps, and that they had better join the Household Division. 'The Army', commented a senior civilian specialist with the Ministry of Defence, 'is a collection of warring tribes, and the Guards are particularly effective in-fighters.'

In the manning crisis which developed rapidly from 1988, traditional associations were bound to suffer. So

6

many units were under strength that the ill-informed or uncertain applicant found himself steered to where the manpower shortage was most acute. A regiment's local links had to be put aside in order to keep front-line units fully manned. The Royal Armoured Corps switched to a virtually national system of recruiting, acknowledging only a direct family connection. Such was the regional imbalance between north and south that the Queen's Division used Geordies from the old Northumberland Fusiliers recruiting area to boost its desperately under-strength Home Counties battalions.

Even territorially jealous Scottish regiments followed suit, although the Scottish Division is the best recruited in the infantry. Glaswegians, known as 'Wegians', supplement Highland battalions. The diversion of recruits to under-strength battalions led to a saying in the Scottish Division that at Glencorse, their depot, the regiment in most urgent need of topping up could easily be spotted, because the bulk of the recruits on parade would be wearing its coloured hackle (a small feather plume) on their glengarry or tam-o'-shanter. More recently, however, Army policy has changed course. Recognizing the importance of local connections, it is again doing what it can to send recruits to the regiment of their choice, and allowing groups of friends to be posted together. So bad has the situation become that a £250 bonus on completion of training is planned for anyone joining the infantry (the Queen's shilling has increased five-thousand-fold) and entry standards have had to drop. 'You can't train an empty bed space,' say veteran recruiters.

When the demographic trough began to intensify competition amongst employers, the Army's need to attract potential recruits before they reached school-leaving age became even more acute. The Director of Army Recruiting in the Ministry of Defence is the equivalent of the marketing director of a large organization. He has a range of career products to sell and a budget to allocate between

7

the basic selling tools: point-of-sale material, pamphlets, local promotional activity and national advertising.

'Advertising', said a senior officer, 'is only the front bit of our campaign.' Promotional activity consists mainly of providing attractive foretastes of a military career. Army youth teams take parties of schoolchildren off canoeing, fell-walking or climbing, activities for which fewer and fewer teachers have either the training, or indeed the inclination, since they risk vilification in the press should there be an accident. Regimental KAPE teams (Keeping the Army in the Public Eye) take round light armoured vehicles for youngsters to scramble over, arena display teams perform at public events, and mobile display teams stage exhibitions with weapons and simulators to provide trigger experiences in both senses of the term. And each year the Royal Tournament provides the services' most spectacular recruiting promotion.

The competition before the recession, when some companies in the south-east even provided computers to get a foot in the classroom door, prompted the Army to step up its efforts aimed at eleven- to fifteen-year-olds. The Army's recruiting organization started a 'young responders' club' with a membership card, newsletters and competitions with command tasks to do at home. Members can collect points 'and get freebies like a camouflage pen' or special offers on records of military bands. Public relations opportunities such as the *Combat '89* competition on television (which 'had a very positive effect') are milked energetically, with advertising linked in wherever possible.

A number of anti-militarist teachers and local education authorities refuse to allow recruiting teams near their schools. 'Short of shooting the lot of them,' one officer joked philosophically, 'there's not a great deal we can do about it.' Most careers advisers, whom the Ministry of Defence encourages to visit junior training regiments, are not opposed to the Army, but they remain uneasy about the signing up of boys at such an impressionable age. They understand the need for a minimum commitment, but still believe that a sixteen-year-old (the age for a junior soldier: adult soldiers must be over seventeen) simply cannot envisage what his life will be like. The Ministry of Defence's reply to any charge of cradle-snatching is that boys must be brought in around school-leaving age, since that is when they start their careers. And in any case all recruits have a 'window' period in training during which they can leave without obligation.

Some teachers also feel that recruiting sergeants, along with Army advertising and displays, mislead potential entrants by emphasizing only the exciting parts of service life. This complaint of oversell is shared by training establishments, and some of the Army's advertising material, it must be said, is not easy to reconcile with its own stated objective of 'giving the public full and fair information on the advantages, and disadvantages of a Service career'.[1] Cinema and television advertising for both the regular and the Territorial Army gives a glamorized and unrealistic picture of life, but to expect the disadvantages to be emphasized in the present recruiting climate would be over-optimistic. Army recruiters reply that they have first got to get boys into the careers office, where it is up to the sergeant and the information videos to point out any disadvantages.

For twenty years, recruiting offices used to send applicants to two Army personnel selection centres – the main one at Sutton Coldfield, the other in Scotland – where, over two days, they did a much more comprehensive battery of intelligence tests and a final interview. Now the system has returned to direct enlistment at recruiting offices, this time with the aid of computers. This should at any rate reduce the time an applicant spends hanging around until he is formally offered a place; it is a period of uncertainty with a great deal of time for second thoughts, particularly after a night in the pub with friends liable to deride his decision to join up.

One colonel said with enthusiasm that careers could be

booked 'like an airline ticket', but this may still be rather a wishful thought when the Army's computer network is also in the throes of reorganization. The testing process is also being brought up to date. Electronic systems will save time and reduce human error. For the intelligence tests, using 'touch-screen technology', the applicant will prod a coloured box on the screen to indicate his answer. But gadgetry can do little to help the personnel selection officer who conducts the final interview – usually a former sergeant major who has received a late-entry commission. However hard he tries to put boys at their ease, most answers come in monosyllables. Personnel selection officers tend to develop verbal tics: one fatherly character could not stop saying 'fair enough' after every answer. The interview always seems to end with: 'Now, have you got any questions you'd like to put to me?' – followed by a slightly uneasy silence, after which the boy shakes his head.

Many officers and NCOs remain uneasy about the demise of Sutton Coldfield as a selection centre. Some of the original arguments for the old centralized system are still valid. Perhaps the key one was that recruits must 'have time to make up their minds in an Army environment'.[2] A recruiting office cannot give them a taste of Army life. To compensate, the Army now tries to organize 'familiarization visits' both for boys and their parents. 'The parents', observed a colonel, 'are vital allies. If they've seen the place, and what it's like, they can tell their son to get on with it when he complains it's too tough.'

St George's Barracks at Sutton Coldfield, with its parade grounds and superannuated tanks and field guns on concrete plinths, has not closed down: instead it has become a remedial centre. Ten-week preliminary education courses are provided for those who fail the comprehension tests. A major observed that with six million illiterates in the country measures like this were clearly needed. The trouble was that the cost and effort required might be too great.

Sutton Coldfield already ran a two-week physical development course to improve the often pathetic levels of those who failed the fitness test. In the cold early morning, officers and NCOs could be seen standing on the edge of the huge asphalt square, yelling robust encouragements as flagging seventeen-year-olds, their breath sobbing, their faces and knees puce, the flabbiest with agonized expressions and cradling their sides from stitch, staggered or limped past. For many, perhaps even a majority, this was probably the first time in their lives they had had to run a whole mile.

The feeble state of the boys on the physical development course rules out a programme of solid PT, so for the rest of the time they are given a taste of Army life, starting with the shock of reveille at 6.30 and breakfast at 7, followed by room inspection and some elementary drill. The NCOs in charge never cease to be amazed by the fact that several boys in each intake decide to throw in the towel because they cannot face getting out of bed on time. But the only cruel touch in the programme comes on the first day: immediately after a good lunch, the boys are marched off to see a film with the memorable title of *Too Fat To Fight*.

The dramatic improvement in fitness and self-confidence often achieved in two weeks can work as an effective word-of-mouth recruiting campaign, although the expense is considerable. A less obvious advantage, which cannot be costed, is the chance to reduce the infectious sense of resentment amongst young soldiers regretting their decision to enlist. Despite the opportunity to leave during basic training, many continue to claim that they did not know what they were letting themselves in for. There can, however, be little doubt about their disenchantment. In answer to the question 'Is life in the Army what you expected it to be before you enlisted?' only 14 per cent of soldiers in 1988 answered 'better' or 'much better'.[3] This shows a striking decline from 1975, when, in answer to an almost identical question, 59 per cent of young single soldiers found life in the Army better than they expected.[4] Such a dramatic change in attitude reflected the greatly raised expectations of the 1980s as much as any disillusionment with a declining 'quality of life' inside the Army.

According to both officers and NCOs, recruits have 'some very peculiar views of what the Army's like'. More could certainly be done to disabuse them of some of their misconceptions, yet the extent of the latest generation's video view of the world is deeply disturbing. Sergeant instructors are continually astonished by their lack of touch with reality.

CHAPTER 2

The Culture Shock of Basic Training

An observant recruit arriving at the barrack gate for the first time will quickly realize that he is entering a different world with different priorities. The flagpole and the flowerbeds are aligned in parade order. Marker stones are freshly whitewashed. On the wall of the guardroom veranda, fire-hoses are perfectly coiled. Alongside, on a row of hooks, hang fire-buckets, their pillar-box red clashing with the bright blue doors.

For most recruits, certainly the sixteen-year-old juniors, this will be their first taste of living away from home. Except for the 'army brats', few know what to expect. Most are taken aback by the barrack block's lack of privacy and dismayed by the functional bareness of brown linoleum and iron cots. The rooms and corridors have the hollow echo of school. Walls of institutional pale green are broken only by noticeboards with photographs of officers they should learn to recognize. There are also posters with badges of rank and regimental insignia. Sergeant instructors add home-made versions, with their capbadge drawn on cartridge paper accompanied by a stencilled slogan, such as 'The Sign of a True Professional'.

Cold water is soon poured on misplaced hopes or dreams. 'Some of them honestly seem to think', said one commanding officer disturbed by the element of fantasy which recruiting sergeants do little to discourage, 'that they're going to live in a Butlin's holiday camp and become Rambos overnight.' At the Guards Depot, a favourite story in the sergeants' mess was of a sixteen-year-old who turned up believing he had joined the junior wing of G Squadron, twenty-two SAS.

Adult recruits, those aged over seventeen-and-a-half,

go to the depot or training regiment appropriate to their regiment or corps for basic training, now called the Common Military Syllabus for Recruits. This universal ten-week course, the Army's lowest common denominator, is supposed to teach the basic infantry skills to every entrant for every arm and service.

The 'junior army', a collection of apprentice colleges and junior leader regiments designed to train technical specialists and future NCOs, generally takes boys from around sixteen. It includes four apprentice colleges (Royal Engineers, Royal Signals, Royal Electrical and Mechanical Engineers and Army Catering Corps), four junior leaders regiments (Royal Armoured Corps, Royal Artillery, Royal Engineers, and Royal Corps of Transport), and four junior infantry establishments. The Scottish Division and the King's Division have a combined junior battalion at Ouston, and the Queen's Division and the Prince of Wales's Division have one at Shorncliffe. The Light Division, like the Guards at Pirbright, has concentrated all its training for adult recruits and junior leaders at Flowerdown, near Winchester. Small 'capbadges' which cannot justify their own establishments blister on to others. The Army Air Corps trains its junior air troopers with the Royal Armoured Corps at Bovington and its adult recruits with the Light Division, while the Parachute Regiment has its own independent junior wing under a Guards umbrella at Pirbright. This side of the 'training army' is, however, likely to be reorganized drastically once the future shape of the Army is determined. Many also expect the number of entrants to decline still further. Junior soldiering, said a staff officer, 'can't compete with Tesco on pay', while the more gifted sixteen-year-olds also seem to be staying on at school longer 'to get more chitties', as one general remarked.

The Guards Depot at Pirbright has been the most intransigent of all in its dedication to traditional standards. It does not provide a representative average of training establishments, but it does offer the best illustration of the dilemma the Army found itself facing at the end of the 1980s and has still not resolved.

Pirbright is a veritable factory. It has a frenetic, production-line air of activity as intakes of school-leavers and adult recruits keep on arriving. Their heads are shorn, giving them the vulnerable air of eagle chicks, after which they are fed into one of the three training companies: Caterham for adult recruits, and Waterloo and Pirbright for junior guardsmen. Together they provide the manpower for the two regiments of Household Cavalry and the five regiments of Foot Guards. The Guards Depot also runs a wing for junior bandsmen, with both a drum school and a piping school. To awake in Surrey just before dawn, with commuter trains to London rumbling past every few minutes, and listen to the sound of bagpipes is a curious experience.

Entirely rebuilt some twenty years ago, the camp's rectangular buildings in black brick give it an austere, uncluttered aspect. With its grass and young birches and views extending to the rifle ranges, there is no reason for the place to feel claustrophobic, but it does.

The peace is continually disturbed by the background chant of recruits carrying out every movement by numbers: 'One, two, three. *One!*' Nobody seems to walk normally. Junior officers saunter, from time to time calling over their shoulder to a disobedient spaniel. Sergeant majors bear down with huge chests and an autocratic imperative. Slim young sergeants move with practised precision on their own or in pairs, twiddling extended pace-sticks beside the right hip like giant brass and wood dividers, though when the same sergeants march a shaven-headed squad in double time from one place to another they appear to take on new, temporarily hysterical, personalities. Meanwhile, the recruits at the bottom of the chain jerk like overwound clockwork toys; their rigidity, on the command eyes right, makes them look as though they have dislocated their necks. And, even while their bodies

15

move rapidly, they have a dazed, uncomprehending look. At first this comes from the shock of what is happening to them. Later, once they have learned to conserve energy by switching off emotionally, a blank expression indicates that a self-protective automatic pilot has taken over.

From reveille at five-thirty to lights out at ten, theirs is a relentless and confusing day. They have hardly a moment to think in this new world of perpetual motion and its accompanying cries: 'Get a move on yourselves!' 'Move, move, *move*!' 'I'll make you move so fast your feet won't even touch the ground!' Between each period they have to double back to the block to change: into service dress for drill, into PT kit for the gymnasium, into combat kit for the rifle ranges. Pirbright's most painful and lasting impressions seem to consist of the drill square and the gradients encountered on runs in the surrounding area. Everything else remains a blur in the memory.

No sooner is tea over than they are back in their barrack block, 'on shining parade'. During shining parade, the platoon NCOs – a sergeant, three lance sergeants and a corporal barrack-room instructor – circle the beds eyeing the kit as it is cleaned. As they do so, they fire off questions on regimental knowledge, including the rank, initials, name and appointment of the officers at Pirbright as well as the tradition, history and dress of the regiment for which they are destined. A Life Guards corporal of horse will concentrate on a junior trooper bound for his regiment, or a sergeant from the Coldstreams on one of his junior guardsmen, making him recite the details of the regiment's thirteen Victoria Crosses.

The little customs that distinguish each regiment are carefully fostered from the beginning, even though this may produce a rather un-Guardslike lack of uniformity: for example, when a group of defaulters is marched in front of an officer for sentencing on minor charges, Scots Guards salute, while others give an eyes right. And officers in the Foot Guards never quite get used to salutes, both indoors and out, from bareheaded junior troopers in the

Household Cavalry, a custom said to date from the time the Marquess of Granby lost his wig in a cavalry charge at the battle of Warburg.

During the first few weeks, up to four hours are spent each evening preparing kit for inspection – much of it devoted to transforming the pimply leather of ammunition boots by ironing, polishing and bulling. The ultimate effect should look like black glass. Days of work can be destroyed in an instant on drill if someone turns the wrong way and stamps on your toecap, though by an unwritten code the stamper has to rectify the damage. Anyone who comes near to treading on a sergeant's boot risks alarming threats, such as having to rebull them there and then on his knees. Not only does the clumsy recruit find himself spending more time on his kit than anyone else, but he will suffer the most on inspection, that constant source of worry to every recruit.

Apart from being shouted at from point-blank range – what sergeant majors call 'a nose-to-nose job' – a guardsman can be charged with having 'dirty boots'. Dirt has little to do with the issue: it simply means that his boots are not shining to the required standard. Similarly, 'dirty hat' may well mean no more than a speck of fluff. Until new guidelines were issued in the autumn of 1989, three faults on inspection automatically meant a recruit was in 'bad order' – an offence which could involve his being marched off under close arrest to the guardroom, known as the 'corner shop', and locked in a cell for a couple of hours as a warning. For a sixteen-year-old junior guardsman, almost certainly ignorant of the Army's true powers over him, the whole procedure was effectively terrifying.

The real pressure on NCOs to bring their platoon up to scratch in drill and turnout comes not from the platoon or company commander, but from the regimental sergeant major and the company sergeant major, a chain of command which is far more likely to inspire furious activity. For a platoon sergeant with a hopeless intake, the prospect of 'passing off the square' in week five, or the RSM's parade in week twelve, is liable to induce a severe case of nervous strain.

Instructors are carefully selected; in theory it is the most prestigious job available to a young sergeant, though the hours alone are enough to explain a dyspeptic tendency. During the most intense part of the course they will be supervising recruits in barracks from six in the morning until ten at night. The effect on marriages can be imagined. Some of the almost fetishistic obsessions of sergeant majors (now officially discouraged) such as bed blocks and the ritual geometry of locker layout, with every article of kit positioned in a prescribed manner, were justified as teaching recruits how to organize themselves, while 'beasting' on the square is said to be an essential test of self-control. It has often been claimed that such pressures make it easier to spot the sort liable to lose his temper and open fire when taunted or stoned on the streets of Belfast, while others argue that they initiate the bonding process vital to any military team by forcing recruits to work together. But these arguments, although not easy to contradict since nobody has discovered a better way to prepare young men to fight without losing their heads, may well be retrospective justification for sticking to the same old system of instilling thoughtless obedience.

In the British Army, probably more than any other, instructors retain a sense of humour, however dubious at times. Instead of attempting to demolish and rebuild, they aim to strip and mould. This moulding process relies more on the individual and his fellow recruits than on the sheer weight of authority. As volunteers, recruits are likely to be amenable. They want to conform to the image of a real soldier – more often than not in the shape of their own sergeant who, as he often makes clear in acerbic fashion, is their parent for the duration since he's the one who has to get them up, make sure they're properly dressed and off to school on time.

Some boys almost come to regard their platoon sergeant as the father they never had, and strive to please him. Yet the insults and similes he directs at them are loaded with sexual innuendo. To listen to sergeants in charge of recruit platoons (PT instructors are incomparably more correct in their language) is liable to make anyone think that the whole Army is obsessed with heterosexual potency.

The relationship develops from a diet of fear and ridicule during the first month to the relative informality which prevails during the penultimate week's battle camp, the climax of the course. Provided the platoon is performing well and has 'not dropped them [their instructors] in the shit', repartee will gradually be allowed. But if anyone takes advantage of this relaxation the old regime will return with a vengeance. Sometimes the punishment is collective, and the platoon itself 'sorts out' the offender. In this way they learn that there are definite limits to familiarity with superiors and a time and place for everything. It is the basis of the Army's unwritten code on which relations between ranks are based.

The other lesson which the platoon instructors will have made them learn in the early chaos of pressure and ignorance is the importance of working together. Outstanding recruits who do not help less competent members, either by lending a hand or offering articles of kit, will receive a hard time until they change their ways. Soldiers have innumerable little ways of dealing with somebody who fancies himself as a star.

Sometimes, with an alarming passion, the younger and more narrow-minded sergeant may find it hard to forgive the outside world's lack of respect for the Army. One, who blamed the post-national service generation of parents who grew up in the sixties and seventies, rather curiously described even his own working-class contemporaries as 'nothing but bloody hippies and flower children'. The parents were responsible for the weakness, both physical and moral, of the recruits the Army was getting. 'They're just about all spineless,' is a common, if sweeping, verdict. 'None of 'em want to stick it.' Even officers complain that 'many are so wet, they burst into tears at the first bollocking'.

The physical state of recruits is the subject on which instructors from the Army Physical Training Corps express their opinions most forcefully. 'Don't be fooled by the media,' said one. 'It's not just the junk food.' Without hesitation, they too blame educationalists opposed to competitive sports, and trace the sharpest decline back to the teachers' strike of 1987.

The physical training instructors seem to find much more satisfaction in their job than the platoon sergeants. They can still make an intake, 'as close to a bunch of spastics as you'll ever see', infinitely fitter and less awkward in a matter of weeks. Gym work (ten heaves to the bar by the end of the course), swimming, platoon runs and assault courses prepare recruits for the combat fitness test which every infantryman has to complete. This consists of an eight-mile 'road-bash' in one hour fifty minutes, carrying a man 100 yards in full kit, and jumping a nine-foot ditch. Whenever possible, they are then marched to the ranges to shoot.

The transformation in physical performance and in drill was, until recently, achieved at a heavy cost in lower-limb injuries. The effects of stamping in steel-shod boots on hard surfaces produced little sympathy in company sergeant majors, whose only comment was liable to be 'They've just got weak muscles.' But the Army has taken action to change such attitudes. 'We've been breaking them,' said a Ministry of Defence specialist. 'Some of our practices have been ridiculous.'

Among a generation unused to wearing footwear with heels, having been accustomed only to trainers, road running in boots can cause damage. Officers also blame the design of the 'boot combat high' which, ironically, was introduced as a result of the excessive foot and ankle casualties suffered in the Falklands. The Army has now realized that inadequate investment in such a vital piece of infantry equipment is worse than a false economy, and new boots, costing five times as much, about the same price as a pair of SAS boots, are being introduced.

In 1990 the overall drop-out rate amongst junior soldiers – those deemed medically unfit; 'culture shock casualties'; the handful discharged on grounds of false attestation, which usually means that the recruit concealed a criminal record when enlisting; the homesick; and those who found the course too tough or the discipline too restricting – ran at 33 per cent for the Army as a whole. The Guards fall-out rate was only 25 per cent, yet for the Parachute Regiment, the Queen's Division and the Light Division it was 50 per cent. Such figures can, of course, be interpreted according to point of view. The Royal Electrical and Mechanical Engineers enjoyed the lowest rate of loss at only 19 per cent. The most encouraging development is that the wastage rate for recruits on medical grounds has dropped dramatically to around 1 per cent.

In all training establishments, the first rush of applications for PVR (premature voluntary release) comes with the opening of the 'window' which allows them to leave after twenty-eight days. The next comes after the first spell of leave when a return to discipline and hardship from the comfortable ease of home seems unbearable. A final wave of juniors applies to leave just before the window closes at six months. For adult recruits the window is open only between week eight and week twelve.

Whenever a young soldier announces that he wants to leave, the permanent staff try in turn to persuade him to stay – platoon sergeant, platoon commander, company sergeant major, company commander. They all say much the same thing: 'Don't throw away the effort you've already made.' Officers usually end up with 'Now I want you to go away and think about this very carefully for a few days and come back and discuss it with me again.' But, once a soldier has said that he wants to go, he seldom changes his mind. As an inducement to stay on beyond the window, the Army wants to offer a bonus of £250 'on completion of training'.

21

Permanent staff instructors dislike the window system as an unsettling influence. They feel its only purpose is to help the recruiter clinch his sale by arguing that the recruit can always change his mind, so why doesn't he give it a try? In their view, it is an extra hook which only catches the wrong fish. But such a view only shows that the sergeants' mess in many training establishments has found the full implications of the manning shortage and the change in attitude of recruits very hard to accept.

Nothing appalled instructors throughout the Army more than the publicity about bullying in 1988 and the consequent measures to combat it. Their outbursts were often a little confused, but the underlying anger and nervousness was unmistakable. They were genuinely afraid of a scapegoat court martial. Their fears, probably exaggerated but by no means baseless, centred on a 'stitch-up' by a recruit who could not take the pressure of training and, desperate to leave, would ring his mother. 'The worst-case scenario', said a company sergeant major, 'is if Mum then rings her MP, or one of the tabloids.' On a more everyday level, some instructors claimed that the more streetwise boy now exploited the atmosphere of official concern with indirect hints of denunciation.

In most instances the allegations collapse in confessional tears once the company commander has talked to the boy on his own. But there are still occasions when NCO instructors overstep an ill-defined mark and an example has to be made.

Part of the problem comes from the tail end of an illegal, though quietly ignored, system of justice as old as the Army itself. In many regiments, a sergeant would offer the miscreant a choice: either 'accept my punishment' – usually a thump administered behind the vehicle sheds – 'or the company commander's', which almost certainly meant a fine. 'I'll take yours, sarge,' was the usual resigned reply. Few nowadays are guilty of much more than making a recruit run round the block naked with only a mess tin for modesty, with the result that the majority feel falsely accused. 'You've only got to prod one of the little bastards with a pace-stick,' complained one aggrieved sergeant, 'and you can be well and truly done for it.'

There is no doubt that Guards sergeants' messes are seriously worried at the decline in the quality of recruits. They are particularly alarmed because they know that their system cannot survive without good NCOs. They clearly fear for the future of the Household Division as they know it. The Foot Guards are the least disposed to accept that things will have to change if they are to attract and retain anything like enough men for their battalions. They may, as a result, find themselves the victims of their own standards.

Until 1988, shining parades at Pirbright required recruits to bull boots sitting to attention astride the bed – an uncomfortable position to say the least. Now they are allowed to polish 'at ease'. Officers pointed to this as a significant reform, but NCOs saw it only as a lowering of standards, and as an almost personal slur, in that it cast doubts on the system which had made them what they were.

The guidelines introduced by Headquarters UK Land Forces in the autumn of 1989 were designed to make training establishments reconsider their practices because too many recruits were leaving. The more mindless aspects of traditional training, particularly such time-wasting requirements as bed blocks for inspection each morning, were strongly discouraged. This new policy of handling recruits more gently was called the 'soft launch'. Military discipline was to be introduced more gradually. Sergeants were told not to shout at recruits for the first three weeks when they did things wrong; they were not to put them on a charge, but should sit them down and patiently explain everything. Not surprisingly, the reaction to such reforms in the bar of the sergeants' mess was heated.

Since then, the more far-sighted sergeants have accepted

the reality of the situation and the official line which is that the objective is not to try to maintain standards on arrival, but on output. If the material is deficient, then the Army must start off with remedial training, and catch up later on. Blitzing a squad into line no longer works with this generation. A number of the new breed of young sergeant majors have noticed that traditional methods of moulding now seem to be counter-productive in the longer term. The change in the recruit between arrival and output may look impressive, but all too often it is superficial. Especially amongst junior soldiers, what used to be known as the 'maturing machine' has proved nothing of the sort: a basic immaturity is more likely to become entrenched. The more modern formula of adventurous training, providing it is imaginatively organized and led, is the best way to bring them on.

The Royal Engineers are much less vulnerable than the Guards. They enjoy the theoretically ideal recruiting combination of trade qualifications with a military image. The name combat engineer suggests it all – demolition work, bridge-laying under fire, and the chance to join a para or commando squadron.

Their junior leaders' regiment at Dover is still housed in a run-down barracks built during the Second World War. The blocks, constructed in thirties Georgian style, show every sign of make do and mend. Military cosmetics such as whitewash and the odd splash of bright paint only draw one's eye to the dilapidation. Yet, although the barracks have the unmistakable air of an establishment with an undecided future, the atmosphere is noticeably less oppressive.

The permanent staff at Dover have a much easier task. They are not faced with such low intelligence gradings. And, although the training and discipline the recruits receive is certainly tough, it does not have the mechanical quality which is so dispiriting at Pirbright.

Like their contemporaries bound for the Guards, sapper

junior leaders are shaken by the rigorous intensity of
training, and they too cause their instructors to mutter
about declining standards, though not on the same scale
as at Pirbright. In common with other arms, members
of the permanent staff who have recently served in
Northern Ireland are usually the least forgiving. One
senior lieutenant was utterly unrepentant about the 45
per cent drop-out rate in his troop: 'I'm not going to
allow anyone to pass out of this place if there's no way
I could rely on him in Belfast.'

Middle-ranking officers seem the most conscious of
dealing with a generation that is completely different
from anything the Army has ever known before, yet has
its paradoxes.

The 'post-baby-boomers' do not believe in staying with
a career, yet are extremely qualification-conscious. They
are much more sceptical than their predecessors about
authority, they question orders and they have much
higher expectations of pay and conditions – partly out of
a rootless ambition and desire for instant professionalism.
Not surprisingly, this makes the Army, with its belief in
public service and long-term commitment, very uneasy.

The basic programme of fitness training, drill, skill-at-
arms, first aid and signals (usually regarded as the most
boring subject) is universal, though units other than the
Guards try to cut down on drill to increase the time spent
on skill-at-arms.

Junior leaders also receive classroom instruction in
map-reading from Royal Army Educational Corps officers.
But the main work of these teachers is to prepare them
for the junior army education certificate. The more able
should be able to get the corporal-to-sergeant Education
for Promotion Certificate under their belt.

Those who are backward in mathematics and English
receive extra tuition, but probably the most pertinent
subject is called 'life skills' – insurance, bank accounts,
hire purchase and loan sharks. The heedless way in
which a sizeable minority of young soldiers rush into

debt, particularly when posted to Germany, is a major headache. It is only natural that a junior, exulting in his first pay packet, should blow several weeks' pay in a single night out to impress his friends. But when it becomes an established habit as an adult soldier, and he continually turns up at the company or squadron office expecting a loan, senior NCOs and officers begin to despair.

In the Royal Engineers over 50 per cent of sergeants and around 90 per cent of regimental sergeant majors are former junior leaders. Old hands in sapper regiments claim that they can immediately spot a junior leader on arrival because his turn-out will be better than that of an adult recruit. Yet some instructors at Dover are a little uneasy at the effects of their own training. 'I know I shouldn't say this,' remarked one of them, 'but they're just moulded – clones. You can look at a squad and it won't take you a second to spot who their instructor is.' Perhaps regimentation at such an early age prevents junior soldiers from developing self-discipline naturally. They appear either to react against the system later or they become unusually dependent on an external discipline. Senior NCOs in different arms have observed that junior leaders seem to show much less initiative than might be expected.

The Army has always been a great believer in team games. On most Wednesday afternoons in junior leaders' regiments and depots there is compulsory sport – football, rugby, hockey, cricket, basketball. The walking wounded and all those 'excused boots' are assembled on the touchlines to cheer, or rather scream, their side on. Many establishments offer the opportunity to ride, sail, and even try free-fall parachuting.

Adventurous training – the Army's potentially very effective character-building recipe of canoeing and rock climbing – may well be enjoyed more in retrospect than at the time. Most recruits are glad to have been forced to do something they would never have imagined possible, but only a minority of 'gladiators' acquire a taste for it.

In addition to the basic adventurous training package, platoon or troop commanders usually plan to take their boys off walking in the Lake District or on Dartmoor for a long weekend. Many junior leaders also learn hobbies like woodwork, but few keep them up. They risk being teased on arrival at their unit, where hobbies are thought cissy.

For both adult recruits and junior leaders, the climax is the passing-out parade, to which parents come from all over the country. The next stage, the 'special-to-arm' course, provides a grounding in the equipment of his future unit in the field army. A signalman, for example, trains to be a linesman, a trooper to be a tank driver or gunner. Sappers go on to Hawley, near Farnborough, where they qualify as combat engineers. A young infantryman is taught his trade in greater depth along with the other weapons to be found in a rifle company. But a young guardsman, more often than not, goes straight to a battalion on public duties. An officer at Pirbright said bluntly: 'The only trade they take out of here is the Mark I Drill Boot.'

At seventeen or eighteen, few young soldiers dream of becoming an RSM, and then obtaining a late-entry commission which could take them as far as major, or even lieutenant colonel in a few cases. Their aspirations are far more immediately focused. They want to put their training into practice; to be tested, as their instructors have continually drummed into them, by the only test that counts – by 'the real thing'. Now that the Gulf war is over, 'real soldiering' can once again be found only in Northern Ireland.

CHAPTER 3

The Life of a Single Soldier

Leaving a training regiment or depot is rather like leaving school. With the most restrictive part behind him, the young soldier looks forward to joining the field army at last. For a junior leader, the whole process has taken around fifteen months since signing up. His expectations therefore tend to be much higher than those of an adult recruit, who has come through the system in just over six months.

From the guardroom, the new arrival will be directed to his company (or squadron or battery) to start on a round of interviews which, in the course of the next few days, will include most of the following: company commander, company sergeant major, platoon commander, paymaster, RSM, adjutant, and even the commanding officer. They will issue the usual encouragements and warnings, principally about the dangers of drink, debt and Aids. Officers tend to finish their homily along the lines of 'what you get out of life here will depend entirely on what you put in'. The old-fashioned sort of RSM, fortunately a declining breed, still places his faith in a more traditional form of motivation. In his view, appealing to a private's reason or better nature should be left to 'the long-haired armies in Nato'.

At the company office, the new arrival will be allocated to a platoon. And after another ration of advice from the platoon sergeant, probably the most pertinent of all, he will be taken over to the accommodation block by the corporal in charge of his section, shown his bed space and introduced to his future comrades.

This is a crucial moment, for first impressions may well dictate how he will be treated. Having probably joined the Army for comradeship and the confidence of the group, the opinion of his fellow soldiers is far more important to him than those of officers or NCOs. The length of time it takes to be accepted varies considerably. This does not just depend on the individual. A newcomer will often find it harder in Germany, because soldiers abroad become creatures of habit and platoons are more clique-ridden. Acceptance may take as long as six months. In the armoured corps the process is much quicker: the cramped conditions within a tank tend to make a crew get on together from the start.

The infantry also has a greater belief in the individual proving himself before he becomes part of the group. Virtually every unit has some sort of initiation test or rite. Some are completely above board, or even form an official tradition. In the Royal Regiment of Wales, for example, recruits have to stand on chairs and eat a large raw leek on St David's Day. Unofficial practices, on the other hand, can be much more dubious, however long-standing they may be. Preying on the credulousness of new arrivals or getting them drunk is almost universal. Once they are drunk, they may be forced to swallow horrible concoctions or submit to degrading tasks back in the barrack room. A vicious element begins to creep in as soon as the process involves sexual humiliation. This may take the form of relatively petty persecutions like bootblacking a victim's balls, smuggling in a prostitute to make the shyest perform in front of the whole platoon or, in very rare but highly publicized extremes, buggery with a broomstick.

The investigation into bullying ordered by the Adjutant General established that, while most cases of brutality by NCOs occurred in the training army, initiation ceremonies were limited almost exclusively to the field army. Several officers have suggested that the two problems are linked, and that the practices described may well have increased over the last few years, partly because young soldiers coming in 'are that much wetter', with the result that the selection process has suffered. This view is voiced even more strongly by soldiers. 'They're nothing but a bunch of fairies joining now,' was a fairly typical remark.

The adjutant of one regiment which had suffered a spate of bullying concentrated his attention on the victims rather than the perpetrators. Studying their records and reports, he found that they were always the least confident. In many cases they had been 'back-squadded' – put back a class – in basic training and only just scraped through. Another target was the more effeminate young soldier. This presumably comes from that intense fear and loathing which aggressively male groups have of their own homosexual potential.

Officers usually describe bullying in terms of 'the pride rejecting the lame cub'. A company commander in a Highland regiment recounted how he had to send a young soldier home, because he seemed to have 'a death wish' in the way he infuriated everyone by letting them down. And the officer commanding an independent field squadron also described how he had 'a real waster'. 'All the others want to pan him. Sometimes it seemed as if he was just asking for it. You virtually have to put the guy in protective custody until you can ship him out. In the old days if you had a lame duck, you could always slip him into the officers' mess [as a waiter or barman] but it doesn't work like that any more.' Far fewer soldiers are now employed in officers' and sergeants' messes.

The group rationale is to try to drive out weaker members who may let them down, particularly in Northern Ireland. Some junior ranks privately continue to justify their treatment of newcomers: 'Fucking up deserves a thump,' they say, with an air of knowing understatement. One or two even took a perverse pride in the newspaper coverage of such misdeeds.

These self-appointed guardians of the flame believe (perhaps without exaggeration) that they are only doing to others what had been done to them. Yet one cannot help suspecting that their attempt to purge the weak from their midst is, in fact, a sneaking admission of inadequacy, an attempt to weed out weakness in themselves. Initiation ceremonies of the worst sort are much less likely to occur in organizations like the paras or commandos, if only because both the elimination of weaklings and the group bonding process have been publicly and officially carried out during a very tough selection course.

Generals were genuinely shocked by the practices described at the courts martial in 1987 and 1988. Studies recommended that the number of permanent staff instructors in training establishments should be increased to relieve the pressure on them. More members of the Women's Royal Voluntary Service were employed to give young soldiers a less intimidating figure with whom they could discuss their problems and complaints. The Army's hierarchy was also disturbed at how little senior NCOs and company officers knew of what went on. Yet many experienced regimental officers believe that such vices have always existed and will never be entirely stamped out. The most effective measures in the field army were taken by units on their own initiative. Each new arrival is now allotted to a senior soldier or lance corporal, who has to report regularly on how his charge is getting on. This is almost certainly the best way of breaking up the barrack-room pack.

If war is the natural state of man, as many senior Army officers argue, one must also accept that bullying is the natural state of man in an aggressively male group: just after the series of courts martial in the British Army in 1988, a report appeared in the Russian press of a teenage Red Army recruit who 'shot dead seven of his comrades in a train after being bullied, tortured and sexually assaulted'.[1]

Racial harassment is an equally vexed issue. The Army, which is trying hard to bring in more recruits from ethnic minorities, is deeply embarrassed and angered by the tabloid treatment of the subject. Yet senior officers do not like to admit how little can be done.

Military life is likely to appeal to teenagers with skinhead prejudices, and one or two vitriolic characters are enough to stir up trouble against a black recruit. Once again, self-appointed guardians of the barrack-block flame think that to chase out blacks is to defend the honour of the regiment. They get away with it because the soldier's code against grassing is almost as strong as the underworld's, and because NCOs and officers often prefer not to acknowledge what is happening.

Racism, however, is not endemic. Much depends on a curious chemistry. Scottish regiments have a reputation for loathing blacks, yet they have a great affinity for the Gurkhas, presumably because they are fellow highlanders and play bagpipes. Fijians have always got on well in the British Army. (A Fijian corporal in my squadron, a gentle giant, was one of the best-liked characters in the regiment. Once, when a group of Dutch soldiers insulted him in a bierkeller, every 11th Hussar in the place waded into the attack on his, and the regiment's, behalf. They recounted the incident with huge satisfaction on the tank park next day.)

In the Parachute Regiment or the Royal Marines, racial harassment is relatively rare, once again because entrants are judged much more by the way they bear up under the arduous selection procedures. Overt racism is also likely to occur less when there are already a number of coloured soldiers serving in the unit, mainly because other newcomers are not prey to a frightening isolation. If the Army is to send members of ethnic minorities into the Guards, then it must not send in one token figure at a time, doomed to draw all the fire. (Although no figures are available, some officers are certain that the number of black soldiers has declined in the last decade. One Green Jackets officer estimated that nearly 10 per cent of their soldiers were black in the 1970s. Apart from the Green Jackets and the Parachute Regiment, the only infantry regiments with a noticeable number are south-eastern and Midland regiments, nearly all in the Queen's Division.)

The revelations of the last few years have demonstrated one thing beyond doubt: the old claim by RSMs that nothing moved in the barracks without their knowing was spurious. One former commanding officer admitted that those in authority knew little of the 'subculture' which existed 'after hours', and what they did know they kept quiet about. Looking beneath the surface was 'like turning over a great flat stone', with prostitutes sometimes smuggled in, and wild drinking parties in which soldiers go in for a drunken striptease known as 'doing the Zulu warrior', during which they pour beer over each other.

Once a young soldier has been accepted into the group he will become a firm upholder of its ethos – which as often as not means its prejudices. 'There's a hell of a lot of needle between regiments,' said a lance corporal in the Parachute Regiment. Certain regiments nurse irrational dislikes for each other which develop into a self-perpetuating tradition. One county battalion which slugged it out with another in Munster after Exercise Lionheart in 1984 still remembers the fight with pride.

Although disastrous for the Army's public image and for Anglo-German relations, such episodes greatly strengthen regimental spirit. They may excite mixed emotions in many an officer's breast, but for the young soldier such events are real and the focus of his pride. For him, traditionally revered battle honours belong in an officers' mess or regimental museum, and El Alamein is almost as distant as the Alma, Waterloo or Dettingen.

The most striking aspect of the Army today is the yearning for service in Northern Ireland. All through training, sergeants try to instil a sense of urgency by yelling at recruits that unless they sort themselves out the IRA will do it for them as soon as they get to Belfast or south Armagh. Service in the province is consequently seen as the proving ground, if not the culmination, of their existence as soldiers.

New arrivals in a battalion recently returned from the province listen eagerly to Falstaffian tales in the junior ranks' club. They long for the excitement of 'real soldiering', to prove something to themselves or to a girl, and, perhaps most important of all, to be part of the group

33

by earning the Northern Ireland medal. Those without it admit to feeling naked on parade alongside the others.

The deployment for Operation Granby prompted a wider range of emotions. The more imaginative soldiers were subdued. In that autumn of 1990, Iraq's chemical arsenal and fighting experience in the war against Iran suggested a very unpleasant war ahead. But, for the less reflective, the great thing was to be part of the team sent out for this, the ultimate World Cup.

This yearning for action is of course heightened by the boredom of barrack life, whether in a sprawling military suburb in England or amidst the soulless landscape of winter in northern Germany. Up well before dawn, the infantryman will probably have to set off on a three- or six-mile run, whatever the state of his hangover. After a shower comes breakfast – a full fry with baked beans if he does not feel too bilious – followed by block inspection and company parade.

There is much less time for drill now. Sergeant majors complain that the programme is so full that they have hardly any opportunity to prepare for the annual competition or the regiment's battle honour parade. In Fallingbostel, I watched a CSM of the Staffords, determined not to lose the opportunity, drilling his company on the square in three inches of snow. Snow had begun to fall again and the scene was blurred in grey and white. Only the dark forage caps stood out. The bass drum, like all the other sounds, whether shouts of command or stamped feet, had a muffled, eerie distance.

The far more elaborate security measures instituted after the IRA attacks of 1988 impose an increasing strain on regiments both in the United Kingdom and in Germany. During a state of maximum alert, a major unit may have to provide over sixty men per day. For a minor establishment, like a base workshop or an ordnance depot, where over half the personnel may be civilian, soldiers can find themselves on 24-hour guard duty every three days. Officers are seriously worried at the effect of the downward spiral. Manpower shortages mean losing even more qualified men.

The Army has been slow to compensate by cutting down on non-essential duties. Official visits, whether from generals, politicians, or foreign dignitaries, can take up a considerable amount of time. Headquarters and signals regiments are often the closest to hand for filling the odd hour or two of an important visitor's programme. Guided tours with a demonstration of 'normal working' and an inevitably platitudinous question-and-answer routine create a good deal of cynicism. Soldiers have their own names for such occasions, such as 'peanut-time' or 'zoo-time'. The 3rd Royal Horse Artillery estimated that during eight months in Cyprus it received 111 official visitors, including 65 stars-worth of generals. Gunner officers had already suggested jokingly that, to save time, one regiment should be designated 'official visits regiment' for the whole of the Royal Artillery.[2] Yet although soldiers consider most visits a waste of time, with politicians and generals giving themselves a nice warm feeling that they are in touch with the men on the ground, they are the first to complain that they have been forgotten, especially during a tour in Northern Ireland. There, they generally appreciate brief, informal visits – providing sergeant majors do not insist on a major clean-up beforehand.

In a mechanized regiment, whether tanks, armoured reconnaissance, artillery, engineer or even armoured infantry, much of a normal working day will be spent on the vehicle park. The infantry loathe serving in armoured personnel carriers as the PBAI – the poor bloody armoured infantry. They consider maintenance a demeaning business, and count off the days before they can return to what they see as their natural existence in fire-teams out on the ground, instead of being cooped up and thrown about and deafened in the back of roaring monsters like the Warrior infantry fighting vehicle. 'If I'd wanted to be a fucking tankie,' runs the frustrated footslogger's lament, 'I'd've fucking well joined 'em.'

A platoon sergeant's chief problem is getting the rest of the section to help the driver maintain their Warrior properly. In the unmodernized vehicle sheds, fumes, bad lighting and numbing cold in winter do not encourage sustained effort. 'Skiving' can go far beyond a pretence of going through the motions. Whenever possible, some soldiers climb inside the vehicles and catch up on sleep.

Almost everyone is killing time, first of all until Naafi break, then lunch, and finally tea, which marks the end of the working day. Tea, the soldier's evening meal, is available from five to six in the canteen, or regimental restaurant as it is sometimes grandiosely called. A number almost deserve the title. Cleverly camouflaged with trellis, plastic ivy and striped canvas awnings, they would not look out of place in a holiday camp. Others still suffer the chilling effects of pale blue walls, painted pipes and expanses of stainless steel serving counters.

Unless he is on guard, or detailed as duty driver, a soldier is free for the evening. He will wander back to his barrack block to change into civilian clothes, and, if sensible, prepare his uniform for the next morning. This may mean giving a quick polish to his boots, throwing his shirt and grease-impregnated overalls into the washing machine, or, if he is a clerk or storeman, ironing the pullover and light trousers of his barrack dress.

In Germany, the old 'Hitler' barrack blocks were slowly being converted and refurbished in a programme which goes under the leadenly self-conscious title of Operation Humane, but with the imminent withdrawal of a large part of the Rhine Army this will stop once the present programme is completed.

These solidly built Wehrmacht buildings, with Mauser rifle racks still clearly visible in embrasures along each corridor, were taken over by the British in 1945 and have housed the Rhine Army ever since. The new system, which is a great improvement, consists of converting each corridor, half a floor, into a self-contained 'flat' for twelve single soldiers. Each flat has its own multiple bathroom as well as a utility room with a washing machine and tumble dryer. The soldiers share the flat, three or four to a room. The harsh overhead lights have not changed, but the floor is now carpeted, and soldiers have their own duvets, some with startling patterns on the cover, such as an attacking tiger, or an oriental girl in provocative pose. In between the tall metal lockers for personal possessions, each bed space is crammed with hi-fi systems, televisions and video recorders. Webbing and helmets are hung from hooks, and the walls around are festooned with the plastic-looking breasts of centrefold pin-ups.

Some soldiers say that there are still too many occupants for real privacy, but the improvements have been generally welcomed. The lockable front door makes it possible to escape a sergeant looking for soldiers for extra duties. Each soldier has his own key and there is a doorbell for visitors. Some reactionary sergeant majors still insist on regular room inspections, though most senior NCOs, realizing the intense resentment that this causes, take a much gentler line: they feel it right that the 'singlies' should have a place to call home, and they respect their privacy providing there is no trouble. Soldiers complain they are treated like children, but officers and NCOs point to the small minority – the proportion varies widely, often according to regiment – who are their own worst enemies and make life difficult for everyone else.

In the United Kingdom, the conversion programme is less advanced. Barrack blocks are mostly of the old dozen-beds-to-a-room variety and often in a bad state of repair. A colonel in Aldershot recalled that when a team of police came down to the Parachute Regiment's barracks to take statements about the bomb explosion at Tern Hill, they took one look at the accommodation they were offered, standard for single soldiers, and booked into a nearby hotel. In another, perhaps apocryphal, story, the

Army offered the Home Office one of its camps to take an overflow of prisoners, but officials from the prison service declined it, saying: 'We couldn't put prisoners in there. There'd be a riot.'

Women are not allowed into barrack blocks in any circumstances. The rare incidents of gang rape will prevent any easing of that regulation. This does not, of course, mean that women are not brought in, but like drink, which is also banned, most officers and NCOs prefer to overlook it providing there is no trouble. British barracks are not dry, like some US Army bases. Each unit will have a junior ranks' club, in theory the soldiers' Naafi-run equivalent of the corporals' or sergeants' mess. Some resentment is inevitably caused by the fact that a beer there often costs more than in the sergeants' or officers' mess because the Naafi has to pay full overheads and wages. (Although a company limited by guarantee, the Naafi – the Navy Army and Air Force Institutes – was founded as a form of co-operative. Soon after Mrs Thatcher's government first came to power, the Naafi appeared an obvious and attractive target for privatization. Its civilian directors, backed by senior officers, found themselves having to explain patiently to disbelieving ministers that it was not the government's to sell.)[3]

Other drinking dens are sometimes permitted in the form of company or squadron bars, barrack rooms which the soldiers do up themselves with fake beams and wall plaques and even horse-brasses. But nothing compares with getting out of barracks, if only to drink the same brand of beer in a similarly decorated bar a few miles down the road. In Germany, the beer is twice as strong as in Britain and not much more expensive.

Only the 'marrieds' – otherwise known as the 'pads' (from 'married pads') – go out for a meal. The 'singlies' do not waste time or money on food, except a take-away in England, or in Germany a cardboard plate with greasy bockwurst and chips to soak up some of the alcohol.

Amongst the Jocks, particularly the Glaswegians, there appears to be an almost Slavic compulsion to drink themselves into oblivion on these occasions. It is a ritual with little appearance of pleasure.

A real night out in Germany means going to a disco. But the discos where local girls go will not let in British soldiers – and the larger the garrison, the colder the welcome from the local community. Worst of all is a place like Hohne, a vast complex of semi-identical barracks with flat empty fields on one side, pine forest behind and the site of Belsen concentration camp on the southern perimeter. There is no nightlife in nearby Bergen, the town whose population was brought at bayonet point by British troops to bury the corpses in 1945. And Bergen's streets are deserted once the shops shut.

Several years ago, an enterprising Welsh Guardsman – every regiment seems to have at least one capitalist *wunderkind* – bought himself out, and borrowed enough money to set up a disco called Mic-Mac's, catering for his former comrades. The fittings were kept simple, robust and, where possible, screwed to the floor so that they could not be used as missiles, and the largest members of his regiment were hired as bouncers. Few women go near the place. 'You don't go to Mic-Mac's to dance!' explained a lance bombardier.

The weekends are the worst time for the single soldier in Germany, as senior NCOs will admit with genuine sympathy. Shops shut at lunch time on Saturday, and going out offers little more diversion than gazing in windows. Back in camp, the 'video vegetables', with packs of beer cans ranged like a stockpile of grenades beside them, settle down to an average of six tapes by Sunday night. These will be swopped around between rooms to save on rental charges. Most of the films they have seen before, the favourites countless times. Sex and war are the most popular: whether *Pussycat Pleasure* or *Rambo III*, soldiers will always say that they are 'good for a laugh'.

The video vegetable is a fairly recent phenomenon. In the past, British soldiers used to amaze their officers with their ability to chat up girls abroad in spite of, or more likely, because of their atrocious rendering of the language. Quite a few, certainly the older ones, still manage satisfactorily if only by profiting from the number of foreign girls who want to perfect their English.

The less streetwise resort to 'whore-hopping binges' – ranging from 50DM for a 'quickie' in Hanover to 150DM or more for the full treatment with Jacuzzi off the Reeperbahn in Hamburg, or around the Stuttgarterplatz in Berlin. The medical recklessness of soldiers, particularly after a few beers, is alarming. Condoms are scorned, in spite of campaigns organized by the Royal Army Medical Corps, and Aids publicity appears to have had little effect. (The Army, not surprisingly, refuses to say how many soldiers have been diagnosed as HIV positive.)

Condoms are issued free when battalions are sent abroad, but apparently wives have protested that this gives official approval to infidelity. But official approval or disapproval is unlikely to change the nature of the British soldier. Even in Germany, which has a thorough approach to health care, the VD rate in infantry battalions can reach well over 5 per cent of junior ranks at any one time. A six-month tour in Belize, where hygiene is primitive to say the least, can produce much higher figures.

The real problem is that it is very hard for a young soldier to have a normal relationship with a girl when he is with the Army. The macho ethos of a barrack room, with its pin-ups and videos, is more likely to produce braggartry than a satisfying relationship, and the practical conditions and regulations of his service mean that, unless his girlfriend has a flat, they are limited to making love in a car or 'going tactical' in the bushes. Postings abroad and the disruption of a relationship also take a toll. In some battalions – the infantry experience the most sudden moves – a custom of pinning a 'Dear John' letter up on the company noticeboard has arisen as a gesture of defiance.

In the United Kingdom, the problem is not so acute. There is no language barrier, and even in remote camps enough soldiers have cars to share rides home at the weekend, assuming most of the regiment still comes from the traditional recruiting area. The exodus on Friday afternoon is almost total. Only the unlucky stay behind – those on guard, or those whose weekend has been effectively wrecked by duties, such as a KAPE team taking vehicles to a local show or a sub-unit detailed to act as enemy for a Territorial Army exercise. Over-frequent or last-minute jobs like this can wreck a promising seduction, and when single soldiers talk about leaving the Army because of discipline this is usually what has rankled most.

Another reason for staying in barracks is quite simply a lack of cash. Yet, although soldiers in Britain feel financially worse off without local overseas allowance, the debt problem in this country is not as serious as it is in Germany. Within a very short time of arriving in his unit in Germany, a young soldier will often decide to emulate his new room-mates, whose quarters are stacked with hi-fis, televisions and video recorders. He will go off to the Naafi, obtain a chargecard or budget account card, and order his own. Few bother to work out whether they can afford to service such a debt on their pay, and in spite of the classes devoted to 'life skills' in training they seldom calculate how much interest they will be charged. Sometimes they end up paying over 25 per cent when they could get a loan at only 3 per cent from a German bank. Officers and senior NCOs become exasperated with the Naafi for making credit so easy – to which the Naafi replies that its terms are no worse than any other British store group, and that it has to compete – but most of all they hate the salesmen who tie gullible young soldiers up in hire purchase contracts way beyond their means, and then expect the Army to act as their debt collectors.

A large minority of soldiers soon fall behind on their payments and throw final demands in the bin, hoping the problem will somehow disappear. Once a young private is in this state of mind, he may well allow his insurance policies on his kit, his life or his car to lapse. Kit insurance is vital when a pair of mislaid binoculars can set him back £150 on top of a fine, yet fewer than half of junior ranks keep a policy going.

The financial nihilism of a few hopeless characters can reach legendary levels. One young gunner recounted with bravado how he negotiated the maximum loan of four times his monthly salary from the local German bank to buy a car, spent the money, then bought the car on credit, wrote it off in a crash, and promptly blew the insurance money before the hire purchase company discovered what had happened.

Most regiments have had to institute a system whereby all junior ranks must register any debt or loan. Soldiers once again complain that this is treating them like children, but the officers concerned would be only too happy to be rid of a constant headache. In the worst cases, a soldier who gets into serious trouble is 'grounded'. The paymaster will take control of his finances, allow him no more than £10 a week in pocket money, and allot the rest of his pay to the most pressing debts.

Sergeant majors recount with resignation how most of the single men are broke by the tenth of the month, and how a few blow the lot the moment it comes in – perhaps even £200 to £300 in a night. Unused to cheque books, many soldiers still cannot resist the notion that having cheques is the same thing as having money, even though a bounced cheque is an offence under military law.

Not surprisingly, given the generally lower educational standard, the situation is worst amongst infantry privates. For them it is a game, even a sort of virility symbol. A dozen privates in a battalion in Germany once managed to draw their whole month's pay twice over from two separate branches of the Kreissparkasse on the afternoon it was credited to their accounts. They regarded the operation as a great achievement, almost a British victory; the fact that the bank promptly refused all further credit to soldiers in the surrounding regiments as well only improved the joke.

Troopers and gunners are sometimes as bad as infantrymen. There is a certain Jack-the-lad kudos to be gained out of leaving unpaid bills behind when posted out, as German businesses unwise enough to give credit have discovered. Only among members of the more technically qualified corps does the level of responsibility and self-discipline increase significantly. Apart from their better standards of education, they suffer much less from the competitiveness of boys trying to prove they are men.

Any army which tries to mould uneducated teenagers straight out of school is bound to end up having to spoon-feed them. In spite of its claims to act as a 'maturing machine', the training system seems to deprive them of the chance to learn for themselves.

Debt can lead to desperate reactions like theft and desertion, but such offences are comparatively rare. The large majority of the Army's disciplinary problems stem from drink as a result of boredom, a point highlighted by the commandant of the Military Corrective Training Centre at Colchester and strongly endorsed at regimental level.

The pattern appears consistent. In Germany, adjutants estimate that around 80 per cent of the charges dealt with by the commanding officer are 'drink-related in some way'. One or two put the figure even higher. Crimes of violence – common assault and actual or grievous bodily harm – are nearly always committed after heavy drinking. Absence without leave, then extending into desertion, in many cases results from a soldier doing something stupid when drunk, like trying to break into the Naafi. He then panics and 'does a runner'. RSMs complain that soldiers don't accept punishment as they used to; nowadays they 'dream up Walter Mitty stories' even when lying only digs them in further.

Fighting is much more of a problem in infantry regiments, above all in those which cultivate an aggressive image. (The league table appears to be infantry, artillery, engineers, armoured corps.) Fights happen either in barracks within the platoon or company, or outside against members of another regiment or civilians, particularly figures of dubious authority such as night-club bouncers. There is an increased use of head-butting in fights, which senior officers view with great concern, and it is now treated almost as seriously as wielding a bottle. From time to time there is a truly horrific incident. But the whole question of violence in Army ranks must be seen in context.

It appears prevalent to the outsider because the tabloid press finds that the subject sells well – much more than the impressively large sums of money which soldiers raise for charity. (The British soldier's unpredictable alternation between the odd bout of mindless violence when drunk and spontaneous kindness when sober is one of his most perplexing traits.) Some of the sensational stories are totally distorted, if not invented. For example, the allegations in 1988 that Rhine Army soldiers were largely responsible for the violence of English football supporters was a myth, as the German police later confirmed. And, although a true statistical comparison is hard, young soldiers are probably no worse than most of their civilian contemporaries, even allowing for the aggressive nature of their training.

There are carefully prescribed limits to the punishment that can be awarded within the regiment. The commanding officer's orders, sometimes known as the CO's bloody assizes, take place whenever there are enough miscreants: its frequency depends on the regiment, where it is stationed, and how long it has been there. A Scottish battalion going through a bad patch in Germany might hold one or more a week, dealing with anything up to twenty men at a time, whereas the commanding officer of a cavalry regiment happily ensconced near its home area in England might punish as few as a dozen men in a year.

Every soldier has the right to elect for trial by court martial on any charge involving loss of pay – roughly the equivalent of the civilian's right to opt for trial by jury.

Very occasionally an awkward customer, knowing that the upheaval and cost cannot possibly be justified, will ask for a court martial when charged with something trivial – but he will usually find himself being given the maximum number of restrictions of privileges and extra guard duties instead. It is hard to beat authority at its own game.

Boredom is clearly the greatest danger facing a peacetime army, particularly in Germany now that few believe that the Russians will 'come over the fence'. Aware of the importance of getting the soldier off the vehicle park and giving him a challenge, recent and present commanders put greater emphasis than ever before on adventurous training. Some regiments now rent a hut in the Bavarian Alps, where they send groups of up to twenty at a time for cross-country and downhill skiing in winter, and climbing and canoeing in summer. The main drawback is that the emphasis on getting as many soldiers through as possible for the lowest cost leads to a production-line approach, so, having done it once, few soldiers want to go again. According to field army units, ambitious officers tend to exploit the opportunity to play the numbers game and make their mark with the next headquarters up the chain of command. Only the prospect of a very different sort of experience, such as an expedition abroad, is likely to stir the imagination.

But more worrying than boredom to regimental officers and NCOs is the apathy prevalent amongst young soldiers. Only a minority takes advantage of the German language courses, and many of these give up when they find it requires concentration. 'It's hardly surprising when you think about it,' remarked one young officer. 'Most of them can't even handle English grammar.' Many soldiers take a crassly British pride in their 'squaddy German', which achieves its basic purpose with 'knock ine beer bitter' (*noch ein bier bitte* – another beer please) and 'dunk a fieldmouse' (*danke vielmals* – thanks very much) when the glass arrives.

Yet there are always notable exceptions: soldiers who make use of every spare moment to explore the country and get to know Germans, hobbyists and collectors (not just of militaria), explorers, climbers and the sportsmen. The variety and quality of Army sports and expeditions is as high as ever. Some group is always either climbing in the Himalayas, crossing the Sahara or canoeing in the Rockies. The Army is making efforts to increase the numbers and variety of these to counter the restrictive life in Germany.

For some soldiers, the experience of the Army, and particularly the male solidarity, is so intense that they apply to rejoin a year or so after leaving. A private in the Parachute Regiment who had come back in said he missed his mates: 'That's why I didn't fit in civvy street. They're not friends. They're just people you know.' Some, on the other hand, regard their years in the Army as utterly wasted, while others leave having acquired skills and, above all, self-confidence. Most see their time with mixed, but on the whole philosophical feelings. 'When you look back on it,' said a private in the Gordons who was about to leave the Army, 'the best times are the worst times, if you know what I mean. You can have a good laugh. You make a lot of good mates. You've got to – you're living together.'

CHAPTER 4

Of Stripes and Crowns
and the Sergeants' Mess

'It's not much of a war,' ran the Army's joke about Northern Ireland before the Gulf crisis, 'but it's the only war we've got.' Officers talk of it as the best training area they could hope for. 'They grow up very fast out on those streets,' said a captain. 'You can see a real difference in a matter of a few weeks.' 'We can't nanny them here,' said a company commander. 'We're not up against a Fantasian enemy this time.' The implications are clear: a tour of duty in the province not only provides a taste of the real thing, it offers the ideal selection process for junior commanders.

The contrast between the no-nonsense operational conditions in Northern Ireland and the traditional method of training soldiers in peacetime reveals a significant paradox. The Army prides itself on the speed with which it can turn boys into men. Parents are often amazed at the transformation, yet the standard system of training often leaves a puerile streak behind the confident exterior. Lacking control over his own fate, the young soldier's devil-may-care attitude to anything important is entrenched by the way he is treated. 'When you mould them through depot,' said an impressive young RSM from the Parachute Regiment, 'you find they're less able to accept discipline.'

More and more senior NCOs are at last becoming aware of such contradictions. A company sergeant major in Belfast said that 'in UK and BAOR, sergeants almost have to treat soldiers like children, because it's the system'. In Northern Ireland, where there was a real job to do and soldiers had to be treated like adults, they responded like adults. And when they received additional responsibility with promotion, they behaved accordingly. Not surprisingly, the Army's continuous research programme into soldiers' attitudes clearly demonstrates that the level of job satisfaction rises steadily rank by rank.[1]

Spotting the sergeants and sergeant majors of the future is one of the most important and difficult tasks facing regimental officers. Potential in one of the quieter members of the platoon or troop may suddenly become apparent once his self-confidence has developed. Loud, irresponsible types are usually incurable, but not always: sometimes one of them suddenly reforms, astonishing everyone, including himself. The hardest choice comes when obvious candidates are few, and there are other considerations to take into account: in the present climate it is important to keep a good soldier, who will 'vote with his feet' unless he receives a stripe.

Regiments without the advantage of Northern Ireland service have to rely on the traditional peacetime method: recommendation followed by a junior NCOs' cadre course. Once a year, the unit will have a promotion conference in regimental headquarters at which the company, squadron, or battery commanders put forward the names of their candidates to the commanding officer. He will consult the regimental sergeant major, a figure whose power of veto is almost as great.

On a given date, the soldiers selected for the junior NCOs' cadre will report to the training wing to start their three-week course. The climax of this should consist of field training, perhaps a week of platoon attacks and patrolling at Sennybridge for a United Kingdom-based infantry battalion, or, in the case of an armoured regiment in Germany, a few days' troop tactics on Soltau or Sennelager training areas. Whenever possible, regiments try to include some adventurous training as well. Assuming they pass – something is very wrong with the selection system if more than a handful fail – the relevant manning and record office will be informed and their promotions published on noticeboards in regimental orders. They can then 'put up their stripe'.

The rank of lance corporal is the most precarious rung on the ladder. A commanding officer can 'bust' one without referral to higher authority. And, since the 'lance-jack' continues to work and live, if single, alongside his former equals, he must quickly establish the right basis of give and take. He has to ensure that 'the lads put their back into it', however unpopular the job, but if he becomes officious then they will 'close down' in silent protest and he will lose credibility with his superiors as well. Sometimes an individual who has been passed over for promotion may try to stir things up, but in general soldiers are unusually free from envy. If one of their number goes for a commission and passes into Sandhurst as an Army entrant, they are pleased for him.

Judgement and tact are perhaps even more important in an NCO than in an officer. If he is fair, and does not mess soldiers around, they 'won't drop him in it' by treating him with disrespect in front of a superior. And if one of their number is a shirker or skiver they will usually sort him out themselves. Within the platoon or troop, formal justice has always been viewed as a last resort, in some ways an admission of failure.

Military law is not the blunderbuss that some of its critics allege. If metaphors have to be made, it is more like a machine-gun covering the whole of no man's land during an unofficial cease-fire. To start shooting every time someone on the other side strayed forward of the agreed line would be impracticable, and even counter-productive or dangerous. But the system has to open fire whenever a serious threat arises, and feels obliged to uphold the proprieties if a senior officer or civilian witnesses happen to be present.

Recently, however, many sergeant majors and company officers have found that soldiers contest charges at every opportunity – according to old quartermasters, even more so than the barrack-room lawyer of National Service days. If the lance corporal who reports them then becomes confused and uncertain, he will be 'in for a real ear-bending' afterwards in the sergeant major's office. According to a battery sergeant major, junior NCOs were 'now afraid to exert pressure' as a result.

For a promising soldier, promotion to lance corporal should come after about four years' service and promotion to corporal after about six years' service – though these periods are being reduced as more NCOs leave the Army for better paid jobs and less of 'the embuggerance factor' outside. Regimental officers and sergeant majors are increasingly uneasy at the youth and inexperience of many of their replacements.

The step from lance corporal to corporal is more significant because the soldier achieves a tactical command in the form of a section or tank. As a result, training is much more formalized, with most of it taking place outside the regiment under the auspices of the arm or corps. Courses, the NCO soon finds, dominate his career, and remorselessly punctuate his family life.

The infantry organizes section commanders' courses. They come in two parts: the demanding six-week section commanders' course at Brecon, for which a considerable amount of fitness training is required in advance, and the weapons and range qualification course, also lasting six weeks, run by the Small Arms School Corps based at Warminster. The armoured corps runs a tank commanders' course at Bovington, and almost all the other arms and services have their own equivalents.

The rank of corporal – 'full screw' in slang – is the halfway stage between junior ranks and senior NCOs. A corporal with any ambition has his eye on the sergeants' mess, and the corporals' mess styles itself accordingly. The mess itself is seldom a separate building, but often consists of the whole upper floor of a typical barrack block, perhaps above the Naafi shop and junior ranks' club. Inevitably the focal point is the bar, which is often lavishly equipped and decorated. The room will be lined with wall plaques, and there are usually gaming machines, a darts board and a snooker table. An area beyond may well have a small dance floor and at the other end of the room are rows of easy-stack chairs ready for a mess meeting.

Mess meetings discuss everything from subscriptions, usually about £5 or £10 a month, to planning social events. The corporals' mess often tries to rival the sergeants' mess over the two major fixtures: the summer ball and the Christmas draw. Themes are popular for the summer ball, and a real pride is taken in the imagination, time and money devoted to converting the gymnasium into 1920s Chicago with theatrical backdrops. One Royal Corps of Transport corporals' mess spent over £3,500 on food and decorations alone for a single evening.

For a young soldier moving up the ladder, the corporals' mess provides a first taste of Army social ritual. The degree of informality permitted depends very much on the regiment and on the RSM, who takes a close interest in their behaviour and dress: jeans and track-suits are usually banned.

Corporals are frequently invited to the sergeants' mess for darts and snooker matches and, occasionally, a formal dinner. This offers them a sort of apprenticeship and, as one RSM said, 'It gives me a good chance to see those I want in my mess in the future and those I don't.'

In an army that is more qualification-conscious than ever before, a corporal hoping for promotion to sergeant needs a range of certificates, as well as the necessary recommendation in his annual confidential report. (All soldiers must see and initial their confidential report. It is possible to appeal against the reporting officer's verdict, but in practice only the most flagrant injustice is likely to be remedied.) To stand a chance, he needs to have passed a written exam, the 'education for promotion certificate', passed the necessary trade tests – for a sergeant in an armoured regiment that means gunnery, signals and driving and maintenance – and qualified as an instructor. Once again, the commanding officer will allow the RSM a right of veto at the promotion conference. The final decision, however, lies outside the regiment with a promotion board at the manning and record office.

Career blockages seldom occur now in the higher ranks. This is due to a 'vacuum effect' caused by too many sergeants and warrant officers leaving the Army, or receiving late-entry commissions to make up shortages of Sandhurst-trained officers. Nowadays, an NCO moving up satisfactorily should be promoted to sergeant after about eight or nine years' service, instead of eleven or more as in the past. Many make it much more quickly. Not surprisingly, considering its effect on their own status as well as on their families' way of life, non-commissioned officers treat the whole subject of promotion with great seriousness. Checks to advancement can cause deep resentment, particularly if it is felt that the regimental sergeant major may have had a hand in the matter.

The increased rapidity of promotion has led to a much higher proportion of the sergeants' mess being under the age of thirty. RSMs under thirty-five are not uncommon nowadays. Regimental officers and sergeant majors are worried that the relative lack of maturity and experience of newly promoted sergeants makes it harder for them to take in hand a platoon or troop commander fresh from Sandhurst.

Sergeants already have quite enough responsibilities – preparing vehicles and equipment for major events such as the annual review of the unit, gunnery camp, a major exercise or, most time-consuming of all, organizing the 'handover' of equipment, stores and accommodation to the next regiment – to devote as much time to a new officer as used to be the case. At crucial moments in the programme, the last thing they need is energetic ignorance from a twenty-year-old lieutenant. Young officers, particularly those with a hint of the Hooray Henry, are often known as 'Ruperts'. Some sergeants' messes privately nominate a 'Rupert of the year': the biggest prat in the regiment with a pip on his shoulder.

Officially, the best appointment for a sergeant is as an instructor in a training establishment, while a posting to Sandhurst is considered the crowning honour. The screening of candidates for junior regiments and depots is very careful: any record of violence on a charge sheet, however far back, eliminates a candidate immediately. Yet, however highly regarded training posts might be when NCOs are considered for promotion, they themselves show little enthusiasm for the work. (Young officers, on the other hand, object less to training jobs, and take full advantage of the fixed holiday periods to organize trips abroad.) A sergeant will often find the hours hard to stomach; those in charge of recruits may have to spend up to sixteen hours in barracks. As a result, he sees almost nothing of his children, his wife complains that he's only home to eat and sleep, and they both miss friends from the regiment.

A sergeants' mess, especially one outside the United Kingdom, is much more a centre of social life than the officers' mess. Many officers remark how the sergeants 'take that sort of thing incredibly seriously'. But they do not acknowledge how much things have changed. In many regiments, the best parties and all the life are in the sergeants' mess, while officers' messes have become characterless in comparison.

For a start, sergeants, under the leadership – some would say under the whip – of the regimental sergeant major, a man who has immense influence over their lives, often invest a great deal of time and money in home improvements, such as building a new bar, when they take over a barracks from another regiment. Very soon, their new mess is decorated with regimental prints and appropriate military paraphernalia. A gunner mess will have highly polished brass shellcases as cylindrical gongs, and sawn-off shellcases as ashtrays, while the Army

Air Corps may have an old propeller. Wall plaques are ubiquitous, except perhaps in the sergeants' mess of a Guards or cavalry regiment, where such items are rather despised. A cavalry sergeants' mess has a very clear idea of its own dignity. The RSM of a lancer regiment remarked with a certain hauteur that the establishment they had taken over from a regiment of dragoon guards was not what he considered a proper cavalry mess. By the time he and his sergeants had finished rebuilding and redecorating, and installed their paintings and showcases of silver, it put most officers' messes to shame.

For a recently promoted sergeant, the unfamiliar surroundings and customs can be daunting. A newcomer lives in fear of forgetting a mess meeting called by the RSM, or passing the port in the wrong direction at a dinner night. With its socials and games nights – such as snooker and darts against the local police – mess life eats into time otherwise spent with wives and family. It is also expensive. What with subscriptions, contributions to charities, over £200 for mess dress, mess bills including as many as two formal dinners a month, new sergeants joke uneasily that they can't afford the pay rise. Not surprisingly, their wives resent such extravagance when, as a family, they are supposed to be paying off debts, or saving up for a house or a new car.

Most wives, however, appreciate the meticulously planned, and often lavish, events such as the summer ball. One Parachute Regiment mess organizes hen nights. The husbands serve the dinner, and afterwards they do the washing-up while the wives enjoy their 'entertainment' behind closed doors. Fancy dress parties seem to be a general favourite. If the sergeants' mess is known to be organizing an *'Allo 'Allo* party, with everyone dressed as their favourite character, or a Naughty Nineties dance, rumours of the RSM's wife turning up dressed as Fifi la Gitane fire the imagination of the whole regiment from the colonel down.

The RSM's wife can in fact be rather a sad figure, because the other wives steer clear of her. And her life is not made any easier if her husband is imprisoned by a rigid self-image. One RSM, explaining his position in the mess, said: 'Familiarity breeds contempt, so I can't allow myself to break down the barriers. It is lonely, though, because you can't let them see you as you really are.'

The tenor and customs of a mess are largely predetermined by regimental attitudes. Some are very relaxed and civilian in outlook, more like a club, while others appear to be living in another world based on a vision of officers' messes which no longer exist.

The drill sergeants at Pirbright, who instruct other NCOs from the rest of the Army, operate the all-arms drill course with a system of 'voluntary fines'. Each major mistake on the square costs a bottle of specially labelled 'Driller's Port'. After work on Friday, all the sergeants on the course have to assemble with their fines and drink them together. Clearly unfit to drive home that evening, they seldom reach their wives before Saturday lunch time, out of pocket and with a wicked hangover. 'Tradition'll be the death of this man's Army,' was the verdict of one sufferer. (In the Foot Guards, port seems to have acquired a symbolic importance. Some RSMs, as concerned about their voice as an opera singer, traditionally take a swig of port before a parade 'to oil the larynx'.)

After about four years, a sergeant has at least a 60 per cent chance of promotion to staff sergeant. And after another year or two, nearly 70 per cent of staff sergeants go on to become a warrant officer class II, the official rank of a company or squadron sergeant major. And 60 per cent of them make it to warrant officer class I – the official rank of a regimental sergeant major – or are appointed to a late-entry commission – what some young officers from Sandhurst rather churlishly call 'a retread officer'.

The late-entry commission is an amplification of the old quartermaster commission. In the past the commissioning of sergeant majors was for specified appointments such as quartermasters, directors of music, riding master in the Household Cavalry, instructors in gunnery of the Royal Artillery, survey executive officers in the Royal Engineers, and master-at-arms in the Army Physical Training Corps. In practice they were used in a variety of other posts relevant to their administrative experience, mainly running the regiment's 'rear echelon', such as the motor transport section, then perhaps later as a major, commanding headquarters company.

Smaller, more specialized parts of the Army, such as the Royal Army Medical Corps, need administrative officers with man-management experience, and they inevitably look to regiments like the Guards with a record for producing good warrant officers. Indeed, the Guards complain, albeit with a strong streak of pride, that their sergeants' messes appear to be regarded as late-entry officer factories for the rest of the Army.

The dramatic acceleration in commissioning warrant officers began about ten years ago, when they were needed to fill the first 'black hole', created by the exodus of Sandhurst-trained officers. But the measure was not regarded a great success, and the Royal Artillery became uneasy at the longer-term effects of 'creaming off the sergeants' mess'. Nearly 30 per cent of the officers commissioned in the year 1990–91 came from the sergeants' mess. In the Royal Signals, the most seriously under-officered of all corps, just over 40 per cent came from the sergeants' mess.

Officer shortages, above all at the captain level, still cause serious concern. Infantry battalions, re-equipping with Warrior infantry fighting vehicles, had to have second captains in each company to command the 'wagons' when their occupants were dismounted. But several commanding officers discovered that late-entry captains were often disastrous in a tactical role. Having never been allowed any command experience in the field, they were liable to panic. The lesson certainly appears to be that, for anything other than straightforward administrative jobs, commissioning from the ranks must take place earlier. But that, RSMs reply, simply means removing the best young sergeants before they have had a chance to contribute where it really matters.

With increasing justification, RSMs are convinced that the sergeants' mess is the heart and the repository of regimental values, principally because officers are now too concerned with their own careers. If the sergeants' mess is allowed to run down, then the whole basis of the British Army is eroded. This is what might be described as a self-sealing truth, particularly in an institution where emotive perceptions can be much stronger than reality.

The RSM, who may well believe that he has reduced his own chances of a late-entry commission by going on to the top rank in the regiment, has a very strong sense of obligation. He is likely to be regarded by the officers as a 'great regimental character' – as is, though with a good deal of irony, his sidekick, the provost sergeant.

Because they must be seen to uphold the system, the two of them find it hard to resist acting the part, like the official executioner. The provost sergeant is hardly expected to overflow with liberal sympathies. The post was once a sinecure for 'the old and bold', but the relatively new breed of younger provost sergeant seems to enjoy styling himself on a B-movie version of the SS, with the peak of his forage cap down over the eyes.

The traditional RSM, obsessed with appearances, will make soldiers' lives much more laborious and irritating than is necessary. Eager to escape his office in regimental headquarters, and to emphasize how much he loathes paperwork, he will summon the provost sergeant by telephone; then, after adjusting their forage caps on the steps, sticks tucked under their arms, they will proceed on their rounds. These relentless inspections of company areas force company sergeant majors to send out work parties in case a couple of pieces of litter become a major symbol of decline.

Mercifully, this sort of diehard is gradually disappearing.

A growing number of RSMs have realized that they do not need to live up to an alarming stereotype to achieve results. They also know that, although maintaining standards is important, the Army is no longer in a position to mess soldiers around. If too many vote with their feet, then the regiment itself is at risk.

CHAPTER 5

Married to the Army

The official relationship between the Army and soldiers' wives developed in the latter part of the nineteenth century, when long periods of service overseas and Victorian sensibilities changed the camp-following practice of centuries. 'Regimental harlots and seamstresses' were dragooned into married respectability, and, providing she conformed to a pattern of behaviour prescribed by officers' wives and the chaplain, Judy O'Grady received official recognition and a measure of charity.

The British Army has never suffered total defeat and disintegration. As a result it has never had to make a clean break with the past. Cold War deployment in Germany replaced the distant stations of imperial commitment, and in Britain, the Army, with its housing and medical services like a prototype version of the welfare state, managed to insulate itself from many of the social changes ushered in after 1945. Since then, like other British institutions which seemed to work satisfactorily in their time, only spasmodic improvements were considered necessary.

Conditions of married service have of course improved considerably in the post-war years, but during the same period the expectations of the whole country and of women in particular have changed still more. Following the introduction of the 'military salary' in 1970, and the wider availability of married quarters, a much higher proportion of servicemen married young. The aspirations and attitudes of Army families gradually became closer to those of civilian society at large. The Army underestimated the long-term implications of these developments. When the number of servicemen leaving because of their wives' unhappiness became a problem several years later, an independent

59

study was commissioned. But the recommendations of the Spencer Report of 1975 were not accepted by the Army Board. Missing this opportunity to put right some of the Army's more unenlightened practices postponed the problem to a less forgiving generation of wives, thereby increasing it considerably.

By 1985, once the recruiting boom of 1980 and 1981 had tailed off, it again became clear that too many trained men were leaving because of 'distaff influences'. The Adjutant General of the day, General Sir Roland Guy, commissioned Colonel Michael Gaffney to study the problem in detail.

The Gaffney Report, written with his wife, who accompanied him, was a remarkable document. With painful honesty, Gaffney admitted how commanding officers – he did not spare himself – refused to acknowledge the reality of wives' complaints. In a way, the most interesting implication of his report lay less in the immediate results than in the revealing reactions his words provoked. At first, the system as a whole demonstrated a powerful inertia when certain articles of faith, above all the paternalistic nature of the regimental system, were called into question. Not surprisingly, considerations which directly affected decisions regarded as exclusively military, such as deployment, stuck most firmly in the Army's gullet. The more hostile critics clearly felt that the Army should not go in for this sort of self-examination, and derided the findings accordingly. But, although many over forty displayed that visceral misogyny or affectionate contempt so common among previous generations of British males, younger NCOs and officers, particularly the better educated, were much closer to the more egalitarian views of their civilian contemporaries.

The Adjutant General did not allow the Gaffney Report to disappear into oblivion. His successor, General Sir David Mostyn, pledged 'fully to implement the recommendations made', and a number of changes have come about.[1] One of the more symbolic is that a wife is at last called Mrs Smith on official forms and no longer 'Wife of Private Smith'. But, although there has been a marked improvement in attitude over the last couple of years, a shift which the Gulf war should have accelerated, many of the worst problems still facing service families are beyond the power of generals. Many of the worries and complaints of Army wives can be solved only with increased spending at a time of constantly reduced budgets. More than a few are common to housing estates all over Britain. Others come with the job.

Lacking control over his own fate, a young soldier's devil-may-care attitude makes a very dubious virtue out of necessity. He will look forward to a spree after a long exercise or tour, or to a change of posting, but any attempt to plan for the future seems a pointless exercise, given the arbitrary nature of service life.

Sudden upheavals affect the infantry more than anyone else. For the first few years at least, young soldiers take pride in the idea of a go-anywhere existence: many have joined the Army because of their inability to settle down in civilian life. But a sudden decision to marry does not make their restlessness go away, not when they are still so young.

Senior NCOs and warrant officers despair that 'young lads who can hardly look after themselves' come back from two weeks' leave having married virtually on the spur of the moment. Often they are simply afraid of losing a girlfriend. Many rush to marry just before a posting. 'They've no idea what they're taking on, some of them,' said one company sergeant major. 'A young lad can come into my office and announce he's hitched up with a woman nearly ten years older with two children of her own, so can he have a quarter large enough please, sir.' He admitted that many soldiers married just to get some privacy – 'there's no way they can court from a barrack block' – yet he did not add that the practice of picking on single soldiers for extra duties, simply because they were closest to hand, also played a part.

★

A private soldier tends to classify women in three categories: prozzies, slags and the girl from home whom he'll
marry. They only really go to prostitutes when abroad,
either 'because there's nothing else', or because they treat
it as a form of sightseeing. It offers the chance to brag
later about 'the local girl' they had a good time with. The
slag is a girl who hangs about the barracks and goes with
soldiers. She will soon find herself a bad, if not cruel, joke.
They relish describing her as 'really rough', accompanied
by some disobliging simile – an old favourite used to be
'She's got a face like a grenade range'.

Another possible bride, seldom imagined in advance,
is a foreigner. Soldiers bring back wives from almost
everywhere the British Army goes. Germany is the most
obvious example. Out of 65,000 married soldiers and NCOs
worldwide, about 2,500 are married to Germans. The effect
over the years is best shown by the fact that some 40,000
former British servicemen are estimated to have settled
in Germany, the vast majority in Westphalia. The size of
this community reflects the reluctance of young German
wives to leave both *Heimat* and *Mutti* when their husbands
have to return to the United Kingdom on posting. Their
unhappiness away from home appears even more intense
than that of young British wives abroad.

A regiment on a six-month unaccompanied tour in Belize
may return with up to a dozen wives. The odds against
such marriages succeeding are heavy, but some survive
against all warnings that 'she only wanted a ticket out'
– the sergeants' mess of one artillery regiment still had
several Belizean wives from a tour there a dozen years
before. Most soldiers, however, still prefer to marry the
girl from home. Unfortunately, one of her chief attractions
– that she has not been out with other soldiers – is likely to
prove a major disadvantage: she will have even less of an
accurate idea of Army life than a recruit.

The young Army bride, sometimes no more than seventeen or eighteen years old, is naturally excited at the
prospect of changing her life at a stroke. She can throw

over her job in a supermarket or factory and escape the petty arguments at home. If her fiancé's regiment is in Germany, accompanying him abroad seems like one long holiday, while the idea of her own house or flat makes her glow with adult pride.

But arrival in north Germany, particularly in winter, with the flat landscape and pine forests covered in snow, can be utterly demoralizing. She knows nobody in this strange, empty and rather eerie country. 'Most of 'em just cry and cry for days,' said a young sapper. 'Mine certainly did.' Often the husband cannot cope emotionally, so he storms out in a show of disgust to rejoin his mates for a night's drinking. 'They think they can get married', said a Scottish company sergeant major, 'and still act as a single laddie'.

After the initial tears and recriminations, a new phase of rows will start. The military married patch, with financial problems as the chief cause of domestic dispute, is little different from its civilian equivalent. When the couple first met, the young soldier probably exaggerated the amount of money he earned and bragged that he would soon be buying a car; and, not having saved for the marriage, he probably borrowed more money over and above his outstanding debts to pay for the ring and some new clothes as well as for various celebrations and the honeymoon.

Once in their quarter, the young couple usually want to replace the issue furniture and buy a television. In what is known as the 'Schrank syndrome', young soldiers and their wives in Germany buy huge cabinet and wall unit assemblies (*Schrank* in German) on credit; but when they return to married quarters in Britain they often find the rooms are too small, and 'end up with the best furnished garden around'. Credit is also easy with his Naafi card, but they soon find that with the repayments and, above all, the interest charges, they have barely enough money for food at home, let alone a night out.

A few couples will be dragged down by the vicious circle, even into the hands of loan sharks. In extreme cases the soldier may be discharged from the Army as SNLR, or 'services no longer required'. The majority struggle on resentfully, still failing to understand how or where their money went. Some young soldiers will be lucky, and find that the girl they married is strong enough to take their affairs in hand and cut spending until all debts are paid off. For them, marriage really is a salvation. They become more responsible in other ways and are soon promoted, providing a fitting end to a moral tale.

The biggest welfare worry on the married patch inevitably centres on the youngest wives. Contrary to the Army's wishes, in Britain they have become increasingly isolated in virtual ghettos, as corporals and sergeants have bought their own houses and moved out, thus reducing the most immediate source of help and advice. Like the rest of the country, the Army has been experiencing the accelerated disintegration of the working class. An alarming division has arisen between those who make it and those who don't, between the successful ones – highly competent and articulate NCOs and their wives, rising rapidly in the social and economic scale – and an increasingly helpless underclass.

Sometimes this division can be made worse by the existing hierarchical system. Junior ranks, those least likely to afford a car, or to encourage their wives to drive, are frequently allocated the quarters farthest from camp. Both in Britain and Germany, these outlying estates are badly served by transport since few civilian bus systems take account of service establishments. Access to competitively priced shops is therefore greatly reduced. In Germany, wives tend to stay close to home because they have not mastered even the most basic phrases. Those quartered in German 'hirings' are the most isolated of all. They resort to 'the catalogues' – shopping by mail order instead of going out.

Lack of money is only part of these families' problems. Lack of experience is far worse. Some teenage wives, having never acquired the simplest skills, are helpless. Their husbands are also emotionally out of their depth when their wives become depressed, while barrack-room advice on marital problems can be crude, to say the least. 'My advice to the Jocks', said a platoon sergeant in a Highland regiment, 'is get her fucking pregnant, then she'll have something to do.' He paused for reflection, then admitted: 'But with some that's good advice, with others it's not.'

The young wife usually has no mother handy to turn to for advice about her baby when it comes, and the cases of neglect disturb both service and civilian social workers. One indication of the scale of the problem was given in 1988, when the North-East Essex Health Authority, which covered the large Colchester garrison, analysed its records over six years and found that the infant mortality rate was twice as high in Army families as in civilian. ('Army mothers tended to be younger than other mothers . . . more of them smoked . . . and fewer intended to breastfeed their babies . . . Significantly more Army families had a history of marital stress or violence, or both.')[2]

Sometimes a young wife never fully recovers from the shock of her new surroundings. Out of touch with her family, and often painfully shy, she can have great difficulty in making friends. Her husband may also warn her against snooping by social workers or other wives, particularly those of NCOs and officers, with the result that she closes the door to everybody and becomes a virtual recluse. According to a senior psychiatric nurse, a major in the Queen Alexandra's Royal Army Nursing Corps, 90 per cent of their patients in Germany were wives and only 10 per cent soldiers.

If a young wife has a child, or her husband is away for six months on an unaccompanied tour, wives' club members and representatives from more professional welfare organisations such as SSAFA (The Soldiers', Sailors' and Airmen's Families Association) will call to make sure she is all right. The balance between intrusion and a respect for privacy is always difficult when somebody refuses help, and SSAFA staff are almost overwhelmed by the volume of work.

For many wives, the disadvantage of SSAFA is its close relationship to the chain of command. It has a duty to report certain matters to commanding officers, so confidentiality cannot always be guaranteed. SSAFA is obliged to report anything involving security and subversion (the IRA has made a number of attempts to infiltrate the Army over the years) or anything which could make a soldier unfit to carry out his operational role. The worries of those in authority that mental instability, alcoholism or drug-taking could be concealed in an organization equipped with weapons and other potentially lethal equipment is perfectly understandable, but the anxiety on the part of soldiers' wives that the slightest whisper of domestic problems to the commanding officer may ruin their husbands' careers creates a greater danger that personal problems will be even more desperately concealed.

Commanding officers and headquarters are uneasy about social work outside 'a proper regimental paternalism', as one garrison commandant put it. This is due partly to a prejudice against the idea of busybodies or 'bearded weirdies' delving into regimental matters, but more to a belief that the operational fitness of their men overrides any other consideration.

Home-Start, a civilian scheme to befriend and advise young wives, was extended with official funding from the personnel branch. Offering complete confidentiality, yet run by specially trained Army wives, Home-Start is a reasonable compromise, satisfying both sides. When carefully set up, it certainly appears to work well, but the scale of the task is daunting.

The other Army-funded initiative which has proved effective is the HIVEs (Help Information Volunteer Exchanges). A mixture of information desk, citizens' advice bureau, coffee shop and clearing house for voluntary activities, the garrison HIVE provides a much less intimidating point of contact than officers, senior NCOs or civilian officials.

The spread of HIVEs and Home-Start, first in Germany then in the United Kingdom, along with a community midwifery scheme run by SSAFA and employing service wives, offered the first tangible results of the Gaffney Report. The position of the Army wife has only just started to change. Until recently, some Rhine Army staff officers regard the US Army notion of 'spouse satisfaction' as a joke, but the Americans showed themselves incomparably more professional and far-sighted by taking the problem seriously. The US Army always enjoyed a great advantage in having a much lower proportion of married personnel in Germany, most of whom volunteered to go there; they have also had more money available; but the difference in attitude was revealing. Soon after the Gaffney Report appeared, a bachelor brigadier responsible for Rhine Army welfare joked to a senior member of the Federation of Army Wives that far too much time was devoted to the problems of wives, so he intended to set up a federation of Army bachelors. If nothing else, the Army has learnt since then that the dissatisfaction of wives can put the whole system at risk.

The main advantage of life on the married patch is the solidarity between wives at difficult times. The Gulf war provided the most outstanding example, but of continuing importance is co-operation during an unaccompanied tour, or when the regiment packs up to move. A block move is considered easier to bear because everyone is in the same boat. But a wife whose husband is 'trickle-posted' individually to a new unit, particularly someone attached to another capbadge such as an Army Catering Corps cook, feels doubly vulnerable to the power of military bureaucracy. The chances are that the husband has been sent on ahead, so the wife has to manage the move with young children all on her own. 'The Army', said a wife active in welfare work, 'still thinks regimental, but forgets that half the Army is on attachment.'

The complaints made about married quarters all to often seemed trivial to senior officers and civil servants, but the cumulative effect on those who have to live in the unmodernized variety can be deeply demoralizing. For a start, most of the older estates have a drab uniformity, although the quality and size of accommodation in Germany is on the whole much better than the dismal style of early welfare state architecture which still predominates amongst the 37,000 quarters in Britain. Some wives (many fewer than before) burst into tears when they see what they have got to live in on returning to this country.

Large garrisons such as Tidworth and Aldershot have long been surrounded by slum dwellings, but, although a lack of funding slows things down, a determined programme of rebuilding has been under way for several years. In Aldershot the Goose Green development and Talavera Park represent an enormous improvement, both in design and quality. 'There, they've finally got it right,' said the commanding officer of a parachute battalion, emphasizing the comparison with the accommodation for his single soldiers.

Even without the roads named after battle honours, some of which have the depressing ring of back streets in a run-down northern town, the traditional married patch is instantly recognizable as Army issue with all the front doors painted the same. So is the furniture. The discouragement of individuality extends to decoration. Only four regulation colours, which somehow manage to be both acid and pastel at the same time, are permitted. One major improvement has finally been accepted. New houses and flats for soldiers and NCOs' houses have fitted carpets instead of the ugly floor tiles which the Army used to have specially made in a showpiece of what might be termed conspicuous false economy.

The wives' feeling that they were 'institutionalized', to use Colonel Gaffney's term, was increased by the lack of respect for privacy, and a sensation that the families officer or estate warden was always checking up on them. The military mentality was also deep-rooted in most branches of officialdom dealing with quarters, since most of the civilian supervisors are retired warrant officers. A wife may still receive a ticking-off for any breach of regulations, such as not cutting the grass. But nothing arouses greater resentment than the indignity of 'marching out'. This ritual of inspecting the quarter on departure, although necessary, often seemed to bring out the authoritarian worst in housing staff. Bedsprings were inspected for dust, as if wives were recruits on barrack inspection, and 'charges raised' for every mark or stain. Problem families could leave a house in a terrible state, for which their successors would otherwise suffer; nevertheless, the accommodation service accountants, nearly always retired sergeants or sergeant majors, provoked so much frustration that in 1989 they were told to improve their image.

Marching out is only one of the trials. Constant moves create a strain on individuals and family life which should not be underestimated. A late-entry captain and his family calculated that in the course of eighteen years' service he had been absent for the equivalent of eight years, they had moved twelve times and the eldest child had attended nine different schools. The 'turbulence' can affect children badly, and disrupt their education considerably. More and more families now opt for boarding-schools, even though the financial burden is considerable on a corporal's or sergeant's pay. A boarding-school allowance is provided, but this seldom covers anything like the full fees, except at one of the more dubious establishments which exploit the service family market.

Wives felt treated like 'excess baggage'. At times an officious mentality could almost make an anomaly in allowance regulations appear the fault of the soldier or wife concerned. Some administrators seemed to forget that soldiers and their families have not asked to be moved, but are simply following orders. Moving procedures have now improved and the system works well in the United Kingdom, but the underlying attitude of military bureaucracy can still remain ungenerous at times.

The delusion that soldiers' lives and aspirations could be determined by imperial ukase has been extraordinarily persistent. A colonel in the Ministry of Defence expressed his dismay at the number of senior officers who argued that soldiers should not be allowed to marry so young. 'Do they honestly think we can still play God?' he said. No civilian organization could have got away for so long with treating its employees and their families in such a manner. Even if many complaints have not yet been remedied, the important point now is that, willingly or reluctantly, the system has started to move in the right direction.

The Army had certainly had enough warnings from its own research to show that it could not count on that sturdy blend of loyalty, fatalism and dogged good humour much longer, especially amongst the new generation of officers' and soldiers' wives. The message was received and understood by most senior officers, yet the Whitehall preference for tinkering, usually a cosmetic package with emollient declarations 'on a no-cost basis', has not disappeared.

Some garrisons have changed little. Whether in the United Kingdom or Germany, the chief problem is usually one of size. Not only do large garrisons become introverted and cut off from the civilian population, but families are spread out around a variety of housing estates where the re-establishment of regimental communities is virtually impossible.

To make the most of garrison life, the British Army attempts wherever it is stationed in the world to recreate a form of provincial society which has virtually disappeared in Britain. Energetic characters have always run activities like the saddle club, glee clubs, amateur dramatics, arts and crafts, cookery classes, flower arranging, lectures, group outings, coffee mornings, bring-and-buy sales, youth clubs, boy scouts and girl guides. But all these wax and wane depending on the enthusiasm of individuals posted in and out.

Meeting places such as a 'Rendezvous Café' are organized by the Wives' Club; a thrift shop is run by volunteers, as are the library, crèche, and keep-fit classes. The initial impetus has traditionally come from officers' wives, who are expected to take on the do-gooder role. They tend to take over out of a sense of responsibility, and run things in a jolly, well-meaning way, but few can avoid the very British middle-class habit of unintentional condescension through exaggerated politeness. Wives of soldiers and NCOs find themselves expected to play the part of customers, and in the end only a small group takes part. 'Sergeants' and soldiers' wives', said a colonel in Germany, 'don't like taking orders now from officers' wives.'

Rank-consciousness has certainly not disappeared, especially in smaller communities, yet the pattern of the past is changing with the new generation of officers' wives in regiments. A young major commented how much his wife had disliked the commanding officer's insistence that the wives of other ranks should call officers' wives 'Ma'am'. Officers' wives now tend to consider 'good works' embarrassingly dated. Social work, they believe, should be left entirely to paid professionals. Even more significantly, a new generation of corporals' and sergeants' wives has emerged. Extremely competent and articulate, and often as well or better qualified than many officers' wives, they no longer feel obliged to defer. As a result they are running more and more activities themselves and speaking out in forums such as the Federation of Army Wives. A business lunch organized by the wife of a commander-in-chief, with a corporal's wife taking all in her stride, including a colour sergeant waiting on her, provided a striking impression of even greater change to come.

The Federation of Army Wives was started in the wake of potentially dramatic events. During the economic crisis towards the end of the Callaghan administration, servicemen's pay and allowances lagged behind so much at a time of high inflation that large numbers of families were on social security – 8,000 in the Army alone. A protest movement began with a group of Navy wives in Plymouth and this snowballed. Following a rally in Hyde Park and a march on Parliament, the House of Commons lobby was overrun with pushchairs.

The more militant wives, especially those in the Royal Navy, called for military trade unions to be formed, as in one or two other Nato armies, an idea which appalled generals. But the heat was taken out of the situation when the new Conservative administration moved rapidly to give the forces a substantial pay rise.

Calls for a union fell away amongst soldiers' wives, yet many of their underlying dissatisfactions had not been solved. Aware of feelings below, yet knowing the intransigence of senior officers and officials, especially to anything they might have regarded as a militant feminist lobby, Lady Kitson, the wife of the then Commander-in-Chief UK Land Forces, General Sir Frank Kitson, started the move to bring Wives' Clubs together into a more effective organization.

Reflecting its anti-political origins, the Federation of Army Wives almost leans over backwards to avoid offending male sensibilities. Jokes about having to convince people that they were not going to burn bras on the steps of the Ministry of Defence suggest how self-conscious they were. But that they should continually feel obliged to declare loyalty to the Army and its chain of command reveals a good deal more about the attitudes of officers than of wives. FAW members are the first to say that they have received nothing but encouragement from the highest levels. Any lingering resistance comes lower down.

The Federation of Army Wives is funded by a Ministry of Defence grant (another post-Gaffney measure) and its basic function for the Army Board is to keep soldiers from leaving. In return, the FAW's role as a polite pressure group is accepted, both at the Adjutant General's conference and with government departments such as housing, social services and the Property Services Agency.

Its main work is to provide a network and a forum for wives as well as a liaison with the personnel branch at each headquarters. It has its own self-financing magazine, *Neighbours*, with a print run of around 50,000 copies. But their most imaginative schemes consist of a computer skills course known as FOCUS, which will eventually enable wives to work from home via modems, and FRED, a database to match wives' skills with jobs available in and around garrisons, both at home and overseas. In its own interests, the Ministry of Defence should invest far more in training wives in information technology, not just for family morale, but because the Army itself is desperately short of trained personnel. The failure to offer specialist pay to soldiers trained in information technology when the country as a whole faces an estimated shortfall of 100,000 computer operators by 1993 means that civilian companies can poach with ease.

It is hard to imagine a family wanting to live in its own house or a wife wanting her own career being controversial subjects in the civilian world, but in the Army they have had far-reaching implications.

During the autumn of 1988, the Army Board strongly reiterated its belief in the merits of accompanied service. Allowances were restructured to discourage the growing practice of wives staying in the couple's own house, while the husband commuted home at weekends from wherever he was working, even in some cases from Germany. Although these revisions had a certain logic, the impression given was that the Ministry of Defence had changed its policy and no longer wanted to help Army families to buy their own homes but preferred them to stay in quarters. Together with other anomalies, the package as a whole 'generated a great deal of heat'.

At the time, generals were genuinely surprised at the reaction, amongst both officers and NCOs, but this only strengthened the impression that some of them refused to acknowledge changes in society as a whole. The idea that the Army could isolate itself from outside pressures, such as the need for two incomes to pay off a much higher level of mortgage, or the desire of a new generation of wives to continue their own careers, was widely described as 'Canute-like' or 'adopting the ostrich position'.

Senior officers feared that wives' careers, house purchase and a family life outside a military environment were bound to civilianize the Army, and this forced them to defend an increasingly untenable state of affairs. Personal priorities have changed within the Army, just as they have in the world outside. More and more officers and soldiers want to share in the early life of their children. But, as with many other family-related matters, this can still produce a defensive rigidity within the hierarchy. The Army, which has a really excellent record for dealing with straightforward compassionate cases, such as a parent's death, is distinctly reluctant to allow soldiers home for something like childbirth, even when a young wife is nervous and alone.

From a wife's point of view, accompanied service means that she can seldom hope for anything better than a temporary job which is usually unsatisfying and ill paid. There are very few careers, apart from medical or social work, which can be maintained once a husband is posted abroad. If there are any jobs going in the military administration, many NCOs' wives complain that officers' wives always end up with the best ones. And all service families need a second salary to help with extremely high mortgage repayments.

Those who get on to the housing ladder soon find themselves in conflict with official views and allowance regulations. 'We're pulling in three directions,' a general acknowledged, 'with a policy of accompanied service while the Government's selling off married quarters and we're encouraging soldiers to purchase their own homes.' While the Government wants to hold on to as few married quarters as possible, generals are concerned for the future. Married quarters, they feel, are essential to the continuance of accompanied service and also to the integrity of the regimental system. And senior officers, not surprisingly, have private misgivings that any lodging allowance provided in lieu by the Treasury would prove utterly inadequate in southern England, where the shortage of houses is serious.

The Ministry of Defence, meanwhile, is disingenuous to pretend that everyone in the forces who buys a house can then let it and carry on accompanied. Some do and manage very well, but they are mostly officers, and not the majority of servicemen. NCOs often install their parents instead of tenants. But both officers and NCOs are bound to feel a strong urge to live in their own houses permanently after the disruption of half a dozen moves. This marked shift towards a civilian normality means that the tradition of regimental communities following the flag is seriously threatened.

Army marriages are often not helped by their origins. Many begin with whirlwind romances during a brief period of leave; to be separated by military duty only heightens the poignancy of the moment and encourages promises to marry at the first opportunity.

Army couples seldom have an opportunity to get to know each other properly. Very few manage to live together first, and only daughters of servicemen know anything of married patch existence. Moving around often appeals to a new wife, but after marching out of the umpteenth quarter she is liable to transfer her disillusionment to the man.

She may well feel unfairly trapped. Her life is controlled by the Army. She is almost as subject to its whims as her husband, yet she is never a truly accepted part of it. If she has a place in the order of battle, it is as the most overlooked rear echelon of all. Her husband, meanwhile, experiences a far more intense existence: he goes to interesting places, and enjoys a comradeship which seems calculated to exclude women.

Any wife accepts that military duty must take precedence over everything else. But she may well become exasperated when off-duty activities such as sport and 'socializing' also take precedence over family life. Before long, she may find it hard to distinguish between the paternalistic, often patronizing assumptions of the Army and those of her husband.

The Army husband is evolving, particularly in the more specialist arms and corps. But within the more traditional combat arms, and above all in the infantry, the old-fashioned husband, the sort who expects traditional meals with 'half a pound of joined-up meat' a day, is a persistent breed. If he ever voices his views on the place of women in mixed company, civilians are liable to assume that he is at least half joking. Even the attempts at humour are revealing. An officer recorded with horrified amusement how when the subject of Army wives came up in a pub, an old and bold corporal replied along the following lines: 'Women? We don't want them in the Army. They should all be kept in a great big compound in Aldershot so we just draw one out whenever we want.'

Some middle-aged officers and NCOs suspect some sort of feminist conspiracy against the Army. Their misogyny is not a pretty sight when it comes out. Women are seen as a political threat in their own right, whether pacifist demonstrators, environmentalists objecting to an increase in Army training areas, or feminists criticizing masculine values. Any disparagement of macho ideals seems to touch a particularly raw nerve in the Territorial Army. The Regular Army, living in an insulated world of its own, seems on the whole to feel less threatened.

The fact that so many of the younger Army wives have influenced their husbands to leave only increases suspicions of some Lysistratan plot to destabilize this most male of male institutions. But the 'dinosaurs', as Colonel Gaffney privately dubbed them, are just as likely to treat women officers and NCOs with little respect. And, although a number of younger officers hold views on women that would make most civilians gulp, male supremacist values are atrophying as they become distanced from reality. The fact that the Army needs to double the number of women in its ranks can only accelerate the pace of change. This civilizing process is also a civilianizing process. A captain in the Queen's Regiment joked that since women had become such a problem the only solution was a homosexual army along Spartan lines.

The bored or ill-used wife who 'plays around' has always existed. But a love of gossip in small communities and the sex-obsessed mythology of barrack-room, mess and married patch can exaggerate the phenomenon out of all proportion. Not long ago garrisons in Germany buzzed with tabloidesque tales of a couple of sergeants' wives part-timing as truck-stop hookers.

The trouble very seldom arises when wives are genuinely worried about their husbands, such as during a Northern Ireland tour or during Operation Granby. It happens during long exercises, or when regiments are flown off for field training in Canada or Kenya, or a six months' unaccompanied tour in Cyprus or Belize. For the wives who seek this sort of diversion, seldom more than a handful in each unit, an element of petty revenge undoubtedly plays a part as they imagine their husbands enjoying themselves in the sun and taking up with local girls.

A yearning for excitement, even danger, must also play a part, for some young wives take crazy risks, such as cruising in the favourite discos of their husbands' regiments. Word soon gets about – a few members of each regiment are always left behind, such as regimental policemen, clerks or storemen – and the cuckolded husband will be 'filled in on what's been going on' as soon as he returns. The errant wife is liable to face a rough reunion.

Regimental police have no jurisdiction in married quarters and cannot be summoned to sort out a 'domestic'.

Members of the Royal Military Police have to be called instead. Whenever possible the RMP duty room will alert the unit's families officer in the hope of solving the problem by diplomacy. If the husband is drunk or unbalanced by rage, he will be taken to the guardroom and locked in a cell until he has cooled down.

Soldiers in general, and infanteers most of all, remain a bunker of double standards. Often proud of their own infidelities, many instinctively believe that an unfaithful wife deserves to be 'slapped around a bit'. In relatively small Army communities, the long collective memory of such incidents can prove even more disastrous for the marriage.

For the husband as well as the disgraced wife, the best solution is a posting far away from the snide remarks and sidelong looks. Whenever possible, a regiment will do its best to give the couple a fresh start. But this is not easy in an infantry battalion or a cavalry regiment, since they lack the size and diversity of the artillery, engineers, signals or any of the large logistic corps which can cross-post almost at will. But transferring a couple with problems to another unit can all too often be the bureaucratic equivalent of pass-the-parcel.

Infidelity by either party is of course only one of many reasons for a relationship breaking down, and even then it is often a symptom of something else. Yet, whatever the cause of failure, the wife is at a grave disadvantage. Her husband will move back into barracks. Counselling will then be arranged for both husband and wife. If the couple has not become reconciled after three months, the soldier will then sign form AFO 1700, known to officers as the 'I-divorce-thee, I-divorce-thee, I-divorce-thee' form. This is then countersigned by his commanding officer, after which the wife is given ninety-three days to vacate the married quarter. If the house is needed, as is almost always the case in Germany, she will be forced to take up the offer of a vacant quarter back in Britain, which can mean substandard accommodation next to an abandoned camp or airfield, usually miles from anywhere. If she refuses to vacate the married quarter she is deemed an 'irregular occupant'. At the beginning of 1990 there were said to be nearly 800 'irregular occupants' in the United Kingdom alone.

Conditions could hardly be worse for someone trying to recover from the shock of a broken marriage, especially if she has small children. Her financial position may well be a nightmare as well, since the husband is obliged to pay for the married quarter only during the ninety-three days. Maintenance must be secured by a court order. And the reaction of social security officials to a wife returned from abroad is often unsympathetic. The local council may argue that they are not obliged to house her since, in their terms, she has made herself homeless, while the Army says that, given the demand for married quarters and the financial restrictions imposed upon it, no other course is possible. Wives feel that this tied-cottage system puts them entirely at the Army's mercy, and that some husbands even use the threat of an AFO 1700 to 'keep a woman in her place'.

Service life exacts a heavy toll on marriages. The divorce rate is not as high as has sometimes been suggested, but it is still on average 18 per cent higher than that for England and Wales, without allowing for divorces which take place just after a soldier has left the Army.[3] A former commanding officer pointed out that the divorce rate does not indicate the true level of service marriages in trouble. 'An artificial cement holds many couples together,' he said. And yet, in spite of the strains, it would be very wrong to depict all service family life as unhappy. Army couples often become much closer than those in other professions or walks of life. Their marriages have proved strong. Colonel Gaffney described them as 'vulcanized' because 'they've been through fire'.

Ironically, while the Army Board was insisting on accompanied service, unaccompanied tours in Northern Ireland and the Falklands were increased in length from four months to six. For the Ministry of Defence, the chief attraction of unaccompanied service is economic. Maintaining families overseas is very expensive. In fact it would not be surprising if Hong Kong became another six-month unaccompanied posting in its last few years of colonial rule.

Wives find adjusting to these long separations particularly difficult. And the attitude of many husbands does not help. One of the great bad jokes of Army life is the husband announcing, without turning his gaze from the television, 'Oh, by the way, pet. I'm off to Northern Ireland for six months tomorrow.'

The often ill-concealed relish which a husband may show at the prospect of 'real soldiering' exasperates a wife even more. She has to live with the uncertainty of what might happen to him, which in many ways is harder to bear than the danger he faces. The problem is often made worse by the husband's account which is dramatized to gain some attention. Highly coloured stories about service in Northern Ireland are another standing joke in many battalions. One company commander commented that statistically there was a greater chance of being killed in Germany, only traffic accidents didn't have the same glamour.

A six-month unaccompanied tour of any sort is no laughing matter for a wife. Suddenly she has to cope not only with the domestic side of life, but with all the minor repairs and paperwork and bills as well. She also has to be both father and mother to the children, which means that when her husband returns, a relative stranger, the children avoid him and instinctively go to their mother.

Rows often occur when the husband, probably suffering from strain after a Northern Ireland tour, tries to reassert his authority over the children. After six months it takes time for a family to get back together. And, in spite of all the macho declarations of married soldiers about what they are going to do when they get home to the wife, there is often sexual uneasiness on both sides. Hardest of all for the wife is when the husband complains that she has changed. She has had to develop two personalities, the first to cope on her own when he is away, and the second to mollify his ego, making sure he does not feel redundant at home when he returns.

Deployment to the Gulf with Operation Granby prompted some officers to assume that wives would go into the same gear as when their husbands were away in Northern Ireland. This was simplistic. Few of the younger wives in armoured and artillery regiments sent to Saudi Arabia had known a tour in Northern Ireland. And even those infantry wives more used to the strain found the Gulf deployment difficult to handle. Nobody knew how long their husband would be away so they could not pace themselves. And fears for their safety were much greater with the threat of chemical weapons. But the greatest worry remained that of battle stress, or post traumatic stress disorder – the fear that they were 'all going to come back changed men'.

For some the gradual development of the war in clear stages helped them come to terms with the danger; for others it made it all the more agonizingly drawn out. The threat of war was 'always at the back of your mind', one wife commented, 'but when it arrived you never really knew how to take it.' The loneliness lying awake at night was hard to bear, but perhaps not as wearing as having to stay cheerful for the children the whole time.

The stress on children was almost certainly greater than for a Northern Ireland tour. Because of the constant television coverage, disturbing fantasies easily developed, with constant playing at soldiers. Malicious rumours might start in the playground telling a child that news had just come through about his dad.

Rhine Army headquarters made preparations for informing next of kin since it would be responsible for passing on 'casualty information' to units. In each unit a specially trained CVO, or casualty visiting officer, would be alerted via a radio pager. They would then set out for the married quarter accompanied by an assistant casualty visiting officer, who was really another wife from the regiment to provide initial comfort and help.

More important, wives did not feel abandoned or forgotten. The scale of the effort, both official and unofficial, made to help them was as reassuring in its way as the practical results. The Ministry of Defence set up an information service for wives and friends of servicemen in the Gulf on BBC Ceefax and assisted helplines. Members of the royal family visited barracks and married quarters. Camcorders, provided by British companies, were used to record messages for husbands in the Gulf from families in the major garrisons affected by the deployment, principally Hohne, Fallingbostel, Soest, Osnabrück and Minden. The scheme was so popular that more camcorders were sent out to Saudi Arabia to allow soldiers to record their messages for wives and children back in Germany.

The families officers and stay-behind parties of the regiments excelled themselves. They laid on handymen ready to fix appliances, shift furniture or help with luggage, and they organized repair and breakdown services for cars and better transport to and from medical centres and camp. Roast-beef Sunday lunches were provided for families once a week. All this helped bring families together far more effectively than during any previous unaccompanied tour. In fact a significant number of wives who decided to move back to the United Kingdom to sit the war out with their own families at home found that civilian sympathy was of little help. Many decided to return to garrison life where all the other wives were suffering similar anxieties.

The demands of Operation Granby dramatically revived the Army ideal of the regimental family. Like their regiments in the desert, the regimental family showed itself at its best. The issues were clear, few complained and everyone got on with their job. Mercifully, casualties in the Gulf were far lighter than anyone had dared hope, so the worst test did not arise. But, if losses had been heavy, the solidarity shown would have probably been even stronger, assuming, of course, that they were not the result of a major blunder by senior officers. Nevertheless, the exceptional nature of Operation Granby should also act as a reminder that, although traditional military values may revive in exceptional circumstances, the day-to-day life of the Army will continue to be dominated by a growing civilian ethos.

Part Two

TO BE AN OFFICER

CHAPTER 6

Officer Selection

In the grounds of a Regency house in Wiltshire, groups of young men, and occasionally young women, can be seen clambering over obstacles of scaffolding painted red and green, using different lengths of plank and rope to form makeshift bridges or cantilevers. These activities might seem to be some sort of ritual ceremony of British improvisation, but the purpose behind it is both serious and effective.

Each member of this particular group of eight wears a coloured tabard with the individual's number front and back. Before each obstacle, or 'command task', a leader is designated. He has to work out a plan, brief the rest of the team and direct the crossing of a notional chasm with a burden, usually a weighted oil drum. The team leader is trying hard to keep his head while demonstrating bags of what used to be called OQ or 'officer quality'. If he is a bluffer, or issues orders in an officious fashion, he stands little chance: it soon shows when others do not like working with him.

A disaster, such as the bridge collapsing with half the team and the burden dropped into an imaginary ravine, does not necessarily matter. What counts is the way the leader reacts: whether he gives up, blames others, or rallies the survivors to start again. On what might seem little more than playground structures, the twin pressures of time and responsibility force the participants to reveal themselves in a fascinating way. Every nuance of confidence and panic is familiar to the directing staff, from the apparently shy character who suddenly shows his qualities to the huge, self-confident rugger player whose brain freezes at the critical moment.

There are two members of the directing staff with this group – a tall major from the Light Infantry and a lieutenant colonel from the Royal Military Police. The major's manner is one of studied disinterest. His exhortations are restricted to 'Gentlemen, you have only two minutes left' – a remark which invariably prompts frantic responses from the candidates. 'Come on, everybody, get a grip!' His body moves slowly, but his eyes are in constant motion, watching the candidates, glancing at his watch and ceaselessly making notes on his clipboard. The scarlet-bereted military policeman, a more general overseer, is much more active. He does not have to take so many detailed notes. He moves round the outside of the group, sizing them all up from every angle. This seems to suit him. He is an amusing character with rather a wicked grin.

When one remembers that the revolutionary era of the 1960s and 1970s never touched the Army, it seems ironic that officer recruitment should have suffered during the second half of the 1980s – the years of triumph of the Right. 'Thatcher's children', as a number of senior officers dubbed the yuppie generation, showed little taste for a permanent career in the Army, and many of those who joined were sceptical of its values.

Ever since the 1960s, the Army has been seeking to attract more applicants from state schools. Northerners, especially, were deterred, feeling that life in an officers' mess was not for them and that a regional accent would disqualify them. 'They see it as a foreign country,' said a colonel at the Regular Commissions Board with genuine regret.

In a partially successful attempt to counter this belief, the Army invited headmasters and career advisers to Sandhurst to hear how things had changed. Yet throughout the 1970s and early 1980s the number of officer cadets from public schools remained high. With various fluctuations, they made up about half the entry, although representing only 6 per cent of their age group. This imbalance was not due to favouritism at the Regular Commissions Board; if anything, its members slightly discriminated against those from independent schools on the grounds that they should be more self-assured in the first place.

The public school, with its mores and hierarchical system, had always been a natural preparation for Army life. One old joke claimed that a former public schoolboy immediately felt at home either in barracks or in prison because they were just like the old place. The tradition of muscular Christianity in Dickensian conditions may have faded, but such schools still encourage the sports which foster competitive teamwork, debating societies which develop a capacity for argument, and the prefectorial system which instils the confidence – or arrogance – for giving orders. Meanwhile, the egalitarian ethos prevalent in most state schools over the last twenty years ran counter to all notions of élitism. Several schools have apparently given this as their reason for refusing to provide reports on Army candidates. Those from the state sector are also deterred by their ignorance of Army life. Most public schoolboys obtain a much better idea through relatives or friends and are less put off by the Army's class mystique – a phenomenon which by now owes rather more to cinematic cliché than contemporary reality.

During the latter half of the 1980s, applicants from public schools began to appear in much smaller numbers. Eton has always been the best represented, due mainly to the fashionable ideal of a short service commission before going into politics, or the City, or running the family estate. The number of Etonians slipped from around a hundred a year a generation ago to less than twenty, and Wellington, once regarded almost as Sandhurst's junior school, produced only a handful each year.

Outside Guards and cavalry regiments, subalterns from such backgrounds became very rare, and even some cavalry regiments opened their doors to a degree unimaginable a few years before. The usual explanation for this was a collapse in the ethos of public service over the last ten years. 'It's now a race to get their noses in the trough,' said a gunner major in 1988. Whether a sweeping judgement or not, the Army's hope for 'a reverse rat-run' in the wake of stock market crashes did not come up to expectations.

Another break in the chain was the unprecedented reluctance of serving officers to recommend the Army as a career to their sons. These developments came to a head quite suddenly, and promised to change the nature of the Army dramatically. The percentage of Sandhurst entrants from public schools in the 1989 September intake was down to its lowest level ever. Then suddenly, in 1990, a recovery took place, with 40 per cent of entrants coming from independent schools. It is, however, far too soon to say whether a significant return to traditional concepts of public service has started to take place at the end of what will inevitably be regarded as the Thatcher decade.

The British Army, more than any other, has always been against the idea of making officer applicants serve first in the ranks; it cannot now do so, because the present generation, especially the graduates, would not accept it.[1]

The Army has generally aimed for a basis of 60 per cent of its subalterns as regulars and 40 per cent short service, but the present ratio, while improving from its worst levels, is around 30 per cent regular and 70 per cent short service. A short service commission is for three years. It can be extended or converted into a regular commission if the individual decides that he wants to make the Army his career, and his regiment is keen to keep him. Regiments have therefore been burdened with the responsibility of persuading short service subalterns to sign on as regulars. Those fortunate enough to be rich in officers, such as the Parachute Regiment, can even afford to take a good look at their short service officers first and then invite those they really want to convert to regular. But most cavalry regiments, which have been spending on average about eleven years at a time in Germany, have become particularly vulnerable. One commanding officer remarked that after a few years in a place like Hohne or Fallingbostel 'You've got to persuade them that they're bloody Rommels to get them to stay on.' Now, even after the Gulf war, convincing them that the 'heavy army' in Germany has a future is very hard.

Unlike soldier applicants, few of those interested in becoming an officer go to an Army careers office to begin with. The more serious candidates find out what they can from friends or relations or careers masters before cutting out the coupon in a colour supplement advertisement and sending it off.

The Ministry of Defence uses a handling company, which receives the coupons, feeds the details into a computer, and then sends off a personalized letter with a comprehensive application form and information pack. Replies are passed to the appropriate schools liaison officer, many of whom are retired majors. They will then get in touch with the applicant and tell him about the different methods of entry to Sandhurst and arrange for him to visit a regiment.

The number of schemes available is bewilderingly various. There are scholarships to help candidates at fee-paying schools, undergraduate bursaries and cadetships to assist students through university before going to Sandhurst, direct entry by graduates and non-graduates for either regular or short service commissions, and women's courses. There are also opportunities for outstanding young soldiers recommended by their commanding officers. These Army entrants, or 'notice engagement soldiers' as they are called, account for a steadily increasing proportion of the Sandhurst intake: in 1990 there were just over eighty, representing around a quarter of the non-graduate entry. The Royal Army Educational Corps at Beaconsfield runs a potential officer development course to help prepare them for the Regular Commissions Board.

The Army even has its own sixth-form college at Welbeck, the seat of previous Dukes of Portland. Welbeck's seventy-five entrants a year, mostly 16-year-olds, are principally destined for the technical corps. After Sandhurst and a few years' service, the majority of Welbexians then take a degree at the Royal Military College of Science at Shrivenham, the Army's own university. At a cost of over £20,000 per boy for the two-year course, Welbeck College ends up more expensive than Eton, but by catching them young it provides the only effective way of recruiting enough technical officers.

The Army needs to train 800 short service and regular officers a year through Sandhurst, 200 of whom should have engineering degrees. Targets are set by arm and corps. For example, the Royal Armoured Corps needs about a hundred a year, the Royal Artillery eighty and the Royal Corps of Transport about fifty. In 1989 the output had dropped sharply to just over over 600 officers commissioned during the year. The Royal Armoured Corps achieved less than three-quarters of its target and the Royal Artillery less than two-thirds. But in 1990 the intake at Sandhurst recovered to 768.

Some believe that, whether or not the officer shortage is over, a serious re-evaluation of appointments is inevitable. One colonel in the Ministry of Defence remarked that the traditional definition of jobs entirely by rank was 'based on the days when officers were assumed to be intelligent and soldiers to be thick, and never the twain should mix'. The Royal College of Defence Studies recently examined the question, and the subject is often discussed informally at Staff College. The goal-posts have been quietly shifted in some headquarters to allow a warrant officer to do a captain's job. But if NCOs are to command a platoon or a troop on a regular basis, or act as battle captains, then training methods for soldiers need to be changed to encourage a different mentality at a much earlier age. For the moment it appears that the Army would prefer to leave the system as it is and make up numbers by commissioning more soldiers from the ranks.

The Army rejects another form of substitution even more

firmly: that of the technical officer without a 'command function'. No matter how many candidates with brilliant qualifications fail the Regular Commissions Board, an officer, in the Army's eyes, must always be a leader and a soldier first. For example, in the Royal Signals, the argument runs, there may be a certain number of technical posts which do not strictly require command skills. But, if they were filled by a new category of officer limited to those posts only, then they would form a ghetto and reduce the fluidity of postings as a whole. They and the Intelligence Corps, the two combat arms with the highest proportions of specialists, dislike the idea of an etiolated back-room breed.

Some candidates do not choose their regiment or corps until they are at Sandhurst, but most begin a semi-official round of exploratory talks with regiments before they go for interview at the Regular Commissions Board. A number go on a potential officers' course designed mainly to bring on borderline cases and 'have a closer look at them'.

The best-known is Brigade Squad, which the Guards run from Pirbright. This eight-week stint puts potential officers through a concentrated version of a guardsman's basic training, culminating in a week's battle-camp. The Royal Corps of Transport also runs a widely respected course for infantry, Royal Engineer and Royal Signals candidates as well as its own, called the Potential Officer Candidate Troop.

The Parachute Regiment, which has always had one of the highest applications per vacancy, does not devote much time to borderline cases. It simply interviews possible entrants and sends them out for two days and a night with a couple of corporals 'for a little taste of field activity' to see 'if they've got a bit of bloody spark in them'.

In virtually all cases, candidates are put through what is known as a pre-RCB, a preliminary interview and test session along the lines of the Regular Commissions Board itself, which, for almost all officer applicants except

Army scholars and Welbexians, is the great obstacle before Sandhurst.

The Regular Commissions Board and its obstacle course is situated at Westbury in Wiltshire. Leighton House, the main building which serves as officers' mess and conference centre, is an imposing but not very beautiful house, with a Victorian conservatory and large rooms which have not been improved by the Property Services Agency's idea of appropriate decoration: the heavy mess armchairs and sofas in imitation leather do not look right on a mauve carpet.

The front of the house looks down on to parkland, and mature trees conceal the obstacle courses with their scrambling nets and brightly painted scaffolding. At the rear of the big house, on either side of an immaculately macadamed road, are rows of wooden huts built in 1950. In good Army style, everything is clearly labelled with red painted signs.

The candidates, of whom there are up to forty-eight at a time, stay in adjoining huts. When there are female candidates, Women's Royal Army Corps NCOs have to be drafted in to deter any attempts at 'nocturnal fraternization'. Candidates are treated as officer cadets. They have their own dining-room and ante-room – the mess equivalent of a drawing-room. And, as a finale to the course and a future taste of mess life, they are given a formal dinner with silver from the officers' mess, decanters of port and the loyal toast. A sergeant major is on hand to advise on etiquette. 'The only change we've had to make', said a Fusilier colonel showing the preparations, 'is to give them toast melba instead of rolls.' He gave a slightly lopsided grin. 'Doesn't have the same ballistic properties.'

The system for evaluating each candidate over three days is impressive. Both sensible and humane, it shows the Army at its best. The pattern has not changed a great deal since 1942, when the basic idea was copied from the Germans and then refined by Army psychiatrists. Although a production-line system – up to six groups of eight go through every week – the degree of attention given to each individual is considerable. Meticulous marking systems with in-built checks and balances prevent the distortion of a result through personal feelings. A civilian expert described it as 'a highly reliable procedure. It doesn't matter who you're assessed by.' He added that research on subsequent careers showed that it even had 'a predictive validity'.

The Board is looking for a good all-rounder. Brilliant individuals may be mercurial and have a serious flaw. A 'cool problem' is a weakness that can scupper any candidate. One of the Army's favourite sayings is that 'an officer's got to be able to think on his feet'. Short of re-creating 'terrible circumstances', the tests provide probably the best guide to those who can and cannot think clearly under pressure. The Central Electricity Generating Board has shown great interest in copying the system for choosing its nuclear power station managers.

The brigadier who acts as president takes care to emphasize that they are not trying to select embryo generals but platoon and troop commanders. Tests concentrate on each candidate's intellect, practical sense and personality. Intellect is not judged just by academic achievement, but by a combination of intelligence tests, the results of which are combined to form an Officer Intelligence Rating from nought to ten. Seven is average, below five is an almost certain failure, and anyone who scores as high as ten 'is likely to be useless on the practical tests'. Very occasionally, an individual with a brilliant academic record receives a low intelligence rating on his written tests. But the apparent paradox may well be resolved during the project stage, when a candidate is made to justify his thought processes. Under pressure, his mind freezes, or 'goes into loop'.

A sense of the practical is tested in problem-solving projects indoors and on the obstacle course with command tasks. Personality is assessed during all these activities and in at least three individual interviews. There are also group discussions on a variety of subjects – the environment, South Africa, trade unions and Northern Ireland appear to be favourites – with the emphasis on coherent argument rather than political opinion. The most dreaded task is a five-minute lecturette on a given subject at short notice.

The supervising officers, the major and lieutenant colonel, watch to see how each person reacts within the group as well as on his own. They take note of those who irritate others, of the bluffers, and of those who are unsure of themselves. Meeting with the vice-president and colonel from the Royal Army Educational Corps, they vote amongst themselves after the first day on likely passes and failures. Experience has shown them that this premature assessment is all too often proved wrong. The second full day, when the candidates come under more pressure, is much more revealing. A previously reticent character may suddenly come out of his shell, while the most self-assured turns out to be 'an empty vessel'.

'Regiments still complain indignantly when we fail Colonel Henry's son,' remarked one of the board vice-presidents. ' "He's just the sort we're looking for," they'll insist.' But the interviewers keep a particularly careful watch on candidates from military families – those said to have Army tattooed on their bums from birth – because they may be there largely out of parental pressure. 'If their heart's not in it, then the kindest thing we can do is to fail them.' The problem in any case seems likely to decrease, with far fewer officers advising sons to follow in their footsteps.

Some personality traits, such as an overbearing arrogance, are judged irredeemable. The sort of cadet who at Sandhurst used to be voted 'the officer most likely to be shot in the back by his own men when going into battle' should certainly be eliminated at this stage, but a few are bound to get through. Faults in the other direction can be rectified with training. The Army has found that the old idea of a born leader standing out from the start is seriously mistaken – the Iron Duke's unflattering school reports are cited in evidence.

Once the Army discovered how much leadership can be developed, often in the most unlikely individuals, it set up a special training scheme based at Sandhurst called Rowallan Company for borderline cases from the Regular Commissions Board. This twelve-week course concentrates on character building through canoeing and rock-climbing and other adventurous training activities. The 60 per cent who pass Rowallan go on to the proper Sandhurst course well prepared and confident. On average they perform better than those who passed the Regular Commissions Board first time, and three have won the Sword of Honour. The Army is pleased with the experiment from every point of view. Most important of all, it has provided over 1,200 officers who might otherwise have been lost.

The overall shortage of officers forced the Regular Commissions Board to pass 60 per cent in 1988 as opposed to only 48 per cent the year before. They admitted they were handing on more responsibility to Sandhurst (eliminating unsuitable candidates halfway through training is a much more expensive option), but circumstances allowed no alternative. By 1990, they were in a position to revert to more traditional standards.

Like others along the officer selection chain, Board members became acutely aware of the change in attitudes during the second half of the 1980s. Careerism started early. A number of candidates who attended were there only because they wanted the offer of a place at Sandhurst to increase their bargaining power with a civilian employer. However flattering in its way, this little ploy was not appreciated when the cost of running the Regular Commissions Board averages well over £1,000 per candidate, but it was impossible to guard against. Altogether around seventy-five a year of those offered places never turned up at Sandhurst.

The directing staff also became inured to shock at the offhand approach of many. Some have been known to turn up with earstuds and designer stubble. Out of the twelve personality categories in the final scoring, they would be marked down on two: 'awareness' and 'military compatibility'. As Sandhurst and regiments found to their disquiet, 'Thatcher's children' did not score highly in these areas. Needless to say, fingers are now kept tightly crossed that the unexpected improvement in officer recruiting, both in numbers and in attitude, will develop further.

CHAPTER 7

Sandhurst

Two memories, I found, remained vivid after more than twenty years. One was the rhythmic slap of weapons on 'present arms', followed by the crunch of a hundred boots hitting the ground in unison. (Are all humans susceptible to the hypnotic effect of mass cohesion?) The other was entirely individual: the sickening dread of pain and failure low in the stomach, waiting for the start of the inter-company assault-course competition. Of course, the moment you were off, your body became numb. A fall meant nothing more than a winded sensation. You could be pouring blood and not notice it.

In full battle order, with helmets and webbing, and slung rifles bouncing awkwardly against the kidneys, we ran across slippery logs over streams, swung on ropes and swayed out of control on the scrambling nets. Worst of all was to misjudge the take-off at the twelve-foot wall and flounder against its rough, wet face. All the time there was a background accompaniment of hoarse shouts to each other, and the cries of our physical training instructor, Staff Sergeant Jennings: 'Come on, Mr Beevor, sir! Don't be such a ninny! Mind over matter!' And you would pick yourself up out of the mud where you had sprawled, and stagger on, secretly and impotently vowing vengeance. Your lungs and your chest felt as if they would burst, or implode – it was hard to tell which.

At the finish, you stood bent over, quivering like a new-born foal, gasping for breath, and spitting whenever you could. Then we formed up in two ranks and were off again on the 'march and shoot' – march meant breaking into a run every other hundred metres. By the the time you reached the firing point on the ranges, you doubted if you could hold the rifle into your shoulder properly, let alone control it sufficiently to aim straight as the Figure 11 targets slid up, showing a charging infantryman with Tartar features.

As I look at the smug expressions in our group photograph, I still cannot understand how we won. In any case, the cup looks pretty small for such a terrible effort. Not that I would have said anything of the sort then. You had to a show a proper company spirit. That meant cheering yourself hoarse at inter-company boxing matches notable only for their unsubtle slogging. But to endure a fearful hammering and then put on a manly smile at the end earned you lots of Officer Quality points. Privately we all despised such sham enthusiasm. There was only one loyalty, and that was to our future regiment. We lived for the day when we would put on its uniform.

Curious contrasts abound in Sandhurst's 900 acres of grounds on the Surrey–Berkshire border. A beautiful area of lakes and woods, landscaped by a follower of Capability Brown, adjoins typical military training terrain of pine, gorse and bracken. Yet it is the architecture that produces the greatest incongruity.

The mixture includes Old Building, long and white with its imposing neo-classical Grand Entrance, late-sixties shoeboxes in textured grey concrete with bunker windows, and then behind the Edwardian imperial sweep of New College – in which the endless majolica-tiled corridor has traditionally been described by cadets as the longest public lavatory in the world – extends a jumble of purpose-built blocks, a last handful of Nissen huts almost approaching the age to attract a preservation order, and a shifting population of Portakabins.

This confusion unintentionally conveys the growth and upheavals of the last twenty years. Sandhurst, from running a single two-year course for regular officers only, absorbed during this period two other officer cadet schools and accumulated a variety of other responsibilities in parallel.

This time of fitful yet apparently perpetual change began in 1972 when Mons, the training school for short service officers, closed. The traditional, rather civilized pattern of Sandhurst life altered out of all recognition. Candidates for both regular and short service commissions, mostly eighteen- or nineteen-year-olds who had achieved at least two A levels at school, trained together as officer cadets in a highly intensive programme which attracted criticism within the Army as little more than a 'sausage machine'.

Today, the standard military course takes eleven months. A special course for graduates started in 1982, and now lasts just over six months. (Graduates at Sandhurst are probationary second lieutenants, not officer cadets.) Three years later Women's Royal Army Corps officer cadets transferred to a new wing at Sandhurst after their college just down the road closed down. Sandhurst also became responsible for a very mixed bag of short courses. These include the academic part of the junior command and staff course for captains, Territorial Army and Army Cadet Force officer training and the professionally qualified officers' course (chaplains, doctors, dentists, vets, and lawyers), originally dubbed the 'vicars and tarts' course by the permanent staff. Organizing all the curricula without clashes, and housing such a throughput, became an administrative nightmare. Altogether accommodation for up to 1,600 had to be provided during the year, in addition to the mainstream officer cadet intakes and the permanent staff.

A visitor to Sandhurst could not fail to notice the relentlessness of the timetable. The pressure on both cadets and permanent staff was emphatically conveyed by shouts of command and the rhythmic crunch of boots as platoons were marched or doubled from drill to military law, from skill-at-arms to the signals wing, from map-reading to the assault course, followed by a shower and a rapid change before a war studies lecture back in the warm – a contrast which has always led to cadets dropping off to sleep. In the case of women officer cadets, PT has to take place at the end of the morning or afternoon so that their hair has a chance to dry, an extra complication to the nerve-racking complexity of the programme which causes unsympathetic comment in headquarters.

The new system, which is supposed to remain in place for a minimum of five years from 1989 to give it a chance, is probably the best compromise between the often conflicting and near-impossible tasks laid upon Sandhurst since the old two-year course for regular officers ended nearly twenty years ago. The great irony is that, after years of effort to achieve a reasonable degree of cohesion and stability, the Army's future role and requirements now face fundamental re-examination.

The main course at Sandhurst, the eleven-month standard military course which has three intakes a year, is housed in New College and Old College. In 1990, a little over half were entrants from school and those who had done one of the potential officers' courses. Army entrants from the ranks made up just over 17 per cent, a proportion certain to increase still further, Welbexians had dropped to just over 11 per cent, and the remaining 16 per cent consisted of overseas students, mostly from Commonwealth countries. (Army entrants receive a short service commission which can later be converted to a regular commission on the recommendation of their commanding officer.)

The standard graduate course shares the concrete ugliness of Victory College with the women's course, both of which last a little over six months. Since the graduates, most of whom are around twenty-one to twenty-three, are older than the school entrants, they are entitled to two and a half years' seniority and a corresponding increase in pay. But the Army's inducement of accelerated promotion for those with a university degree has inevitably created rivalries and jealousies both at Sandhurst and within regiments. Officer cadets on the standard military course tend to regard graduates with a mixture of jealousy and disdain, convinced that the Army pampers them unnecessarily.

Suspicions are not limited to fellow cadets. Officers of the directing staff tend to see graduates as less committed, even fickle, for they have a noticeably higher drop-out rate. Anything up to 10 per cent leave during the first week. They are also thought to be the most interested in 'looking after number one'. (This is remarked on far beyond Sandhurst. A colonel in the Military Secretary's department which deals with officer appointments commented: 'The Army's spent too much time looking after Mr Flyer. It's now got to look after Mr Average.') The NCO instructors also complain that they are 'always questioning everything'. For their part, the graduates soon tire of the heavy jocularity: 'Come on Mr So-and-So, sir. With all that brainpower and all those degrees I'm sure we can solve a simple little problem like putting a rifle back together correctly.'

To reduce ill-feeling between the standard military course and the graduates, Academy Headquarters has arranged for them to be brought together wherever possible both in training and in competition. Another Sword of Honour is now presented to the top cadet on each graduate course as well – the keenest rivals for it are known as 'blade-runners'.

Sandhurst's chief task will always be 'to develop the qualities of leadership and to provide the basic knowledge required by all young officers of any arm or service so that after the necessary specialist training appropriate to that arm or service they will be fit to be junior commanders'. Although cumbersome in expression, this aim is met by a far more relevant syllabus than in the old days. Civilians might find it disturbingly pertinent, particularly in such subjects as counter-revolutionary warfare, but the Army will reply that this is just a product of the times. Two decades of bloodshed in Northern Ireland have left little option.

Officer cadets are much better prepared for the culture shock of their first weeks in the Army than recruits. They are far more likely to have spent time away from home, they tend to be fitter, and they arrive expecting life to be very tough. In a complete reversal of the average recruit's experience, most admit to finding it much easier than they had envisaged. According to former members of the permanent staff and cadets, the pressure was eased considerably during 1988 and 1989, some say far too much. Bulling has been virtually abolished, and the workload generally reduced so that cadets, for the first time in nearly twenty years, once again manage to spend several nights a week in London. Exercises are still tough, but nobody seems to fail for performing badly. 'People who should be binned are getting through,' said a newly commissioned subaltern.

The one thing from previous generations that has definitely not returned are the ritual humiliations of basic training. As punishment for 'dirty kit', the junior intake might find itself pushing pencils down corridors with their noses, while if the platoon was late on the square the cadet sergeant from the senior intake would subject it afterwards to 'changing parades', where for a couple of hours they would be made to change from drill order into PT kit, then into combat kit and back to drill order, with twenty press-ups for the last man standing to attention outside his door.

This prefectorial system, known as the cadet government, is now long buried. Basic training is completely in the hands of sergeants from the Guards and line infantry battalions, but it is an unconvincing imitation of the real thing. Newcomers to the permanent staff are a little overawed by Sandhurst's mystique, and their threats and insults lack conviction, as if they were actors fresh from drama school. Non-commissioned members of the permanent staff also have to treat officer cadets to a 'sir' each time they address them, but the Guards sergeant majors still manage to load that monosyllable with disrespectful irony. 'You call me sir, and I call you sir', runs the old chestnut; 'the only difference is you mean it, and I don't!'

The domination of Sandhurst life by a Guards sergeant-ocracy, dedicated to maintaining the standard of drill as the best in the world, has been greatly loosened. Officer cadets see slightly less of their platoon sergeants and more of their platoon commanders, who now take a more active role in training.

The platoon commanders' relatively low profile had nothing to do with idleness, or incompetence. Most former cadets admired them, and generally considered them 'the best officers in the Army'. The trouble was that at Sandhurst, with all its training wings and specialists, they had little chance to instruct their charges apart from indoor subjects such as military law, and 'customs and courtesies', and outdoor subjects such as tactics. Yet, although they do more now, their only prolonged contact comes on exercise.

Recent changes have also brought a breath of reason in other areas. The pursuit of physical excellence to the point of officer cadets carrying 50 per cent more weight than in the standard Combat Fitness Test has now been curbed. Sandhurst's record in lower limb injuries was one of the worst in the Army. But competitive sports – on Monday and Wednesday afternoons, with major fixtures on Saturday – have not lost any of their importance in the character-building recipe. The ferocity of Army rugby remains reminiscent of Jorrocks's comparison between hunting and war, except perhaps that the danger appears rather more closely matched. During one particularly violent encounter long ago, a cadet from Kenya was heard to yell from the sidelines: 'God, I like to see all you white wogs killing each other!'

The old academic part of a young officer's education has been either dramatically cut back or postponed. Contemporary affairs and war studies are little more than an introduction to what they will come back to on the junior command and staff course. The conventional warfare aspect seems well constructed and relevant. But the quarter of the course devoted to revolutionary guerrilla warfare and 'the challenge of terrorism' is astonishingly dated, with studies of Mao, Giap, Castro, Che Guevara and Carlos Marighella. The lecturer's self-conscious joke, that when he was at university posters of Che Guevara seemed to have been issued to students on arrival, failed even to raise a polite laugh.

Although the theory may be superannuated, the training for counter-revolutionary warfare is much more up to date. FIBUA (fighting in built-up areas) is realistically simulated during a week in abandoned married quarters not far away, which now serve as a surrogate for west Belfast. Cordon and search, soft riots, hard riots, barricade-clearing, house search, vehicle check-points, patrolling, suspect vehicle drill and key personnel guards are all included. The enemy, whether in the form of a rioting crowd with bricks and petrol bombs, or a sniper in black balaclava appearing momentarily at a window, come from units in the Aldershot area. The officer cadet temporarily acting as commander soon discovers that a television camera team is tracking every incident. He is then forced into a roadside interview. That evening the Communications Studies Department responsible for this simulated media coverage puts out a news programme recording the day's events, and the hapless commander of the hour squirms in mortification at his performance.

At the opposite end of the training scale come 'customs and courtesies', under the general subject of leadership. They provide an interesting picture of how Sandhurst and the social basis of the Army has changed. Major General JFC Fuller recalled how, just before the turn of the century, 'When I went to Sandhurst we were not taught to behave like gentlemen, because it never occurred to anyone that we could behave otherwise.'[1] Twenty years ago a company commander would gather members of the senior intake together in the ante-room, rather as a housemaster would assemble leavers to talk about the dangers of alcohol and loose women and how a gentleman should conduct himself.

The only thing which sticks in my mind from our company commander's little homily on behaviour was that an officer should never ask for a Coca-Cola in the mess.

Today, the subject of behaviour is taught in a far more structured form, and the course comes in 'packages' like almost everything else which stems from a training directive, whether man-management or first aid and health and hygiene. Company commanders nowadays feel that the much wider social basis of the officer corps means that there are 'a lot more rough edges to knock off' – though one writer described the Sandhurst approach as 'the perpetuation of a squirearchical ethos long after the squires have departed'.[2]

The behaviour package includes 'introduction to good manners', 'customs and etiquette', and 'invitations and thank-you letters'. Subsequent periods cover 'mess procedure', 'behaviour at dinner nights and guests', 'conversation' and 'after-dinner'. The Guards and cavalry clique amongst the cadets may still raise their eyebrows in amusement at the earnest note-taking around them, but this shrink-wrapping of social codes into 'training packages' seems to symbolize not the preservation of that world known to previous generations, but its final passing.

This side of the Sandhurst officer factory is known as the 'chameleon effect'. Cadets are taught to dress to a middle-class average in their civilian clothes. Regional diversity disappears into the nasal monotone of corporation man: during a communication studies period on television technique a cadet with a wonderful West Country accent joked about the inevitability of losing his. But this conformism is superficial. Cadets today tend to play the part expected of them, but not much more, and then only because it is necessary to their careers. Only the least confident allow themselves to be remoulded in the Army's image. This change is not restricted to Sandhurst – the staff at RAF Cranwell have found exactly the same attitude amongst their cadets.

The notion of a code of values in the services, passed on like a sort of social DNA chain, suddenly appeared to have crumbled in the late 1980s. But that lingering minority of cadets who show no less enthusiasm for traditional soldiering and regimental tradition than their father's generation may find themselves less out on a limb. They are, however, still the ones most likely to find that their idealism leads to 'a very cold shower', particularly if on reaching their regiment they find that their soldiers 'just don't want to know'.

The sudden drop in ethical standards in society as a whole has caused serious concern in the Army, which has a greater horror of dishonesty than the police. Sandhurst has experienced a marked rise in cases of 'financial impropriety' amongst cadets, including credit card fraud. A general who was very much concerned with officer discipline said he had been horrified above all by the refusal of culprits to see that they had done anything wrong. A Guards commanding officer remarked that there had probably always been the odd bad apple in the past, but now it seemed as if the Army had also been infected by the utter unscrupulousness which had become prevalent outside in the last five years. Whether, with the indication of another sea-change, this decreases again will be interesting to see.

Commanding officers and colonels of regiments take a close interest in the progress of those joining their battalion or regiment on passing out of Sandhurst. They also interview other cadets who have not yet made their choice of regiment or corps.

The climax of the course at Sandhurst has always been the Sovereign's Parade. The officer cadets who are passing out leave the parade ground by marching up the steps of the Grand Entrance and into Old Building. The adjutant, a major from the Foot Guards, rides his grey charger up the steps behind them and then down the long corridor, where a couple of soldiers wait with shovels at the ready to clear up behind the horse. In the past, cadets were deemed to have received their commissions the moment the doors of the Grand Entrance closed behind them.

Many years ago one fledgling officer wanted to take revenge on a sergeant major by trying to put him under close arrest. History does not record the outcome, nor Sandhurst's embarrassment at having allowed such an appalling character to become an officer. But, ever since, cadets have not received their commissions until midnight, by which time members of the permanent staff have disappeared with the end of term.

That evening, just before the commissioning ball, as the fledgling officers dress in their brand-new regimental mess kit for the first time, the pip on each little epaulette is covered with material tied in a bow to await its unveiling at midnight. However beautiful their dresses, girlfriends know they take second place in the peacock parade of new uniforms, with Guards, line infantry and most of the corps in scarlet jackets, the Light Division and Gurkhas in rifle green, gunners in dark blue faced in red, and then the chaos of the cavalry, high-necked jackets and rich waistcoats trimmed in gold, scarlet jackets for dragoon guards, midnight blue for hussars and lancers, and skin-tight overalls with thick double stripes down to the swan-neck spurs which catch in dresses. Seen through drunken eyes, the varied mass of uniforms provides a constantly shifting kaleidoscope.

The Edwardian elegance is, however, restricted to the uniforms. Champagne, when it is not being sprayed around, is more often drunk from the bottle than the glass. At midnight, when girlfriends pull off the cache-pips to turn cadets into officers, the rite of passage can become quite orgiastic. 'I know we all behaved badly in our time at Sandhurst,' remarked a very unpompous infantry officer, certainly not the sort to indulge in expostulations of the *O tempora, O mores* variety, 'but we didn't bloody well have it away on the grass opposite the Grand Entrance.'

CHAPTER 8
Young Officers

After leaving Sandhurst on a wave of euphoria and champagne, the newly commissioned second lieutenant is usually allowed two or three weeks of what used to be known as embarkation leave. During this time he will assemble the rest of his trousseau.

The uniform allowance seldom covers the cost of everything if purchased new, especially for infantry and cavalry regiments. An officer has to have shirts and hats as well as service dress (No. 2 dress), mess kit and all the seldom-used accoutrements such as Sam Brownes and sword frogs, though only regular officers are expected to buy their own sword, claymore or sabre. Wherever possible the regiment itself will help out from a store of second-hand uniforms donated by officers on leaving. The gunners at Larkhill, for example, run a very effective recycling operation.

Many in the infantry and cavalry resist the idea of standardizing uniforms, which they see as a dangerous step towards a homogenized officer corps. But, leaving aside any arguments about the future of the regimental system, the expense of mess dress, which few officers wear more than four or five times a year, is increasingly hard to justify. It is in any case an uncomfortable, unflattering (for all except those with tiny bottoms) and thoroughly antiquated apparel at the best of times. As more and more officers contend, a far better solution would be to adapt Sandhurst No. 1 dress, the blue patrol, for both evening and ceremonial use.

The uniform allowance is clearly inadequate for the smarter regiments. Their sartorial complexities are still tended by tailors around Savile Row and Sackville Street. Forage cap, sidecap and No. 1 dress cap come from Herbert

Johnsons's, long known as Herbie J's. A loan or a parental contribution is often the only recourse for unmoneyed young officers joining cavalry and many infantry regiments. Private incomes are seldom expected today. The commanding officer might well suggest to parents that they buy their son a car, because he would not be able to pay for one on credit on top of his other expenses. Certain regiments, notably the Household Cavalry and the Royal Scots Dragoon Guards, have always attracted rich officers, but that does not mean they would refuse a penniless one, particularly if he is good or has a strong family connection. Officers in the Foot Guards or cavalry regiments may or may not have private money. Everything, of course, depends on the tastes of the individual: although far cheaper in the Army than outside, polo and skiing are still expensive sports.

Once the young officer has bought his uniforms, and impressed or amused his girlfriend with a private view, he awaits a posting order telling him where he is to report.

Sandhurst trains everyone to command an infantry platoon as a grounding rather than a qualification – 'Infantry tactics are used as a medium to teach leadership qualities rather than to teach tactics themselves.'[1] Subalterns are therefore sent (usually after a short spell with the regiment to focus their ideas) on a three-month special-to-arm course. The special-to-arm course, whether that of, say, the Royal Engineers at Chatham, the Royal Signals at Blandford, or the Royal Corps of Transport at Aldershot, will train them on the specialist equipment they will be in charge of in their regiment.

Armoured corps officers, after spending a few weeks with the regiment, begin their troop leaders' course at Bovington. In the old days they would have gone there straight away, but many cavalry subalterns, still on a post-commissioning high, went to too many parties and failed to concentrate during vehicle maintenance and gunnery lectures. The short spell with the regiment makes them realize how little they know, and how hard they will have to concentrate. But the traditional diversions of young cavalry officers, racing back to London at night, do not seem to have disappeared entirely. No less than seven cars were written off during a recent course.

Newly commissioned officers in the infantry usually spend six months with their regiment before going off to Warminster for the platoon commanders' battle course. Officers destined for the Parachute Regiment face the toughest time. Before parachute training at Netheravon, they have to pass the 'P Company' course of physical endurance. A young Guards subaltern's first taste of regimental life is more likely to consist of marching round 'the Birthday Cake' outside Buckingham Palace in bearskin and tunic than of platoon attacks on Salisbury Plain with their faces smeared in green and brown 'cam cream'. Those joining a battalion already in Northern Ireland will find themselves doing a very different sort of course at Ballykinler before they are allowed on the streets of Belfast or Londonderry.

Twenty-odd years ago, when most of the present commanding officers joined their regiments for the first time, a freshly commissioned subaltern was treated very much like a new boy at school. In one or two messes nobody spoke to him for several months, and captains over breakfast would answer with frosty stares if he said so much as 'good morning'.

Some regiments stationed in Germany used to play practical jokes on innocent newcomers. A favourite was for them to be collected from the airport by a couple of officers dressed up as scruffy soldiers, who then behaved in a thoroughly insubordinate manner to see how they reacted. One of the most elaborate tricks consisted of warning a group of three newly arrived subalterns that they would be dropped off as a standing patrol that night on what was the 'inner German border'. After a long drive in the back of a Land Rover with the canvas roof fastened down, they were led forward in a crouching run to a waterlogged ditch where they were told to hide. Ahead was a wire fence with arc lights and guards patrolling with dogs. Keyed up at this first sight of the enemy and proud of the duty entrusted to them, they ignored the freezing conditions and scrupulously noted all movements until dawn. Only when they were collected for breakfast in the mess did they discover that they had spent the whole night observing the camp ammunition compound a few hundred yards down the road.

Today, the officer initiation rituals organized by senior subalterns are much less imaginative. Most of them are little more than a crude drinking test. Hideous concoctions are prepared, although some stick to the tradition of a bottle of champagne drunk unswizzled and without stopping, often from a ceremonial piece of mess silver such as a fox's mask or a presentation bowl or cup. These little rituals are liable to end messily if not unpleasantly. Officers in one cavalry regiment found themselves in serious trouble when the son of the colonel of the regiment collapsed after drinking a whole bottle of whisky.

The sergeants' mess, eager for a share of the fun, usually invites the latest batch of 'young Ruperts' over to test their capacity. For the subaltern who knows what lies ahead, it is an awesome prospect. The wise line their stomachs with a pint of milk before they leave. To make it out of the door upright is a point of honour, even if you have to crawl the rest of the way back to the officers' mess.

Partly because of the difference in age, but mainly due to a difference in attitude, the officers' mess has always tended to be far more boisterous than the sergeants' mess. Brawls of mess rugger, or getting round the outside of the ante-room without touching the floor, and other forms of compulsive bravado – what is still sometimes known as 'showing form by numbers' – occur mainly in the combat arms. But the origins of this behaviour always used to stem more from public-school rowdiness, whether or not those involved went to one, than from military machismo.

Messes have often been strikingly reminiscent of an Edwardian country house. They share that characterless masculinity of sporting or military prints, club armchairs, an upholstered brass bum-warmer round the fire, a billiard room – now used for snooker or television – and a lavatory lined with group photographs and group caricatures. Other aspects evoke a more tempting comparison with the Edwardian nursery, where romping children were ministered to by servants in a confusion of utterly ill-disciplined dogs, while adults stayed well out of the way except on set occasions. This is reflected in turns of phrase redolent of the schoolroom, or even playroom – for example, gunner officers referring to a colleague who has resigned his commission in a huff say that 'He threw his teddy in the corner'.

Yet such cosy impressions are rapidly becoming dated. Traditional custom in most regiments is dying on its feet mainly because the new generation of officers, like most outsiders, have started to see it as an anachronism. They are no longer beguiled by the eccentricities and are far more interested in their 'conditions of service', in other words their perks. Their predecessors led a life in which being well looked after, with time to indulge sporting or adventurous interests, had always been a tacitly accepted compensation for low pay. Yet that early slogan of Mrs Thatcher's administration – 'deprivilegize the civil service' – almost certainly hit the Army hardest of all.[2] The cuts and economy measures of the last ten years have both reduced mess staff and greatly increased the individual officer's workload – a combination which has reduced mess life to a utilitarian and soulless norm far more effectively than all the socialist governments since the war.

Of equal significance was the relative lack of interest shown in mess life by the generation of 'Thatcher's children'. Many would prefer to live out of camp in their own flat, either sharing with civilian friends or installed with a girlfriend, while most of the 'rough diamonds' have little time for what they regard as a public schoolboys' institution. A major in the Parachute Regiment remarked that some junior officers would be 'just as happy to eat in the Naafi or the cookhouse. The mess doesn't mean anything to them any more.' The revival in public school entry seen during 1990 may well slow this trend, but it is unlikely to reverse it entirely.

The platoon or troop sergeant has traditionally been the newly arrived subaltern's mentor. In many cavalry regiments a second lieutenant did not take command of the troop until his sergeant and the squadron leader considered him ready. In a systems-oriented army, he takes command straight away because the appropriate training packages are deemed to have qualified him.

Sergeants are also younger now, and so find it harder to make a self-assured subaltern acknowledge their experience. Yet for a junior officer the success of this relationship is still just as vital. Without the support of his sergeant he will find it very hard to learn to handle soldiers and enjoy their company. Despite all its advances in man-management training, Sandhurst can never provide a true foretaste or guide to the fascinating subtleties of that first command.

In Northern Ireland there is always the risk of a new subaltern wanting to prove himself in front of 'the Toms'. 'If you've got a headstrong platoon commander who thinks he's going to rule the world . . .' began one company sergeant major, then left the scope for disaster unspecified, perhaps because he had a particular example in mind. But, although subalterns are considered much more pushy, a general impression of them acting like Wall Street Masters of the Universe would be unfair. In any case, the subaltern's urge to indulge in *Boy's Own Paper* heroics to prove himself has always dogged every army.

If the sergeant is not around to restrain him – in Northern Ireland platoons are split – then soldiers will not shrink from the task, especially if their lives are put needlessly at risk. It has been known for a gung-ho subaltern to ignore orders to keep away from a particularly dangerous area, only to be told by his soldiers that if he wants to go on, then 'you can bloody well do it on your own . . . *sir*!'

The first thing any subaltern must recognize is that he cannot bullshit his soldiers, and that he does not know all the answers, however many courses he has been on. If he fails to learn this from their sceptical gaze on the first morning, then he is in for a hard time.

The British soldier has always survived on a sick sense of humour, which is no doubt a form of self-protection as old as war itself. His ability to crack jokes under appalling conditions never ceases to amaze officers, for whom he should be the best reason for being in the Army. And yet a number of officers now fear that the humour is disappearing, and not just because of that ubiquitous refrain from both officers and NCOs that soldiering isn't fun any more. They detect an apathy, a lack of spark and initiative, in many of the soldiers joining today.

But if recently joined soldiers are different, then their platoon and troop commanders have changed dramatically, as officers right up to the highest level of command have observed. In their view, the most significant shift is in the relationship between subalterns and their men. Captains are generally the most critical of a tendency towards what the Americans first called 'nine-to-five soldiering'. Clearly, numerous exceptions exist everywhere, and they may well increase significantly, but in their view junior officers now make little effort to get close to their soldiers and take less interest in their welfare. They knock off work at 4.30 to play squash together, and organize sport or other activities for their soldiers only when pushed into it.

Perhaps the best illustration of the contrasting attitudes came from a young NCO in the Royal Artillery. His regiment was on battle group exercises at the British Army Training Unit Suffield (BATUS) in Canada, a vast area where, for three weeks at a time, combat arm regiments from the Rhine Army can train separately and then together with the minimum of restrictions. It provides a unique opportunity in which everyone should be working flat out together, especially on maintenance at the end of the day, yet all the junior officers in the battery slipped away the moment the self-propelled guns had returned to camp. The anger of the gunners at their officers' behaviour was increased by the fact that the three men 'track-bashing' in overalls on the headquarters tank of the cavalry regiment they were supporting consisted of the commanding officer, the adjutant and the RSM. Their own subalterns did not reappear until next morning – dressed in khaki caps, service dress trousers, and highly polished shoes.

Senior officers began to discover in the late 1980s that any form of remonstrance had little effect; it merely confirmed the young officer's belief that the Army was completely out of touch. His most common complaint was the lack of attention paid to his career. Senior officers were flabbergasted when twenty-two-year-olds strolled up to ask about their best career move. 'We never gave a thought to that sort of thing,' said one colonel, 'at least not until we were in line for Staff College.'

Commanding officers try to tell subalterns to forget about their careers and enjoy soldiering while they can. 'A platoon's probably the best command they'll ever have,' said one, 'but they just don't believe me when I tell them that.' 'They're too impatient,' said another; 'that's why they've got so little commitment. If things aren't working fast enough for them, then they'll be off. The graduates first of all.'

The same general who had been disturbed by cases of financial impropriety was also appalled that young officers now refused to accept that it was 'bad order to put your leg over someone else's wife'. A typical reaction when reprimanded was to say that 'If I worked for ICI no-one would give a bugger'. (Officer cadets at Sandhurst are warned that the battalion or regiment is a family which

117

no officer should bring into disrepute through sexual misconduct with the wives of other officers. In the case of a divorce, commanding officers have to provide a certificate guaranteeing that this has not undermined 'good order or military discipline', that catch-all phrase of military justice. If he considers that it has been undermined, then the offending officer will be dealt with under Army General and Administrative Instructions, commonly known as AGAIs, a disciplinary procedure for dealing with the misconduct of officers not covered by the manual of military law.)

Much of the friction came from a new generation's open scepticism about sacred cows and conventions – an attitude that provoked stuffier officers to burst out with 'It's like joining a club. You can't pick and choose the rules.' Majors and colonels also complained that subalterns fail to maintain sufficient dignity in front of their soldiers, and that they are much too familiar. One cannot help suspecting that this was in fact a euphemistic way of referring to the change in officers' backgrounds. 'The person who is being led', said one colonel, voicing a common conviction amongst older officers, 'does not believe in being led by a bigger version of himself. He wants his officers to be different.' Such a belief may well contain a large measure of nostalgia. Soldiers used to prefer gentlemen officers, not because they looked up to them as gentlemen, but because they were more likely to be easy-going, and less officious; and yet, as another officer pointed out, a gentlemen nowadays has to be just as pushy.

Despite such litanies of dismay, an unrelieved portrait of self-centred 'military yuppies' would be unfair. A number of qualities cannot be denied them. Apart from their disconcerting self-assurance, they are on the whole much better educated and much more professional and articulate than their predecessors. If they are to be judged, it must be in the context of their own generation.

They have tended to stay in touch with contemporaries from university and school to a degree unimaginable in those not very distant days when the Army was isolated from civilian society, seeing itself as a vocation more than as a career. This contact with friends outside has influenced their political as well as their social attitudes, and they question almost everything as a result. 'It's a hierarchical society,' said a gunner colonel in one outburst. 'We're not a bloody soviet!'

A number even question such basic articles of faith as the British Army's presence in Northern Ireland. This does not mean that they sympathize with Irish nationalism or pacifist ideals; but they cannot accept that an entirely open-ended commitment can be, or should be, maintained. Many more, however, look at the work from a purely professional angle: 'It's the most satisfying thing you can do.'

The ambition of young officers is frequently misunderstood. Their critics do not seem to appreciate that they are under far greater pressure to succeed than previous generations. Ambition is probably more defensive than aggressive. 'We're now thinking ten years ahead,' said a subaltern in the Foot Guards, 'and worrying ten years ahead.'

One of the ways in which they look ahead – and here they are far more clear-sighted than their predecessors – is to the prospect of marriage in a military environment. They soon have a foretaste of the problems ahead, when one weekend after another planned with their girlfriends has to be cancelled because of some last-minute duty or regimental commitment. And, however much she may enjoy coming to regimental parties or weekends, the idea of becoming an Army wife is a very different matter.

Even the most dedicated soldiers now dislike the idea of inflicting their way of life and their brother officers' wives on someone they love. And those who stay in after marriage are far more likely to encourage a wife to keep her career. A subaltern in the Royal Engineers who had been singled out as the most promising in his regiment expressed the dilemma when he admitted in private his intention to leave: 'The Army is no place at all for a married man. If I was going to stay single it would suit me very well. It's a great shame because I don't want to leave and the idea gives me a physical feeling of being torn in two.' The problem, he felt, resulted largely from official attitudes: 'Generals seem to expect us to marry a brigadier's daughter who's been bred for the job.' He then wondered how many brigadiers' daughters were prepared to marry an officer nowadays – a question that was later echoed by several senior officers who remarked that their daughters had no intention of marrying back into the Army. In any case, the Army demanded 'the right sort of wife' – one who had no independent existence and no career of her own, who did not mind being 'wheeled out for regimental occasions' and keeping quiet the rest of the time. 'But the last thing I want', he said, 'is to marry someone who's only interested in coffee mornings and flower-arranging. A Mrs Lieutenant So-and-so who's expected to run the wives' club.'

The adjutant, the commanding officer's staff officer responsible for personnel and discipline in the regiment, also oversees the subalterns. In the interest of fairness, subalterns are fined the same rates as soldiers or NCOs for offences such as losing an identity card or a pair of binoculars. The only difference is that their fine, because it is not statutory, goes towards the officers' mess silver fund, the Army Benevolent Fund or a children's charity. Most minor breaches of discipline are punished with a number of 'extra orderly officers' or 'extra pickets', as the Foot Guards still call them.

The job of orderly officer is as unpopular amongst officers as guard duty is amongst soldiers, and yet it is a far less irksome round. The officer usually spends the night in a special room in the mess with a telephone by the bed. During an uneventful night, he has to get up only once to check the guard and sentries after the ten o'clock staff parade. But a 'domestic', or a soldier being locked up for drunkenness, may lose him several hours' sleep.

Debt is now as great a danger for subalterns as it is for their civilian contemporaries. With credit endlessly on offer, investing in an expensive car tax-free in Germany can rebound if the officer is posted back to Britain unexpectedly: many find themselves having to sell at a loss when faced with customs duties and an end to British Forces' petrol coupons. More established forms of overspending result from mess bills and entertaining girlfriends. A tradition of betting bottles of champagne on almost anything from who will marry first to a sweepstake on gunnery results – the details are recorded in the wager book – has persisted into a world where few officers have private means. This can sometimes encourage an outlook which has little to do with economic or social reality. Second lieutenants may also try to imitate free-spending young captains whose disposable income is considerably greater. A couple of nights out in Hamburg, Berlin or even London might well cause their mess bill cheque to bounce at the end of the month.

Once a lieutenant has completed two years as a platoon or troop commander, he should attend his first specialist course, such as signals, reconnaissance (always known as recce) or gunnery. A variety of other jobs open up to him, some favoured, some despised. The most unpopular of all – 'a real nothing job' – is that of assistant adjutant, a position now filled frequently by young women officers used as 'manpower replacement'.

The most sought-after appointment in cavalry and infantry regiments is commanding a recce troop or recce platoon, usually mounted in fast armoured vehicles, such as Scimitars, and acting as a reconnaissance screen. The most independent group in the regiment, it carries an aura which is both swashbuckling and seriously military. Other appointments in regimental or battalion headquarters include those of signals officer, a post usually described with mixed feelings of the could-be-worse variety, intelligence officer and operations officer. The ops officer, either a senior subaltern or junior captain, can be described roughly as the commanding officer's adjutant in the field. Much of his work in barracks is planning exercises and the fulfilment of outside commitments, such as providing the manpower for site guards and civil assistance tasks.

The choice of jobs outside the regiment is very restricted, which is something of a blessing for commanding officers short of subalterns. The only standard ones are as platoon or troop commanders at a training regiment or depot. The shortage of infantry platoon commanders in the late 1980s produced one beneficial side-effect. Battalions which must be up to strength for a priority task, like Northern Ireland, made up numbers with subalterns from other capbadges, both within the infantry and outside. Attached service helped inter-arm co-operation in other fields, even if this new fluidity between capbadges worried staunch believers in the regimental system.

A commanding officer with the regiment's future at heart must balance his requirements with the career needs of his subalterns and captains. A limited pool can make this extremely difficult for some regiments. But if there are to be suitably qualified officers to command companies or squadrons, and later the regiment itself, he must first of all persuade short service officers to stay on, since there are still so few regular officers on entry. This may require 'some judicious arm-twisting', such as reserving the interesting jobs for converts and shunting those who resign into less congenial ones.

Conceding that the officers' mess is the unmarried officer's home, the much less stuffy regime of today allows a subaltern to invite his girlfriend in, providing she behaves; he can even arrange, with the permission of the president of the mess committee (usually a senior major), for her to stay the night in one of the guest rooms. To avoid a breach of discipline, he must corridor-creep if he wants to sleep with her. Subalterns sees this as a rather unnecessary and demeaning hypocrisy, while the Army prefers to regard it as a necessary element of discretion. But whatever the respective merits of openness or discretion, the compromise reveals that this is the only way an old-fashioned institution can bend without appearing to drop its standards.

A young female officer, on the other hand, would be unwise to count on such indulgence. And another form of double standard comes between officer and soldier. Even in the new flat-style accommodation block, the single soldier could never really call his quarters his home. There are no guest rooms available for his girlfriend, so if he brings her back for the night he could find himself 'tapping the boards' in front of the commanding officer, while a subaltern caught *in flagrante delicto* would be humorously ticked off.

Nevertheless, a subaltern is just as likely as a soldier to lose his girlfriend when posted to Northern Ireland, the Falklands or Germany (the Gulf was different, partly because of the national mood, and partly because of the media attention it attracted). Yet when a young officer gets his 'Dear John' letter, he does not pin it up on the noticeboard like 'the Toms'. He is more likely to suffer in silence and vow to leave the Army. The sense of disillusionment is heightened by memories of the romantic ideal – what a former SAS officer called 'the white charger and Sir Lancelot bit' – which originally brought him into the Army.

CHAPTER 9

Onwards and Upwards

Those who deplore the career-consciousness of young officers cannot blame it entirely on self-interest. A former colonel commandant of the Parachute Regiment, General Sir Anthony Farrar-Hockley, left the commanding officers of its three regular battalions in no doubt about their responsibility. To secure the future of the regiment, they had to make sure that junior officers studied hard.

Twenty years ago, officers finishing the old two-year course at Sandhurst breathed a sigh of relief and looked forward to some enjoyable soldiering unclouded by homework. Today, their further military education starts almost as soon as they have finished their young officers' course. All subalterns, short service and regular alike, have to submit two essays a year to their commanding officer whatever the circumstances. Those on anything up to eight patrols a day in Northern Ireland think it unfair that they should have to sit down and cudgel their brains 'instead of crashing out like the Toms'. And hardly has a regular subaltern finished his first tour as a platoon or troop commander than he starts on the syllabus which leads to Staff College.

Over the last two decades, determined attempts to improve the training of the officer corps at all levels have been generally successful. Many argue, however, that the systems approach has gone too far. One training package after another was introduced, often without allowing enough time for the proper teaching or absorption of the information, as Sandhurst found to its cost. Many officers thought that the British Army had become 'the most over-instructed army in the world'. One colonel in charge of specialist training at an arms centre remarked that people seemed now to believe 'that you can't do anything until you've done a course, which really is nonsense'.

With Staff College as his goal, the ambitious young captain has to study for the different phases of the Junior Officers' Training and Education Scheme, pass the exams and, ideally, accumulate the right experience to impress selection boards later. The most useful appointment for anyone aspiring to command a regiment is that of adjutant.

The adjutant is the commanding officer's personal staff officer. He deals with manning, promotion, discipline, postings, and leave, and oversees the orderly room, which is run by the chief clerk, a staff sergeant. Adjutants work the longest hours in the regiment, if only because the telephone never stops ringing and 'people keep sticking their head round the door'. Referring to the daily bombardment of petty matters as the 'niff-naff', they find they can get down to real work only after five o'clock when everyone else has gone home.

The main requirement for captains in a regiment is to fill the post of second-in-command in a company, squadron or battery, but they are in such short supply that promotion has become greatly accelerated. Artillery regiments are particularly worried by the knock-on effect this can have. A graduate with only a couple of years' service who is 'being raced ahead beyond his experience' is likely 'to make a balls-up, get a bad confidential [report] and then leave as a result'. The alternative of commissioning warrant officers in large numbers, usually known as 'creaming off the sergeants' mess', is considered a bad short-term solution which has already been over-used.

Some parts of the Army are less short of captains than others. The Royal Corps of Transport, for example, is fortunate in having junior commands with a good deal of independence, which persuades many to stay on for the managerial experience. The Royal Electrical and Mechanical Engineers, whose light aid detachments form part of every mechanized unit, have even more semi-independent commands. But captains in logistic corps like these generally have less choice about leaving than their combat arm contemporaries. Many, in particular those who went to Welbeck before Sandhurst, are bound to the Army by a five-year contractual 'time-bar' after completing a degree course at the Royal Military College of Science at Shrivenham. As a result, the 'black hole' comes later on the logistic side than in the combat arms.

In an ideal world, a regiment should have a slight surplus of captains so that as many as possible can be spared for at least one tour outside the usual round of appointments, either with their regiments or on the staff or as instructors. This gives them an opportunity to volunteer for loan service as instructors or advisers with foreign armies, for a flying tour on helicopters with the Army Air Corps, or for service with special forces. With this very end in view, the Parachute Regiment has consciously overstepped its limit on officer recruitment whenever possible; if there were too many subalterns as a result, they were lent to short-staffed regiments for tours in Northern Ireland.

In 1987, the Military Secretary, Lieutenant General Sir Patrick Palmer, well aware of the importance of variety at this stage in an officer's career, took steps to promote the scheme further. He also underlined the Army Board's guarantee that such experience would help rather than hinder an officer's prospects at selection boards for promotion.

Loan service offers the greatest variety, with up to about 150 officers instructing or advising in over twenty countries. Loan service teams can range from 100 officers and NCOs down to single-man missions. The largest and best known is in Zimbabwe, training Mozambique government forces as well as the Zimbabwean National Army. The British Army's success in uniting the rival guerrilla groups into a single force led to a request from Namibia that a team should train their post-independence armed forces and, with the agreement of both the United

Nations and South Africa, an advance party left in January 1990. Oman, Brunei and Saudia Arabia are also major clients. The rest of the teams are spread mainly across the Middle East and Africa, with three in the Caribbean and another three in the Far East. A flying tour with the Army Air Corps is liable to complicate an officer's career, since it takes up about four years in the pre-Staff-College period. It also creates complications for the regiment: not only does it lose a senior subaltern or captain for all that time, but in most cases it loses him for good. Whether true or not, he will almost certainly feel that he has greatly reduced his chances of promotion within his old regiment. And, if he really enjoys life as a helicopter pilot, he will either transfer to the Army Air Corps or decide to continue flying outside the Army at a much higher salary.

A tour with special forces usually means the Special Air Service, but there is also the alternative of volunteering for 'special duties' in Northern Ireland. The special duties tour lasts around two years, including training, and attracts higher rates of pay. Service with the SAS is no longer 'seen as a career foul' for officers. After the Iranian Embassy siege, Mrs Thatcher looked into the question and gave firm instructions that selection boards should consider such experience a benefit rather than a disadvantage. The tour, including training, lasts for around three years, during which time the subaltern or young captain serves as a troop commander in one of 22 SAS's sabre squadrons based at Hereford.

Given the acute shortage of captains in many parts of the Army, such military sabbaticals have become a strain on the system. Commanding officers and the Military Secretary's department are torn between the manning requirements of the mainstream and the need to keep good captains in the Army by giving them interesting opportunities. But under pressure the long-term need is bound to lose to the short-term imperative. The less interesting jobs are usually those which have to be filled first, with the result that more and more officers decide that 'the Army's no fun any more' at a time when they may well be considering marriage and are therefore reviewing their future.

If the Army has lost its fun over the last ten years, it has certainly lost a good deal of its glamour. Not so very long ago, romantic young women used to dream of a military wedding with a guard of honour in full dress uniform, their swords, sabres or lances forming an arch outside the church door. A few no doubt still do. But the recent change in attitudes has been striking: even the Sloane Ranger who rather despised a proper job has become a relatively endangered species. A young officer's girlfriend is likely to have a full career, and she often earns more than he does. The wives of graduates are usually graduates themselves: on a recent Army Staff Course at Camberley, 60 per cent of officers' wives were graduates.[1]

For a newly married officer's wife with no previous experience of Army life, the first taste can prove something of a shock, particularly if she has come straight to a Rhine Army garrison from London. An artillery officer described the wife of a captain in a Highland regiment – smartly dressed and 'a real looker' – as she gazed around at the Naafi supermarket on a Monday morning in appalled disbelief. The shelves were half-empty, making the place resemble 'something out of Eastern Europe'. The general impression was probably not helped by the dazed expressions of fellow trolley-pushers, wearing those stretch velour tracksuits which only seem to accentuate bulges in the wrong places.

After London, Army married life is a suburban existence in a military environment. And, because the regimental system prides itself on its parochial nature, the effect may be stifling for those not used to it. Lasting friendships are made, but much depends on attitude and common interests.

Graduates, and particularly those who have had to abandon their careers, are likely to react against a 'Stepford Wives conformity' which previous generations accepted as inevitable, if not normal. The polite banality of conversation at coffee parties amazes them. They find the range of subjects very restricted – babies, the best and worst quarters people have experienced, garrison activities such as amateur dramatics, and mutual friends. Those who consistently hark back to times in more interesting places are known as the 'when-wees', because they load their conversation with reminiscence: 'When we were in Hong Kong . . . When we were in Cyprus.'

The friendships made are, however, the greatest and most enduring benefit of service life. They are also vital to make the difficult times bearable, especially during moves or when husbands are away on unaccompanied tours. With any luck the new arrival, however 'un-Army', will find one or two kindred spirits. But more and more now try to escape the wives' club and garrison dinner party circuit. They concentrate instead on friends outside the Army; in Germany this can of course be very difficult.

Loyalties are strained, mainly because the regiment's claims seem omnivorous. The wife may feel that they go far beyond the call of duty and that a form of moral blackmail is used on her husband, making him need to prove that he has 'a positive attitude' and is fully part of the team. Much depends on the regiment. A good commanding officer – good in the sense of the longer-term interests of the regiment – will ensure that his married officers and soldiers are not kept away from their families more than is absolutely necessary.

Domestic problems seem to be hushed up more in the Army than in civilian life. This is partly because the institution as a whole has an instinctive aversion to washing dirty linen in public, and partly because it is a profession in which weakness of any sort attracts a doubly dangerous stigma. For an officer above all, financial worries, marital problems, depressions or psychological stress bring an added fear of career failure.

One officer's wife active in the welfare field felt that the polite fiction that 'officers don't have problems, they don't have child abuse and they don't have violence in the home' made life intolerably difficult for the women concerned. Afraid of harming their husbands' careers, and thus the whole family, and afraid of encountering disbelief, they were loath to confide in anyone within the regiment. In Germany, perhaps even further from home in the imagination than in reality, a wife faced with a crisis feels much more vulnerable.

From the point of view of a wife's career, Germany might as well be the other side of the world. Only a handful survive a posting there. The Civil Service has shown itself a sympathetic and wise employer by counting the period of the husband's tour as a sabbatical. But few private companies are prepared to show such flexibility. Wives who cannot find work say they almost feel like kept women, while the modern breed of husband feels guilty that his career has been responsible. Many officers' wives also consider that the Army, or the government, is a bad employer because it still expects something for nothing from them in a welfare role, and the salaries offered for jobs within the garrison or headquarters bear little relation to standard rates for the work, either in Germany or the United Kingdom. They resent the underlying assumption that, to avoid harming their husbands' careers, 'we aren't going to chain ourselves to the railings'. (It is a phrase used with revealing frequency in different contexts.)

In the long run, the Army is the principal loser. The need for two salaries to cope with a mortgage can make the wife's civilian job vital. Many officers calculate that even if they had to take a cut in salary outside the Army they would still be better off as a couple.

'The Army wife is a vanishing breed,' said a colonel's wife. 'My generation just followed the flag and did good works. In those days we weren't saving for houses. But the financial ball game has completely changed, and now we're no different from any civilian wife.'

One general admitted that the Army had tied itself in a Gordian knot. On the one hand it was demanding that flexibility of posting and the tradition of accompanied service be maintained, and on the other it was advising officers and NCOs to purchase their own houses as soon as possible because they could expect no help from the government. The first two fulfil the Army's need for operational efficiency and morale and therefore take priority. But house purchase is the family's need, and by definition takes second place. House purchase has become an even more emotive subject within the Army than outside. A commanding officer in the Parachute Regiment remarked with mild amazement on 'the panic of 25-year-olds if they don't own any property'.

There is in fact only one candidate for married life in the Army who knows what to expect, who accepts the ethos and the social and military imperatives without question, and who can often be co-located with her husband so that both salaries go towards their mortgage – a woman officer. They, however, are in relatively short supply, and a double military marriage is not to everyone's taste, even if the idea of a mixed guard of honour outside the church carries a certain piquancy.

Wifely dissatisfaction is certainly not the only reason for a captain's decision to leave. 'You do the most enjoyable bit first, which is commanding a platoon,' ran the typical argument. 'Then it becomes more and more administrative. So you ask yourself, why be sitting behind a desk when you could be doing it in civilian life and earning a lot more?' This point of view, however, is likely to become rarer during the recession while jobs remain hard to find, and the pay rise in April 1991 for captains to £23,000 a year has no doubt helped. Perhaps even more of a carrot to stay on is the knowledge that a brigadier's salary was increased to £50,000 a year, a rise of 18 per cent no doubt designed to hold out this luminous figure to those on the ladder below.

Younger officers react to complaints about deteriorating standards of loyalty with the argument that loyalty is a two-way business, and many feel that their loyalty has been exploited. Certainly graduates, whether or not prompted by their wives, are indeed more likely to compare the Army's conditions of service unfavourably with those on offer in civilian life. Conditions of service, or 'the quality of life' as almost everyone calls it when they become heated on the subject, have declined noticeably. This, more than anything else, convinced younger officers that the government was not interested in keeping them. A female captain, a graduate who had worked in the Ministry of Defence, compared the conditions of work there in an office 'which was too depressing . . . it hadn't been painted for seventeen years' with what a civilian could expect. 'The perks are now in civilian life,' she emphasized, 'not in Army life.' What rankled was 'not the fact that they're not there, but the fact that they've been taken away.' Younger officers, unlike their seniors, no longer regard the Army as a way of life, but as a career which has to deliver.[2]

The general who had spoken of the Gordian knot problem on house purchase described an address he had given to the Junior Command and Staff Course in 1988. After his talk, he asked if there were any questions. A young captain in the audience stood up and asked: 'General, why do you stay in the Army?' Recovering from the shock of the question, he replied that he stayed in for a number of things, but above all out of a sense of service. 'They thought these reasons were unutterably quaint,' he said, more in dismay than in anger. The speed of social change, he acknowledged, had taken the Army utterly by surprise. 'We've been caught with our pants very far down.'

Senior officers now hope that 1990 marked a real change in mood in the country, and that the ethos of what political commentators call 'Essex man' is in retreat. How far that retreat goes, and how far traditional notions of public service return, will be one of the fascinating questions of the next few years.

CHAPTER 10

Staff College

Staff officers have seldom attracted a good press in the British Army. Officers facing Rommel in the Western Desert referred to the uniformed bureaucrats back in Cairo as the 'Gaberdine Swine' and in Flanders regimental officers in the trenches cursed staff officers as red-tabbed asses heedlessly sending men to their death while comfortably billeted far behind the lines. That depth of distrust, even if vastly diminished, still colours the system to this day. Unlike the Bundeswehr, with its separate staff corps, the British Army maintains 'a single staff concept', which means that officers are continually moved between regimental soldiering and staff posts – whether in a headquarters or a department of the Ministry of Defence – to ensure that the disastrous division between the fighting soldier and the administrator never arises again.

Staff College, which the Army's most promising officers attend for a year around the time of their promotion from captain to major, is designed more as an initiation into the function of command than the black arts of military bureaucracy. Each year, over 500 officers enter the age bracket for selection. Half of them are not qualified because of earlier exam failures, while those who did pass them all, including the captain-to-major promotion exam, face the new staff selection test designed to show how they reason under pressure. The final choice is then made by the Staff Selection Board, which re-examines their confidential reports from commanding officers and allots places accordingly. Out of about 270 officers, 120 are chosen. The vast majority of places are awarded on merit alone. The last few are 'top-ups by corps and guys on their last chance who are given a lift'.

For a number of officers, winning a place at Staff College produces a dilemma as well as satisfaction. If they take up their place they become subject to a three-year 'time-bar', which means they will not be allowed to resign until they are in their mid-thirties. And, since they will be eligible for a pension from the age of thirty-seven, there are strong arguments for staying on for a few more years. But to leave the Army after the age of thirty-seven is very different from leaving at twenty-eight or twenty-nine, when interesting jobs are still within their grasp and adapting to civilian life holds no fears. The Army is finding to its dismay that every year some of its brightest captains turn round at the last moment to decline the offer of a Staff College place and resign.

The Army Command and Staff Course is split into two. The first part, mainly military technology, takes place at the Royal Military College of Science at Shrivenham before officers go on to the Staff College itself at Camberley.

For Shrivenham, an officer is allotted to one of three streams, according to his technical qualifications and potential. Those on Division I must have a technical degree, either from university or from Shrivenham itself. Division II, a slightly longer course of eleven months, is usually for officers with a technical background but without a technical degree. And Division III, 'the dross' in the eyes of technocrats, consists principally of combat arm officers almost innocent of scientific knowledge. Opinions on this two-month course differ sharply. A company commander from the Coldstream considered it 'a very well taught and very valuable course', while a Parachute Regiment major said he regarded Division III as a complete waste of time; he 'just didn't understand a word. It was gobbledygook.' One general, the director of a major arm, complained that 'the trouble with Div. III is that they look upon themselves as technical idiots with a great deal of pride.'

Weapons staff officers, those who work on all aspects of

introducing new weaponry and equipment for the procurement executive, in research establishments or on the staff of the Deputy Chief of the Defence Staff (Systems), will be chosen from Divisions I and II. Only about a dozen jobs, mainly research and development in telecommunications, are 'Div. I defined'.

Each year, early in March, the three divisions meet up at Camberley. The Staff College building, which dates from around 1860, is a very solid imitation of a French château of that period. There the British Army contingent, around 120 strong, mingle with the outsiders, 10 officers from the other services – 3 Royal Navy, 3 Royal Air Force and 4 Royal Marine officers – and nearly 50 overseas students selected and paid for by their governments. (Government policy of making foreign governments pay the fullest price possible on courses may have backfired in one important area. The subsequent Canadian demands that the British pay the full market cost for their training facilities in Canada at Suffield and Wainwright are said to be not entirely unconnected.)

The outsiders arrive up to two weeks early to receive a crash course of initiation into the mysteries of the British Army. The subject is a difficult one to teach in a short time, for, as one gunner colonel said on the subject of its federal nature, 'There is no such thing as the British Army. At Camberley, foreign officers are amazed by all the different uniforms.'

A third of the overseas students are from Commonwealth countries, a third from Nato countries and a third from elsewhere. The scheme is run by a committee on which the Foreign and Commonwealth Office is represented. Nationalities and their proportions vary, except that there always seem to be 3 Americans and 1 Israeli. The potential for irony is considerable. Once there was an Iraqi officer who, having attended the Russian staff college, was able to correct the directing staff's 'Orange Force' scenarios; while an Argentinian graduate of the course later became General Menéndez's aide in Port Stanley, where he surrendered to a fellow student from Camberley. The fate of the Iraqi officer is unknown.

Language can sometimes be a problem. One or two candidates arrive unable to understand a single lecture. Wherever possible, they are rushed off to the Royal Army Educational Corps Centre at Beaconsfield for intensive instruction, but they seldom manage to catch up. Most, however, are well chosen. The Indian and Pakistani officers selected are amongst the top students to have qualified through their own system, and the German officers are particularly good.

The course is intense. On average students need to do several hours' work each evening, which is not much fun for their wives. Most of the work is done in syndicates of ten, with one lieutenant colonel as their DS (directing staff). The syndicates are mixed as evenly as possible, both by capbadge and nationality, to encourage 'all-arms thinking'. 'The diversity's a good thing,' commented one recent graduate. 'You need that depth of experience and strong disagreements. You don't want that party-line bland assumption that all's well with the world.' More and more middle-ranking officers, especially the young turks just out of Staff College, are now saying that the old regimental system, with senior officers still influenced by loyalty to their old regiments rather than to the Army as a whole, has become a serious liability. In their view vital reforms are stymied by an unofficial lobby system, in which generals, tied to the interests of their old regiment or arm, cannot make objective decisions.

In the last few years, Staff College has proved a notable forum for military thinking. The original suggestion and impetus for a military doctrine for the British Army came from members of a course there, and a paper embodying their recommendations was forwarded to the Chief of the General Staff, General Sir Nigel Bagnall, who was keen to stimulate clear thought on all-arms operations. The Falklands conflict had revealed some key gaps, and the emphasis within Nato on Land/Air operations showed up the lack of intellectual framework in the British Army.

Under Bagnall's active direction, *The British Military Doctrine* was written by a gunner colonel who had just graduated from the higher command and staff course, and a Foot Guard major who had been among the Staff College proponents of the idea. They visited headquarters in Britain and Germany for discussions with formation commanders, and after a number of drafts, mainly to ensure that the document was comprehensible to a mythical average officer they named Captain Podsnap, it was published by Bagnall's successor, General Sir John Chapple, in September 1989.[1]

According to an old jibe, Staff College only turned out petty generals. Whether true or not in the past, training today is restricted to a set objective: 'To develop the professional knowledge and understanding of selected officers in order to prepare them for majors' and lieutenant colonels' appointments both on the staff and in command.' Any teaching of generalship is to sense 'what being a general is all about', so that they can understand the staff role better. The more arcane subjects, such as 'operational art' (basically the co-ordination of tactical plans to achieve strategic success), although covered, are not studied in detail until the higher command and staff course before promotion to brigadier. Less than a third of the course is devoted to staff work: the real emphasis is on command, which is why the course was renamed to include the word in 1989.

The nine-and-a-half month course consists of four terms, each between six and nine weeks long. The first covers the nuts and bolts of administration, staff duties and organization. The second is entitled 'Basic Tactics' and includes a European tour of battlefields and Allied headquarters. The third covers counter-revolutionary warfare and out-of-area operations.

The counter-revolutionary warfare package occasionally

includes anti-terrorist and public order map and telephone exercises planned with students from Bramshill Police College. Telephone exercises, like telephone battles, take place indoors in a series of fully equipped operations rooms linked by telephone; the directing staff provides an initial scenario, then builds up the crisis or battle with contact reports of incidents or contacts with enemy troops. A large town is borrowed in detail, given another name, then set in another part of the country so that nobody can take it literally; Aberdeen, for example, might be set in Wales.

The out-of-area part includes a tri-service period with visits to the Royal Navy and Royal Air Force. Syndicates then plan and mount an unexpected out-of-area operation along Falklands lines – the archetypal 'come-as-you-are' war. A country like Albania is chosen, less for politically symbolic reasons than for the way in which its difficult coastline and bad communications increase the 'embuggerance factor'. At times like these, the contribution of officers from the other services is invaluable.

Whatever the prognostications for the post-Cold-War world, the fourth and final term concentrates on general war operations in a European setting, only now with intense study of the land/air battle lessons from the Gulf war. The climax to the term is an elaborate telephone battle from division up to army group level which lasts for four days and nights with only one break to reorganize between phases. The term 'telephone battle' belittles the effort and scale of Exercise Right Cross. A syndicate of Bundeswehr officers comes over from the Führungsakademie near Hamburg to represent the flank division of 1st (German) Corps. A syndicate of American officers flies in from the command and general staff course at Fort Leavenworth to play the part of 1st (US) Corps Headquarters. (This group of majors, all with strong jaws, sincere expressions and close-clipped fair hair and dressed identically in combat fatigues conjured up visions of an Ollie North look-alike competition.) The RAF Staff College at Bracknell sends a team to represent the Second Allied Tactical Air Force. The

Soviet Studies Research Centre advises on the scenario and 'Orange Force' tactics. And the communications studies group at Sandhurst videotapes and broadcasts regular television news bulletins during the four-day battle.

Division and corps headquarters work from separate operations rooms. A stage with cubicles runs round the four walls, leaving a well in the middle for the huge 'bird-table' of joined-up maps. In the cubicles, each component of the headquarters staff, manned by officers appropriate to the arm or corps, receives information, calculates, confers and then sends orders down the line. From their seats the officers can refer to the plastic-covered maps below them where map-markers, busy with red and blue chinagraph, update enemy and own-force positions. They work entirely from ground and air reconnaissance reports of Fantasian movements rung in from a central control room.

Despite surprises, the overall course of the battle is predictable enough. Blue forces, forced to withdraw in the face of the Fantasians' overwhelming superiority, finally stabilize the front and launch a devastating counter-blow. All it lacks before the credits roll up are storm clouds blown away and the musical accompaniment rising in a triumphant crescendo.

An important part of the course consists of lectures and presentations. The different combat arms and Ministry of Defence directorates, such as recruiting, manning and training, bring down teams to mount presentations, so providing a good platform to get a message across to the next generation of commanding officers. Before the Gulf war, the gunners, for example, used to take the opportunity to emphasize that just because they cannot simulate battery fire on exercise battle group commanders should not fall into the trap of disregarding their importance in a real battle. Since the preparatory barrages for 1st Armoured Division in the Gulf, only a gentle reminder is now necessary.

The list of lecturers is varied and stimulating. Speakers

invited to broaden the mind, such as Ken Livingstone, Enoch Powell and Peter Tatchell, spice the principal diet of ministers, generals and sundry experts from the Ministry of Defence. Not all of the 'home team' have been considered impressive. A major in the Parachute Regiment said: 'One or two [of the generals] we listened to in amazement and wondered if we were in the same army.' A sapper officer also described how a senior general, now retired, reminisced at great length about his wonderful time in the Army, serving all round the world in marvellous places, and said how much he envied them at their stage of their career. A number of officers stood up to remind him that all the marvellous postings he mentioned had now gone or were about to go.

At the end of the fourth term, the successful British candidates are awarded the lower case initials *psc* after their name to denote passed Staff College. Together with Nato and Australian officers they stay on for the post-staff term, while the rest of the overseas students return home. The security classification of the material covered is thus able to rise from 'confidential' to 'Nato secret'.

Reactions to the course as a whole are inevitably mixed. Cynics comment that 'It's a six-month course packed into nine months', or that 'Some people just use the course. They want to make their mark to get on'. A significant number genuinely appreciate the experience. 'Staff College does prepare you very well for a Nato job', observed an infantry major who had been sent straight to Northern Army Group Headquarters at Rheindahlen.

A major in the Royal Engineers felt that any decline in the quality of the course was not the fault of the directing staff, who are very carefully selected, in theory from the thirty most highly regarded lieutenant colonels in the Army. 'One of the most depressing things', he said, 'is that with the black hole you get a polarization of ability. There's a very mediocre bunch at the other end which greatly lowers the overall standard.'

At the end of the year, each student is marked. The final grade can play a significant part in an officer's subsequent career, because the Military Secretary's Branch gives Staff College a menu of sixty to sixty-five staff appointments to be filled in what is known as the 'black bag' process. Of these, fifteen are designated 'key appointments' and twenty 'semi-key'.

The key posts available include the 'real plums', such as chief of staff (the brigade major of old) in an armoured brigade in Germany, certain posts in the Ministry of Defence, such as the directorates of military operations or plans, assistant chief of staff at an armoured division, or military assistant to a three- or four-star general. This clearly distinguishes a recipient as a high-flyer, 'going for the stars' of the military firmament.

In a parallel move, Shrivenham selects about thirty Div. I or Div. II members of the course for weapons staff jobs. This will bring them into the world of the Procurement Executive and equipment research and development. Inevitably 'a certain amount of horse-trading' ensues over officers wanted by both sides.

An officer can join the weapons staff ladder only after Staff College. He will specialize in one of four general areas: fighting vehicles and engineer equipment, weapons, guided weapons and electronics, and advanced data processing. Starting as an SO2 (staff major) in a project management team, his career as a weapons-trained officer will alternate between mainstream Army and weapons staff until he becomes a colonel. From then on he is streamed. The vertical chain of the Procurement Executive – policy, operational requirements, feasibility, development, and trials – is centralized under the joint-service Defence Staff, even though many departments deal only in army specifications. The chances of promotion to full colonel and brigadier are much better than average for the rest of the Army, but whether promotion to major general and beyond is easier is open to debate.

Not all officers go on from Camberley to a staff job:

those who had been doing one just before the course usually return to command a company, squadron or battery with their regiment or corps. Most regard this as the best part of their career. They have real responsibility, and yet they are still in direct contact with soldiers (an increasingly rare experience in a career relentlessly punctuated by courses and the need to clock up the right jobs outside the regiment). A sapper major commanding an independent field squadron, a signals major with a detached squadron or an Army Air Corps major in charge of a squadron of helicopters will each feel that he has the best of all worlds because he enjoys a large degree of autonomy as well. With the shortage of majors, an officer may have the chance to command a rifle company or a sabre squadron before he is thirty. To prepare him for the task of handling his new command in the field, he will go on a five-week all-arms tactics course at Warminster just before taking up the appointment.

About a quarter of all Staff College students are majors on arrival. The rest receive their promotion during the course. The importance of reaching field rank is symbolized by the gold braid around the peak of the No. 1 dress cap, although officers in the Household Division and most cavalry regiments wear it from the time they are commissioned. Far closer to the heart of the career-conscious officer today is the different form of confidential report for majors and above. Alongside the boxes for gradings, there is an alternative box marked 'outstanding'. A tick there from the superior officer who writes the report indicates that your career might take you to brigadier and perhaps beyond.

CHAPTER 11
Commanding the Regiment

Until about twenty years ago, the principal objective of a young officer was to command his regiment. Subalterns held the commanding officer in awe. 'The Colonel', as he has always been known, seemed a figure of limitless power. To reach such heights, to become the head of the regimental family, seemed more than enough to satisfy ordinary ambition. Further ascent into the distant and almost mythical world of staff officers and generals struck them as slightly unreal, to be regarded as a windfall, should promotion ever take them that far. Within the reality of the regimental system, the notion of a field marshal's baton in every soldier's knapsack was something which few took seriously.

Camaraderie amongst officers can be misleading. It may be warm and genuine, but it can also serve to camouflage rivalries and antipathies or even become a form of carapace. Evelyn Waugh, whose feelings about the Army ranged from adulation to scorn, described the camaraderie of his generation as a 'peculiar, impersonal, barely human geniality'.[1]

In recent years, the consciousness of success and failure within the officer corps has increased acutely. 'Any social gathering', wrote a gunner colonel, 'offers a snapshot of the yawning gap between the "failed" and the successful.'[2] Promotion to lieutenant colonel is a crucial step. (The Ministry of Defence describes it as 'a satisfactory goal for the good but not exceptional officer'.)[3] To be left on the wrong side of the bottleneck always used to mean a prolonged spell as second-in-command, and then an aimless orbit of minor staff appointments while the boarding-school allowance kept the children at decent establishments. Now, with the axe poised, and jobs hard to find outside, the fear of failure is worse than ever.

There are still many who never make it to lieutenant colonel – and not just those incapable of passing exams. A squadron or company commander who messes up a key attack during battle group training in Canada may find his prospects ruined in a single morning if the brigade commander happens to be there. This sort of disaster often seems to happen to the one person whom the traditionalists in the regiment were hoping to see as the next commanding officer but one. The bottleneck remained, but the contents of the bottle were considerably reduced. 'With black holes moving through the system like bubbles,' said a general, resorting to a different metaphor, the Army suffered a severe and unaccustomed shortage of majors as well as captains. In the late 1980s the Ministry of Defence did an about-turn on policy, trying to persuade the older ones to stay on. But then in 1991 policy changed again, this time to reduce drastically the total of majors and colonels.

Passed-over majors were undervalued as a breed, perhaps because of the dyed-in-the-wool attitudes and preposterous pomposity of a memorable few. But these characteristics are now almost extinct. In an increasingly faceless organization their qualities of loyalty and experience are appreciated. The best example is often the second-in-command of a regiment, sometimes a 45-year-old who can remember the RSM arriving as a recruit fresh from the depot or training regiment. (Unlike policemen, RSMs really have got younger.) Whatever bitterness he may feel at failing to receive that vital promotion, he will hide his feelings and serve the comparative youngster appointed over him to the best of his ability. At times, when expediency is allowed to come before the interests of the regiment, it will be hard for him not to speak out, but he will 'bite his lip', and try to advise the new commanding officer as tactfully as he can.

The shortage of majors presented a double handicap.

A senior staff officer closely involved in the question admitted: 'We've got a serious problem in quality in promotion to lieutenant colonel.'

The appointment of even a relatively small number of mediocre commanding officers can create its own vicious circle. For majors and captains, the reality or prospect of working for 'second-raters just interested in their own career' can influence the decision if an officer is unsure whether to stay on in the Army or leave. One major in line for command, a character considered outstanding by his colleagues, said he was 'increasingly fed up with this growing mediocrity. I refuse to work for someone I despise.' The fear which senior officers had for their careers depressed him so much that he wanted to leave.

The other social changes which hit the Army in the late eighties were an even greater source of worry for the Military Secretary's branch, which manages officers' careers. Its staff may try to 'give the officer a little more say in his own destiny', but the Army found itself very vulnerable to job-market forces. The most acute form of blackmail came from those with badly needed qualifications, such as computer skills. More common, however, was the officer whose wife had a career or was sick of moving house. He was prepared to state point-blank that if he was posted to Germany or the Falklands he would resign. (Ironically, the Falklands came to be seen with a typical dash of black-humoured exaggeration as a sort of Devil's Island for officers and senior NCOs who had announced their intention of leaving, but still had at least six months to serve.)

The threat to resign was seldom mere bluff, and the Military Secretary's branch usually had little alternative but to find someone else to fill the post. Bachelors complained that they received an unfair proportion of unpopular postings as a result. 'We're getting fed up with being shunted about,' said one. 'They assume that just because you're single you've got no family and friends.'

Everyone agreed that this state of affairs was very

unsatisfactory. If nothing else, it indicated a sharp decline in respect for traditional standards of discipline. Yet a widespread feeling had arisen in the officer corps that you have to protect your own interests, because nobody else will.

Promotion to the rank of lieutenant colonel requires positive selection. Unlike previous promotions, it does not become virtually automatic after a set period. The earliest age at which a major can enter the zone for selection is thirty-seven. Anyone hoping to become a brigadier or general should certainly be a lieutenant colonel by the time he is forty – the target age for promotion.

Each January, the Directorate of Manning calculates the vacancies for the year by arm and service. (About a tenth of the total is reserved for an Army-wide merit pool.) In February the Military Secretary's Branch checks the records of every major aged between thirty-seven and forty-eight. They eliminate all those who are ineligible or who have not been recommended. This brings the total down from a maximum of 2,500 to under 1,000. In March it convenes pre-selection boards for each arm and service. The confidential report books (now computerized, with up to twenty pages on the details of each officer's career) of some 400 majors are considered during the next two months. From 179 places in 1989, the quota has shrunk as the Army contracts, with a reduction of 25 per cent in 1990 and then 10 per cent in 1991. Even greater cuts are to come.

Officers from small corps with specialist roles, such as the Intelligence Corps or the Military Police, can be at a disadvantage, and discreet lobbying is often needed by their director to make sure they receive their chance. 'One has to play the system,' said a retired colonel in charge of officer careers. 'Generals think in easily recognizable Army terms. This man's done adjutant and so on.'

Finally in June the board meets to confirm the candidates for the 'Pink List', named after the colour of the paper on which the final list is published. A candidate never appears before the board, and learns the result only when the Pink List is published shortly afterwards. If successful, he can expect promotion with effect from either the end of June or December of the following year.

A new lieutenant colonel's first tour is usually as a grade one staff officer (SO1) or, if specially selected, as an instructor at Camberley or Shrivenham. Just before his promotion, or soon after, he may also attend the Joint Service Defence College at Greenwich.

This seven-month course prepares officers for 'purple appointments' on a joint service staff, and ultimately some form of 'purple command'. Much of the instruction takes a similar form to the Army Staff Course, only with a different emphasis. A number of officers considered the lectures to be the most valuable part of the course. 'It was a purely British course,' said an infantry lieutenant colonel, 'so [unlike at Camberley] speakers were unhampered by security restrictions. We even had the deputy head of SIS.' The only qualification was a strong criticism of the party line put forward by speakers from the Ministry of Defence, trying to conceal how bad things were – officers on the course were apparently exasperated when a senior civil servant insisted in 1989 that there was absolutely no need for a defence review.

As autumn approaches, new lieutenant colonels anxiously await the publication of the command list for the following year. The combat arms have just over a thousand lieutenant colonels, but the number of field army commands is limited. There are, until the reductions announced in the summer of 1991 take effect, 113 regular regiments or battalions, of which 19 are armour, 22 artillery, 13 engineer, 55 infantry, 1 SAS and 3 Army Air Corps. Commands outside the regular field army, such as a Territorial Army unit, do not carry the same cachet later on when an officer is considered for further promotion.

The competition for command is intense, but both good and bad luck can play a considerable part. Much depends on circumstances within each regiment or corps. A rash of resignations can smooth the way for an officer who might at best have been considered borderline a few years ago, while a batch of brilliant contemporaries can block the path of a good candidate who, with a different capbadge, would have had no trouble.

Such bottlenecks are increasingly circumvented by sending outsiders to command regiments whose own candidates are not thought up to scratch. The recipient regiment, however, is unlikely to greet this solution with joy. Many officers and senior NCOs feel that it represents a major step in the erosion of the regimental system. But other officers, particularly the young turks who regard the regimental obsession of the British Army as its greatest handicap, welcome any step towards a purer meritocracy. The old breed of commanding officer, the sort of solid, unimaginative officer who had dreamed only of commanding his regiment, has, however, virtually disappeared. 'You either have to be quite exceptional or political,' said a sapper major. 'If you're a complete dozer, the system will find you out.'

There are some commanding officers who never went to Staff College. They have *sq* for 'staff qualified' after their name in the Army List, not *psc* for 'passed Staff College'. This means that, although they have not attended the Command and Staff Course at Camberley, they have completed two staff jobs, one as a captain (SO3) and another as a major (SO2).

A commanding officer will seldom come straight from a field army unit. In many cases, he will have had two tours away from regimental duties. To reorient him tactically, as well as bring home to him his new responsibilities, he will be sent off on an intensive round of updating and briefing.

A commanding officer designate course at Larkhill is run three times a year for up to eighty lieutenant colonels at a time. Much of the course consists of lectures from senior representatives of different Ministry of Defence departments on anything from the new budgetary system to manning and recruiting. But, according to one colonel, 'The people speaking to them don't seem to realize the effect of what they're saying. Those on the course could see straight through what they were being told and knew it was just whitewash. The facts alone meant doom and despondency.'

A commanding officers' tactics course for officers due to command major units in the field army then follows at Warminster, on the other side of Salisbury Plain. After spending half the week at their own arms centre, where they are brought up to date on developments, they return to Warminster for a series of talks updating them on everything: weapons systems; nuclear, biological and chemical warfare; electronic warfare; support helicopters and air mobility; the UK Mobile Force and out-of-area operations; and tactical theory.

At the end of that week, the 'loggies' – those about to command logistic units – depart, while combat arm officers stay. This brings the course strength down to under thirty. The second week consists mainly of TEWTs (Tactical Exercise Without Troops) and MAPEXs (Map Exercises), concentrating on withdrawal, defence, advance and obstacle crossing. Thus prepared, the commanding officer designate sets off to take up his command.

The arrival of a new commanding officer is sometimes awaited with a trepidation equivalent to that of a new ship's captain. His power may not be quite as absolute, but his influence upon the destiny of those serving under him can easily seem as great. Discussions about his character in both officers' and sergeants' messes are likely to be intense, yet cautious. Anyone who has served directly under him will be closely questioned. Officers may have better access to official information, but the sergeants have their own very effective grapevine; chief clerks in regiments, headquarters, establishments or Ministry of

Defence departments form their own discreet network, while sergeants on courses will pick up everything they can about a relatively unknown officer about to take command.

An officer familiar from previous service with the regiment will prompt highly coloured reminiscences, but an outsider preceded only by a reputation will excite intense speculation. The possibilities are always narrowed simplistically. Which will he be? A 'politician', or a likeable man who will have to be carried, or a paragon – firm yet fair, able and well liked?

Particularly dreaded is an outsider who, from the start, ignores advise. One or two have been known to cancel all outstanding recommendations for promotion, replacing the list with one of their own. This sort of commanding officer is determined to make his mark in as short a time as possible. 'I don't give a damn how Colonel Jeremy did it,' is his angry retort to suggestions. 'This is the way it's going to be done from now on!' His sweeping reforms seem to reflect a perverse pleasure in courting unpopularity, as if to prove his tough decision-making.

No commanding officer mindful of his career can forget that his immediate superior, usually his brigade commander, is the person who writes his confidential report. This may influence him to accept extra burdens on behalf of the regiment without demur because he has to project a positive attitude. He will have to join in the 'numbers game', providing his superiors with impressive figures on the number of courses run, qualifications obtained, open days held, and soldiers sent on adventurous training, but the quality of these activities and, above all, the long-term effect on job satisfaction within the regiment often have to take second place. Above all, he must not rock the boat by speaking out if things are wrong. 'If you create a ripple,' said one former commanding officer, 'then you're embarrassing the chain of command.'

A recent commanding officer argued that only loyalty is holding most of the men in. Lose that and you lose your regiment. The ideal commanding officer wins not only the professional respect, but the affection of those he leads.

The demands made on commanding officers are much greater than ever before. No longer is it enough to be a good infantryman, cavalryman, gunner or sapper. Like the Army as a whole, they are expected to be 'all singing, all dancing' – tacticians who also manage budgets, inspiring leaders who fulfil 'performance indicators'. The job itself can be daunting. An infantry officer, for example, may have to take command of an armoured infantry battalion without any previous experience of mechanized warfare. For someone unaccustomed to the heavy army, taking over a Warrior-equipped battalion feels like a sudden switch to a totally different arm. Out on exercise for the first time, in charge of a battle group with a squadron of tanks under his command and the brigadier breathing down his neck, he will be under a great deal of pressure. The divisional commander will be watching closely, and rival regiments with a strong streak of *schadenfreude* wait for him 'to make a major Horlicks'. 'If you drop a bollock then,' said one who only just survived the experience, 'you've had it.'

The fear of 'dropping a bollock' influences not only exercises. 'We've become so worried about our careers', said a commanding officer in Northern Ireland, 'that nobody dares let their deputies have their heads. We're afraid they will make mistakes, and we'll lose out come confidential report time . . . This fear of making mistakes only saves them up for the future.'

The chance of a spectacular disaster on exercise is becoming rarer, if only because most exercises today are the driest of dry runs. The work-up exercises and live-firing practice for Operation Granby were quite exceptional. Command post exercises, when only headquarters command vehicles and signal units go out, save money and keep environmental damage to a minimum. An even more economical form of practice is run by three battle group trainers, one at Catterick, one at Bovington and one at Sennelager. From these centres, a commanding officer of a regiment and his key officers recce the surrounding countryside, then return to a scale model in a specially converted building where the directing staff subject them to a form of telephone battle.

Given the restraints on major exercises, and the infinitely more bureaucratic environment of budgets and 'efficiency measures', a commanding officer now seems to be judged on criteria other than tactical skills. 'Presentational skills' have become much more important, at times vital to his career. The Army unhappily finds itself in a system where everything has to be measured by pre-defined scales. Graphs and bar-charts are a fine way to measure the output of industry, but how do you measure military productivity in peacetime? To try to do so soon leads to grotesque distortions, as the Vietnam War so vividly demonstrated. Man-days spent on field training can be calculated and charted, but as a guide to a unit's likely performance in the field they are without value. A regiment or battalion has little say in the matter, since formation or district headquarters allocate everything: time, facilities, resources and track mileage. The battalion, or major parts of it, may be absent half the year on a six-month unaccompanied tour in Northern Ireland, Belize, Cyprus or the Falklands. Other commitments not predicted in the annual programme will also be dumped in its lap, but no help can be expected, no lightening of the load elsewhere to compensate.

The Heseltine doctrine of no spare capacity led, in the manpower crisis of 1990, to cases of gross overstretch. A brigade commander pointed to the way a battalion in the United Kingdom may be asked to fulfil up to three different roles. He warned of the consequences of 'having an army on the cheap by getting them to do so many things'. Perpetual overstretch on an already greatly reduced manpower level leads to more soldiers leaving, and so to the sort of disastrous downward spiral which many infantry battalions have experienced.

To add insult to injury, commanding officers are then

told that good leadership is the only way to stop soldiers leaving. The same brigade commander rejected the notion as sophistry: 'It's not a leadership problem, it's a management problem.' Commitments and manpower resources had to be matched up first. He also echoed a common criticism of the budgetary system introduced in April 1991: 'It is unfair to be asked to control your budget if you can't control your commitment.' The government had to decide what it wanted its army to do, then decide how large it should be.

For many commanding officers, an even more exasperating form of sophistry is the succession of directives from headquarters implementing or requesting suggestions for 'efficiency measures'. As an infantry colonel said, 'It's got nothing to do with efficiency at all. It's just a euphemism for saving money at any price.'

Away from statistics and performance indicators, a commanding officer can also distinguish his tenure through the regiment's sporting achievement. As a substitute for the glory of war, this leads to some minor excesses and a disproportionate allocation of time and resources in certain parts of the Army. Some officers and senior NCOs feel that sporting events have become far too much of a regimental status symbol for commanding officers, and that an excessive amount of welfare funds are concentrated on a tiny minority of 'gladiators'.

A number of commanding officers, determined to win the championship for a particular sport at which the regiment excels already, will beg their arms director to intercede with the Manning and Record Office to get him a particular wing-forward or goalkeeper, all for the glory of the corps as a whole. This practice is known as 'packing', and large capbadges such as the Royal Engineers go in for it shamelessly.

Infantry regiments, although much more restricted in team choice, still specialize in a certain sport, sometimes with sustained success. The Duke of Wellington's

Regiment, for example, is known to be rugby-mad. (Its nickname, the Duke of Boots, in fact refers to the Iron Duke's footwear, and not to the studded variety.) They claim – perhaps jokingly – that their application form for prospective officers asks them to specify for which county side they play.

Whether a commanding officer sets out to establish his own particular style, or to work for the continuity of the regiment, he has only two and a half years in this, his last direct command of 'troops on the ground'. 'It went all too quickly' is a common remark. For those who had handed over command in the spring of 1990, only to see their replacement take the regiment into action in the Gulf, the yearning to be back could be intense.

As pressures on the system increase, and regiments come under threat from the Defence Review, the job will no doubt change still further. In short, 'the Colonel' may still be master in his own house, but he is certainly not master of its future. Anyone taking up command could find himself the last of a long line.

CHAPTER 12

Going for the Stars

After commanding a regiment, the next appointment can produce a feeling of dislocation, since it usually consists of a job on the staff of a major headquarters or in one of the many departments of the Ministry of Defence. The change in job may well require much more than a change in outlook. Sometimes a completely different personality is needed. 'Where we are not doing enough', said an expert at the Army Personnel Research Establishment, 'is trying to define what you expect from an officer . . . How do you define requirements which are so very different for an officer in the MoD and in the field?'

The pace of work in the Ministry of Defence is seldom less intense than commanding a regiment. Very few officers have managed to take their 'full whack of leave' in the last five years. (The take-up of leave entitlement is regarded as the best way of measuring overwork.) Army psychiatrists are also concerned at the toll on officers working in the most demanding departments of the Ministry of Defence, but the Army prefers to turn its back on the effects of stress, whether in the field or in the office.

For the former commanding officer, there is above all a strong sense of anticlimax after giving up command. From a position of prestige, responsibility and power, the former commanding officer finds himself a 'half colonel', like a thousand other grade one staff officers, with a desk-bound job. Instead of having his driver greet him with a salute outside his own front door each morning, he probably has to slog in on London Transport like any other commuter.

Self-esteem will certainly be restored for those who are promoted to full colonel, a rank which from April 1991 commanded a salary of £45,000. This is a frontier as

155

well as a step, since they become gazetted to the Staff, no longer to their regiment or corps: Lt Col A. B. C. Smith, Loamshire, becomes Col A. B. C. Smith, Staff (late Loamshire). To demonstrate his new status he wears red 'tabs' on the collar of his uniforms, a red band round his service dress cap, and the Army symbol of lion and crown as a non-denominational capbadge. But tribalism retains its grip. Senior officers hang on to as much of their regimental uniform as they can. A Green Jacket will remain recognizable by his black buttons, a Highlander by his kilt and tam-o'-shanter, a Foot Guard by his groups of buttons, and a Para by his beret. A senior officer from the Royal Hussars, on the other hand, will feel obliged to leave behind his Cherrypicker trousers, if only because the crimson clashes dreadfully with the red tabs.

The minor change in nomenclature from half to full colonel camouflages its importance. One officer was amused at the difference it could make. Having been correctly billed as a lieutenant colonel for a series of fact-finding visits round the Army, he then received promotion at the very last moment. On several occasions staff officers and commanding officers kept him waiting when he arrived at a headquarters or unit, until alerted to his true rank.

A colonel destined for field army promotion, such as brigade commander or the chief of staff at a divisional headquarters, is sent on a two-week senior officers' tactics course. Like those for company commanders and commanding officers, it is run by the all-arms tactics wing at Warminster.

For those singled out as flyers, there is the twelve-week higher command and staff course which began in 1988 at Camberley. That first course included Brigadier Patrick Cordingley, who commanded seventh Armoured Brigade on Operation Granby. Only fifteen British Army officers, mainly full colonels aged from forty-one to forty-four, attend each year. The Military Secretary decides on each candidate. They are joined by one or two Royal

Navy captains, one or two RAF group captains, and a colonel from each of four allied countries such as the United States, Australia, the Netherlands and Germany. The American connection is important. Their School of Advanced Military Studies lent stimulus to the idea.

After the standard course at the US Army Command and General Staff College, Fort Leavenworth, the brightest officers are picked for this further year. Once trained up in US Army doctrine, covering every aspect of operational art and the land/air battle, 'they're sent out two by two like animals from the Ark', according to a Light Infantry colonel who had instructed there. Known as the 'Jedi knights', their mission is to spread the word at US head-quarters around the world. They are said to exert a large degree of influence, and American generals were soon seen arriving at Nato conferences closely flanked by their pair of Jedis. (Another nickname for graduates from the School of Advanced Military Studies is 'inner ringknockers'. West Point graduates are known as 'ringknockers' because they are said to rap their West Point fraternity rings on the table to make a point during conferences.)

Characteristically sceptical of a system with such Jesu-itical undertones, the British Army produced a syllabus closer to the Bundeswehr's Führungsakademie than to its American counterpart. Eminent military historians and senior scientists from Shrivenham were also involved in its elaboration. The scientific contribution is vital, since one of the phases – the future battlefield – examines models for the land/air battle up to the year 2020, and includes an exercise in planning defence budgets accordingly.

As a course devoted more to theory than to execution, the higher command and staff course requires consid-erable background reading – an average of 240 pages per day. The programme of lectures is intensive and varied. Academic lecturers have included Corelli Barnett, Professors Laurence Freedman, Sir Michael Howard and Martin van Creveld. The military speakers have tended to consist of field marshals such as Lord Carver and

Sir Nigel Bagnall, army group and corps commanders, admirals and air marshals to give the course a strong joint-service emphasis, and weapons system experts. As if to underline the overwhelmingly Nato emphasis (only one of the nine phases is devoted to out-of-area operations), the Commander-in-Chief Central Region, a German general, is one of the star attractions.

The culmination of the course is an indoor computer-based wargame against Soviet operational manoeuvre groups. Far more sophisticated than the older chess-board version, this system is 'geographically smart'. Every map square is minutely subdivided in hexagons, which, programmed according to the difficulty of the terrain, automatically slow down or ease the cross-country movement of armoured formations. 'Army Group Wargame' now runs with a compatible air game developed by SHAPE technical centre to practise inter-service liaison in battle. They are both 'attrition-smart', and instantly work out the loss rate of aircraft from missile batteries, or the casualties inflicted by a multiple-launch rocket system attack on an enemy concentration.

The social side of the course – some of the lectures by senior generals are after-dinner speeches – is also regarded as important. Not only do army commanders have a chance to meet the next generation of brigade commanders but, even more important, the future brigade commanders get to know each other very well. The cachet of being 'HCSC trained' is already considerable. Fortunately, the character of the British Army makes their development into a self-regarding élite unlikely. The missionary fervour of the Jedi knights is also hard to imagine. Initial resistance to a military doctrine was based on the notion that this was 'not the British way'.[1]

The Royal College of Defence Studies is very different from the higher command and staff course. For a start, it is for officers about two years further on in their career, usually colonels and brigadiers. It lasts a whole year and does not deal with operational matters at all. According to a former senior civilian instructor – an ex-ambassador – 'It conveys the general environment in which defence decisions are made. You assume they know their own subject in depth, so you teach in breadth.'

The Imperial Defence College, an innovation pushed by Winston Churchill in 1922, was the first joint-service establishment of its kind, and the first course of twenty-five officers in 1927 included Auchinleck, Alanbrooke and Sholto Douglas. The college moved in 1946 to premises of considerable grandeur in Belgrave Square. Seaford House, redone soon after the golden age of Edwardian ostentation by the Lord Howard de Walden of the day, has a double-return staircase in green onyx almost worthy of St Petersburg.

The course sets out to 'study the world from a Western defence point of view', but it is also intended to be 'a mind-stretching exercise'. Speakers are invited from both sides of an argument: government and opposition, left-wing nuclear disarmers and Pentagon consultants, and both Arab and Israeli speakers on the Middle East. (Officers from Arab armies study alongside colonels from the Israeli Defence Force.) Apart from lectures by academics and other experts, much of the course-work is done in seminars, private study and papers prepared on specialist subjects. A number of visits are laid on during the course of the year to headquarters and ministries abroad as well as in the United Kingdom. In 1990, members of the RCDS course visited Soviet army, navy and air force units – at the time a notable step in the dismantling of Cold War positions. The syllabus, which embraces economics, industry, politics, strategic philosophy and superpower relationships, evolves constantly, with a major shake-up proposed every five to ten years.

Army candidates, usually ten out of a course of nearly eighty, are chosen by No. 2 Selection Board and confirmed by No. 1 Board. (One of those on the 1989 course was Brigadier Christopher Hammerbeck, who took command of the 4th Armoured Brigade in time for its deployment to the Gulf.) A similar number come from the Navy and the Marines, as well as ten from the RAF. In addition there are usually a couple of assistant chief constables, half a dozen senior officials from the Ministry of Defence, a handful from the Foreign Office, and then up to forty foreign officers or defence officials from any of twenty-six countries. The biggest contingents are from Australia and the United States. The same selection process chooses candidates for defence fellowships, a programme instituted in 1969 by Denis Healey. One of the first to benefit was Brigadier, later General Sir Frank, Kitson who wrote *Low Intensity Operations* during his year at University College, Oxford.

The past significance of the course can be read in the Army List. Virtually all infantry generals of three- or four-star rank, especially Green Jackets, have *rcds* after their name. But the success of the higher command and staff course has rather eclipsed its glory. One senior officer joked that for someone who has done the Higher Command and Staff Course, 'the ideal is to be selected for RCDS, but be too busy to attend'.

The promotion pyramid inevitably narrows towards the top, and will soon narrow still further, but some steps are larger and more competitive than others. Much depends on your capbadge. Approximately one lieutenant colonel in six makes it to brigadier in the combat arms, as opposed to one in twelve in logistic corps.

Promotion to brigadier is divided between 'command board' (those to command a brigade in the field army) and 'green pool' appointments. 'Green pool' promotions are for colonels from all arms and services up to the age of fifty-two who will not command a brigade.

The candidates for brigade command considered by No. 2 Selection Board must be between forty-three and forty-seven years old. Occasionally a lieutenant colonel is promoted, leap-frogging the rank of colonel. Three or four names are put forward for each appointment, and the final decision is made by No. 1 Selection Board, which consists of the four members of the Executive Committee of the Army Board and the two commanders-in-chief. They are not simply choosing a brigade commander: they are choosing a candidate for three-star rank, perhaps even a future member of the Army Board.

'If history tells us anything', wrote General Sir John Chapple in his introduction to the 1989 higher command and staff course, 'it is that defensive alliances are invariably surprised tactically or technically in the opening round'. Few would disagree with him, and many majors and colonels emphasized the point with considerable feeling at the end of the 1980s.

In an age when a war can last only a few weeks or even a few days, they were acutely aware that the British Army's tradition of muddling through and 'getting it right in the end' no longer stood a chance. The right formation commander had to be in place on day one. They were worried that incumbents had little chance of learning the job: one brigadier said that, with the restrictions on exercises, a brigade commander in Germany could do little more than command a garrison. On the other hand, an officer who had recently commanded his battalion in Germany pointed out that an incompetent brigade commander would soon be shown up on command post exercises, battle group trainers and the new computer-based simulation exercises.

Nevertheless, the idea that careerists were more likely to get through to formation command had become very strong by the end of the decade. 'If you're a good tactician', said a colonel who had recently commanded an armoured regiment in Germany, 'it doesn't count for anything, but if you're a good politician, then you'll get on.' Although unstinting in his diatribe against the 'political' senior officers, he admitted that 'a few bloody good ones still manage to get through. I don't know how, but thank Christ for the Army, they do'. He went on to repeat the opinion of a general he particularly admired: 'The moment we get a war we're going to have to sack most of the brigade commanders and generals, but there won't be time.' (The belief that commanders only interested in their careers are disastrous operationally was held very strongly by the police as well at that time. The riot at Broadwater Farm in October 1985 seems to have brought this out in a dramatic fashion.)[2]

Such opinions were not restricted to 'the next fixture': they extended to 'come-as-you-are' wars such as the Falklands conflict. Criticisms of the initial stages of the campaign were far more severe than outsiders might expect. One infantry officer, who had studied the battles in great detail, voiced his dismay at 'the early cock-ups'. 'Of course, by the end,' he acknowledged, 'everything went like clockwork. Wireless Ridge worked like the DS Solution [i.e. went entirely according to plan], with armour, artillery and infantry integrating perfectly. But are we going to have to go through this process in every war?' Though not on this occasion, almost every discussion of that sort in the year or so before the Iraqi invasion of Kuwait seemed to end with the comment: 'The trouble is we've been at peace too bloody long.'

One thing has certainly changed from the days when the British Army was described as lions led by donkeys.[3] Generals today are seldom castigated as stupid. In fact that sometimes back-handed accolade, a 'thinking general', has fallen out of use precisely because the phenomenon has become so much less unusual. A general today is far more likely to be criticized as a 'politician', or given that Kitsonian epithet, a 'paper general'. The main target for the ire of officers' and sergeants' messes has been the refusal of generals to warn politicians of the damage caused by relentless rounds of economies. 'They're just looking upwards,' was, and still is, a common lament. A widespread feeling existed that the Army was being destroyed by the sophistry of 'efficiency measures'. A number of officers argued in the heat of the moment that generals should be prepared to speak out and resign if necessary. 'But of course none of them will' was the usual comment. If some of this cynicism was well founded, some was unjust, no doubt an integral part of 'the chain of contempt' which runs in the opposite direction to the chain of command. Envy undoubtedly played a part – though less than might be imagined, for even the strongest critics of the promotion system acknowledged the excellence of a number of senior officers.

Not all the criticisms have been stilled by a long way, but even the deepest cynics had to admit that, when the moment of truth arrived with the ground offensive against the Iraqi army, 'it certainly went all right on the night'. Military professionalism, that over-used word during the previous decade, was shown to have substance as well as form.

Another cause for complaint about the selection of senior officers is restricted to certain corps. Middle-ranking members of the more technical arms and services resent the self-perpetuating supremacy at Army Board level of infantry and armour, followed by gunners and sappers. (The Royal Signals, Army Air Corps and Intelligence Corps make up the other combat arms. All arms are combat, one might say, but some are more combat than others.)

The more technically minded young turks coming out of Staff College are now challenging the traditional assumption that only field experience of infantry and armour qualifies you for the highest appointments. A three- or four-star general from outside the main combat trinity of infantry, armour and artillery is almost unknown, unless as Master General of the Ordnance, on the Procurement Executive. The only two field marshals in the last thirty years who were from neither the infantry nor armour were both gunners.

The questioning of traditional assumptions about leadership is most strongly echoed in branches such as the Army Air Corps and the Royal Corps of Signals. A Royal Signals officer won the 1988 commandant's prize at Staff College for a paper on the subject.[4] His theme was that 'within the present system one might conclude that for the cavalry or infantry soldier the field marshal's baton rests somewhere near the top of his knapsack; that for the gunner or sapper it nestles in the lower layers waiting to be rediscovered, while for the sizeable remainder of the Army it appears to have dropped unnoticed through a hole in the bottom'.

The arguments advanced by both sides are, of course, very subjective. Hints of old-fashioned prejudice often appear close to the surface. Most infantrymen and cavalrymen, for example, still think of technocrats as backroom boys there to serve their needs. And many of them see the Royal Signals, with their high proportion of Welbexians, as uncharismatic and middle-managerial in character.

The appointment of a brigade commander in Germany from the Royal Signals produced baffled expostulations amongst professional armoured tacticians. Their view was that if they themselves did not have the knowledge or experience to command a signal squadron, let alone a signal regiment, then how could a signaller be expected to command an armoured formation?

A form of catch-22 is bound to operate against those without infantry or armour experience. A senior officer who has not commanded a squadron of tanks or a company of armoured infantry at different levels will not be able to appreciate what is happening on the ground. Even officers who have commanded armoured reconnaissance regiments, or an infantry battalion in an unmechanized role, are said to lack the right experience.

But both sides agree on one thing: change cannot be imposed through a policy of positive discrimination. It has to come up through the system, with a greatly increased cross-posting between arms to give the most promising officers, no matter what their capbadge, the chance of commanding infantry and armour on the ground.

A cynic might whisper that few relinquish power voluntarily. Armour and infantry would either find last-minute reasons to frustrate this, or rely on the power of inertia to preserve the old pattern. But things are now starting to change, albeit slowly, and they may well move very much more rapidly when fundamental questions about the future manning and deployment of the Army have at last been faced. Changes in tactical doctrine demand changes in attitude as well as in equipment priorities. The emphasis on the land/air battle and the recently acknowledged importance of air-mobile formations mean that the armoured corps and infantry cannot play down the Army Air Corps' combat role for very much longer.

On the other hand, a major withdrawal from Germany was expected to have an even greater effect, leaving the main members of the 'heavy army' – the Royal Armoured Corps and the Royal Artillery – extremely vulnerable. They would bear the brunt of the ensuing reductions. 'If you don't put your armour in Germany, where do you put it?' said a cavalry general. And with severe cut-backs in re-equipment programmes, combined with both budgetary and training restrictions, an army largely confined to the United Kingdom could only pay lip-service to operational art.

Even before the Berlin Wall came down, the armoured corps' influence had already declined sharply. In 1981 it had four four-star generals and five three-star generals; by 1991 this was reduced to only one four-star and two three-star. How far the armour-heavy slant of the Gulf war will go to slowing the decline is impossible to predict.

The infantry was expected to suffer comparatively little in the withdrawal from Germany, since only twelve of its fifty-five battalions were stationed there, but the announcement of a reduction of around 19 battalions was larger than anticipated. Nevertheless, with its grip on command unshaken, infantry influence is likely to increase still further.

The future leadership of the Army is effectively decided by No. 1 Selection Board. Its key responsibility is 'to submit

165

to the Secretary of State for Defence, through the Minister of State for the Armed Forces, the names of officers considered suitable for promotion to the substantive rank of major general and for commands and appointments in that rank'.

The Chief of the General Staff is president of the Board, and its members are the Adjutant General, the Quartermaster General, the Master General of the Ordnance and the two commanders-in-chief. The Military Secretary acts as secretary. One senior staff officer added that it also served in the more private function of a 'talking shop' with no civil servants or politicians present. 'Its only constitutional role is appointments and promotions, but if the CGS has got a knotty problem he'd be a fool if he didn't take the opportunity to discuss it with his colleagues.'

The suspicion that No. 1 Selection Board is bound to operate as a self-perpetuating élite is not limited to technocratic young turks. More and more officers throughout the Army are dismayed by the stranglehold of lobbies, both by arms and regiments. In their view, the Army's federal nature leaves it divided and therefore at a severe disadvantage when facing up to the Navy and RAF, as well as the civil servants in the Ministry of Defence.

Capbadge loyalty is particularly strong in the present generation of senior officers. They were mostly captains in the late 1960s when so many regiments were amalgamated or disappeared. In most cases the experience was not a happy one. A general, therefore, in his patriarchal role of honorary colonel or colonel commandant of a regiment, feels doubly bound to do everything he can to safeguard its identity. One way is to make sure that it will have other members in senior positions 'to fight its corner' in the future. This makes the system, as every general admits, a thoroughly tribal one.

Few dispute the advantages of the regimental system as a tool for recruiting, and the steadying influence it exerts in battle is envied by both the US Army and the Bundeswehr. Few, however, envy its ramifications.

The RAF believes the promotion system is permeated by regimental patronage with 'its tentacles reaching right to the top'. 'To us it's incredible,' said an air marshal. This was not a case of inter-service rivalry. His acknowledgement that 'we've got a bloody good army' was clearly genuine. The Royal Navy, meanwhile, is hugely entertained by the Army's tribal intricacies and internal rivalries.

Within the Army, the success of the Green Jackets provokes resentment and suspicion of a self-perpetuating élite, dubbed the 'black mafia' – black being the colour of their uniform buttons. A Guards general, on the other hand, said that there was nothing sinister in their success. They had produced a lot of highly qualified officers over the years. 'Good officers breed good officers,' he said. 'They make sure that the younger ones pass exams. Nobody in my regiment ever bothered about exams.' And in any case, he added, it now looked as if their winning streak was coming to an end. In 1991, the Light Division was the second most under-strength both for officers and for soldiers out of the six infantry divisions.

No. 1 Selection Board is seen as a college of cardinals. Favourites to become generals have been picked out and encouraged ever since they commanded their regiments, when estimates were made on whether they had two-, three- or four-star potential. Given the loyalties of the regimental system, complete objectivity would be too much to hope for. 'Patronage does come into it,' said a general who has taken part in the deliberations. Apparently, if the officer came from a particular regiment, 'there was a good deal of "Oh, yes, so-and-so, he could command a brigade." Not enough searching questions are asked.' He then added: 'There's far too much over-grading. It's been proved statistically.'

Concern about a more literal freemasonry seems to be conspicuous only by its absence, and yet freemasonry is still strong in parts of the Army. One leading mason said that when he joined every member of the Army Board was a mason – he would not say how things stood today. The truth would appear to be that freemasonry in the Army is mainly a social activity in an already clubbable society, and much less of a power network than in some other organizations.

The next step up from brigadier is to major general, but they have become an increasingly threatened species over the last quarter of a century. In 1967 there were ninety-seven; in 1991 there were fifty-five, a figure soon likely to drop much further. Very few major generals have field army commands. There are the divisions allocated to Nato, the appointment of Commander Land Forces in Northern Ireland, and joint-service commands overseas, such as Hong Kong, Cyprus and the Falklands when the Army's turn comes round. Other major generals preside over military districts or directorates general in the Ministry of Defence, or they are the directors of a major arm or service, such as the Director of Infantry, or commandant of Sandhurst, the Staff College or Shrivenham. Another major general is chief of staff of UK Land Forces, but the most important and the most powerful major general in the Army is the Assistant Chief of the General Staff. The post of ACGS is really a three-star appointment (the old Vice Chief of the General Staff) held by a two-star general. The holder is probably destined for four-star rank.

Most major generals on their last or penultimate job in the Army, want to be remembered for having raised, or at least maintained, standards. This includes maintenance of the respect and dignity they regard as due to the rank. A number feel that the onslaught on privilege in the public service has gone too far. Very often a house goes with the job – nothing very grand, but usually larger than a commanding officer's house. Many already have their own houses ready for retirement in Hampshire or Wiltshire, often within easy commuting distance, but wherever possible they occupy the official house to prevent the Treasury 'flogging it off'. One general remarked apropos of this constant chipping away at 'the trappings of office' that it removed the incentives for those who came after them. 'You always find', he said, 'that just before you get there they've taken away the staff car.' But, following the greatly increased pay scales for senior officers in 1991, an increased onslaught on trappings is liable to accompany the culling of figurehead appointments.

Only two major generals receive knighthoods automatically: the KCVO in both cases. They are the General Officer Commanding London District and the Defence Services Secretary, a job rotated between the Services, who is responsible for liaison with Buckingham Palace over appointments.

Several senior officers have made the point that the further up the ladder you go, the less effect you have. By this they mean that rank does not necessarily relate to power. A colonel, sometimes even a major, in an influential post can wield far more influence than all those generals whose levers are not connected to the central grid.

The British Army hierarchy is frequently accused of 'rank inflation' and military bureaucracy.[5] But comparisons with a much larger organization such as the US Army can make the ratios of generals to soldiers look more disproportionate than they are. Rank inflation comes largely from the insistence of arms and corps on maintaining as high-ranking a director as they can manage – two stars for major arms directors, and one star for small corps. Arms directors argue that this is necessary so that they can talk as equals to their opposite number in the US Army (shades of the wartime alliance). The small corps have an additional reason. Squeezed out of the big jobs, they feel they must keep at least one job of brigadier's rank to act as an enticement to potential officers; otherwise they will never attract anyone with ambition.

Statistically, just over one major general in five will make it to three stars, but this does not present a true picture. Since almost all lieutenant generals are infantrymen (seven out of nine in 1991), this means that one infantry major general in two is promoted, and virtually nobody else. 'The blade of the infantry', said one of their generals with unrepentant amusement, 'is honed rather sharper.' Only one lieutenant general has come from the logistic corps in the last twenty-five years and, to the frustration of the Royal Signals, none of their members has made it beyond two stars, even though they once had seven major generals together.

Promotion at the highest level provides a subject of endless fascination for middle-ranking officers, especially those who fancy their own chances. Reminiscences of well-known figures who have made it are often accompanied by pet theories. A discussion about an armoured commander with original ideas and a forceful personality prompted the view that 'too powerful a general scares his staff', which means he can risk getting dangerously out of touch. But another forceful armoured commander, Field Marshal Sir Nigel Bagnall – always referred to in this sort of conversation by his nickname of 'Ginge' – was respected as a general who was 'on receive, not on send'.

Career routes provide another subject to intrigue form-spotters, particularly now that UK Land Forces at Wilton is bound to become more important than Rhine Army headquarters at Rheindahlen. There are of course numerous exceptions, and unexpected crossovers, but a pattern often emerged, particularly in the heavy army, which was bound to contain a self-perpetuating element. 'It would be very difficult', explained a Rhine Army general, 'for someone who hadn't commanded a division to be corps commander.' Then, at the next step, Nato insisted that as commander of the Northern Army Group the candidate for commander-in-chief BAOR must have commanded either a division in Germany or the corps itself. All of which only served to emphasize how vital that 'black bag' appointment after Staff College can be.

Similarly, to become Chief of the General Staff it is usually essential to have been the commander-in-chief, either in Germany or England. Like all the other senior promotions, these appointments are decided by No. 1 Selection Board, and approved by the Secretary of State. Clearly, the outgoing Chief of the General Staff 'has a major say' in the choice of his replacement, but there must be a reasonable consensus; despite its tribal rivalries, the Army abhors a power struggle. About once every ten years or so, it is rumoured that the most likely candidate has been thwarted by jealousy, horse-trading or a straightforward dislike of his ideas. (Both General Sir John Hackett and General Sir Frank Kitson were said to have been blocked in this way, but the stories may well have been merely a rumour or greatly exaggerated.)

The Chief of the General Staff will not lack for honours. Like one or two other full generals, he will almost certainly be appointed an ADC General to the Queen. He will also be promoted from KCB to GCB and, on retirement, will become a field marshal. (Apparently Field Marshal Montgomery wanted the custom of subsequent promotion to be stopped after his own elevation.)

Depending on the Navy and Air Force chiefs of staff, the Chief of the General Staff stands a one-in-four chance of promotion to field marshal as the Chief of the Defence Staff, the only five-star appointment on the active list. The fourth contender is the Vice Chief of the Defence Staff, and in 1991 Field Marshal Sir Richard Vincent, a former gunner, went from VCDS to CDS.

The rank of field marshal sometimes brings a peerage on retirement, but far more useful than the House of Lords attendance allowance is the tradition of field marshals remaining on full pay until their death. Even then, there is the consoling image of the sort of funeral at which the British Army excels, with a gun carriage, a bearer party and his field marshal's baton on a velvet cushion. Of all Napoleon's aphorisms, the marshal's baton in the knapsack was one of his most instantly appealing but, on reflection, less convincing images.

Part Three

COMMAND AND CONTROL

CHAPTER 13

Whitehall Warriors:
The Ministry of Defence

Between Whitehall and the Embankment stands the Ministry of Defence Main Building. It is a monolithic structure from the 1930s. Muscular, large-breasted women in stone surmount the north entrance, presumably symbols of fertility from the days when the Board of Trade had half-tenure. At least the style falls short of the totalitarian architecture of that decade, but it is still not a place designed to lift the spirits.

Amidst the grey-suited stream of officers and civil servants arriving each morning from Charing Cross or Westminster underground stations, those from the Army are the easiest to pick out – not least by their highly polished black shoes. Until not very long ago, many Army officers wore tweed suits on Friday, whether or not they were going away to the country for the weekend.

Inside the entrance, a notice proclaims the present state of alert against terrorist attack. Seven-foot-high metal turnstiles and doors of bullet-proof glass are ranged on either side. To enter, a plastic pass has to be inserted into a panel on which a code is then tapped out. A small coloured light winks and the door clicks open with a hiss.

Other Ministry of Defence buildings in London are probably no more attractive, yet they do not have the same air of nervous energy. Although some officers clearly thrive on departmental cut and thrust, most seem to feel uncomfortable when close to the centre of politics and power.

The chain of command starts with the Cabinet's Defence and Oversea Policy Committee. Its decisions guide the

Secretary of State for Defence. He in turn has under him two ministers of state, one for the armed forces, and one for defence procurement. And they are both assisted by one junior minister each – a parliamentary under-secretary of state.

These five politicians head the Defence Council (see Fig. 1), which has the appearance of the Ministry of Defence's own Cabinet, but has tended to be more a symbolic than an active forum. Field Marshal Lord Carver described it as 'that august but little used and not very useful body', claiming that it met only once during his time as Chief of the Defence Staff – for a group photograph.[1] A member, such as the Chief of Defence Procurement, is virtually the head of a ministry in its own right, while the Office of Management and Budget, which is responsible for long-term costings, is really the Ministry of Defence's internal version of the Treasury. The Financial Planning and Management Group, comprising both military and civilian chiefs, is the highest decision-making forum in non-operational matters.

The nature of the Ministry of Defence has been greatly influenced by its evolution. During the Thorneycroft–Mountbatten reorganization of 1963–4, the Ministry of Defence subsumed the Admiralty, the War Office, and the Air Ministry. This combined super-ministry was supposed in those days to be like a trident, in that each Service continued to have its own minister, while the Secretary of State kept a firm grip on the shaft.

But bringing the service chiefs under one roof did not stimulate co-operation. If anything it brought a new edge to old rivalries. 'The history of the Ministry of Defence', said Sir John Nott, 'is the history of the war between the RAF and the Navy.'[2] Instead of separate Navy, Army and Air Force estimates, there was a central 'pot of gold', as senior officers so quaintly put it, over which to do battle. 'The old adage', said an air marshal, 'that we're all at each others' throats in the MoD is true where money is concerned.'

Mountbatten, the first Chief of the Defence Staff, found that his recommendations for central control had been sapped. As little more than chairman of the Chiefs of Staff Committee, his power hardly extended beyond a deciding vote in the case of deadlock. In a characteristically paradoxical move, the service chiefs united to guard their fractious liberty by insisting on consensus. The creation of the Defence Staff – the 'Centre' – simply shifted the battle out of the trenches and into a triangular no man's land.

Little changed for some time. The Healey defence review of 1967–8 concentrated on cutting regiments in the post-colonial retreat and did not really attempt to tackle the question of command, while the Mason defence review of 1974–5 tried to reorganize the field army, at that stage overstretched by the Northern Ireland commitment. The first attempt to revive the Mountbatten plan was John Nott's defence review of 1981. It became far better known, in fact, for his attempt to establish defence priorities clearly, to the Navy's disadvantage and fury. 'The Navy is misnamed the silent service,' commented an Army officer on the Defence Staff. 'They vilified Nott.'

Nott stopped the practice of each Service being assigned its own individual minister and established the present system. He also excluded the chiefs of staff of the three Services from the Cabinet's Defence and Oversea Policy Committee, though they could still be invited whenever necessary. But the key to political control of the Ministry of Defence lay in strengthening the Centre and doing away with a consensus which only produced what he called 'lowest common denominator decisions'. Changing the trident metaphor, Cerberus had to be wagged by his tail.

It is not an easy tail to grip. A senior RAF officer who had just explained the vital importance of tri-service integration, and spoken approvingly of the way 'Heseltine knocked the Services' heads together', then added: 'Of course, it should never fundamentally threaten the reason why people join a Service, nor the individual character and *modus operandi* of that Service.' To paraphrase Saint

Fig. 1. The Higher Organization

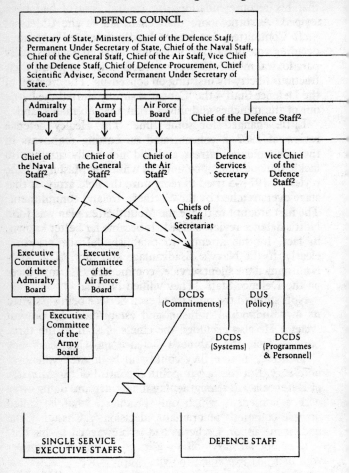

DEFENCE COUNCIL

Secretary of State, Ministers, Chief of the Defence Staff, Permanent Under Secretary of State, Chief of the Naval Staff, Chief of the General Staff, Chief of the Air Staff, Vice Chief of the Defence Staff, Chief of Defence Procurement, Chief Scientific Adviser, Second Permanent Under Secretary of State.

| Admiralty Board | Army Board | Air Force Board | Chief of the Defence Staff[2] |

Chief of the Naval Staff[2] — Chief of the General Staff[2] — Chief of the Air Staff[2] — Defence Services Secretary — Vice Chief of the Defence Staff[2]

Chiefs of Staff Secretariat

Executive Committee of the Admiralty Board

Executive Committee of the Air Force Board

Executive Committee of the Army Board

DCDS (Commitments)

DUS (Policy)

DCDS (Systems)

DCDS (Programmes & Personnel)

SINGLE SERVICE EXECUTIVE STAFFS

DEFENCE STAFF

178

of the Ministry of Defence

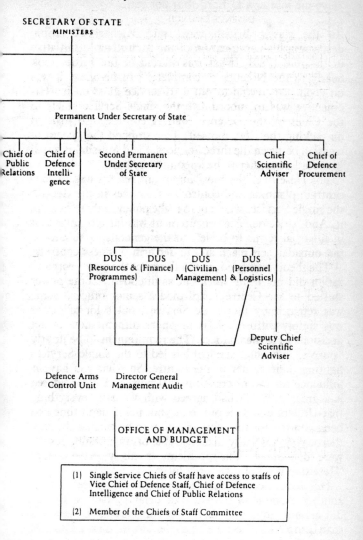

SECRETARY OF STATE
MINISTERS

Permanent Under Secretary of State

Chief of Public Relations

Chief of Defence Intelligence

Second Permanent Under Secretary of State

Chief Scientific Adviser

Chief of Defence Procurement

DUS (Resources & Programmes)

DUS (Finance)

DUS (Civilian Management)

DUS (Personnel & Logistics)

Deputy Chief Scientific Adviser

Defence Arms Control Unit

Director General Management Audit

OFFICE OF MANAGEMENT AND BUDGET

(1) Single Service Chiefs of Staff have access to staffs of Vice Chief of Defence Staff, Chief of Defence Intelligence and Chief of Public Relations

(2) Member of the Chiefs of Staff Committee

Augustine on chastity, the general attitude seems to be: 'Give me jointery, O Lord, but not yet.'

'In the classic British way,' said Michael Heseltine, describing his continuation of the Mountbatten initiative in the mid-1980s, 'what was started in the Fifties took nearly to the Nineties to complete.'[3] In his view, it was no good just 'trying to put a tri-service gloss on it'. His objective was to subordinate the single Service chiefs to the Chief of the Defence Staff. Heseltine also insisted on picking the CDS himself. This stopped the system of rotation between the three Services. Field Marshal Bramall was the last soldier to be appointed by turn.

For Heseltine, the most important reform was to concentrate planning and control of resources in the Centre: the single Services were not to make policy, only to execute it. And, since defence procurement was far too important in financial terms to be left to the generals, it should be put outside their reach and under firm business controls.

The theory was good, but in the event the great reorganization did not quite work out as intended. 'Some power shifted to the Centre,' explained a senior officer, 'some was retained by the single Services, but a lot of power was simply diffused. It is far more difficult now to get decisions.' He then added: 'The requirement to be utterly "purple" [i.e. joint-service] has led to the single Services fighting their corner in the Centre. So what you have is influence instead of constitutional power.' He considered it a great pity. He had agreed with virtually everything that Heseltine had set out to do, but not enough time had been allowed for the reorganization to be carried through thoroughly. Instantly demonstrable or quantifiable results were demanded. The problem, in his view, was that 'Heseltine is a politician in a hurry'.

Heseltine clearly regarded requests for more time as another example of bureaucratic delaying tactics. But he did acknowledge that the revolution may have been less than complete. 'There isn't a model way to run the Ministry of Defence. Compromise is inevitable. You're not trying to create the best, you're trying to create the best available.'

One of Heseltine's main moves to restrict the power of the single Services had been to replace their three-star vice chiefs of staff with two-star assistant chiefs and, in his view, any future Secretary of State would have to watch out for what he called 'the vice chiefs litmus test'. The Services, he felt, would 'fight like tigers to get back them back', and, if they succeeded, it would signify that all progress had been reversed.

A certain frustration could be sensed at the lack of real control he had had as Secretary of State over key appointments, apart from the very top one. Heseltine acknowledged that the college of cardinals selection system was inevitable. 'The constituency of appointments is a huge flat pyramid. Ministers don't know all the people involved. How can they know them? Most of the most important appointments are too far from the MoD. So you've got to have a college of cardinals working on the top plot . . . Ministers should in any case beware of interfering. But hopefully, when they come to the most senior, they're able to exert an influence.'

Mrs Thatcher also took a close interest in the appointment of Chief of the Defence Staff when the rotational system ended. It is said that she strongly opposed the appointment of General Sir Nigel Bagnall after his time as Chief of the General Staff because he was 'unsound on nuclear theology', having challenged the thinking on her pet subject of theatre nuclear weapons. If this is true (others say his age was a greater handicap), then the Services lost one of their most brilliant and stimulating minds at a crucial moment.

Within the Army, many felt that Marshal of the Royal Air Force Sir David Craig, the CDS throughout the Gulf crisis, was a very nice man, but not a patch on Bagnall. While the RAF is rightly sceptical at the ramifications of the regimental system on Army appointments, the Army feels that the RAF, as the most technological Service, is the least likely to produce effective leaders. One senior officer argued that fast jet pilots, with their super physical reactions, were 'little more than kids who do well in the amusement arcade'. These 'pinball wizards', however brave and cool in action, had no experience of leadership in the usual sense of the term if only because they were guided individually to their target. Yet under the 'master race' system, their career path led them via the command of 11 Group to the very top. Great was the relief in Army circles when Field Marshal Sir Richard Vincent, who had been the Vice Chief of the Defence Staff, took over in the spring of 1991. With the very difficult decisions ahead, the reaction was one of 'Thank God, it's Dick Vincent.'

Every few months an updated internal directory to the Ministry of Defence is published. Resembling a fairly slim telephone directory, it also includes pages of charts – rather like the pedigrees of several intermarried and prolific families – showing the different departments and their satellite directorates. These 'wiring diagrams', or maps, as senior officers tend to call them now, provide an official guide to the streams which flow through the bureaucratic delta. But, to the confusion of the newcomer, the straight lines down the official chain of command do not necessarily reflect the reality of bureaucratic power. The senior officer who spoke of Heseltine's reforms ending up with an increase of influence at the expense of constitutional power emphasized that 'the dotted lines are often far more important than the straight'. Notional dotted lines running diagonally across between different departments and 'bricks' of directorates signify that, although a particular director in theory reports to his immediate superior, the bulk of his work is controlled by another officer in another department altogether.

The key map, entitled 'The Higher Organisation of the Ministry of Defence', closely follows Michael Heseltine's first outline sketched during a flight back from Bahrein.[4] As can be seen, there are four main groupings: the three single Services on the left (still not entirely under the Chief of the Defence Staff), then the Centre itself, then the Office of Management and Budget, and finally the Defence Scientific Staff and the Procurement Executive, which, although independent, work closely together.

The Centre, which comes under the separate control of both the Chief of the Defence Staff and the Permanent Under Secretary of State, has four main departments of which the first two, Commitments (operations) and Systems (operational requirements), have some twenty directorates each. Most are 'purple', but each Service has its own 'brick' of directorates for operational requirements. Then, reporting directly to the Vice Chief of the Defence Staff, is the mainly civilian department under the Deputy Under Secretary of State (Policy). Finally, there is the Deputy CDS (Programmes and Personnel) whose satrapy deals with budget and manpower projections. His three directorates of plans – Navy, Army and Air Force – are single-Service and not purple. Theirs was the unenviable task of producing the recommendations for Options for Change.

The line of operational command goes from the Secretary of State to the Chief of the Defence Staff, almost invariably in consultation with the Chiefs of Staff Committee, to the Defence Operations Executive. Chaired by the Deputy Chief of the Defence Staff (Commitments), a three-star appointment which rotates between the three Services, its members will include the assistant chiefs of the Naval Staff, the General Staff and the Air Staff. Their instructions are then implemented by the Joint Operations Centre, which in turn will instruct the relevant headquarters: Rhine Army and RAF (Germany) at Rheindahlen if Nato interests are involved, Fleet at Northwood, UK Land Forces at Wilton or Strike Command at High Wycombe. Overseas commands, such as the Falklands, Cyprus, Belize or Hong Kong, will also receive instructions by signal from the Joint Operations Centre.

*

The Procurement Executive, although not Michael Heseltine's creation, formed the cornerstone of his reorganization of the Ministry of Defence. He found that however much senior officers disagreed between themselves over resources, they united against the common ministerial enemy. Their main ploy was to exert moral blackmail by presenting manipulative cases which demanded 'horrendous decisions'. (Images of a military version of Sir Humphrey Appleby spring to mind, saying: 'Well, yes, Secretary of State, but you realize we would have to do away with the air–sea rescue service if you want us to reduce expenditure any more.')

Heseltine felt that the only solution was to change the game so that it was no longer loaded in favour of the 'power baronies'. The key was resource allocation, and for that 'you must put the professionals into bat with each other'. The professional he brought in to bat (poacher turned gamekeeper would have been just as apt) was the entrepreneur Peter Levene, who had built up his own company in the defence field, United Scientific Holdings. Levene, who has since been knighted, soon proved himself 'a formidable operator, a born bargainer'.[5]

Levene's task was to introduce a more rational and, above all, businesslike approach to spending a budget which now runs at over £8 billion a year on equipment and spares for the three Services. Despite much covert resistance from both civil servants and senior officers, Levene was made Chief of Defence Procurement. A lack of enthusiasm for these reforms persists to this day in the middle reaches of the system, according to one general, yet Levene had still managed to bring about 'a huge sea change in our attitudes. We're trying to run things much more as a business.'

Although the Chief of Defence Procurement reports to his Minister of State and to the Permanent Under Secretary of State, he has direct access to the Secretary of State for Defence and, on an informal basis, to the Prime Minister himself. He does not report to any of the service chiefs. In fact their heads of weapons and equipment – the Controller of the Navy, the Master General of the Ordnance, and the Controller Aircraft – are his direct subordinates, as are the heads of research and development establishments. He is, in short, 'a four-star civilian' with a satrapy independent even of the Centre and its five-star supremo, the Chief of the Defence Staff.

Parallel to the Procurement Executive, on what might be called the financial and technical wing of the Ministry of Defence, is the Office of Management and Budget under the Second Permanent Under Secretary of State, and the Defence Scientific Staff under the Chief Scientific Adviser. Both these men are also four-star civilians and members of the Defence Council. When a major project is requested by the relevant operational requirements branch in the Centre, all three departments are involved.

For example, in grossly simplified terms, if a new armoured vehicle is wanted, the Directorate of Operational Requirements (Land) 1 discusses the technical aspects with all relevant departments, including that of the Chief Scientific Adviser, and funding with the Programmes Staff and the Office of Management and Budget. Only then would it assemble the justification for the project. Once the requirements and funding have been agreed in principle, the project as a whole is then studied by the Chief Scientific Adviser and the Equipment Policy Committee before a full presentation to the Minister of State for Defence Procurement. If he agrees, the project passes to the Procurement Executive and its land branch under the Master General of the Ordnance. The relevant director general, in this case the Director General of Fighting Vehicles (DGFVE), will then be told: 'There's your money, there's your brief, come back in so many years with the kit.'

The slowness of the process causes great frustration in the field army. An Army Air Corps major remarked that 'the half-life of technology at the moment is a lot shorter than the British procurement system.' But although there is 'tremendous inertia in the system', as

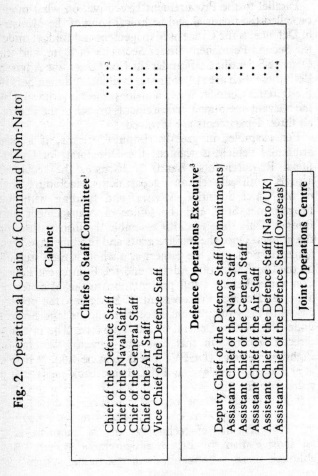

Fig. 2. Operational Chain of Command (Non-Nato)

Cabinet

Chiefs of Staff Committee[1]

Chief of the Defence Staff
Chief of the Naval Staff
Chief of the General Staff
Chief of the Air Staff
Vice Chief of the Defence Staff[2]

Defence Operations Executive[3]

Deputy Chief of the Defence Staff (Commitments)
Assistant Chief of the Naval Staff
Assistant Chief of the General Staff
Assistant Chief of the Air Staff
Assistant Chief of the Defence Staff (Nato/UK)
Assistant Chief of the Defence Staff (Overseas)[4]

Joint Operations Centre

(Royal Navy)
HQ CINCFLEET
(Northwood)

(Army)
HQ UK Land Forces
(Wilton)

(Royal Air Force)
HQ STC [5]
(High Wycombe)

CBF Cyprus [6]
Army/RAF**

CBF Belize
Army*

CBF Falklands
RN/Army/RAF**

CBF Hong Kong
Army**

CBF Gibraltar
RN**

1 In addition to the permanent members listed, other senior officers, such
  as the Chief of Defence Intelligence (a three-star appointment), will attend.
2 Number of stars indicate rank. For example, a three-star joint-service
  appointment could be held by a vice admiral, a lieutenant general or an air
  marshal.
3 It must be remembered that the role of the Ministry of Defence is to
  direct commanders: the commander on the spot commands. The temptation
  to interfere in operations has increased greatly with satellite
  communications.
4 Other senior officers will attend as required.
5 STC – Strike Command.
6 CBF – Commander British Forces. For details on overseas commands see
  Chapter 18.

187

a general acknowledged, far more care has to be taken with equipment whose sophistication and expense increases with almost exponential growth. And, as General Sir Peter Inge pointed out, 'frequently a new weapon system is part way through its development cycle when it is overtaken by what is apparently an even more effective system or counter to it, thus many weapons are obsolescent before they are in the hands of the soldiers'.[6]

One of the most important considerations is the human factor, and since 1981, when the US General Accounting Office reported that up to 50 per cent of US Army equipment was ineffective through inadequate consideration of the end user, much work has been done by the Army Personnel Research Establishment at Farnborough. Testing soldiers' performance under extreme conditions, and with the application of 'cognitive ergonomics', equipment can be designed to allow for human error, which means that instead of being solidly 'soldier-proof' as in the old days it can now be 'soldier-friendly'.

Defence procurement has to reconcile far more conflicting interests than any commercial enterprise. Budgetary considerations, although enormous, represent only one aspect, and the image of civil servants tussling with officers determined to 'gold-plate' or 'over-spec' their precious new kit is one-sided and nowadays exaggerated. Many interest-groups try to influence the final decision, from one of the other Services to the Department of Trade and Industry to the buy-British-at-all-costs lobby in Parliament and the press. 'Nevertheless, the system's beginning to work,' said the same general. 'It's only not working because we're not letting it work.'

Struggling over 'the pot of gold' may be the chief reason for the system's complications, yet many within Westminster and Whitehall feel that the armed forces demand and get far too much already. John Nott thought that pride had always played a large part, especially in Germany, where the Army continually made comparisons with the other Allies. 'What matters is looking good in your uniform and driving up in your new [armoured vehicle] and holding your head high . . . Resources were constantly poured in . . . The whole psychology of the Army was to compete with the Allies on kit.'

A senior staff officer in the Centre was particularly irreverent. 'Generals are like children in a toyshop,' he said. 'They want all the toys but can't afford the batteries.' Although great fun, the Dinky Toy theory of defence procurement is not entirely fair. Soldiers want the latest armoured vehicle just as scientists want the latest laboratory equipment. The real problem is competition between the arms and services. An armoured general is bound to see a new tank as the overwhelming priority, an aviation general argues equally strongly for his attack helicopter, while for a gunner general the multi-launch rocket system is far more important than all the rest. The gunners' case for more kit provoked the retort that they had already 'done very well', having been allowed to raise a new air defence regiment, which rather revealed the continuing capbadge fixation of generals who are supposed to have risen above the fray.

Divided by these capbadge loyalties, the Army is at a severe disadvantage when facing the other two Services. 'The Navy and the RAF are top-down systems,' explained one departmental director. 'The Army is a bottom up organization, because of the regimental system, and this puts us at a tremendous disadvantage . . . The RAF play the system very cleverly.' This view is echoed with feeling throughout the Army. The RAF, several Army officers remarked, somehow always manages to obtain the best equipment available. One or two commented that they often wangled Range Rovers when the Army would get only Land Rovers. Before the Gulf war, the jealousy prompted very unfraternal comments about the cost of replacing crashed Tornado fighters, and how much better the money could be spent.

But all this only goes to emphasize the old tribal truths. The idea that an officer in the Centre can forget the colour

189

of his uniform is as much a fiction as the idea that an Army officer leaves behind his regimental perspective on promotion to colonel. 'We are all prisoners of our own experience,' acknowledged the same officer cheerfully.

'The MoD produces a distinctive type of civil servant,' wrote Peter Hennessy in his book on Whitehall, 'a particularly tough breed, though not because war planning requires the harder type. It has more to do with constant battles.'[7] John Nott saw them as 'totally unlike Treasury civil servants, who write beautifully, but are very other-worldly . . . Civil servants in the Ministry of Defence were much more committed than anywhere else. They were advocates for their particular Service, and not dispassionate at all. They even seem to have imbibed the service discipline. They stood up when you entered a room and almost leapt to attention as if you were a general. The idea of anyone in the Treasury doing that was unthinkable.'

Perhaps the difference is also explained by an almost besieged feeling, an isolation from the rest of Whitehall. The Ministry of Defence, Nott felt, was disliked because 'they spend so much money . . . Alone in Whitehall the Ministry of Defence has a block budget and it cocks a snook at the Treasury. Every other department has to go cringing . . . It also has the power. It can beat off the others including the DTI [Department of Trade and Industry] which has a watching brief on procurement.' The Services are also privileged in another way. 'Ours is the only ministry', the air marshal emphasized, 'where the specialists have direct access to ministers – you can't imagine teachers having access to the Minister of Education. That's why we're used to getting on with politicians.'

A number of people, both in Westminster and in the Army itself, have remarked that the Ministry of Defence suffers from an instinctive fear of the truth, whether good or bad, while the field army is much more robust. An officer on the Defence Staff commented that the trouble was that 'civil servants always tend to jump at their own shadows'. But this is not enough to explain that often obsessively guarded manner. Unlike the more overtly political variety of other countries, the Ministry of Defence's secrecy owes much to that traditionally British fear of frankness, an instinctive dislike of having even the most lightly soiled linen washed under public scrutiny.

Inevitably, there may also be a complete difference in outlook between civil servant and Army officer, sometimes causing deep distrust. 'The managers for the Army', said a brigadier, 'are the civil servants, and they cut things without regard to the effect it will have. They don't feel responsibility for their actions . . . They just massage problems. The buck's passed upwards. It's not us, it's the minister.' Other senior officers feel that civil servants unfairly receive the brunt of the Army's frustrations. If there were tensions, a general said, they were mainly over money, and that was the Army's fault. 'We don't know the cost of anything.'

A recently retired colonel who emphasized that 'we are very well served' by civilian officials in the Ministry of Defence added that if there were problems of understanding it was because 'they cannot quite comprehend the [Army's] system', which in their eyes was often illogical. And a senior civil servant working for the Ministry of Defence on the scientific side made the following observation: 'With an Air Force officer I would be used to arguing on a technical level, and he would respond in the same way. With an Army officer I can present sound technical arguments until I'm blue in the face, but if he doesn't trust me I'm wasting my time. It's pure gut reaction . . . It's a cultural thing in the Army. They're a band of brothers and if you haven't made the rapport you have great difficulty getting your point across.'

The two most important civil servants on Options for Change, Richard Mottram, the Deputy Under Secretary of State (Policy), and Roger Jackling, the Assistant Under Secretary (Programmes), aroused a widespread visceral distrust amongst Army officers who did not know them, but they made the rapport and won the respect of those officers who worked alongside them.

The Army Department within the Ministry of Defence is really an integrated version of the old War Office, with its independence greatly reduced. The full title of the Army's own cabinet is the Army Board of the Defence Council. Its members include all five members of the Government – the Secretary of State for Defence, the Minister of State for the Armed Forces and the Minister of State for Defence Procurement, together with the two Parliamentary Under Secretaries of State – the Chief of the General Staff, the Second Permanent Under Secretary of State, the Adjutant General, the Quartermaster General, the Master General of the Ordnance and the Controller of Research and Development Establishments. The Executive Committee of the Army Board (ECAB) is responsible for the 'detailed management of the Army'. It numbers the four military members of the Army Board, the Second Permanent Under Secretary and the Assistant Chief of the General Staff. The Master General of the Ordnance sits on the Army Board and on No. 1 Selection Board to represent the weapons staff side, yet his department is part of the Procurement Executive, not the Army Department. The Chief of the General Staff, according to a former incumbent, 'is only *primus inter pares* on the Army Board – significantly less regarded as the boss than the First Sea Lord in the Navy and the Chief of the Air Staff in the RAF'.[8]

The Army Department consists of four main blocks: the General Staff, which reports to the Assistant Chief of the General Staff (hence his remarkable degree of power); the Adjutant General's Department; the Military Secretary's Department; and the Quartermaster General's Department (see Chapter 25).

At first sight, the General Staff appears a bizarre collection. It includes everything from the Army Historical Branch to the Director SAS, but broad categories can soon be spotted. There is an administrative and academic side (General Staff Secretariat, Army Board Secretariat, Historical Branch – known predictably and unjustly as the 'hysterical branch' – and Soviet Studies Research Centre), an operational side (Director of Military Operations and Director SAS), a command, control and engineering side in support (information technology, Signal Officer-in-Chief, Engineer-in-Chief, Military Survey), a directorate-general dealing with both the Army's organization and its reserves, and a directorate-general responsible for policy on training, exams and doctrine. The operational side is, of course, the most important and the most powerful.

The Adjutant General ranks after the Chief of the General Staff, and is the only other member of ECAB always to have four-star rank. His department is one of the largest in the Ministry of Defence, mainly because the Army is by far the most labour-intensive of all three Services – 'You can't put machines into Northern Ireland,' said a general to emphasize the point. It is responsible for all aspects of manpower resources, recruiting, pay, conditions of service, and discipline.

The two pillars, or perhaps pyramids, of his organization are each headed by a two-star general – the Director General of Army Manning and Recruiting and the Director General of Personal Services. (The latter title provoked a number of predictable jokes when *Personal Services*, the film about 'Madame Cyn', came out since both the Chaplain General and the Provost Marshal (who is responsible for policing and, under another hat, punishment) belong to his province.

The DGPS's most immediate subordinate is the Director of Army Service Conditions, a one-star directorate with heavy responsibilities for discipline – both policy, in the form of regular reviews of military law, and casework, including the appeal procedure of courts martial – and the welfare of single soldiers, married soldiers and their families. The most contentious responsibility of all, pay and allowances, belongs to the 'number-crunchers' in PS10 who handle pay and the infinitely more vexed question of allowances. They advise the Army Board on policy options – the different ways of distributing the cake – but options are usually hobbled by a host of bureaucratic and inter-service complications. If the Army is given something or denied something, the Treasury will say, then the same must go for the Navy and the Air Force. One cannot help suspecting a streak of Whitehall revenge for all the times the Services have thwarted them. In theory at least, pay should not be a contentious issue since it is regularly adjusted by the Armed Forces Pay Review Body: PS10 provides the relevant data on the comparability of Army pay against a basket of notional equivalents in civilian life, and then an independent quango comes to an independent recommendation. The mechanism finally managed to calm the rumblings with the pay awards of April 1991.

The first Military Secretary to the Commander-in-Chief was appointed during the Napoleonic Wars. His specific duties covered 'promotion and patronage of the Army'. In 1904, when the post of Commander-in-Chief was abolished on the recommendation of the Esher committee, the Military Secretary was attached to the Secretary of State for War and the appointment lost much of its power. Since then his main task has been to organize the selection boards and oversee the promotion and appointments of officers. (Connoisseurs of the black mafia conspiracy theory, who believe that the Army has secretly been taken over by the Green Jackets, can point to the fact that since 1815 twelve out of fifty-three Military Secretaries have come from the Light Division, and no less than three out of the last nine from the Green Jackets.)

Over the years there have been several attempts by the Adjutant General of the day to have the Military Secretary's Department included in his empire, but none has succeeded. The Military Secretary's office, together with the fateful boardroom in which officers' careers are made and unmade, is situated on the eighth floor of Main Building. His department, however, is based at Stanmore in a low-rise military sprawl of wartime accommodation which has all too clearly been extended several times past its due date.

A key general acknowledged that senior officers seemed to move around at a ridiculous pace, and that nobody really knew why. They seldom had time to get to know anyone properly. Those marked out for the top, the flyers, had the least time of all in which to settle into a job before being rushed on to the next promotion. As they circle higher into the star bracket, alternating between staff and command appointments, the rhythm seems to accelerate.

The system causes a good deal of unease, and not only amongst the less successful. 'Everyone's looking upwards,' said a colonel. 'They're all scared of dropping a bollock,' said another. 'The problem is', said a brigadier, 'that it's often much safer to do nothing . . . the MoD is very far removed from the coalface.' More seriously, there was 'an attitude of always looking to the next job'. In other words, officers were mainly interested in having something to show by the time their confidential report was written; the long-term consequences of their actions were disregarded.

The number of out-and-out careerists is probably quite small. But the minority is bound to set the pace, and others are forced to follow. (To judge by the toll from stress, nobody could accuse officers in the Ministry of Defence of slacking.) The Army has been sitting uncomfortably in an era in which personal ambition suddenly became respectable, even admirable, and 'efficiency measures' were demanded by politicians. For officers with more traditional loyalties, the idea of showing enthusiasm for schemes which they knew were hurting the Army 'at the coalface' was hard to stomach.

Michael Heseltine declared that generals themselves should decide how to restructure their organization and make the economies required. Asked if it was not unfair to give them such responsibilities without control of their commitments, he said that if there was a serious imbalance between commitments and resources then 'their task should be to keep putting it in writing and standing up'. He then added: 'But at the end of the day they must obey orders.' Neither morale nor job satisfaction were key issues: 'The underlying barometer is always pay.'

Heseltine appeared to misunderstand the Army's nature. Both politicians and civil servants frequently fail to grasp an obvious, but essential, point stressed by nearly every writer on military matters. Some men may join for the money in peacetime, but to be effective when they are needed they cannot be employees in uniform. To give them the necessary courage, they must have a collective self-confidence, based on emotive beliefs which may well be irrational and even obnoxious in the eyes of many civilians. But one thing is certain: an army, to mix a paraphrase, does not march on its pay scales alone. 'If you turn us into a monetary organization,' said a major from the Parachute Regiment, 'you get a monetary mentality.'

Ministers, civil servants and senior officers are passing through the most important and difficult period of decision-making the Army has known since the inter-war years. The process will probably 'go several rounds' in both senses of the term, and it will be very painful. Although the Army put some of its brightest and best officers into the Directorate of Army Plans and Programmes, the odds were stacked against them with the field 'full of sacred cows'. It is hard to redesign an army for the future when the British habit of compromise and loyalty to existing structures is so ingrained.

CHAPTER 14

BAOR: 'The Next Fixture'
Indefinitely Postponed

An impressionistic sketch of the huge headquarters complex at Rheindahlen should include 'the big house' of Joint Headquarters – its white façade has a rather Festival of Britain attempt at grandeur – clumps of silver birch trees, car parks, garrison sports fields, churches and social services of various denominations, a Naafi supermarket and row after row of German-built married quarters with addresses like Appleby Walk and Wellington Road. Yet many of those who have served there, to say nothing of the field army, have tended to see Rheindahlen as a state of mind.

On the edge of the greatly diminished Hardter Forest, between Mönchen-Gladbach and the Dutch border, this capital of the British archipelago in Germany retains a cheerless and dated air. The military cemetery has a different poignancy from those that are full of war dead. The graves, some of which date back nearly forty years, contain the remains of soldiers and their families who died away from home. Many Germans saw the British presence in their country as our substitute for the Raj lost in 1946.

Rhine Army Headquarters, according to an infantry major who had served there, was 'a self-perpetuating anachronism – they're all bloody good at justifying why the headquarters should stay'. It was really just 'a halfway house' between the Ministry of Defence and the 1st (British) Corps, whose headquarters were in Bielefeld. None of the other Allied corps in the Northern Army Group had this intermediate level. Basically it was 'just a post-box'. The disbanding of Rhine Army headquarters and the splitting of its functions between the headquarters of Bielefeld and the Ministry of Defence was rejected in 1984 on the grounds that 'severe operational penalties would result'. In its 1989 report into the cost-efficiency of the Ministry of Defence, the National Audit Office – Whitehall's auditors – still did not sound very convinced.[1] Now, it has little time left to run.

Not everyone shuffled paperwork between London and the forward troops. Many departments, following the first law of bureau-dynamics, felt obliged to create their own, demanding statistics from subordinate headquarters who had to demand them from units, and then pass them back. The lamentable state of the Army's data-processing systems made this a wasteful and cumbersome process. And few officers, especially the ROs or retired officers, were likely to say that their jobs could be dispensed with. One colonel remarked that Rheindahlen as a whole had an 'RO mentality'. Younger staff officers especially were scathing about the ROs' addiction to their perks – petrol coupons, tax-free cars, duty-free cigarettes and drink – and claimed that the main challenge in their lives was to extend their appointments for as long as possible.

A large part of the headquarters, at least for the moment, still deals with the administration of personnel and families. One senior officer described himself as 'a sort of Pooh-Bah, because I'm Lord High everything else . . . minister of housing, minister of finance, attorney-general, minister for social security and education and vehicle licensing'. His main problem was the dispersal of the garrisons, which he described as 'a population the size of Reading spread over an area the size of Scotland'. This produces its problems. In some cases children have to spend two and a half hours travelling each day to school and back. Hospital visits can take a whole day because the British military hospitals have not followed the shift in garrisons for reasons of economy – Osnabrück, with over 10,000 troops and several times that number of 'dependants', is without one. In another uncorrected 'historical illogicality', married quarters are often far away from barracks, isolating families without cars, or wives who cannot drive. The 1975 Spencer Report described the conditions in the Rhine Army as 'a recipe for social distress'.[2]

Accounts of the system's shortcomings and heavy-handedness were, and to a degree still are, very depressing. But to allocate blame to individuals, even those Colonel Gaffney once described as 'defending the indefensible', would be pointless. Military administration of essentially civilian matters, and above all welfare services, has never been successful. The priorities are utterly different. 'We've got to run an army,' said a senior officer shortly before the Berlin Wall came down, 'not a strength-through-joy camp.' Three factors combined to change attitudes during 1990 and 1991: the severe loss of manpower, often prompted by the dissatisfaction of wives; the collapse of the Warsaw Pact, and thus much of the argument that welfare must be subordinated to operational priorities; and the genuine enthusiasm to help the wives of men in the Gulf which arose at all levels in the autumn of 1990.

The contrast between Rhine Army headquarters at Rheindahlen on the Dutch frontier and the headquarters of 1st (British) Corps at Bielefeld, 130 kilometres closer to the old Cold War frontier, was always unmistakable. On the edge of the Teutoburger Wald, corps headquarters was closer to its own units, ringed by the garrisons at Herford, Detmold, Sennelager, Paderborn, Münster, and Osnabrück – the largest British garrison anywhere, larger even than Aldershot. As a field army headquarters, unencumbered by the bureaucratic tail, the organization was, of course, much tighter, but so too were the attitudes. Now its future, like that of Rheindahlen, is one of great change as the new Nato system of multi-national corps and a rapid reaction force begins to take shape.

To maintain interest, let alone a sense of urgency, after the revolutions of 1989, has been very difficult. 'A soldier,' generals are fond of saying, 'is only happy when he's soldiering.' Soldiers indeed look forward to exercises, not just as a break from the depressing monotony of maintenance on the vehicle park, but as the only test of training short of war, and therefore the validation of his existence.

In theory, the annual programme starts with platoon or troop tactics, followed by company and squadron 'schemes', gradually working up to a large exercise in the early autumn for part of the Rhine Army. The sub-unit work-ups – 'a bit of right-flanking, two up and bags of smoke' – on the overfamiliar wasteland of Soltau training area stir little enthusiasm. 'Soltau becomes deadly for them,' said a troop leader.

A measure of excitement could be stimulated on exercise when the enemy came from outside the unit, but that happened only on the larger schemes, which have now become as politically obsolete as the Four Power agreement. Nothing kept soldiers on their toes better than the possibility of the SAS or the Parachute Regiment 'putting in' a night attack. A scrap with troops from an Allied army was relished and long remembered. To the horror of exercise umpires, mock battles with German Panzergrenadier battalions or Belgian para-commandos sometimes turned into real fights with fists, boots, rifle butts and, on at least one occasion, even bayonets. And infantrymen love the idea of duffing up 'tankies', who in revenge have been known to pursue them in their armoured vehicles if they catch them in the open.

In spite of all the conviction their officers tried to put into their briefings, fictional scenarios of a Fantasian operational manoeuvre group striking across the Weser left soldiers unmoved. The main subject for discussion afterwards was whether the spot chosen for their tactical hide was near that village with the gasthaus which they slipped off to the year before. Exercises are supposed to be dry, but during stand-down officers will usually turn a blind eye, providing soldiers 'don't tear the arse out of it and get caught'. The eleventh commandment is far more important than the precise disciplinary code laid down in *The Manual of Military Law*. In the meantime, they retreat to regimental headquarters for 'a glass of cold tea'.

The Weser-Bergland triangle, which lies between Hanover, Bielefeld and Göttingen, was well-trodden and well-tracked ground before the end of the Cold War in 1989, but that had little to do with the paucity of training value in the big exercises. The lumbering choreography of whole formations meant that regiments sat around for anything up to a day or more. 'The larger the exercise, the less the benefit to the guy on the ground,' said a major in the Royal Tank Regiment. 'The only advantage of the large-scale FTX [formation training exercise]', said the commanding officer of a gunner regiment, 'is that it imposes realistic buggeration factors on the staff.' A sapper captain was much more cynical: 'They don't play for real, they play for training directives.'

The restrictions imposed so as to avoid provoking an increasingly intolerant German public had already drastically reduced the realism of the big exercises in Germany by 1988. To avoid churning up fields – farmers no longer welcomed the 'second harvest' of compensation – tank squadrons sat nose to tail, seldom allowed off the road. In 1988, even fast-moving armoured reconnaissance regiments found Exercise Iron Hammer 'very low key' compared to those of previous years, and the following year Exercise White Rhino (soon dubbed Green Rhino) was drastically diluted as a sop to German public opinion. It proved the forerunner for a new hybrid between a traditional field exercise and a command post exercise in which only headquarters vehicles move out into the field. This was defined as a CFX, a command field exercise, in which token bodies of troops and vehicles – a platoon, for example, represents a whole battalion – make the moves ordered by exercise control, rather like a Chinese emperor's game of chess in a large square-tiled courtyard with human beings as chess pieces. By the autumn training season of

1991 the deployment of formations outside the existing training areas of Soltau and Sennelager had effectively ceased.

Environmental regulations were already severe in the Federal Republic. The digging of latrines was forbidden, and Portaloos had to be shipped in at considerable cost. The local fire brigade had to be summoned to clear up any chemical or fuel spillage. A military vehicle with an oil leak was likely to be reported by a civilian driver – most probably an exasperated motorist stuck behind a convoy – and the commanding officer of the regiment would be fined. At first, the rather lax British found all this very officious, but they have had to learn to live with the restrictions, whether on the movement of military vehicles at weekends or low-flying aircraft. 'The Germans are not friendly,' said a company sergeant major, 'but I can see why they're not friendly.'

The British Army has two alternatives: to train elsewhere, or take greater advantage of the technological advances in simulators, which, in a specially adapted tank turret or helicopter pilot's seat, can recreate combat conditions with remarkable realism. Since the loss of training rights in Libya in 1971, the only unrestricted area for Rhine Army regiments has been at Suffield in Canada. BATUS – the British Army Training Unit Suffield, near Medicine Hat – is otherwise known as 'the dust bowl'. Its huge tracts of rolling country, where the Blackfoot tribe once hunted buffalo, offer almost ideal facilities for a battle group at a time. Suffield's only disadvantage is the severity of the winters which shortens the training season, and the Ministry of Defence has been looking into examining the possibility of borrowing another major training area from a Nato country in the Mediterranean region, and now possibly the Gulf in order to keep an occasional presence there.

Using tanks, artillery and armoured personnel carriers maintained at Suffield, battle groups flown over from

Germany work up through an intense three-week programme, culminating in tactical live firing, with tanks, infantry and artillery 'playing it for real' with an Army Air Corps flight in HELARM support firing missiles. Soldiers love it, and few complain about the hard work involved, but the relatively short season means that they go there from Germany only once every three years. Above all, the British Army has envied US Army facilities, which has a reproduced 'Red Army' brigade based at Fort Irwin in California to act as enemy. It is equipped with Russian vehicles and Russian uniforms, organized along Red Army lines and using only Red Army tactics.

Senior officers are far from blind to the problem of unrealistic training in Germany. 'We must be more imaginative,' said a gunner general. 'Range firing should be done tactically.' Many agree with him. They also feel that the vogue for competition can reduce training to a form of military Olympics. Winning has become more important than learning.

As the threat of real war decreases, Nato armies seem ever more desperate to try to keep up an interest in training through competitions. The best is almost certainly the Boeselager Trophy, the Bundeswehr's competition between armoured recce regiments, which has prompted many imitations. There is the 'cop shoot' at Hohne for military police, and even an international canine biathlon for dog-handlers, organized at Sennelager by the Defence Animal Support Unit, RAVC. Divisions have their own competitions – for example 1st Armoured Division, whose symbol is a rhinoceros, has the Rhino Trophy – and staff officers continually rack their brains for more ideas.

Convinced that competition results may be reflected in their confidential reports, commanding officers are liable to devote too much time and resources to bringing a picked handful of their soldiers to peak condition for a contest which bears little resemblance to real field conditions.

The worst example of the 'Olympics' syndrome is the biggest: the Canadian Army Trophy for tank gunnery, a competition between Allied armies which takes place every other year. The Americans' feverish will to win has become legendary – the trophy has been dubbed 'the Superbowl of tank gunnery' – and US Army teams were spotted secretly videotaping the ranges for their simulators so that picked tank crews could practise with every tree and bush in place, effectively making a mockery of training for war.

The Rhine Army, having not won the competition since 1970, pulled out after a disastrous performance in 1987. Until the fire control system on the Challenger has been improved, British tanks stands no chance against the German-built Leopard 2, which, in 1989 took the first five places. Even though the Challenger's performance in Iraq was much better than feared, there was still no question of entering it again in 1991.

The Americans are far ahead of the British in the field of simulators for tank gunnery and driving – a technology which saves not only the countryside, but also a good deal of money in the long run. (The British are not helped by governmental accounting procedures, which discriminate against 'spend-to-save' measures.) A main battle tank simulator is now capable of achieving an astonishing degree of realism and for those who take part – closed down in a real turret – traversing and engaging Russian T80s appearing in the gunner's sight before they fire back stimulates an even greater urgency than live firing. The American Simnet (simulation network) allows tank crews stationed near Nuremburg to fight tank crews stationed in Kentucky over pre-filmed terrain, such as their Cold War Oberfälzer Wald front, all via satellite.

After Tom King's announcement on 14 September 1990 of the 7th Armoured Brigade's deployment in the Gulf, the switch from playing at war produced some suitably striking contrasts. All the financial restrictions of a peacetime army suddenly vanished, from limitations on track mileage to the rationing of ammunition. The German authorities also dropped restrictions on the use of Hohne ranges, except for a silent hour during morning service on Sundays. Windows rattled for almost a fortnight from the constant booming of tank guns fired by the Royal Scots Dragoon Guards and the Queen's Royal Irish Hussars and the 155mm M109s of 40th Field Regiment. It was probably the most concentrated expenditure of live firing in peacetime.

Soldiers from other regiments were brought in to help so that 7th Armoured Brigade units could concentrate on the job in hand. The Queen's Own Hussars did the 'ammo bashing' on the ranges to speed firing practice, while men from the 4th Royal Tank Regiment sprayed Challenger tanks and Warrior infantry fighting vehicles a 'custard yellow'. Other regiments in the garrison, for example the 1st Regiment Royal Horse Artillery in Hohne, took on guard duties and other chores.

For those going to the Gulf, feelings were clearly mixed. With the estimated strength of the Iraqi forces, and the threat of chemical weapons, most officers experienced a very proper unease at what lay ahead. The whole history of warfare is a history of nasty surprises, and for political reasons the Allies were vulnerable to hiccups of any sort. 'We are in the midst of contingency planning for the Gulf,' wrote a senior general closely involved in last autumn's preparations. 'Goodness knows where it will all end.'

On the other hand, there was inevitably something of a St Crispin's syndrome. For those not necessarily abed, but certainly far away, to be absent from the regiment at such a time was particularly frustrating. 'The rest of the Army wishes it were there,' said a cavalry officer at the height of the battle. 'Most of soldiering was rather like being a surgeon, but never being allowed to operate . . . It's not a question of giving your eye teeth to be there, but you always wanted to know how you would measure up.

'Your family is of course very relieved,' he went on, 'but at the same time it's very hard to come to terms with not being there.' He felt it was even harder on armoured corps officers than on the infantry, who had already had the chance to test themselves in Northern Ireland.

Initially, the most disappointed man in the whole Army was Brigadier Tim Sulivan, formerly of the Blues and Royals and a graduate of the Higher Command and Staff Course. He had been due to take over 7th Armoured Brigade, but to avoid a change of command just after the formation deployed in an operational theatre he had to let Brigadier Patrick Cordingley carry on all the way through. General de la Billière, however, not wanting to lose his services, had him appointed as the senior British representative on General Schwarzkopf's staff.

Certainly, many of the soldiers could not quite repress their excitement, even though the jingoistic enthusiasm of the Falklands send-off was absent. (Paradoxically, the Falklands was a far riskier venture.) Influenced at least a little by all the Desert Rat headlines in the tabloids, some young soldiers went off to have tattoos made of the insignia just before they left. One unfortunate realized just too late that the German tattooist had not inscribed his chest over the jerboa with 'Desert Rat', but with 'Dessert Rat'. Perhaps, like a misprinted stamp, it will acquire a rarity value.

For those left behind, the Gulf war evoked both pride in those out there and cynicism at their own lot. As well as 1st Armoured Division and other engineer and artillery regiments, almost every regiment sent men, either individually or as formed sub-units to bring the armoured brigades up to war strength. Bandsmen left to man the armoured ambulance detachments and provide manpower for the field hospitals, and other soldiers went out with the depressing label of 'battle casualty replacements'.

As the barracks emptied, the rest of the Rhine Army was left even more undermanned than before. Guard duties increased, and, with armoured vehicles stripped to the hull to provide enough spare parts for Operation Granby, 1st (British) Corps ceased to be militarily effective for the duration. Many officers and NCOs reflected bitterly at the effect of the last few years of economies. It was not much of an exaggeration to say that the Rhine Army, with four divisions, could put only a single reinforced armoured division into the field for its first real test in forty-five years. Nobody needed reminding that the division could never have been sent to the Gulf if 1990 had not been the year of Gorbachev.

Throughout 1990, Berlin was the focal point for developments in Germany, if only because of its unique status – virtually a padlock designed to prevent reunification. During the Cold War, Berlin was an occupied city. The Kommandatura of the military government, the Allied Forces Day Parade and the precedence of British, French or American military police over the German civil police, maintained the status quo of 1945 in circumstances so different as to be almost surreal. Members of the 2nd Regiment Royal Military Police controlled the crossing points to the East and 'swept' the Helmstedt autobahn link to West Germany, while infantry battalions were responsible for patrolling the Berlin border. Even as East and West Germans celebrated on top of the Wall, an infantry company and a troop of Chieftain tanks were fully 'bombed up' for war on forty-five minutes' notice to move. But the final meeting at the Allied Kommandantura took place on 2 October 1990, and at midnight that night Allied authority over the four sectors came to an end.

Seldom in history have foreign troops remained on foreign territory following its conquest with the consent of its people for as long as the Allies in Germany since 1945. The relationship, though firm, has not always been easy. Lord Ismay's notorious definition of Nato's purpose when its first Secretary-General – 'To keep the Russians out, the Americans in and the Germans down' – lingered well beyond 1952. For nearly twenty years the attitude of British officers was sometimes little better than that of a benign occupying power. As late as the mid-1960s a well-wined captain became famous for thumping his restaurant table in the Vierjahreszeiten in Hamburg and bellowing with huge amusement: 'My regiment captured this bloody city and I want better service!'

British self-esteem declined to more appropriate levels during the 1970s – more or less in line with the exchange rate, which fell from over ten marks to the pound to around three. Only the blinkered could ignore the fact that, during the dark days of the balance of payments crisis, the Bundesbank saved sterling from total collapse. Today, only the British squaddie, his vision of recent history shaped by comic strips and war movie stereotypes, is likely to remind 'Herman the German' that he lost the war. And yet traces of the Ismay doctrine linger on even among officers. One said that Nato had 'a dual purpose', of which the second part was 'to prevent a resurgence of the German Reich', yet then admitted that 'the British Army can be extremely parochial' and expressed genuine admiration for the Bundeswehr.

Anglo-German social activities – known to the British as 'Anglo-Banglo' – work at different levels in different ways. At the smart end polo and equestrian events, particularly in 1st Armoured Division's area north of Hanover, a centre for German horse-breeding, plays a large part. Very rich Germans appear to enjoy the company of impoverished cavalry officers. They usually win the matches, partly because they can afford better ponies, but perhaps also because of their ruthlessly competitive spirit. And if there is a patronizing heartiness in their hospitality afterwards, the British do not seem to mind.

Garrison saddle-club events and the large horse show at Bielefeld have always attracted a great many Germans, but smaller-scale and less sophisticated events also help to build good relations. Some of the Anglophilia, cynics suggest, is prompted by the hope of duty-free alcohol, but the friendliness of those Germans who do take part seems quite genuine. Anglo-German clubs designed to foster the right feelings are the responsibility of the service liaison officers. Descendants of the Allied Control Commission, they come under a major general based in Bonn, and organize anything from Burns night suppers to truly Germanic programmes of conspicuous consumption – coach outings, lasting a day or a weekend, which are little more than gasthaus crawls cum eating competitions, won by whoever puts on the most weight.

So far, the British Army has been spared the American approach to 'host-nation relations', which, according to a senior officer at Rheindahlen, consists of producing daily statistics on the number of servicemen who have had a meal with a German national, or even – though this may be something of an exaggeration – said 'Good morning' to one. Senior British officers tend to rely on dinner parties for the local bürgermeister or regierungspräsident (the chairman of the local Land government), while sergeants' messes have continued, in their far-sighted fashion, to entertain the local police.

The best proof that not everyone has disliked serving in Germany can be found in the sergeants' mess – in 1989, a Royal Artillery warrant officer returned to England having served in 1st Armoured Division for twenty-two years, all his adult service.[3] But most single soldiers in Germany seem to feel that they are missing out on their youth to little purpose between the vehicle park and the barrack block – 'You just see lives going down the Swannee out here,' said a trooper. It is hard not to see a single soldier's experience of Germany today as symbolic. Unable to exercise over real countryside, his training will be increasingly restricted to the screen of a battlefield simulator; unable to make contact with real girls in Germany, he is likely to resort even more to video sex. For many, this doubly onanistic existence will not last much longer. The Rhine Army as an institution will be replaced and forces in Germany pared down, with regiments amalgamated and withdrawn. Whether changes such as the rapid response force for British troops give a new point to soldiering in Germany only the next few years can tell.

CHAPTER 15

'The Next Fixture'
Transferred to the Gulf

Early in July 1990, a month before Iraqi forces invaded
Kuwait, a team from the Ministry of Defence crossed the
Atlantic for Global War Game '90 at the US Naval War
College at Newport, Rhode Island.

War Game '90 should have been the last of a quinquennial
cycle, but, since the collapse of the Warsaw Pact made the
theme of the cycle redundant, it was decided instead 'to
brainstorm a world-wide range of problems affecting the
world in the Nineties'. About as much attention was paid to
the nationalism of the Soviet Union's borderlands and the
Balkans as the Middle East. At one point, while everyone
was studying a chart of the US Army's order of battle,
and discussing future reductions in defence spending, a
senior representative of the State Department made a
soon-to-be-remembered remark: 'I'd sure hate to be the
chairman of the Joint Chiefs in the late nineties who has
to go to the President to explain why we couldn't whip the
ass off the Iraqis.'

In the days following the Iraqi invasion of Kuwait on 2
August, the Joint Operations Centre found itself working
round the clock. At that stage, the Iraqis were thought to
be redeploying for a second-phase strike down the east coast
of Saudi Arabia. The Defence Intelligence Staff, working
closely with the Americans, took nearly two weeks to
establish for certain that Saddam Hussein had no plans
for a second invasion.

The politicians needed to know what formations could be
deployed to the Saudi Arabian border and how quickly. A
rapid deployment to the Gulf had been tested in December

210

1986 with Exercise Swift Sword in Oman: this three-week scheme involved the 2nd Battalion of the Parachute Regiment and a naval force led by the aircraft carrier HMS *Illustrious*. But the Kuwait crisis was hardly a bushfire war. To have thrown 5th Airborne Brigade in against Iraqi armoured divisions would have been a futile gesture, and the idea was rejected. The only troops sent immediately were satellite communications (SATCOM) teams from the 30th Signals Regiment at Blandford, which had provided the British contribution to the UN force in Namibia. They left on 9 August.

In the Ministry of Defence lights were on all through the night. The Joint Operations Centre soon found itself performing a job for which it had not been designed. 'The wash-up reports on Corporate [the Falklands operation]', said one staff officer, 'were the most read documents in the building.' But Operation Granby soon proved very different from Operation Corporate.

Although out-of-area and unexpected, Operation Grandy was not entirely a 'come-as-you-are' war (the hurried adaptation of central region equipment and tactics to a distant theatre). Of course, desert conditions required a number of vital modifications to equipment, especially filters, and the issue of special kit, such as desert boots, goggles and Arab *shemaghs*. But there was time to prepare and the desert terrain was even more favourable to the equipment and the Allied land/air battle system than the European battlefield for which it had been designed. With no troops desert-trained apart from the SAS, the main concern was acclimatization, but the Allies were extraordinary lucky at the way Saddam Hussein boxed himself in, politically as well as militarily, allowing them to pick the timetable.

Direction of operations passed to one of the joint headquarters to administer – RAF Strike Command at High Wycombe. With Marshal of the RAF Sir David Craig as CDS, Air Chief Marshal Sir Patrick Hine at the Joint Headquarters, and Air Vice Marshal Bill Wratten as Commander British Forces during the build-up, Operation

Granby began to look like an RAF show. (The RAF, to the annoyance of Army officers, refused to use the Permanent Planning Group at Aldershot which had been set up for this type of emergency.) But once the Cabinet decided to commit ground forces in the shape of an armoured formation, the light-blue chain of command was broken.

Curiously, the two most senior commanders of the armoured force deployed in the Gulf, Lieutenant General Sir Peter de la Billière and Major General Rupert Smith, both came from the 'light army', the former from the SAS and the latter from the Parachute Regiment. Mrs Thatcher is said to have intervened directly in the selection of the Commander British Forces Middle East. Apart from General de la Billière, the other two leading candidates were Lieutenant General Sir Michael Wilkes, a former gunner, and Lieutenant General Sir Richard Swinburn, a former 17th/21st Lancer. Wilkes, who had commanded an armoured division in Germany, was the Commander UK Field Army. Swinburn, after commanding 1st Armoured Division in Germany, had become Assistant Chief of the General Staff in 1989; then, in 1990 he was appointed to take over from General de la Billière as GOC South East District in Aldershot, the home of out-of-area operations. Swinburn's principal reputation was for the originality of his thinking on armoured warfare. His orders groups were said by members of his division in Germany to have been far more stimulating than any seminar at Staff College. Yet, while acknowledging the brilliance of his ideas, some of his officers felt that he went too far. He was known as 'a Challengers-must-fly man', because he believed that the future lay not with attack helicopters but with flying tanks armed with electromagnetic guns as main armament.

Although General de la Billière was retiring from the Army, Mrs Thatcher wanted him to stay to command the British forces in Operation Granby. Having known him during the Iranian Embassy siege, when, as a brigadier, he was Director SAS, she had complete confidence in him. In Army eyes too, General de la Billière was an unusually good choice (unusual if only because officers, with their visceral distrust of bureaucracy, tend to suspect that the best candidate for a job is passed over as a matter of course). Much was made in the press of his SAS career, of his decorations – a DSO and two MCs – and of his fluency in Arabic and knowledge of the region. Yet just as important in the eyes of those under his command was another reputation: he had never been a 'political' general interested only in furthering his career.

General de la Billière's appointment was unlikely to give him a major role in the creation of strategy, for primacy was bound to remain with the Americans, but it put him in a position to apply an emergency brake, or to offer quiet advice. This he did, having won General Norman Schwarzkopf's respect very quickly, and he per-suaded Schwarzkopf to make several minor, yet important, changes to his plan, which the British thought 'worryingly complicated' in its first draft. Apparently, Schwarzkopf had envisaged Allied divisions crossing each other's line of advance until Billière pointed out the potential for chaos.

At press conferences during the build-up to war, Billière's reticence, both natural and professional, was frustrating for journalists. Their photographers focused on his SAS sand-coloured beret and the distinctively shaped SAS parachute wings, but missed a more important sartorial touch. He wore a stable-belt of navy, scarlet and pale blue. This tri-service symbol provided an early sign that he was there to uphold inter-service co-operation as much as the multinational alliance. Behind-the-scenes criticism of the way senior RAF officers had handled the early stages of Operation Granby needed to be laid to rest. (The criticism of senior RAF officers was not limited to the Army: fighter pilots too appear to have been unhappy with the management of operations.)[1] For a man of action, he proved an unusually good diplomat.

Major General Rupert Smith was one of the first paratroopers to have broken the 'heavy army' stranglehold on key appointments in Germany when he commanded first 6th Brigade, then the 1st Armoured Division. He had tough acts to follow at 1st Armoured Division. Both his predecessors, first Swinburn then Major General R. N. Wheeler, went on to that most powerful job of Assistant Chief of the General Staff in extremely rapid succession. But Smith, although a paratrooper, was well grounded in the latest developments of the land/air battle and multinational operations. He had just come from Staff College, where he had been deputy commandant during a period of fertile reassessment and been responsible for the Higher Command and Staff Course.

The commander of the 7th Armoured Brigade, Brigadier Patrick Cordingley, a man punctilious both in courtesy and military detail, was a graduate of the very first Higher Command and Staff Course in 1988. Cordingley was also a 'Skin' – a 5th Inniskilling Dragoon Guard, and 7th Armoured Brigade traditions were very important to him. His Desert Rat shoulder flash, presented to him by a veteran, had seen service throughout the North African campaign and the pennant on his tank had accompanied 7th Armoured Division to Germany in 1945.

On 23 October, the anniversary of the Battle of Alamein, he sent a telegram of greeting from the Gulf back to the annual dinner of the 7th Armoured Division officers' club. Among the generals and colonels present were Field Marshal Lord Carver and, representing continuity in the form of a younger generation of serving officers, Brigadier Christopher Hammerbeck, the new commander of 4th Armoured Brigade, who did not then know that he and his men would also be going out to face the Iraqis in the desert in the second phase known as 'Granby 1.5'. That night, as the dinner-jacketed assembly applauded the telegram from the Gulf, few believed it would come to war. The feeling seemed to be that Saddam Hussein would probably withdraw from Kuwait at the very last moment, having caused the maximum 'buggeration factor' to everybody concerned.

Hammerbeck, tall, fair-haired and with the build of a

rugby forward, arrived in the desert wearing the black beret of the Royal Tank Regiment. Unlike another senior officer from his regiment, his looks have saved him from the nickname of Blackadder and his chief of staff from that of Baldrick. This also saved a good deal of confusion since both names were used for the temporary camps established at Al Jubail, after Tent City became Baldrick Lines.

The build-up of forces in the Gulf had an unreal, 'phoney war' quality, mainly because of that pervasive assumption that Saddam Hussein would pull back at the last moment. Servicemen greeted distinguished visitors with placards such as 'Wot, no Kate Adie?' while the *Sun* newspaper ran one of its inimitable campaigns – 'Knit Your Hero a Willy Warmer.'[2] Under the heading of 'host nation relations' in Saudi Arabia, the Christian religion, alcohol and pictures of female bodies had to be kept out of sight. One vehicle parking site in the desert was moved so that camels could get at their favourite scratching pole.

American soldiers, identically clothed in their 'chocolate chip' desert camouflage, helmets and sunglasses, were amazed by both the tribal diversity and the scruffy lack of uniformity in British dress: the Desert Rat tradition of the 'Two Types' cartoon had not entirely disappeared. Regimental idiosyncrasies, such as the high, gold-braided officer's tentcap of the Queen's Royal Irish Hussars (which fellow cavalrymen say makes them look 'like dago dragoons'), were sported on suitable occasions.

From the beginning, when US Marines played host to the advance parties, there were few problems of Allied co-operation. The British 1st Armoured Division was seen as a useful addition to the Allied forces, but also as a powerful talisman. British victory in the Falklands and the SAS performance at the Iranian Embassy had created a reputation for getting it right, which the US Army, acutely conscious of its own débâcles in the last quarter of a century, greatly envied.

The American taste for collecting badges and souvenirs

created a lively market. Anything with the red jerboa on it, from official brigade badges to T-shirts from Scottish regiments of a Desert Rat playing the bagpipes, fetched even a US Army camp bed or a Walkman stereo. (The jerboa industry at home included cushion-cover embroidery kits designed by the Royal School of Needlework; it would have been interesting to know their exchange rate in the desert.)

On a more basic level, British rations were highly prized by American soldiers, whose MREs (Meals Ready to Eat) were in such disfavour that they were known as Meals Rejected by Ethiopians. US soldiers were impressed by British supply and engineering services, and by convoy discipline. They also liked the phlegmatic approach. Some of the younger British soldiers, on the other hand, preferred American brashness and boastfulness to their own officers' cultivation of wry understatement. British military eccentricity, such as the commander of the artillery group using his shepherd's crook to sketch plans in the sand, almost certainly appealed more to the Americans and the media than to British soldiers.

'The friendly forces' were indeed remarkably friendly considering how disparate the coalition was. In the early days some British officers rather predictably referred to General Schwarzkopf as 'General Blackhead' until they realized that there was rather more to such a bull of a man than his physical stereotype and sound bites. At the beginning, there was a good deal of evasiveness and unease in political and media circles about the British contingent coming under US command, with the fear that the British might be led into a US adventure. (American senators, however, have pointed out that this concern was rather paradoxical after Mrs Thatcher told President Bush right at the start that it was not the time to get 'wobbly'.) Soon everybody faced up to the fact that, with all due respect to the Saudis and Prince Khaled ibn Abdul Aziz, the Allied chain of command would be a sort of Nato on the Gulf with Schwarzkopf as the equivalent of an American

SACEUR. It worked because 'Stormin' Norman' was smart enough to listen with an open mind.

For British armoured regiments the heavy rain in the weeks before the battle made the ground unpleasantly reminiscent of Soltau training area. Yet seldom has the British Army had a better opportunity to practise dress rehearsals in place so shortly before the opening night, largely thanks to the superiority established by the Allied air forces. A mock 'Saddam Line', with berms, fire-ditches and minefields was constructed by sapper field squadrons to practise the assault. And on day 21 of the war the 20,000 men and 160 tanks of the 1st Armoured Division practised going, not over the top, but through the berm.

Nothing concentrates the mind like the imminence of going into battle. Soldiers, no different from their predecessors over the centuries, sought privacy to write what might be their last letters home. Many in this notoriously irreligious profession turned to religion, thus enabling regimental padres to invoke their favourite comparison between the Army and God – that people forget about both until they really need them. Some soldiers managed to pack a little bravado into the admission of being 'shit scared', but if any cockiness remained it was of the nervous joke variety.

Confidence was instilled by the hammering the enemy were getting from the air – 'poor buggers' was the reaction of soldiers as they saw the B52s going over, vapour trails in a blue sky, to bomb the Republican Guard – and by seeing that the kit worked. Goggles, body armour, and especially the widely respected quality of British NBC (or 'Noddy') suits against chemical attack had a cumulative effect on morale. The cynics from Soltau found that their tanks worked far better than expected, partly because the spare parts were at last available, but also because the tanks were being driven regularly and no longer suffering from 'track-milageitis' when under-used vehicles broke down the whole time. But curiously indirect preparations for the

217

big moment, even positive ones such as the arrival of the Coldstream Guards and the Royal Highland Fusiliers to guard prisoners of war, were all reminders of the unknown reality to come.

Like all armies prior to battle, the important thing was to keep busy, even if it consisted of zeroing guns, servicing vehicles, cleaning weapons, having haircuts, or even playing 'nerdles' – an improvised cross between a coconut shy and ice hockey (see Glossary for full details). Pipe Major Bruce of the Royal Scots Dragoon Guards offered piping lessons, but he did not have that many takers. Household Division officers and NCOs zealously upheld the practice of foot inspection – one might be tempted to regard the practice as fetishistic traditionalism if it were not such an ageless necessity. But, despite all the contrived and real distractions, the overextended period before the ground offensive was a time for reflection. Their surroundings probably encouraged the mood. 'The desert', observed one cavalry officer, 'seems to make everyone an amateur philosopher.' Kate Adie, having been adopted as 1st Armoured Division's unofficial mascot, repaid the compliment with an emotional, yet understated, eve-of-battle broadcast in which she described them as a 'thinking army'.[3]

Commanding officers, conscious of the presence of the press, may have wondered about the right balance when delivering their final address from the top of a Warrior or Challenger, but in the end most returned to the essence of what their predecessors had probably said before the battles of Assaye, Omdurman and Alamein. 'I know, and you know,' said Lieutenant Colonel Ian Johnstone of the Royal Scots to his men, 'that we will never let the Regiment down.'[4] It was very different from US Army cheer-leading slogans. (Among the tackiest was a banner at an airbase reading 'Send Us In To Kick Some, Or Send Us Home To Get Some'.)

Brigadier Patrick Cordingley, standing on top of a Warrior infantry fighting vehicle to speak to the Staffords formed up in a hollow square, would never have talked of 'getting Saddam by the nuts'. Instead he said: 'It's going to be noisy, it's going to be frightening and I would expect it to be chaotic . . . I think the battle will probably be quite quick, though not everyone agrees.' He told them to be bold and aggressive so that they took prisoners, not casualties.[5] Afterwards, the companies marched off, raising a light dust cloud as they returned to their positions and vehicles.

Not surprisingly, most just wanted 'to get it over and done with'. During the shuttle diplomacy between Baghdad and Moscow, which started just as the ground offensive was imminent, Brigadier Christopher Hammerbeck spoke out strongly in a television interview about the danger this posed to the morale of the soldiers about to fight. Almost as if in answer to his call, President Bush announced his ultimatum. And, as the deadline of midday local time on 23 February approached, a desire for the Iraqis to withdraw probably outweighed the fear of anticlimax in most soldiers. Yet, as the deadline expired, one senior Army officer described what lay ahead as 'the last great adventure', which was only marginally less embarrassing than the senior RAF officer quoting the St Crispin's Day speech in *Henry V*.[6]

Operation Granby, as a cavalry officer proudly asserted, could not have been a better chosen name since they had indeed gone 'bald-headed at the enemy'. Cordingley's advice that boldness saved casualties was sound, and General Schwarzkopf's plan was impeccable.

This is not the place to provide a full account of 1st Armoured Division's part in the hundred-hour campaign, but a few outlines are worth drawing. On the second day of the offensive, the point units of the division followed lanes blasted by the Americans through Iraqi front-line defences.

First went a reconnaissance screen of the 16th/5th Lancers, accompanied by artillery forward observation officers and forward air controllers. Then came the lead formation, the 7th Armoured Brigade, with its battle groups formed from two regiments of Challengers (the Royal Scots Dragoon Guards and the Queen's Royal Irish Hussars) and a battalion of Warrior-mounted infantry (the Staffordshire Regiment). The 4th Armoured Brigade, which was 'infantry heavy' (the Royal Scots and the 3rd Battalion, the Royal Regiment of Fusiliers in Warriors, and the 14th/20th King's Hussars in Challengers), followed close behind.

To Brigadier Cordingley's astonishment, the point armoured unit, the Queen's Royal Irish Hussars, covered the first 25 kilometres into Iraq in under an hour. No resistance was encountered until that evening. Waiting until just after nightfall, the Scots Dragoon Guards battle group launched an attack on a communications complex sited near a water-hole. 'Conditions were absolutely appalling,' Cordingley recounted. 'It was pitch black and raining. It was difficult to see through thermal-imaging devices and near-impossible to see with the human eye.'[7] The battle group destroyed a number of tanks and dealt with the equivalent of two infantry companies in bunkers – the Staffords throwing in phosphorus grenades – before pushing on to the main objective. 'Behind a berm was clearly a large tented area which might be a hospital, so the battle group asked permission to withhold their attack until first light when the target could be identified.' To wait until dawn was clearly a risk, but fortunately no nasty shocks awaited them. A propaganda vehicle was brought up and a few warning shots with messages in Arabic calling for surrender had the desired effect.

By the time the British rear echelon went through the berm an improvised sign announced 'Welcome to Iraq'. Beyond they found that fluorescent light sticks placed by the military police marked the route through the minefield. The Iraqi defences were not nearly as formidable as they had first appeared and, thanks to air support, they were not covered by fire. Nevertheless, Allied preparations were so thorough that as the rear echelon vehicles queued up they were told by a military policeman, only half-joking, that the road ahead would be 'tarmacked with a McDonald's halfway along it'.[8]

With no fear of air attack, the bulk of the division was able to follow along in a huge nose-to-tail convoy. The sight of tail lights stretching forwards into the distance made one sergeant major remark that it was 'like the M25 on a Friday night'.[9] Many experienced a sense of anticlimax after having steeled themselves for semi-imaginable horrors, but also a sense of profound relief.

The other objective, codenamed 'Zinc', was devastated by a 23-minute barrage from multi-launch rocket systems and three regiments of artillery, then the battle groups of the Irish Hussars and the Staffords mopped up.

The next day they moved against Objective Platinum. American A10 'Warthogs' attacked first, then the Queen's Royal Irish Hussars charged through and Iraqi armour, in the words of the Staffords' commanding officer, scattered 'like bloody pheasants bolting'.[10] The battlefield became chaotic. Sappers found themselves running into T55 tanks in a dust storm, while the Staffords destroyed a number of armoured vehicles with their Milan anti-tank missiles.

Next morning, the division crossed the Wadi-al-Satin into Kuwait, and received the ceasefire order soon after reaching the Basra road north of the carbonized 'traffic jam'. In the course of three days, the 1st Armoured Division had advanced over 300 kilometres, destroyed up to two hundred tanks, about a hundred armoured vehicles and a hundred artillery pieces mostly from the Iraqi 12th Armoured Division. To split the bag between arms – artillery, Army Air Corps, armour and infantry – would be impossible. The multi-launch rocket systems firing some 2,500 rounds had the rest of the division gazing in wonder, their feelings split between exultation and pity for those on the receiving end. Night-vision equipment provided a devastating advantage, but well over half the battle, as anyone would admit, had already been won by Allied air power, especially the A10 'Warthogs' and the US Apache attack helicopters.

Air power had not only smashed and demoralized Iraqi armoured formations, it had rendered their headquarters blind by destroying the command and control network and preventing any aerial reconnaissance. A senior British officer remarked in a faintly apologetic tone that the destruction of the Iraqi army 'was nothing less than what was intended, I'm afraid'.[11]

To acknowledge the overwhelming part played by air power does not diminish the professionalism shown by 1st Armoured Division. Perhaps the best testimony to their training was that they were redeployed and resupplied, and prepared to advance to contact again when the ceasefire order came through.[12]

During the battle 4th Armoured Brigade suffered one of the war's worst disasters from 'friendly fire' (what British officers call a 'blue-on-blue' since own and friendly forces are marked in blue on maps) when an American A10 aircraft attacked two Warrior infantry fighting vehicles with its Gatling gun. Nine young soldiers, ranging from seventeen to twenty-one years old, were killed, six from the 3rd Battalion of the Royal Regiment of Fusiliers and three from the Queen's Own Highlanders. In another incident two soldiers from the 16th/5th Lancers were wounded when their Scimitar was hit by an American tank. It was a crushing verdict that the Allies' greatest danger during the battle was from 'friendly fire'.

Almost as soon as the fighting started, soldiers would be startled by scarecrow figures rising out of the ground or looming up in the half-light, with their hands up, then throwing themselves on their knees, emaciated, shivering and wet. A soldier who went out to relieve himself found ten Iraqis emerging from a dugout, their hands raised awkwardly in surrender. Soldiers could not resist whipping out their Instamatics to take 'warries' of Iraqi soldiers surrendering and then photographs of each other on top of shot-up enemy tanks.

After prisoners had been searched for weapons, the

British handed out food, often their own rations. One group of soldiers watched in amazement as an Iraqi lieutenant gulped down a tin of jam scooped out with a fork. At the collection point for prisoners, Coldstreamers, who handed out rations in bulk, could hardly believe their eyes when they saw Iraqi officers seize all the food for themselves. 'You wouldn't treat a dog the way their officers treated them,' one soldier commented.

The British soldier once again showed his sentimental streak when animals were found abandoned. Stray puppies were adopted in Jubail, and in the last moments of the war a cavalry regiment discovered some horses left to starve by retreating Iraqis. They were especially fortunate in the care they received. Although mechanized for over half a century, the cavalrymen still knew how to take care of them.

The less sentimental side of soldiers came out with some of the souvenir hunting amidst corpses on the battlefield. It would seem that the sitting-room conversation piece in quite a few married quarters will consist of camel skulls, until wives summon up their courage to throw them out.

When confirmation came that the ceasefire had taken effect, the release of emotion and jubilation was universal, even if its expression varied according to rank. Whisky to celebrate the moment, camouflaged in a variety of unconvincing disguises, from shampoo to mouthwash, was produced and toasts drunk. Thoughts, seldom held back, quickly turned to home pleasures. A trooper in the 14th/20th Hussars, no doubt speaking for many, announced to the world's press that he was looking forward to 'some serious sex'.[13] 'All the lads want,' said a late-entry captain with the Staffords, 'is to get back home to a warm lady, a warm bed and a warm bath. With a stop on the way for a couple of pints of cold lager.'[14]

One or two did not share in the general jubilation. The most disappointed members of the division appear to have been a tank crew from the Royal Scots Dragoon Guards who steadfastly refused to take part in the orgy of victory photographs. 'We broke down on the way to battle,' Trooper Hanson explained. 'After years of training and months of waiting, our gearbox went just as our mates were going in. I'm sick about it. There's no celebration for us.'[15] Yet the Challengers performed much better than most people had thought possible. In his report to the Defence Select Committee a few days after the ceasefire, the Secretary of State, Tom King, claimed an overall serviceability rate of 95 per cent throughout the battle. But thanks only to the long period of preparation was there the opportunity for the armoured vehicles, especially the tanks, to be driven and fired constantly for several weeks before the battle. This made a very great difference. 'The guys were using the kit the whole time and maintaining it properly,' an armoured corps officer explained. Usually, in peacetime, tanks were just driven round the tank park and put back in the sheds. 'You can't leave a car in the garage and then expect to drive it all the way to Scotland without problems.' On the other hand, there were still no plans to enter a Challenger team for the Canadian Army Trophy for tank gunnery.

With the lenses of the national press and television upon them as the regimental fight for survival hotted up at home, commanding officers made the most of the opportunity for lobbying. Their shameless exploitation of photo-opportunities for regimental ends would have had seasoned PR men shaking their heads in admiration. Lieutenant Colonel Rory Clayton of the 40th Field Regiment had his M109 self-propelled guns drawn up in the form of a huge XL to form the regiment's Roman numerals for an aerial photograph. Infantry battalions, especially those of Scottish regiments, determined to stand out even in the anonymity of desert camouflage and helmets, resorted to extra badges and patches. The Royal Scots wore square patches of Hunting Stewart tartan on the side of their helmet. The Queen's Own Highlanders, in case anyone needed reminding, sewed St Andrew's crosses on the shoulder. 'The Queen's Own Highlanders', remarked one officer, 'banged their highland tambourine more than anyone I've come across.' The Royal Scots Dragoon Guards flew outsize lion-rampant flags from the antennae on their challengers, while the Queen's Dragoon Guards displayed the red dragon of Wales. Even back in Germany the wives played their part. Maggie Denaro, the wife of the commanding officer of the Queen's Royal Irish Hussars, made sure she was never photographed without a regimental sweatshirt with badge and slogan. The Lancastrians of the 14th/20th Hussars flew their rather curious black eagle with its legs out (a bird which gave the regiment the nickname of 'the skipping chickens'), and the Staffords showed their Staffordshire knot, but such English gestures seemed pale against the boisterous efforts of the borderlands.

But for many of those who took part in Operation Granby there seemed to be little point in staying on after the war was over. A desk job, barrack routine, and especially exercises, would feel unbearably petty and anticlimactic after 'the real thing'. There was, in any case, bound to be a sense of aimlessness once they all returned from leave and waited for their armoured vehicles to return from the Gulf.

Officers in the Ministry of Defence, anticipated this *post bellum triste* mood even while the ground offensive was in progress. They speculated uneasily about the number who would apply to leave in the following months. But, not long afterwards, more than one officer observed that at least the alarming rise in unemployment 'outside', which accelerated during the spring of 1991, managed to keep the Army together.

The success of the ground offensive and the very professional performance of officers and soldiers in the 1st Armoured Division should not be allowed to camouflage the state of the British Army when the crisis began. The deployment of a single division, with men borrowed from all over to make up numbers and vehicles cannibalized for spare parts, stripped the Rhine Army to an immobilized hulk. The war reserves of ammunition for the whole of the Central Region were proved to be so pathetically inadequate that the British had to go begging amongst their Allies for more. The 40th Field Regiment, the first gunner regiment to go, had to take 60 per cent of the Rhine Army's war reserve of 155mm shells.

Only the long delay before the fighting allowed British commanders to train their troops properly. This very rare luxury should not encourage the 'army-on-the-cheap' delusion that Territorial Army numbers can be included in the figure of effective fighting forces.

One of the main questions in many minds was how well the new generation of young soldier and young officer would perform. The dismay at the decline in the standard of recruits had led to such outbursts as 'If we had to fight the Falklands again now, we'd lose it.'

The short answer is that both soldiers and young officers performed extremely well. However, the battle was very brief, and the enemy had been utterly demoralized by air attack, so the ground offensive in the Gulf cannot be regarded as the ultimate test. There was, of course, the other huge advantage of intensive training with live ammunition in the theatre before operations began. Commanding officers, very sensibly, did not waste the opportunity. The unprecedented realism of training and the imminence of battle concentrated minds and rapidly dispelled any lingering video fantasies. Young soldiers had to grow up very rapidly.

Young officers also rose to the occasion. All the criticisms that they were a self-centred and feckless generation, which rumbled throughout the Army in the late 1980s, were not borne out in the desert, but, since surroundings and circumstance can make all the difference, not very much was proved either way. The Gulf war may have provided a sadly perfect testing ground for weapons systems, but it did not turn out to be a major test of human endurance for the Allied forces. It was neither long enough nor desperate enough to produce cases of battle stress. But this should not belittle the courage of those who took part. The threat from chemical weapons and the danger of engaging troops who were well dug in, even if greatly overestimated at the time, were real enough to those about to go through the berm.

Fig. 3 The Order of Battle for Operation Granby

1st Armoured Division Major General Rupert Smith
16th/5th Queen's Royal Lancers, Lt Col Philip Scott
32 Armoured Engineer Regiment, Lt Col Alwyn Hutchinson
4th Regiment Army Air Corps, Lt Col F. M. Wawn

4th Armoured Brigade Brigadier Christopher Hammerbeck
14th/20th King's Hussars (Challenger), Lt Col Michael Vickery
23rd Engineer Regiment, Lt Col David Beaton
1st Bn, the Royal Scots (Warrior), Lt Col Iain Johnstone
3rd Bn, Royal Regiment of Fusiliers (Warrior), Lt Col Andrew Larpent

7th Armoured Brigade Brigadier Patrick Cordingley
Royal Scots Dragoon Guards (Challenger), Lt Col John Sharples
Queen's Royal Irish Hussars (Challenger), Lt Col Arthur Denaro
21st Engineer Regiment, Lt Col John Moore-Bick
1st Bn, the Staffordshire Regiment (Warrior), Lt Col Charles Rogers

Artillery Group Brigadier Ian Durie
Direct Support
2nd Field Regiment – 4th Armd Bde – (M109), Lt Col David Radcliffe

40th Field Regiment – 7th Armd Bde – (M109), Lt Col Rory Clayton

General Support
26th Field Regiment (M109), Lt Col Mark Corbet Burcher
32nd Heavy Regiment (M110 8-inch howitzers), Lt Col Peter Marwood
39th Heavy Regiment (MLRS), Lt Col Peter Williams
12th Air Defence (tracked Rapier), Lt Col Peter Villalard

Units in 1st Armoured Division were brought up to strength with detachments mainly from the following regiments. The official policy of 'fighting as friends' was to keep reinforcement sub-units together.

Armoured reconnaissance regiments: A Squadron, 1st Queen's Dragoon Guards, 9th/12th Royal Lancers.

Armoured regiments: Life Guards; 17th/21st Lancers; 4th Royal Tank Regiment.

Armoured infantry: 1st Bn, Grenadier Guards; 1st Bn, Scots Guards; 1st Bn, Queen's Own Highlanders; 1st Bn, the Devonshire and Dorset Regiment; and 1st Bn, the Royal Green Jackets.

1st Bn, Coldstream Guards, 1st Bn, the Royal Highland Fusiliers, 1st Bn, King's Own Scottish Borderers, and 1st Bn, the Prince of Wales's Own Regiment of Yorkshire guarded prisoners and provided a divisional headquarters detachment.

CHAPTER 16

Home and Away: UK Land Forces and Out-of-Area Operations

The headquarters of United Kingdom Land Forces is situated on the edge of Wilton in Wiltshire. Behind high barbed-wire fences, HQ UKLF is a complex of flat-roofed brick buildings linked by concrete paths and a road of immaculate tarmac. Like most military establishments of the Poulson pattern in southern England, it has not aged gracefully, but the lack of grandiosity after Rhine Army headquarters is rather refreshing. It is clearly a much tighter and more economical organization.

In spite of all the changes in Eastern Europe, UK Land Forces still retains its same three war roles: the reinforcement of Nato's central region, the despatch of specialist reinforcement forces (UK Mobile Force and ACE Mobile Force), and military home defence. In peacetime it has four categories of commitments: out-of-area operations, military aid to the civil authorities, all forms of training from the common military syllabus to the higher command and staff course, and 'administering the home base'. The headquarters at Wilton also administers British Army training and Loan Service teams abroad, as well as units in Belize and personnel with the multinational force and observers (MFO) in Sinai.

The Commander-in-Chief UK Land Forces is a four-star general. He is almost always an infantryman and stands a good chance of becoming the next Chief of the General Staff. Immediately below him are two lieutenant generals: the Commander of the UK Field Army, and the Commander Training and Arms Directors.

The Commander UK Field Army presides over nearly

40,000 regular soldiers, just over 70,000 members of the Territorial Army and 6,000 civilians. He may like to regard his force as the equivalent of the corps in Germany, but he will be the first to admit that it is 'not a coherent organization'.

The restructuring of British forces on the continent and at home offers a good opportunity to reduce the potential for confusion, to say nothing of confused identity, when so many units have reported to different chains of command. The 2nd Infantry Division at York, including 24th Air Mobile Brigade, and 19th Infantry Brigade at Colchester, while part of UK Land Forces for administrative and training purposes, have long been under the operational command of 1st (British) Corps in Bielefeld.

With tours in Belize or Northern Ireland, a battalion can come under two or even three different headquarters in the course of a single year (which does not help the system for confidential reports on commanding officers). To complicate matters further, companies and squadrons are also detached from their parent unit for six-month tours or overseas training. Perhaps the most extreme case is 7th Regiment Army Air Corps based at Netheravon, which has one squadron tasked to the UK Mobile Force under the operational command of Nato, another to 5th Airborne Brigade, and two squadrons in Northern Ireland under the Commander Land Forces there. The UK Field Army headquarters at Wilton, not surprisingly, has a hard time making sure that 'the whole thing doesn't become an unstructured bugger's muddle', as a senior general put it.

In addition to its defence commitments, the UK Field Army is responsible for aid to the civil authority. Military Aid to the Civil Community (MACC) involves disaster relief and rescue. Military Aid to the Civil Ministries (MACM) includes the provision of essential services during strikes, for example the ambulance drivers' strike during the winter of 1989–90. 'Military Aid to the Civil Power (MACP) encompasses the use of troops in support of the maintenance of public order and security, and includes assistance to counter-terrorism. Commanders react to requests by the civil power. Owing to the political and legal implications, ministerial authority will invariably be obtained when a military force is committed to MACP, and ministers will take a close interest in the control of such deployments.'[1] Military Aid to the Military Authority (MAMA) essentially means guarding US bases, assisting with 'off-base deployment' and providing support for training.

Until the spring of 1991, mainland Britain was divided into nine military districts, not very different from those established by Cromwell. In all except two cases, these districts matched the areas of wartime regional governments, should control from London become impossible. The District Structure Review eventually aims to reduce the number to four.

These four-super districts will be commanded by a lieutenant general, as was the practice for South-East, Scotland and Northern Ireland. The first of the minor districts to be amalgamated under the measure were North West, Western and Wales, to form a new Western District. Northern Ireland, which was the tenth district, will continue to be separate and report to Wilton 'only on non-operational matters'.

One senior officer, while acknowledging the inevitablity of a shake-up, felt that the way it had been carried out was something of a 'foot-shooting exercise'. If he had been Chief of the General Staff he would have kept the plan in his top drawer until the next round of cuts was demanded.

London District, not surprisingly, was always the most unusual. Its single formation, 56th Brigade, is the strongest in the country. On top of the five public duties battalions, it had three Territorial Army battalions – 10th Battalion of the Parachute Regiment, 4th Royal Green Jackets, 8th Queen's Fusiliers – and 151 Regiment RCT, 217 General Hospital, 221 Field Ambulance and 253 Provost Company

Royal Military Police. The most curious inclusions were the King's Troop Royal Horse Artillery and the Household Cavalry Mounted Regiment, which were over-horsed and underequipped for any serious military purpose.

Created in January 1987, 56th Brigade's first commander was Brigadier Blundell-Hollinshead-Blundell, a Grenadier. Its emblem consists of 'an inverted red sword bayonet set against Dick Whittington's black cat'. The Household Division wanted it to be called 56th Guards Brigade, but once again this attempt at empire-building met firm resistance, and the only concession was to allow the badge to have the shield outline of the wartime Guards Armoured Division.

Sir John Nott always felt that 'Fortress Britain' was the most neglected part of his 1981 Defence Review. Eight years later UK Land Forces 'reviewed military home defence tasks and resources and concluded that there was a current shortfall in the manpower allocated to this area'.[2]

While the bulk of the Regular Army was committed to Nato, the main responsibility for home defence rested with part of the Territorial Army and the 3,000-strong Home Service Force. About half of their effort was allocated to guarding against attacks by Russian special forces, Spetsnaz. This scenario (a favourite Army term) was tested in major exercises such as Brave Defender, which saw the Royal Marines' Special Boat Section fixing dummy charges in the Port of Dover and on to the radio masts above on the white cliffs. In the multiple exercises of 1988, the anti-Spetsnaz precautions included the protection of VIPs. But the Territorial Army will be restructured, and in a number of cases 're-roled', in the Defence Review.

Most regular Army training in this country has more to do with practising operations overseas than with military home defence. Tri-service operations with amphibious assaults on the Scottish coastline have been practised in exercises such as Purple Warrior. Most conventional Army training takes place on the familiar cockpit of Salisbury Plain, which acts both as a notional island off the African coast, ripe for rescue by 5th Airborne Brigade in an out-of-area operation, and as a miniature version of Germany for Rhine Army-designated troops. Salisbury Plain is minute in comparison to the Suffield area in Canada. Armoured recce crews complain that you get to know it like the back of your hand – after advancing in one direction for a bit, you reach the edge of the training area, turn round and come back. Yet, in spite of the Plain's geographical limitations, the British Army's most realistic field training to date started there.

A large exercise may last only a week or less, but it requires many months of planning by staff officers at every headquarters involved. Local authorities and the police must be warned well in advance. Even the Foreign Office will be briefed if the exercise is deploying more than a certain number of troops, because foreign countries may well wish to exercise their right to send observers at the last moment. Interpreters, escorts and transport, from staff cars to helicopters, all have to be laid on. If the press is to be invited, then the public relations departments at every level start preparing programmes several months in advance, and requisition drivers, vehicles and extra escorting officers from within the command. Meanwhile, in the regiments that are going to take part, first the commanding officer and the operations officer, then all the company or squadron commanders, begin to plan their requirements so that quartermaster sergeants can indent for stores, including rations. Blank ammunition is 'scaled' by a higher headquarters – it seems to be the first victim of any economy drive, so there is never enough. The squadron of tanks detailed to act as enemy will paint large red stars on their turrets – a detail which always amused Warsaw Pact observers.

Once regiments and battalions have moved to the

exercise area and taken up their starting positions, and commanding officers have returned from brigade headquarters, an orders group is summoned. Squadron and company commanders then brief their troop or platoon commanders, and finally, in huddled groups, the boys 'at the sharp end' hear what the Fantasians are up to this time.

The scenarios are no more convincing than in Germany, but an impressive advance in realistic effect has come with lasers. When fired accurately, a laser attached to the appropriate weapon sets off a smoke canister on the armoured vehicle it hits, and also triggers a light which begins to flash, denoting a 'kill'. Amongst foot soldiers, each infantryman has a SAWES sensor (small arms weapons effects simulators) attached to his equipment which begins to bleep when he is accurately targeted by an enemy rifle or machine-gun. He can only stop the noise by lying flat on his back – there is a compression pad on his harness – until the sensor is switched off by an exercise controller. The soldier then opens a sealed card denoting his particular injury. On the first Simex in 1988, a number of Jocks from the Argylls, quick to spot an opportunity, started trading their cards once the umpire's back was turned. A death card, the cushiest fate, was the most highly prized.

In spite of the soldiers' jokes, laser simulation provides a sobering and highly effective method of training. Instead of an umpire telling a certain number of men that they are casualties, the rate of attrition is decided entirely by the accuracy of the shooting, so everything is tested at once – skill-at-arms, fieldcraft and even fitness when they have to cross open ground covered by enemy fire. Armoured personnel carriers are shown to be 'communal coffins', and a single engagement can leave a battalion reduced to a fraction of its former strength, sometimes with only an NCO left in command of a company as if it were the first day of the Somme. The overall effect on that first exercise made many wonder how much of the Rhine Army would be left after a full day of fighting. Since then, as officers realize only too well, soldiers need to be reminded of their vulnerability more than ever after the astonishingly light casualties of the Gulf war.

Tests have indicated that soldiers trained with laser simulators stand a far greater chance of survival in action, and the technology is improving all the time. The equipment is expensive – about £10 million for a battle group – but it must be more cost-effective in the long run than the set-piece manoeuvres in Germany, which were becoming hard to take seriously even before German public opinion put a stop to them.

Finding sufficiently large areas in which to train has become a major problem. Environmental and pacifist pressure in Europe has encouraged the Ministry of Defence to export training to less populated regions whenever possible. The increased safety areas required by the longer-range anti-tank missiles make live-firing in Britain more and more difficult. Just as the Rhine Army trains armoured battle groups at Suffield in Canada, UK Land Forces use the nearby Camp Wainwright for battalion groups. And since the early 1980s large training areas in Kenya – the main one is at Nanyuki – have been borrowed for three battalion groups a year. These areas offer either 'dry training' (without live ammunition) or field firing for weapons up to the 105mm light gun. The British pay little: the Kenyan government apparently likes the arrangement, according to a senior officer, because 'it offers continuity and security'.

In Cyprus twenty companies a year can carry out 'dry training' only. Infantry companies go each year to Jordan and Oman. Exercise Swift Sword in Oman, with part of 5th Airborne Brigade, was the only major test of deployment to the Middle East to take place between the Falklands conflict and the Gulf war. The main hope of overseas exercises seemed to rest on Turkey, but after the Gulf war the Government became keen on the idea of regular exercises with Allied forces in the Gulf region. The lure of virtually unrestricted training areas combined with the political advantage of maintaining an off-stage presence has a compelling logic from a Western point of view, but whether Arab opinion will see it in quite the same light remains to be seen.

For field army units in the United Kingdom, one of the most dreaded set of initials is RAAT, the Regular Army Assistance Table. This distributes jobs ranging from acting as enemy for the Territorial Army at weekends and firepower demonstrations to running the ranges at Bisley and a host of other minor tasks. In 1991, this was calculated for the whole Army at 323,000 man-days on top of the normal programme, and this did not include many other extras, such as public relation tours and helping with local events.

Headquarters UK Land Forces insists that 'we are continually reviewing our force levels and commitments', but such assertions provoke bitter laughs at lower levels. 'People take advantage of us the whole time,' said the commanding officer of a Guards battalion in London. The commanding officer of a line infantry battalion said the Army's ethos of 'don't worry, we'll get the job done' meant that they always took on too much: 'We're our own biggest enemy accepting it.' Weekend commitments were the worst – his battalion had not had a single free weekend for four months. Coupled with a tour in Northern Ireland, this caused tremendous discontent among both families and single soldiers. Armoured recce regiments in particular find their services are continually required for Territorial Army exercises so as to lend an air of Regular Army realism. For young soldiers, losing several weekends in a row may mean losing their girlfriends as well, which makes many of them think about leaving. Such constant demands from all directions divide up squadrons. 'England', said a cavalry captain with a large measure of understatement, 'isn't good for regimental unity.'

Some of the tasks, on the other hand, can be welcome. 'We are overcommitted in England,' said a company commander in the Coldstream Guards. 'But it's not all Bisley and prisons. People often forget that some RAAT has very good training value, particularly the [firepower] demonstrations. It's one of the few times one has the chance to see all the kit out of their boxes.' A major in the Parachute Regiment agreed: 'Some RAAT tasks are quite fun, and if they provide us with a new experience then we're very happy.' Gunner and sapper regiments, who rarely get the chance to act as infantry, enjoy the part of 'Hunterforce' on escape and evasion exercises for aircrew who have supposedly crashed in enemy territory, or special forces practising sabotage missions. The chance to rough up some hapless RAF officer – all in the interest of exercise verisimilitude – is just part of the fun.

Overcommitment seems to remain the most serious problem for commanding officers, particularly at a time when they are losing not only soldiers but experienced officers and NCOs. The official view that holding on to them is a 'leadership challenge' provokes strong reactions. 'It's not a leadership problem,' was the retort of one commanding officer, 'it's a management problem.' Another said: 'You're getting an army on the cheap by getting them to do so many things . . . The politicians have got to decide what their commitments are.'

The other cause for unease is the 'management strategy' introduced by the Government in April 1991. Generals profess great enthusiasm for these reforms imposed on most public institutions, but this arouses the suspicion lower down that they are simply reflecting the view of their political masters. 'At last we'll know how much things cost,' said one senior general beforehand, as if this was almost enough to solve problems on its own. Another general, however, cautiously made the very valid point that there must be an incentive system so that when a budget-holder achieved savings he should be allowed to 'apply the resources to achieve the best result in his particular area'. Yet past experience would appear to offer little encouragement: any savings are almost always snatched back. The only incentive therefore lies in the confidential report, not from any satisfaction at improving the system.

Senior officers with the Army's welfare close to their heart are in an unenviable position. Unable to melt the cold resolve of Whitehall above, headquarters can only turn a deaf ear to complaints from below.

The headquarters of UK Land Forces at Wilton, along with its naval and air force equivalents, is a four-star 'joint headquarters', able to command a full tri-service operation overseas. It has its own operations branch – G3 OPS (Nato/Rest of World) – which from the ops room can maintain constant contact with the Directorate of Military Operations on the General Staff and the Defence Staff's Joint Operations Centre. Detailed administrative instructions are meanwhile formulated by the joint force headquarters in Aldershot, which comes under the General Officer Commanding South-East District.

All UK Land Force units are on seven days' notice to move, and at all times there are four battalions on different forms of standby: an 'Adamant' unit for military aid to the civil authority (MACA), a London District battalion for anti-terrorist deployment at Heathrow on Operation Tonnage, a 'Spearhead' battalion group for deployment anywhere in the world, and the 'leading parachute battalion group' for airborne operations anywhere in the world.

Towards the end of the last Labour administration, French and Belgian paratroopers dropped on Kolwezi in Zaire to rescue a number of their nationals threatened by fighting. Soon after the Conservatives came to power in 1979, Francis Pym asked the Army Board if they could mount a similar operation. They replied that they could not. The previous Government had told them not to plan for that sort of capability. The next year, 5th Infantry Brigade was told to train for an intervention role, and after the Falklands conflict it became 5th Airborne Brigade.

Britain's other intervention force is the 3rd Commando

Brigade, which, based on the Royal Marines, is the preserve of the Royal Navy. Ready with nearly two hundred Snowcats for mountain and Arctic warfare in northern Norway – their main responsibility – or elsewhere, should another Falklands-style operation be mounted, the brigade consists of 40, 42 and 45 Royal Marine Commandos, 29 Commando Regiment Royal Artillery and an Air Defence battery, 59 Independent Commando Squadron Royal Engineers, the Air Squadron Royal Marines, an Assault Squadron Royal Marines and the Commando Logistics Regiment.

Few in the Army dispute the toughness or professionalism of the 'booties', as they call them, but many officers are openly sceptical, both about the feasibility of landings on a hostile shore, known as 'over-the-beach' operations, and the cost-efficiency of the Marines as an organization. 'The Marines', said a senior staff officer in the Ministry of Defence, 'are very top heavy. They have nearly 8,000 men to put 2,400 in the field. Their tail and superstructure are very large, since they have three tied generals: a three-star, the Commandant General, a major general as his chief of staff, and a major general commando forces. If the Royal Marines came across to the Army, they could do with half the infrastructure. The Navy', he concluded, 'would be particularly well served if they lost them, but the trouble is, emotion always wins.'

The 5th Airborne Brigade, to many people's surprise, is the only regular formation allocated to home defence in the event of a European war. In peacetime it has to be ready for emergencies overseas, whether for a 'come-as-you-are' war such as the Falklands conflict, or a rescue operation similar to that at Kolwezi.

Centred on Aldershot, 5th Airborne includes the Blues and Royals at Windsor, 7th Regiment Royal Horse Artillery, 9th Parachute Squadron Royal Engineers, two battalions of the Parachute Regiment, the Gurkha battalion at Church Crookham, another infantry battalion, 658 Squadron Army

Air Corps, the Airborne Logistics Battalion, 23 Parachute Field Ambulance and 160 Provost Company.

Training depends on weather and aircraft availability. Often out of fourteen drops planned in a year only about seven take place. A minimum of four are required to qualify for parachute pay of £21 a week extra. 'It may seem a lot,' said a major, 'but when you're standing at the door with 130 lb strapped to your leg . . .'

In action, 5th Airborne would be preceded by a path-finder platoon, using tactical freefall techniques known as HALO (high altitude, low opening) to achieve surprise on the dropping zone. The paratroop units would follow shortly afterwards, a 'stick' of up to forty-five paratroopers dropping from each side of each Hercules, which means that for a full drop the brigade needs about thirty aircraft. (The acquisition of Supacats a couple of years ago – light cross-country vehicles with six wheels – greatly increased the mobility of the first wave.) The non-para infantry, including most of the armoured recce regiment and the rest of the brigade, follow once the units dropped by parachute have secured a landing zone for their Hercules.

Senior officers, and politicians such as Michael Heseltine, have become very enthusiastic about the greatly increased ranges now possible with in-flight refuelling, which they see as 'a real multiplier of capability'. Yet Heseltine's predecessor as Secretary of State for Defence, Sir John Nott, was sceptical about an out-of-area capability. He admitted that he was probably influenced by the way the 'argument always came back to the blessed carriers and why we needed a deep-sea fleet'. Yet there was no doubt that the whole out-of-area capability appealed enormously to the Service chiefs, above all the Navy and the Army. 'I used to call it the Caribbean frigate syndrome,' he said, then added: 'But I suppose as a general you must become obsessed about how you're going to recruit people.'

What really concerned him, though, was the temptation the capability created to interfere in minor outbreaks of chaos. 'As a politician,' he said, 'I am extremely wary of too much emphasis on out-of-area capability. You're very quickly sucked into a disaster like Lebanon when you attempt to alter the politics of the situation . . . It's extraordinarily dangerous.'

After the Gulf war, whose conventional nature was misleadingly reassuring to those brought up on the theories of conventional war, the warning is perhaps even more relevant. We are not on the threshold of a 'New World Order', but of multiple 'Lebanization' – the Balkans, the Middle East, the Soviet borderlands. The world, after being held artificially in splints for nearly half a century by the Cold War confrontation, has failed to develop its own muscles.

Enthusiasm for out-of-area roles is almost certainly misplaced. The peacekeeping role of soldiers will increasingly consist of controlling and forcing back hordes of desperate refugees trying to flee from famine and civil war.

CHAPTER 17

Northern Ireland: The Long War

For servicemen returning from Britain by the Belfast shuttle, Northern Ireland is another country. They are back in the land of 'the threat'.

Inside Aldergrove's new terminal, modern and self-consciously international to attract business to the province, they have to pretend not to recognize each other. Few officers can resist a smile, as if slightly embarrassed by a childish game. They know that they are not very effectively disguised. The combination of accent, short hair, tweed jacket, Viyella shirt and corduroy trousers is unmistakable. And crew-cut soldiers with the odd capbadge tattoo, and a version of plain clothes based on T-shirts, jeans and sportswear, are just as conspicuous in their way.

Although civilian and terrorist alike can spot them easily, the Provisional IRA, PIRA in security force jargon, avoids spur-of-the-moment actions. The real danger for Army personnel results from repetition. The coach bomb which exploded at Ballygawley in August 1988, killing eight soldiers and wounding many more, provided one of the cruellest reminders of such dangers. Observers, or 'dickers', watch for a pattern, after which the active service unit plans its attack and awaits the perfect opportunity, if necessary for several months. They are convinced that time is on their side.

At first sight the route from the airport could be almost anywhere in Britain. The landscape, road signs and traffic are all familiar, but a sudden tailback is more likely to be the result of a vehicle checkpoint than of roadworks.

The checkpoints outside Belfast are usually manned either by heavily armed members of the Royal Ulster

Constabulary, red-faced and thickset in dark green uniform and flak jacket, or by soldiers of the Ulster Defence Regiment in the camouflage combat kit of the Regular Army. Depending on the policy in force at the time, British and UDR battalions either wear camouflage helmets or revert to the beret to give themselves a more human face. Soldiers 'riding shotgun', with head and shoulders out of the top of an armoured Land Rover, keep the old riot helmet with plastic visor. They are a favourite target for 'bricking' when driving through Republican areas.

In Belfast itself, the rare, incongruous glimpse of an Army foot patrol, ignored as the soldiers advance on either side of a busy street, rifles carried across the body, eyes sweeping ceaselessly, the tail-end Charlie watching backwards, can still impress first-time visitors. After twenty years, Northern Ireland continues to exist in the British public's consciousness as dramatic and horrifying fragments of television news. In most of the province for most of the time, there is no trace of 'the troubles'.

'Nothing', observed an infantry major, explaining the Army's job satisfaction in Northern Ireland, 'makes you work together better than a common enemy out there trying to slot you one.' The 'common enemy' in military minds is essentially the Provisional IRA, because it is responsible for most security force casualties. Protestant terrorists usually stick to the less dangerous activity of sectarian murder. According to the Irish Information Partnership, in the twenty years since 1969 the IRA had killed 325 civilians, and loyalist paramilitaries 610.[1] But figures must be treated with care, since much depends on definition. Is a part-time UDR member shot down on his way to work, or an RUC constable, or a prison warder, or a retired serviceman a civilian? Is a terrorist shot by the security forces a civilian? The Army feels that to distinguish too much between the murder of civilians and the murder of security force members is liable to lend an air of military legitimacy to terrorist acts. Headquarters Northern Ireland in February

1991 gave the following casualty figures since the start of the troubles in 1969: 428 members of the Regular Army, 189 of the Ulster Defence Regiment, 277 of the Royal Ulster Constabulary and 1,596 civilians. (The Army's figure for civilian casualties is much lower than those from other sources: one gives a total casualty rate of 2,849.)[2]

On the Republican side, the Irish People's Liberation Organization also concentrates on sectarian killings. This group is a splinter from the Irish National Liberation Army, whose internal feud in 1986 left a dozen of its members dead -- an outcome not exactly mourned by the security forces. INLA was known principally for its ideological frenzy and often irrational attacks.

The PIRA is estimated to have under 300 hard-core activists, but they receive support from anything up to a couple of thousand sympathizers or coerced helpers who watch, steal cars, supply safe houses, prepare firing-points and smuggle weapons and explosives. Its operational arm consists of so-called active service units. The size of these cells, seldom more than five, is dictated more by the number of available recruits than by a predetermined plan. They are richer in weapons than volunteers.

Their arsenal ranges from home-made weapons such as the nail bomb, which can also be filled with 'dockyard confetti', or the 'drogue' bomb (an anti-vehicle grenade with half a pound of shaped explosive packed in a large baked-beans tin fastened to a throwing handle), to Armalite rifles and 'prestige weapons' such as the 12.7mm machine-gun, which has been used against helicopters, and the Soviet RPG 7 rocket launcher. But snap vehicle check-points make shoulder weapons hard to move around, and improvements in rapid forensic monitoring have deterred 'hands-on' attacks. 'Fire an RPG 7 and you glow like Chernobyl,' said one officer.

For attacks on security force bases, the Provisional IRA has evolved its so-called Mark 10 mortar, the sort used in the attack on 10 Downing Street during the Gulf war. This fires a 6-inch shell with 24 pounds of explosive up to 300 metres. A rack of these are usually fixed to the back of a hijacked lorry, which is driven into position, and then simultaneous fuses are set. But for their inaccuracy, the casualty toll would have been a great deal higher.

Helped by shipments from Libya, the PIRA has shifted its tactics to include a much greater use of explosives, which cannot be so easily traced by monitoring devices. As the same officer said, 'You can't be pinged so easily on a bomb.' The man who triggers the device has not usually handled any traceable chemicals – he may not even have to be in line of sight, since a 'dicker' on a crossroads only has to blow his nose or take off his hat as a signal when the target patrol or vehicle reaches a particular point.

Bombs can be detonated in many ways: with a timer, with a tilt mechanism in the case of the 'sandwich-box job' fixed by magnet to the underside of a car, with a command wire, or triggered by remote control; all the parts are commercially available in electronic gadgets for model aeroplanes and opening garage doors. In towns the charge can be hidden in drainpipes, behind loosened brickwork, in a letter-box, under the pavement, in a dustbin or a litter basket attached to a lamp-post, or behind a garden fence. In the countryside, they are concealed in milk churns, culverts, and hedges next to a gap in a fence, or packed into a drystone wall. Larger bombs, often with a smaller charge of Semtex as detonator, usually consist of home-made explosive. Semtex on its own is generally reserved for cleverly concealed street ambushes.

Improvised explosive devices, or IEDs as they are called, are mostly detonated by remote control or command wire. In towns the cable can be run back up a drain pipe and over the roof; in rural areas, it may be buried underground and left in place for several months until required. The Provisional IRA has a particular fondness for remote-controlled devices. Infuriated, however, by the loss of men, sometimes their most valued explosives experts, in 'own goal' premature explosions, the IRA have blamed the Army's electronic counter-measures. They have even claimed that the 1987 Remembrance Day bomb at Enniskillen was set off by the Army's frequency scanning. But that version of events did not last long after parts of a timing device had been found in the rubble.

The greatest danger to the security forces results from the Provisional IRA's fondness for two-step operations – such as an explosion or rocket attack followed by a weapons shoot or, more frequently, a primary bomb or hoax as a 'come-on' followed by a secondary device calculated to go off when reinforcements and assistance arrive. At Warrenpoint in August 1979, the second blast took the death toll to eighteen, the worst disaster ever inflicted by the IRA on British troops.

When the news came through that evening of the Warrenpoint massacre and of the bomb which killed Lord Mountbatten the same day, there was an uneasy silence instead of the usual celebrations and taunts in Republican areas of Belfast and Londonderry. The Catholic community feared a massacre of Cromwellian proportions. Yet one thing is clear from the evidence of the last twenty years: although there may have been lapses in the early days – Bloody Sunday in Londonderry in 1972 provided the PIRA's most emotive and most enduring recruitment argument – it is hard to imagine other armies maintaining a similar degree of discipline and restraint in the face of such provocation.

The most horrific development came in 1990, with the IRA's 'human bomb' tactic of forcing a victim to drive a car full of explosive to a permanent checkpoint while a close relative was held hostage. This caused the death of seven people in the latter part of the year, and the abandonment of a number of vulnerable checkpoints in March 1991.

Headquarters Northern Ireland is at Lisburn, some ten miles south-west of Belfast. Adjoining a prosperously solid suburb of Edwardian brick and laurel bushes on a hill, Thiepval Barracks is protected by high metal screens and barbed-wire fences with warning notices.

It presents a strange mixture of traditional and modern, permanent and impermanent. The principal buildings, also in Edwardian brick, have been surrounded by Portakabin satellites, asphalt heli-pads and huge radio masts.

The approach road is guarded by a system of barriers and blockhouse-like sangars. Armed with rifles, soldiers from the Royal Pioneer Corps in khaki berets check identifications and search cars. All gate sentries in Northern Ireland automatically ask whether the vehicle has been left unattended. A member of the security forces who leaves his vehicle for only a few minutes must check the underside and the rest of the car. The risk of a bomb being smuggled unwittingly into a military base, especially a prime target like the headquarters at Lisburn, can never be ignored.

Although the troops in the province – over 11,000 British soldiers and about 6,000 members of the Ulster Defence Regiment – are technically part of United Kingdom Land Forces, the General Officer Commanding, a lieutenant general, reports to the Ministry of Defence and the Secretary of State for Northern Ireland. He also has local Royal Navy and, more important, Royal Air Force units under command. The RAF fly the 'workhorse' transport helicopters: Puma, Wessex and Chinook.

The Lisburn complex has a wide organizational embrace. As well as the GOC and his staff, it contains the headquarters for the Commander Land Forces (a major general) and his staff, for the Ulster Defence Regiment and for specialist force troops such as the Royal Military Police, the Royal Engineers and the Royal Army Ordnance Corps bomb-disposal teams. It also houses the headquarters of 39th Infantry Brigade.

Each of the three brigades in Northern Ireland has a TAOR, a tactical area of operational responsibility. The TAOR of 39th Brigade includes Belfast and the eastern half of the province except the South Armagh border region. The largest formation, 3rd Infantry Brigade, whose headquarters is outside the city of Armagh, controls almost all the border region. Its TAOR snakes from near Newry in the south-east all the way round to Strabane in the west, some 300 miles along the outer parts of Armagh, Fermanagh and Tyrone. Based on Londonderry, 8th Infantry Brigade, controls the north and centre-west.

Of the ten major British frontline units in the province, at least nine are infantry battalions. The tenth can be an artillery or armoured regiment in a dismounted role. Staff officers from other arms are therefore something of a rarity, and the Northern Ireland command gives the impression of being basically an infantry show. Of the ten infantry units in the garrison, six are 'resident' and four are 'roulement'. 'Resident' means that personnel are stationed with their families in the province, usually for a two-and-a-half-year tour; the relay system of 'roulement' means that the whole unit is flown in en bloc from Britain or Germany for a six-month tour without families.

The day-to-day life of a brigade commander, in fact of most commanders down to company level, is potentially frustrating. 'It's a corporals' war' is the standard comment, because the basic element consists of the four-man fire-team. Once the commander has established tasks and policy, he has to stand back and trust the men on the ground. His job is to co-ordinate and liaise with other authorities such as the RUC, not to direct operations.

At all levels, whether brigade, battalion or company headquarters, there is a background temptation to linger in the ops room – not to scan the incident boards or the perspex-covered maps with TAOR boundaries marked in blue chinagraph but to listen to the radio net. Everyone is waiting in spite of themselves. Either they hope for an arms find or the sighting of a 'top player', or they quietly dread an unforeseeable disaster. As the tour progresses, hardly a conversation takes place without somebody reaching round to touch wood.

When a 'contact' is reported, whether a weapons shoot, rocket attack, mortar 'stonk' or bomb explosion, those in the ops room are seldom in a position to give detailed orders. They will offer advice and call in specialist teams from within the unit or outside. These include dog handlers, Royal Army Medical Corps assistance and casualty evacuation, Army Air Corps reconnaissance helicopters (equipped like some British police forces with 'heli-tele' cameras), Royal Engineer search teams to check for hidden explosive devices, and Royal Army Ordnance Corps bomb-disposal teams. The only independent force troop units they are unlikely to call in are those rather cryptically categorized as 'other agencies'.

The Army in Northern Ireland is divided between the 'green army', which operates openly in uniform, and those who operate in civilian clothes and unmarked cars. One senior officer spoke of 'the field army green, as opposed to the field army you-can't-see-it-now'.

Force troops of 'the field army you-can't-see-it-now' include a troop or squadron of the SAS based at Aldergrove and an Intelligence and Security Group – formerly 14 Intelligence and Security Company – with its teams of volunteers on 'special duties'. (The team involved in the shooting of three men at the betting shop robbery on 13 January 1990 were from this unit.)[3]

The close observation platoons, or COPs, provided by the six resident infantry battalions, stand with one foot still on the green side of the line. Consisting mainly of carefully selected NCOs, their prime role is surveillance. Close observation work involves terrorist recognition, long-range photography and logging the movement of 'known players'. In large towns, most of this is done from sangars built on the top of high buildings. There they wear uniform to be indistinguishable from other soldiers. But the close observation platoons are also sent out by the RUC Special Branch on 'drive-pasts' and 'look-sees', which clearly have to be done in civilian clothes and unmarked cars. The COPs do not carry out 'lifts' or ambushes. As defensive weapons in urban areas they prefer the 9mm Browning pistol and automatic shotguns to the SA80 rifle. Images of the lynching of the two corporals in March 1988 lurk at the back of many soldiers' minds. The fact that they were not involved in surveillance but just happened to choose a very unfortunate route inevitably increased the sensation of 'there but for the grace of God' – what the psychiatrists call 'survivor guilt'.

Apart from the infantry, green army force troop units include the Royal Engineers, the Royal Army Ordnance Corps bomb-disposal teams and the Royal Military Police. In Northern Ireland, the bomb-disposal teams answer alerts in khaki vans with a blue flashing light and a Felix the Cat sticker on the side as a good luck symbol, rather like a US Air Force plane in the Second World War. In common with members of other dangerous professions, the ammunition technical officers (ATOs) who tackle the bombs have their private superstitions. If they feel happy working with a particular team, any change can cause deep unease, particularly if the replacement is thought to be jinxed.

Every call-out has to be treated as a 'worst possible case'. A victim's body discovered in a car boot may be booby-trapped. A hoax car bomb could be a 'come-on' with a secondary device hidden nearby. 'You've got to look at it from the terrorist's point of view,' said an officer with several tours behind him. 'He's always one step ahead, and he can always choose the direction in which he runs. So you've got to look for anything which doesn't fit the scenario.' Ordnance bomb-disposal experts have a chilled respect for the ingenuity of PIRA experts. 'You certainly won't hear any jokes about thick Paddies from them,' a warrant officer remarked.

For the ATO, the first rule on arrival is to establish complete control over the pace of the operation, which means appearing calm and confident even while his brain is working furiously. The worst pressures on him to work fast result from car bombs in a city centre. An infantry or police cordon will have evacuated nearby buildings and blocked off roads, probably causing traffic jams over a large area, so everyone wants to know how soon life can return to normal.

In rural parts, the job can generally be taken at a much slower rate. If necessary several square miles will be sealed off for up to a week to allow a minute search of the area and greatly reduce the possibility of a detonation by a hidden terrorist. In 1988, the main railway line to Dublin was closed for four days over Christmas in an exceptional operation to remove a bomb from a bridge. The infantry cordon in the fields on either side had to stay in place even longer.

When dealing with a large bomb, particularly in a car, the operator, standing up to 400 metres away, will use the 'Wheelbarrow' wherever possible. This miniature tracked vehicle enables him to carry out an initial diagnosis by remote control ('the jack-in-the-box') via its closed circuit camera, and as much surgery with its robot arms and lock-busting gun ('the pig-stick') as circumstances permit. The Wheelbarrow has become very sophisticated over the years (the latest model costs over £30,000) and has saved an incalculable number of lives since the early days of improvisation.

Once the Wheelbarrow has blown open bonnet, boot and side doors – simple hook-ups can prove surprisingly complicated when doors and car boots behave with a bloody-minded obstinacy – the ATO, dressed in full protective clothing, can assess the risk in greater detail. When wearing his 'heavy suit', with its narrow visor, the ATO must not let himself lapse into tunnel vision and forget the danger of secondary devices. The weight of all this protective clothing makes the work very tiring when he has to go back and forth at each stage. In summer, heat exhaustion is a constant risk.

The Wheelbarrow cannot do everything. At some stage the ATO has to handle the detonator and leads. The practice of talking through every movement into a microphone was stopped in 1982 after the death of two operators: having to speak as well as think ahead probably distracted them.

Once the device has been made safe, the ATO brings out the explosive for subsequent disposal – usually a controlled explosion on waste ground. Then, 'the adrenalin still pumping', the team tries to wind down. They need the reassurance of their own company. Old jokes about near misses which 'redesigned' a building yet left them 'shaken but not stirred' provide the best release. Unlike the soldiers who have to clear up after an explosion, ATOs tend not to cultivate a sick sense of humour. Facetious or serious, it is unhealthy to dwell on the consequences of error.

Approximately 400-strong, the Royal Military Police in Northern Ireland has more responsibilities per head than any other capbadge. And, with seventy servicewomen employed mainly as searchers, it has the highest proportion of female personnel.

Most of the conventional military police duties are carried out by the provost company attached to each brigade, while the main internal security support to the field army is performed by the Provost Marshal's force troops detachment, 173 Provost Company. This includes the Special Investigation Branch, close protection teams and a legal affairs branch.

The SIB, amongst its many activities, investigates complaints against the Army and every potentially controversial incident as rapidly as possible. Its teams are under 'great pressure to get it right', interviewing witnesses with the Royal Ulster Constabulary so that their report is 'on the GOC's desk by 7.30 the following morning'. Only then can headquarters at Lisburn brief the Northern Ireland Office before a statement is issued. (Nowhere does the Army bewail the speed of modern communications so much. Radio news can be broadcasting interviews within minutes of an incident, but the official version of events has to be vetted by so many people that sometimes it appears only after the story has left the front page.)

The close protection teams guard generals, ministers, senior British officials and distinguished visitors. Armed with Heckler & Koch sub-machine-guns, they provide 24-hour security. The safety of judges, politicians and other Northern Irish personalities at risk is the responsibility of the RUC. The main task of the legal affairs branch is to organize the recall of servicemen who have left the province if they are needed as witnesses in court proceedings.

Another part of the RMP which is unique to Northern Ireland is its monitoring organization, consisting of a weapons intelligence section, a vehicle intelligence section and terrorist recognition cells. Of most immediate help to a fresh roulement battalion is the service provided by continuity NCOs, known as CONCOs. Working in pairs on the same 'patch' for at least two years at a time, they brief sub-units and accompany patrols for the first few weeks, passing on all the 'local lore'.

Every soldier who serves in the province should have been told the official definition of his task: 'The role of the Army in Northern Ireland is to support the Royal Ulster Constabulary in the defeat of terrorism.'

The RUC came into existence in 1922, following partition. It was the direct successor of the Royal Irish Constabulary, which provided 'the model for a number of colonial police forces', as the force's own booklet relates. From the beginning, the RUC was split between its role of civil policing, similar to any other British force, and its paramilitary role of 'protecting the State from armed subversion'. The Hunt Committee, established in 1969, recommended that the RUC should be disarmed and restricted to its civil police responsibility, but the cycle of violence and resistance to the measure made this impossible. With 8,500 regulars and 4,500 reservists, the RUC – armed with carbines, pistols and sub-machine-guns and mounted in grey Hotspur armoured Land Rovers – represents a small independent army in its own right. The paramilitary nature of the force lies in its origins in the Royal Irish Constabulary, which adopted the rifle green of the Light Infantry who trained them.[4]

In 1970 a Police Authority of around twenty members was set up as a result of the Hunt recommendations. It is supposed to represent the community as a whole and monitor the RUC's activities, its budget (now running at over £400 million a year), and senior appointments in the force. But in practice the Authority has little effective power, as controversies such as the Stalker-Sampson inquiry have shown. One former member stated that they were never allowed to see relevant files. The Authority was made to feel that 'we and the RUC are on the same team and should be pulling together'.[5] The lavish document *Three Years of Progress* published jointly by the Police Authority and the RUC in June 1988, the same month that its Chief Constable, Sir John Hermon, faced the possibility of disciplinary action for refusing to co-operate with the inquiry, only confirms this impression. Moderate nationalists such as the SDLP refuse to work with the Authority because they do not believe it has the power or determination to supervise the RUC effectively.

The RUC is extremely jealous of its independence, as the following statement reveals: 'Operational control and direction of the RUC in the enforcement of the law are vested in the Chief Constable who alone decides the disposition of the police service, the concentration of its resources on any particular type of crime and area, and the manner in which it handles demonstrations or processions. The Chief Constable is not subject to direction on operational matters either by the Secretary of State or the Police Authority.' That he is not answerable to military authority, the passage implies, goes without saying.

The RUC's relationship, both with the government and the British Army, is inevitably a difficult one. This relationship is also important in other ways, for it could well influence those between police and Army on the mainland in a future which many officers believe will resemble what they have faced in Northern Ireland.

In the mid-1970s, when the RUC began to recover from its virtual collapse under the onslaught of 1969, the Civil

Service coined a formula to help rebuild its pride and self-confidence. In 1977 'police primacy' was said to have been restored, implying that it had been officially taken away. It had in fact simply lapsed in those areas where the RUC would not venture out from behind the protection of the Army. Many, both in the Army and the RUC, preferred the rather more accurate term of 'Ulsterization' – in spite of its rather unfortunate echo of 'Vietnamization' – to denote a change of direction, in which British troops would gradually play a smaller role, and their numbers be reduced as a strengthened RUC took their place. The RUC was to be rearmed but this once more gave it a paramilitary appearance, if not a paramilitary role – quite against the recommendations of the Hunt Report. Many within the RUC were worried by this, and opposed the RUC's straddling of the line between civilian police and a paramilitary force; but the RUC hierarchy, inspired by Sir Kenneth Newman, Hermon's predecessor as chief constable, believed strongly that they had to fulfil both roles if they were to take over from the Army.[6]

This straddling of the paramilitary line, with a consequent blurring of responsibilities between the RUC and the Army, is inevitably the source of most of the difficulties and rivalries between them. Senior Army officers believe that the RUC is a good civilian police force (detection rates have compared extremely well with mainland forces) but that it cannot be an effective anti-terrorist force, since its men have neither the training nor the aptitude. The Army does not in any way dispute the notion of police primacy; it simply believes that it is fundamentally wrong, for political, operational and psychological reasons, to expect any police force to fulfil both roles. Yet the quasi-military origins of the RUC still influence its image of itself, and its military flavour is proudly maintained, with sergeant majors from the Irish Guards ensuring a standard of parade-ground drill and turn-out to match that of the Regular Army.

Coloured by the frustrations of liaison, above all in the intelligence field, the Army's opinion of the RUC, and the RUC's opinions of the Army, are very mixed. RUC officers resent the idea of gung-ho commanding officers, freshly arrived in the province with their battalion, wanting instant results. They feel, with justification, that officers on short tours fail to take a long-term view of a situation which the RUC will have to live with long after the battalion in question has gone back to Germany or the United Kingdom. Some Army officers, on the other hand, describe how relations between the two organizations have at times been strained at the higher levels. Several also recite examples of the RUC's 'trade-union mentality'. One senior officer lamented their rigid insistence on an eight-hour shift, which made it much easier for the PIRA to organize attacks on constables going home. He went on to say that the murder of a constable instantly reversed any improvement in confidence, but that eventually he hoped to see them not in armoured vehicles but on foot patrol without a surrounding screen of soldiers. That was the only way to make them look less like a colonial police force.

In spite of the frustrations and disagreements, most Army officers and NCOs have a genuine sympathy for members of the RUC, and speak with admiration of the way they have borne up under 'the long war'. The military police Special Investigations Branch, who have worked very closely with RUC detectives, express great respect for their counterparts, although they too have had their rivalries in the past.[7] But one infantry major, whose battalion had just returned from Belfast, doubted whether the 'appalling bigotry' of many constables would ever change, judging by the way in which they screamed abuse at passers-by from their Hotspur armoured Land Rovers as they drove through Catholic areas. 'Their attitude is entirely wrong,' he said. 'They are inevitably a sectarian force, and they do a lot of harm as a result.' After leaving the province, he had received a letter from a Catholic priest with whom he had got on well. The priest said that, not surprisingly, his parishioners saw British soldiers as an army of occupation, but that their hatred was not personal: 'The Army is alien, but the enemy is the RUC.'

Resentment amongst soldiers and regimental officers focuses mainly on what they regard as the RUC's attachment to its pay and comforts. RUC constables on joint patrols are famous for rubbing in how much they receive on overtime. An RAF group captain recounted how he once went out on patrol with two RUC constables, guarded by two teams from the Royal Highland Fusiliers. Their company commander told him that not only did they have to provide eight Jocks to guard two constables, but the two constables earned almost as much as the eight Jocks put together. 'And what's more,' he had said, 'they all know it.' The RAF officer said that this increased his admiration for the soldiers' discipline all the more.

The difference in conditions of service cause almost as much resentment as the difference in pay. The RUC live mostly in modern purpose-built accommodation, superior to anything known in British police stations, while the troops are still housed, twenty years on, in temporary slums alongside, 'hotbedding' in multiple-bunk berths 'like bloody gypsies'. But, whatever their personal feelings, no member of the Army denies the strain on RUC personnel. Over ten years the annual suicide rate tripled to approximately one in every 2,700.[8]

Hugh Annesley, a Dublin-born Protestant who had been an assistant commissioner at Scotland Yard, succeeded Sir John Hermon as Chief Constable in the spring of 1989. A Catholic Deputy Chief Constable was appointed even though Catholics still represent only 8 per cent of the force. Hopes for the future rose. But then the confirmation that members of the security forces had links with Protestant extremists only seemed to underline the impression that whatever the changes at the top – and Annesley certainly seems to have won the Army's respect – the Catholic community can never see the security forces as impartial until there is a radical change in attitudes lower down in both the RUC and the Ulster Defence Regiment.

But, although fairness is probably too much to expect in a Protestant-dominated society, the RUC's policing, as the Army points out, must be infinitely preferable to the gun-law of sectarian gangs.

The Ulster Defence Regiment is usually described as the youngest regiment in the Army, but this can be misleading since its organization and its restricted role are hardly comparable with those of a British regiment.

Raised early in 1970 to replace the infamous B Specials, the UDR consisted of seven part-time battalions, one in Belfast and one for each of the six counties. The level of civil disorder in 1971 led to the formation of four more battalions, though in 1983 the relative improvement in the security situation enabled the number of units to be reduced to its present level of nine.

UDR battalions form an integral part of the three brigades in the Province. A British Army brigadier is the UDR's commander, although his role is more equivalent to a divisional colonel of infantry, and members of the Regular Army hold the key appointments in each battalion: the commanding officer, a major who acts as the TISO (training intelligence and security officer), the quartermaster and the RSM, along with six senior NCOs. They command and train three categories of UDR member: the permanent cadre of full-time soldiers operating from home who make up nearly half the force, the part-timers whose numbers are being reduced, and over 700 unarmed women soldiers who even take part in patrols. Down to 6,300 strong in the autumn of 1989, the UDR is moving towards a more regular staffing, with candidates now going through the regular commissions board.[9]

UDR operations revolve round guard duties and patrols, usually accompanying a member of the RUC, and snap vehicle checkpoints. The permanent cadre is on duty throughout the day, and the part-timers take over at night and at weekends.

The official line stresses the discipline and impartiality

of the force, but attempts to recruit more Catholics have failed. Catholic membership has fallen from 18 per cent to 3 per cent, largely as a result of PIRA threats and attacks, but also because UDR members actively discourage the recruitment of anyone who is not prepared to declare himself a loyalist. Most alarming of all is the very small minority of Protestant terrorists and their sympathizers who infiltrate both the RUC and the UDR to obtain access to military training, weapons and information. In the late summer of 1989, when the extent of leaked intelligence became clear, sixteen former members of the UDR were serving life sentences for murder, another seven had been sentenced for manslaughter and over a hundred had been jailed for other serious offences, mostly sectarian in origin.[10]

The regiment's casualties, nearly 200 killed and 400 seriously wounded, have mainly consisted of 'close-quarter assassinations' either at home, in the car or while shopping. Families in isolated and predominantly Catholic areas, such as west Fermanagh, live in a perpetual state of siege. They do not know which of their neighbours might be passing information to the PIRA. To endure such a relentless threat requires extraordinary determination and bravery, but it does not encourage an open mind, particularly among those who volunteer following the death of a relative.

Before their arrival in the province, all infantry battalions undergo two months' preparatory training. Other arms, such as armoured regiments temporarily 're-roled' as infantry, have to do at least three months. The programme is run by NITAT, the Northern Ireland Training Advisory Team, and takes place at specially adapted camps, one in south-east England and another in Germany for troops coming from the Rhine Army.

The training is intensive and much more specialized than the counter-revolutionary warfare syllabus at Sandhurst. It prepares officers and soldiers for both urban and rural operations: riot control, prison breakout, street patrol, cross-country movement. It also covers the basic rules – the Blue Card arrest procedure and the Yellow Card conditions for opening fire – and standard skills such as observation, post-incident procedure, cordons, vehicle search, body search and house search. Procedures for securing evidence are particularly important. After a 'contact' they must secure any bodies for forensic examination. And any suspect arrested must be 'bagged' immediately, which means putting plastic gloves on at the same time as handcuffs to prevent him from washing away any chemical traces. For those with several tours already behind them, the NITAT programme provides a very necessary refresher course and updates them on any changes in standing operational procedures and equipment.

Some senior officers feel that commanding officers allow their battalions to take in the training package without sufficient thought. They allow procedures to become an end in themselves rather than a guide: an attitude influenced by the prevailing mood of 'let's not put our heads above the parapet'. This does not mean that battalions automatically react in the same way. The differences in approach can be revealing. English county regiments are certain that their soldiers' more relaxed and chatty approach is the best way to take the steam out of a confrontation. They were long troubled by the aggressive tactics of other units who may have felt they had to live up to an élite image. But there now appears to be a much wider agreement that 'going in hard' can be counter-productive, to say the least. One colonel observed that even 'the coloured beret brigade [i.e. para and commando units], in comparison with the seventies, now act with considerably more tact.'

There are six resident battalions in Northern Ireland, two with each brigade. All have different tasks and operate in a variety of circumstances. Companies can find themselves switched around unexpectedly, so that on one operation soldiers from Belfast found themselves spending eighteen days in trenches in south Armagh.

The resident battalion closest to Belfast is based at Palace

Barracks, Hollywood, which overlooks the lough. Named after the archbishop's palace on whose site it stands, this red-brick camp from the days of empire is encircled by the Dannert wire, arc lamps and closed-circuit television cameras of today. According to an almost certainly apocryphal account, its high-ceilinged officers' mess was originally designed for India, but someone mixed up the plans.

The Palace Barracks battalion is reorganized: headquarters company acts as a manpower reserve and 'shadow guard' in addition to its normal duties, and each rifle company is restructured. When operating 'out on the ground' or as the reserve for 39th Brigade, it should be able to deploy eighteen teams of four men. (Three teams then make up a 'multiple', which is commanded by one of the platoon sergeants or platoon commanders.)

Resident battalions have to pace themselves very differently from a roulement unit. Their companies change round every four to six weeks during the two-and-a-half-year tour; a more precise period offers a target date for an attack during the handover period. (All units fresh to the province or on their last few weeks have to be particularly alert, because PIRA active service units aim whenever possible to strike at the start or end of a tour, since casualties then have a much greater effect on morale.)

The rota usually consists of four stages, each averaging five weeks. Quartered alongside an RUC police station in a security force base, the first company is responsible for a particular 'patch' of West Belfast under the operational control of the Belfast Roulement Battalion – OPCON BRB. This will be followed by a return to barracks as brigade reserve on less than two hours' notice to move. The second company has nine Pig armoured personnel vehicles standing by in case of riots, and would be the first reinforcement deployed in the event of a prison breakout. The third company will be on six hours' notice, thus theoretically allowing it time for training, and would be stood to as a brigade reinforcement for politically exploited funerals, Orange marches or emotive anniversaries. The fourth company is called upon only in exceptional circumstances, because most of its men will be away on leave, on adventure training, or on courses.

With all their talk of 'top players' and 'own goals', officers can make anti-terrorist operations sound like a tricky away match. The second-in-command of one keen rugby battalion defined their aim as 'to ensure that when our guys go out on the street, they're on the top of their form'. This frame of mind no doubt represents a natural way of coping with the idea of killing and being killed. But the undercurrent of excitement has a strong whiff of the Great Game. And when you see regimental insignia painted on the walls of forts as a memento of their service, like those carved in the rock of the Khyber Pass, the Six Counties suddenly take on the guise of Britain's last north-west frontier.

Senior officers are bullish about their soldiers' morale: 'They like the danger, and they like the importance of the job.' Even after several weeks, 'working on occasions over sixteen hours a day, they recover extraordinarily quickly. They come back, have a skinful of ale and a couple of nights' sleep, and they're ready to go again.'

The temptation for senior officers to indulge in slightly idealized images of the irrepressible squaddy is only natural. Soldiers behave differently in their presence, and their own memories of commanding a platoon or company are nostalgically selective. Often they have only a partial idea of what really goes on. For example, some seem not to know about the 'happy snaps' their men take on patrol to send home. Soldiers sneak out Instamatic cameras for shots of each other in 'warry' poses, and if the team passes a suspected terrorist they cannot arrest they might snap him for the album as well. Such pictures help impress their girlfriends with stories of undercover work. 'They're such bullshitters,' said one company clerk, 'it's unreal. When it comes to their letters back home, you'd think they were James Bond and Rambo rolled into one.'

But many soldiers, more than might be imagined from

some of the macho skylarking, think seriously about what they are doing. It can make them a little uneasy at times. For a start, they are self-conscious about patrolling in areas where they know they are hated. 'If you did this in England,' said one, 'people would look at you as if you were daft.' They talk cynically of themselves as 'duty targets' or 'figure elevens' – the man-shaped silhouette used on rifle ranges. And, however much they detest the PIRA, they can see why a young Catholic brought up in West Belfast might want to join. Few have any illusions about the way Protestants have behaved.

Most officers accept these doubts with equanimity, partly because they have never constituted the slightest threat to discipline, and partly because they may share them. One brigadier described how subalterns searching houses in the early days were shaken by the squalor, having 'never seen how the other half lived'. He was convinced that this had 'moderated a lot of attitudes in the officer corps'. But now many shake their heads in disbelief, claiming that even when Catholic families are moved to new, much better housing, they are immediately in squalor again. One or two believe they must prefer it that way, and comment how scrubbed the Protestant houses are, even in the poorest areas. Others put it down to the number of children in each family, sometimes as many as ten, with no money coming in except the dole. 'It's like the Third World out there,' said a captain nodding in the direction of West Belfast. 'It's not Europe, at least not northern Europe.'

Certainly on their first tour, most junior officers view service in Northern Ireland with undisguised enthusiasm: 'It's the real thing . . . we're at last doing what we've been trained to do.' A few soon revise their attitudes sharply and can be very outspoken on the pointlessness, even the counter-productive effect of the whole exercise: 'As far as I'm concerned the aim of this tour now is not to get terrorists, but to get out without casualties. The Irish just aren't worth it'; 'We're the honey, and where we are, there's the IRA'; 'We've dug ourselves into a hole which we can't get out of'; 'I think we've given up thinking of a solution.' One even said: 'The Russians had the guts to pull out of Afghanistan, we should think of doing the same.' But this was more a way of expressing his frustration at the political paralysis than a serious suggestion.

Officers and soldiers alike seem to suffer a confusion of emotions about Republican areas, as though torn between pity and anger. They would have to be very cold fish to carry out a 5 a.m. 'lift' or house search and ignore the children who cling fearfully to their mothers. Perhaps this is what makes them angry. The house they have to take apart after an arms tip-off is still a family's home. In some cases they suspect that, rather like the blank rounds traditionally used in riot control to conceal the marksman, they are making innocent people suffer to hide the identity of an informant. Although the damage is repaired and compensation paid, the longer-term effect on the household, above all the older children, is clear. The PIRA, exploiting this opportunity to increase resentment against the security forces, has resorted to false tip-offs via the confidential telephone number advertised on the side of the armoured Land Rovers.

On the other hand, there are always a few soldiers who enjoy the power to make other people's lives hell. A uniform and the idea of authority was almost certainly what brought them into the Army in the first place. They are the ones most likely to cultivate a sense of vengeance against Republican sympathizers. A good sergeant will grip such a character firmly, but there are occasions when this brand of loathing may become contagious.

'Nobody can hate quite like the Irish' is a common saying in the British Army. Above all the Catholic women, some would add, thinking of occasions when shaken soldiers, tending a comrade maimed by a bomb, are surrounded by a horde, jeering and laughing 'like fat witches'. The foul abuse is 'unbelievable'.

Little boys are their other foe. As soon as they are

big enough to manage half a brick, they will aim at the armoured Land Rovers. More dangerous are the young joyriders, who steal cars and then drive at foot patrols, sometimes mounting the pavement, to make them jump for it. They are liable to receive a baton round through the windscreen. Other games include slapping a plank on concrete when a foot patrol passes, because the noise can be indistinguishable from a high-velocity round. The spectacle of soldiers diving for cover brings the whole neighbourhood out laughing and pointing.

Petty revenge is exacted at times. Anyone caught 'bricking' them is likely to receive 'a good rousting in a dark alley' unless an officer or sergeant intervenes. But systematic harassment is more likely to be the result of military bureaucracy than calculated. If there is an order on the computer to stop and search a particular suspect and his car, the individual concerned will find himself stopped and searched at every checkpoint on his journey. As a result he may take several hours to cross Belfast. Vociferous protests will only make things worse. The soldier on duty, probably short of sleep and irritable, is unlikely to be sympathetic.

The conditions in which soldiers live in security force bases are inexcusably shoddy after so many years. 'If things were like this in a prison,' officers say, almost certainly without exaggeration, 'there'd be a riot.' Accommodation is generally in Portakabins surrounded by blast-proof walls of double-thick breeze-blocks and covered by anti-mortar roofs.

Inside, four men share a windowless and perpetually damp box no more than nine foot by six foot. It has a single naked light bulb, two double bunk beds and a few hooks on which to hang some of their kit. The rest, helmets, webbing and packs, is kept on the floor. They have to sleep wearing ear plugs, because patrols return or go out at all hours. Every word and every boot can be heard through the plywood partitions. The collage of years of Page Three girls provides little insulation.

Cleanliness is a continual problem. There is one ablutions Portakabin for up to a hundred men – showers, basins, lavatories and a single overworked washing machine. Another Portakabin acts as both canteen and TV room.

Discipline is seldom a problem in Northern Ireland. Only 50 out of 400 military policemen in the province are involved in routine duties. But some offences, particularly anything which threatens security, are dealt with harshly. A lost identity card can mean a £400 fine – a huge sum for a soldier with a take-home pay of about £90 a week.

Trouble only really comes as a result of drinking bouts following long periods of duty during which alcohol is banned. Some bases are completely dry; in others the ration is two cans of beer a day. According to an officer in the military police, 'When they get back to barracks, the pads [the married men] go home and have a serious session with the missus, the single ones get smashed.'

Officers in infantry battalions would not, however, agree with his description of the married men. Difficulties often arise on the first evening back, when husbands virtually ignore their wives and go off drinking with the same men whose company they have shared for the last few weeks. Although it may well be better for everyone if the men unwind in their own company, their wives find such behaviour hard to accept.

The disruption to their lives is already considerable. Apart from the company stint on the other side of the city, their husbands can often average 60 per cent 'nights out of bed' on pre-planned duties and emergency call-outs. And the PIRA, to increase the war of nerves as well as stretch the security forces further, bombed some married quarters for the first time in December 1988.

While their husbands are out on duty, wives can never entirely suppress their anxiety. Worst of all is the feeling of utter powerlessness. They cannot help listening to the news on the radio or television. Unlike the cursory reporting of such events in Britain, every bulletin in the province seems to contain some reference to the terrorist threat, even when no explosion or shooting incident has occurred. The strain is considerable: between 10 and 30 per cent of wives prefer to stay behind in Britain, while a number of those who do accompany the battalion spend virtually the whole of the two-and-a-half-year tour without going outside the wire.

For their husbands, the rules of personal security when alone soon become second nature. Unless moving in armed formation, they must wear civilian clothes and travel in unmarked cars. They must never set a pattern by taking the same route or following a timetable. If carrying a weapon for personal protection, it must be concealed at all times. (The bulk of the 9mm pistol makes this difficult. Smaller handguns have been tried, but none can match its reliability and stopping power.)

Attempts to lead a normal existence off-duty with wife and family are far more difficult. Little things, done without thought in Britain, can be dangerous in Northern Ireland. When parking the car, the husband must make sure that he has not left a beret or any other article of kit visible; he has to remember not to give an address in shops, and to explain to his children that they must not point to a patrol and say: 'Look Dad! There's a soldier like you.'

Commanding officers are naturally keen to maintain the continuity of regimental life as far as possible. Sports teams cannot easily be kept together and the life of both messes will suffer when many of their members are often only there 'to crash out' for a couple of nights before starting again. When a newly arrived Guards officer innocently asked what there was to do at weekends, his words rapidly became a standing joke in 39th Brigade. Nevertheless, well-connected officers sometimes receive invitations for the weekend or for dinner from some of the grander families living untouched by the troubles deep in the countryside. A television journalist invited to one of these occasions recorded how pleasantly amazed the officers were to find civilization 'out here'. But, when one of them mentioned this in an expansive mood, his hostess did not appreciate the compliment.

For most single soldiers, time off means the chance to satisfy their two major preoccupations. In Palace Barracks, there is a smart new Naafi disco. Rather like the inside of a chrome steel and scarlet pyramid, it seems incongruously modern in an old barrack building with concrete floors, bulbous radiators and fire extinguishers. There is a lingering smell of stale cigarette ash and split beer. 'These events really are the most appalling cattle markets,' said a major in amused distaste. 'God knows where they pick 'em up.'

On a disco night, the girls turn up at the main gate after filling in a security form. They are searched by 'Greenfinches' from the local battalion of the Ulster Defence Regiment and then go into the guardroom to wait for their boyfriends. Sometimes the soldiers stay on drinking in the junior ranks club, and the furious guard commander, surrounded by a chattering crowd, has to keep telephoning to get them to come down and collect their dates.

The sexual success of the Toms, and the treatment these casual girlfriends are prepared to put up with, seem astonishing at first sight. Ask a single soldier what he likes about the place, and the most frequent response, accompanied as often as not by an adolescent smirk, usually has something to do with the 'friendliness' of the girls. But the truth is that all too many of them are desperate to marry a soldier, which they see as the only way to escape to the mainland. A resident battalion usually leaves with between fifteen and sixty new wives.

Soldiers are allowed out on evenings off, but certain pubs and districts are permanently out of bounds. Precautions are also taken to prevent them congregating regularly in favourite places which would then become a target. Drugs are seldom a problem amongst soldiers stationed in the province. They have been warned in vivid terms of the real danger. Although most of the trade is controlled by loyalist paramilitary groups who have switched to racketeering, a soldier client may quickly attract the attention of the PIRA.

The 'honey trap', when terrorists get girls to entice off-duty soldiers back to a flat, remains the greatest cause for concern. Indeed, if the Army's personal hatred for the PIRA can be dated to any particular incident, it would probably be the ambush which killed three young Scottish soldiers in March 1971. The brutality of that event is still evoked on barrack noticeboards. Soldiers are warned by means of a cartoon strip of a likely scenario, photographs identifying girls currently suspected of similar ploys, and a picture of a murdered soldier's body dumped naked at the side of a road.

The countryside demands a completely different approach; and only a unit on a short tour can sustain the intensity of effort demanded by a patch such as south Armagh, an area long known for lawlessness. In modern times smuggling and guerrilla warfare continue the tradition. There are fifty-one border crossing points, of which only four are officially approved. The most flagrant smuggling operations and European Community agricultural fraud flourish within binocular range of Army observation posts, but witnesses are hard to find. The local PIRA gang, over thirty-strong, is famously brutal. Ireland's version of *omertà* can be just as effective as in Sicily. 'It's real pond life down here,' said one major.

Bessbrook Mill, the security force base for operations in south Armagh, is a huge Victorian flax mill which has been so reinforced with blast walls, barbicans, and inner and outer keeps as to resemble a medieval castle. It has been reconstructed to house up to a thousand men and a small number of women. With ops rooms, offices, kitchens, dining-halls, stores, workshops and an armoury, Bessbrook has become a complete barracks under one roof. The windowless corridors, huge pipes and generators throbbing in the distance make it feel like the deepest bowels of a ship. The soldiers call it 'the submarine'.

Bessbrook is the supply base for operations in south Armagh as well as the command centre. No vehicles can be risked on the roads, so all movement of personnel and stores has to be carried out by air. Even the rubbish is flown out. As a result Bessbrook's heliport is reputedly the busiest in northern Europe. RAF Wessex and Puma helicopters and the Gazelles and Lynxes of the Army Air Corps shuttle in from Aldergrove, then on round the patch.

The outlying areas are manned from satellite security force bases and surveyed from a network of watch-towers begun in 1985. The most famous outpost is at Crossmaglen.

Crossmaglen, or XMG in military abbreviation, is a sin-ister little border town whose inhabitants watch the street from the side of their windows. A lance corporal described it as 'the sort of place you'd expect Clint Eastwood to ride into if it wasn't so fucking cold and wet'.

Adjoining and overlooking the town, the security force base is another fort with corner towers and fifteen-foot-high corrugated iron walls. The walls protect the helipad, and the sentries in the tower sangars watch the town, looking out for suspiciously parked lorries and farm trailers which might conceal a rack of mortars.

Inside the blast-proofed walls of the base, living condi-tions are even more crowded than in Belfast. Allowing for a storage drawer, there is so little space left between the bunks that a soldier cannot lie on his back with his knees up. Apart from a week's leave in Britain, which starts on the milk-run helicopter back to Aldergrove, they have no privacy for six months, and no recreation except pumping iron in the improvised gymnasium or watching videos.

During their tour at Crossmaglen, the multiples (groups of fire-teams) in the company rotate. They man the observation towers for several weeks, then switch to a patrolling cycle and finally guard the base. The base guard provides the sentries, who do two four-hour 'stags' out of

271

twenty-four, and the quick reaction force, which hangs around on instant standby with equipment and weapons to hand.

The work of the observation post towers is probably the most useful, but it is an isolated and boring experience. Two men at a time watch the surrounding countryside and farm buildings through powerful binoculars, telephoto-lensed cameras and closed-circuit screens. The sergeant or sub-altern commanding the multiple visits them frequently to see what is going on, and to keep them alert. There is little room to spare up in these armoured crow's-nests. Mounted on little more than a network of scaffolding encased in corrugated iron, they can sway enough in the wind to cause seasickness. Sandbagged and revetted trenches, with machine-guns on tripods, connect the base of the tower to underground bunkers, where those off duty sleep, eat and watch videos. This may conjure up images of the First World War, but comparisons with Vietnam spring to mind when the helicopter comes in and khaki figures run back and forth from the bunkers, bareheaded and in a crouching run. One of these observation posts is called the 'Hanoi Hilton'.

To increase the deterrent effect of the watchtowers, speculation about the power of their equipment is occasionally encouraged. The Scots Guards were particularly pleased at the rumours which spread following one little charade. A car was stopped at a vehicle checkpoint. The NCO took the driver's licence – in Northern Ireland these include photographs – held it up towards the nearest watchtower, almost a mile away, and asked over the radio for the details to be checked. Back came the reply fifteen seconds later that the holder was clear. The licence was returned with a straight face and permission to drive on.

In Crossmaglen, officers and soldiers are highly enter-tained by the complaints of some hostile locals that infra-red beams and lasers are directed into their bedrooms. But, for all the jokes, it seems likely that the hard-core PIRA has a very good idea of both the extent and the limits of the equipment used. Its intelligence network is unsettlingly good.

Long patrols lasting up to four days provide the best break from the claustrophobic monotony of watchtower and sangar. But they are very hard work. Distances covered on the map and distances covered on the ground bear little relation to one another. The easiest point at which to cross an obstacle or the shortest route across a field are obvious targets for a bomb, and reminding your brain 'not to slip into neutral' requires a constant effort. The countryside, however, beautiful to a tourist, loses its charm when blackthorn fences and barbed wire rip combat kit to pieces. (The Army is less than generous over replacements, and the standard issue of clothing and equipment, although improved, remains fairly basic. Officers in one battalion calculated that for a single roulement tour, the average soldier had spent about £200 on extra kit, a sum he and his family can ill afford.)

These patrols do not consist entirely of movement, however. Part of the time will be spent concealed in 'lurks' to watch for any suspicious movement. One company commander emphasized that it was a war of patience and caution. First-tour subalterns 'looking for a scalp' had to be held in check because they had the 'bravery of innocence'. The RSM of the same battalion was less charitable. 'The last thing we need is thrusting young gentlemen liable to make horrible mistakes.'

Officers often prefer the challenge of rural operations because they are closer to normal infantry work. But soldiers, as one company commander acknowledged, have to spend 'far too much time staring out into the bundu'. For hours on end, a cow crossing the field may well provide the only interest for those watching from a sangar, an observation post or a lurk. In towns at least there are people to watch.

Clearly there is no standard attitude within the Army to the conflict in Northern Ireland. There are those who believe that 'it should be towed out into the Atlantic and sunk' and those who, with longer postings, have acquired a genuine affection for the place and the people. Senior officers point with determined optimism to evidence of rising Catholic disenchantment with the IRA, while younger officers scorn 'lights at the end of the tunnel'. Other wars around the world may come to an end, especially in the new phase of East–West relations, but Northern Ireland, which predates all other colonial conflicts, goes on and on.

Middle-ranking officers, who may have done up to half a dozen tours, appear the most cynical about the province's new-found wealth. Pointing to the BMWs and Mercedes and all the other signs of an artificial boom, they say that perpetuating the conflict seems to be in the interests of powerful people on both sides. The security industry is huge, as is the construction business, but biggest of all are the swindles and protection rackets organized by loyalist and Republican groups alike. 'The whole thing's a thoroughly sick joke,' said a captain. 'The economy's riding high on every form of subsidy going, but it's riddled with hypocrisy and utterly corrupt.' Another officer commented that 'The Prod bully boys and the IRA ring each other up to sort out any rivalry on the ground. The last thing they want are any clashes which might be bad for business.' The head of the RUC drugs squad stated in February 1991 that the two loyalist paramilitary groups, the Ulster Defence Association and the Ulster Volunteer Force, had not only become deeply involved in cannabis trafficking, but they also co-operated with the Irish People's Liberation Organization, a breakaway group from the INLA.[11]

Senior Army officers agree with this picture of creeping corruption, but their conclusions are different, perhaps because they feel obliged to stick to the bullish party line. One pointed out that most organized crime of the Mafia variety started out with nationalist aspirations, which convinced him that the degeneration of IRA ideals would help the security forces win a hearts-and-minds campaign in the long term. But however true this may be, the real

Mafia's strength shows little sign of decreasing, either in Europe or America. Northern Ireland could become the United Kingdom's Sicily. (Perhaps this aspect of the troubles may have some bearing on the increased number of visits to the province by British chief constables.) A senior member of the military police also warned of the psychopathic gunmen – what he called the 'Hungerford element' – who would not give up their activities whatever the political solution.

Amongst NCOs and soldiers, feelings are also mixed, although on a narrower front than amongst the junior and middle-ranking officers. Most soldiers, particularly the younger ones, openly enjoy the work; and, however much they may look forward to a break, few enjoy the return to barrack routine in Britain or Germany. Northern Ireland is the only place where they are not inflicted with the time-wasting trivia of a peacetime army. As for the future, they just feel resigned. The older sergeants and warrant officers have served about ten tours over the last twenty years, and they expect the cycle to continue for another twenty. They accept the pattern because it is their duty, and because service there is good for the battalion. Everyone pulls together, and the system works.

The emotional trigger points have never been caused by casualty statistics, but by personal experience: a friend killed or maimed, or the unexpectedness of a hostile gesture. Soldiers remember feeling far more shocked when spat at for the first time than when shot at. They now laugh at that initial innocence. 'They gob at us and we gob at them,' said one.

To prepare soldiers for the most horrific eventualities, those coming to Northern Ireland receive a package of battle-shock training. This process, an annual inoculation formulated by the Army's psychiatrists, is designed to make them accept the idea of battle shock, and train them to spot it in each other, and to explain how it is best treated. Film and slides also prepare them for carnage, rather like young doctors witnessing operations. The effectiveness of this method was brought out at Lockerbie. The soldiers of the Royal Highland Fusiliers assigned to collecting corpse fragments had just received their training package, and according to a civilian psychiatrist present they coped admirably, suffering no cases of post-traumatic stress disorder at the time.[12] But the 'psychological robustness' of soldiers is very much the product of their own instinct to tackle horrors head on with a sick sense of humour rather than try to smother the effects.

A colonel in the Royal Artillery described how some of his soldiers, given the task of clearing up the corpses of IRA bombers killed in an 'own-goal explosion, picked up a head and played catch with it. And, when a private in the Duke of Wellington's Regiment lost a leg from a bomb, his mates visited him in hospital bearing a bag of jelly babies, each with a leg bitten off. The soldier concerned took it as a great joke, and as soon as he was allowed out of hospital he came thumping into battalion headquarters on crutches. He went into the office of the assistant adjutant, a young blonde female lieutenant, and saluted. 'Can I show you my stump, ma'am?' But the after-effects of service in Northern Ireland, particularly rows at home and even violence, are not easily admitted. It is bound to have a brutalizing effect. Police involved in the miners' strike disorders admitted to acquiring an instinctively aggressive reaction, in some cases even a taste for violence.[13] Perhaps something similar will be true of Britain as a whole, with television coverage of terrorist atrocities unintentionally providing a similar course of desensitizing treatment which may be not unlike the Army's battle-shock training.

There are soldiers serving in Northern Ireland who had not been born when the rioting started in August 1969, yet grim echoes of the Vietnam era have lingered on, including a spoof notice in one headquarters – 'Will the last watchkeeper to leave Northern Ireland please switch off the television?'[14] This, like the echoes of a final outpost of empire, serves to underline the fact that, whatever its exact political status, Northern Ireland has never really been treated by Whitehall as a constituent part of the United Kingdom, but as a post-colonial successor state. It has therefore been neither truly British nor truly Irish. The illusion that the defensive positions across this no-man's-land will be spontaneously dismantled within the Common Market cannot be maintained much longer. After more than twenty years a stark logic seems to be emerging.

Whatever the state of Eire says in its constitution, runs the argument, it cannot want a province which would erupt into a civil war far more savage than anything seen so far; and not even the most fervent Republican expects an Algerian settlement, with loyalist *pieds noirs* resettled in metropolitan Britain. Independence is out of the question, since the Catholic minority would have no protection. If there is to be a solution, it has to be a startling one. Even if historically unfair to the nationalists, the only course appears to lie in complete integration with Britain. But this integration could no longer permit a sectarian power structure. That would mean no Stormont, no Ulster Defence Regiment, and instead of the RUC in green uniforms, with its paramilitary air, there should be a British national police force in blue. It offers the only way to call the pseudo-patriotic bluff of Protestant extremists. From 1921 to 1969, Britain washed its hands of Ulster. Since then, using the Army as a shield, it has been able to keep the worst of the problem at arm's length. Integration clearly has its dangers. It could easily bring the violence and gangsterism of Belfast on to the mainland more rapidly, but to continue hoping for a miracle may well find ten battalions still in the province when the thirtieth anniversary comes round on the eve of the new century.

CHAPTER 18

Overseas: Sunshine and Other Postings

When Denis Healey became Secretary of State for Defence in 1964, Britain had more troops east of Suez than in the Rhine Army.[1] Twenty-five years later, it had less than 15,000 outside Europe, of whom nearly half were Gurkhas. Since then the Gulf war temporarily reversed the trend, but no permanent presence in the region is foreseen.

Of all its remaining foreign bases, the Army seems to feel most at home in Cyprus. The widespread friendliness of Cypriots makes their presence feel like a natural extension of the colonial past. Except at odd moments, the hatred of EOKA days is hard to imagine.

Hong Kong, on the other hand, exerts a strong fascination, but soldiers seem ill at ease there. Belize goes on providing the Army's version of 'the Caribbean frigate syndrome', but seldom has a place had such an air of impermanence. And then there are the Falklands Islands, a far-away colony of which we knew little, until the armed forces had to recapture them at great cost.

Cyprus has all the advantages. Offering both a pleasant climate and a proper job, it embodies the soldier's dream: a holiday destination in combat kit. The 1974 ceasefire line (now known as the 'green line') between the Greek and Turkish forces has held, thanks to the patient presence of UNFICYP – United Nations Forces in Cyprus. For over fifteen years, the white Ferret scout cars and sky-blue berets have acted as a symbol of civilized peacekeeping to an army partially brutalized by service in Northern Ireland.

There are four national contingents in UNFICYP: Canadian, Danish, Austrian and British. The British contingent patrols its sector of the 'green line' around the divided city of Nicosia and mans observation posts overlooking the buffer zone, which varies in width. The contingent consists of an armoured recce squadron, a detachment of Military Police, an Army Air Corps flight of helicopters and half of the Cyprus Emergency Reinforcement Regiment, which is usually an armoured corps or gunner regiment from Germany serving on its feet to give it a break from Rhine Army routine. They are supported by elements from the Royal Signals, Royal Corps of Transport, REME and the Royal Army Ordnance Corps.

The British are the best positioned of all the contingents because they already have a considerable military infrastructure in Cyprus, consisting of over 3,000 troops. Britain retained two sovereign base areas on the south coast, together with certain other rights, under the Treaty of Establishment agreed when Cyprus received independence in 1960. RAF Akrotiri proved invaluable as a staging-post during the Gulf crisis, with over 10,000 aircraft in and out by the time the ground offensive began.

The Commander British Forces Cyprus is either a major general or an air vice marshal. Like his counterparts in Belize, the Falklands, and Hong Kong, he reports to the Centre in the form of the Deputy Chief of the Defence Staff (Commitments). In a crisis he receives his instructions from the Joint Operations Centre.

Security for all bases has to be taken seriously in the eastern Mediterranean region. As a first-line, low-key guard, the sovereign base areas have the Army Depot Police Cyprus, a locally recruited force 150-strong under Royal Military Police command.

British Forces Cyprus also include RAF Akrotiri and the RAF radar site on Mount Troodos, 9 Signal Regiment at Ayios Nikolaos, and a couple of training bases. There are two armoured recce squadrons equipped with ancient Ferrets and Saladin armoured cars to protect the sovereign base areas of Episkopi in the west and Dhekelia to the east. Other troops include a resident infantry battalion, 62

Cyprus Support Squadron Royal Engineers and 16 Flight Army Air Corps at Dhekelia. (They are all supported by 30 Regiment RCT at Episkopi with 10 Port Squadron and 58 Sqn RCT at Akrotiri, together with 48 Workshop REME and 17 Ordnance Battalion.)

With the joint services training centre in the Troodos mountains, and the adventure training centre at Pergamos, soldiers are exceptionally well provided for. They have almost everything: skiing, trekking, gliding, freefall parachuting, sub-aqua and canoeing. Best established of all are those long-term residents, the airwave listeners of 9 Signal Regiment, who have the Famagusta Saddle Club and their own Yacht Club. To the envy of other units, they also have the highest number of servicewomen. Karting is one of the soldiers' favourite sports. Senior NCOs and officers play golf, while cavalry and other officers play polo; before the Gulf war, their team used to fly over to Jordan, where members of the Hashemite royal family are keen players. The uncertainty of the political situation in the Middle East has made such outings rather too complicated for the time being.

Although the empire has gone, traces of its way of life have proved remarkably persistent in those microcosms of England past, served by the British Forces Broadcasting Service, entertained by amateur dramatics, and where a commander's residence still has a name like Flagstaff House. Yet such impressions should not be taken too literally. The eastern Mediterranean does not permit such complacency, and the younger generation of the Army is very different from its predecessors.

The Governor of Hong Kong retains a vice-regal touch in his appointment, for he is also the Commander-in-Chief. Naturally he relies on the Commander British Forces for military advice, and if there should ever be a major difference of opinion they are both in touch with London by satellite.

Commander British Forces Hong Kong is a 'tied Army'

post in the jargon of jointery, and the incumbent automatically assumes the appointment of Major General, Brigade of Gurkhas. Gurkha units represent the bulk of his 7,000-odd force; 48th Gurkha Infantry Brigade Headquarters and the Gurkha Depot are based at Sek Kong. The only major British unit is the resident battalion at Stanley Fort, currently the Royal Welch Fusiliers. The Gurkhas and British troops are supported by the 1,250-strong Hong Kong Military Service Corps, based on Stonecutters' Island, a former Japanese prison camp. These Hong Kong Chinese 'locally employed personnel' are full-time soldiers. The Royal Hong Kong Regiment, on the other hand, is the equivalent of a territorial unit, only about three times the size at close to a thousand-strong. As a reconnaissance regiment, most of its British officers come from the cavalry, which makes the siting of its base at Happy Valley, next to the Royal Hong Kong Jockey Club, particularly apt. Curiously, the regiment's most famous officer was Errol Flynn, whose relatively brief service experience came in useful for a number of roles at his next destination.

British soldiers enjoy Hong Kong, although mainly as an exotic memory to talk about when they get home. The 'marrieds' like the style of life. 'We had a marvellous big house and maid,' said a sergeant nostalgically, after returning to the cramped conditions of an English quarter. Young single soldiers, on the other hand, are preoccupied with their unsentimental education in red-light districts. While the more enterprising take the opportunity to travel during their leave, trekking in Nepal or hitch-hiking round Australia, the main pilgrimage is to Bangkok, comparing its massage parlours with what Hong Kong has to offer. 'The VD rate', said a platoon commander, 'was pretty appalling.'

Soldiers and sailors in the Orient tend to behave like previous generations, largely because they feel it is expected of them. The worst incidents are likely to happen when warships of either the Royal Navy or the US Navy are in port. Brawls escalate in the bars of Wanchai, and after a night of running battles and destruction the whole battalion may be confined to barracks.

But soldiering in Hong Kong has its serious, if not increasingly tragic side. For years Gurkhas, British troops and dog-handlers from the Veterinary Corps' Defence Animal Support Unit have guarded the twenty-two-mile border, arresting each year thousands of illegal immigrants, known as IIs, and sending them back to the People's Republic. It has become something of a ritual – one young officer compared it to a baseball game, as would-be immigrants gathered in the 'departure lounge' on the other side ready to try for a home run.

For newly arrived British soldiers, the experience has usually been unsettling. Their instinctive sympathy for the underdog has largely been influenced by service in Germany where refugees from communism were always applauded and never handed back. A major from the Light Division recounted how very few 'illegals' were captured early on in his battalion's tour. The authorities began to complain, so 'We offered a crate of beer to the section which caught the most, and it was amazing how fast ethics go out of the window.'

In the last few years Hong Kong has also become the main destination for the Vietnamese 'boat people'. Their rate of arrival accelerated, creating huge logistic problems. Nearly 10,000 refugees turned up in May 1989, with more than a thousand in a single day. Since then numbers of new arrivals have diminished greatly, but the problem is very far from solved.

Queen's Gurkha engineers helped built the camps and provide water supplies, the Gurkha Transport Regiment has moved them and the Royal Hong Kong Police has had to cope with riots. It provides a chilling foretaste of the work of security forces in the next century, perhaps sooner, if the pattern of mass migration is further accelerated by climatic disaster.

Border patrols may have 'absolutely no training value' for Germany, but some officers regard them as useful for

Northern Ireland. To keep their soldiers up to the mark, battalions book time on the New Territories training area. This contains the close-quarters battle range at Castle Peak, an elaborate mock-up of streets in a huge diorama of façades. This lozenge-shaped theatre, several hundred yards across and open to the sky, is controlled from a bullet-proof control tower via closed-circuit television cameras and remote control devises. It is a superficially oriental version of those at Hythe and Sennelager.

Heavier weapons cannot be used in the restricted space of the New Territories, and the only ranges large enough for Milan anti-tank projectiles are at Puckapunyal in Victoria, Australia. Visits there are usually combined with exercises involving the Australian Army. An occasional exercise takes place in New Zealand, but most training from Hong Kong is carried out in Brunei.

From time to time, a major tri-service exercise is mounted, with an air bridge of Hercules ferrying Gurkha battalions, supposedly in support of the Royal Brunei Armed Forces. Royal Navy warships provide naval gunfire support and the local version of Fantasian forces are thoroughly confounded.

Apart from maintaining a battalion of Gurkhas based in Brunei, the Sultan's government also acts as host to the Jungle Warfare Wing of the School of Infantry. Training Team Brunei's main activity is running the jungle warfare instructors' course, a section commanders' course, the long-range patrol course, and a survival course for crashed aircrew. (The SAS course is entirely separate.) Once selected NCOs from Gurkha and British units have completed the course, they train their own company, under the supervision of an instructor, on how to survive and fight in the tropical forest.

The school of jungle warfare in Brunei is as much the arbiter in its field as Pirbright is for drill. A team from Brunei, for example, goes to Belize to train the roulement battalion there. It teaches them how to live off the jungle, eating termites and snakes and the leaves of certain trees, how to cope with the 'nasties', whether insect or reptile, and, most important of all, how to avoid self-inflicted 'machete bites' when hacking through the vegetation.

Roughly the size of Wales, but with a population of about 150,000, Belize and its British presence is one of those accidents of history peculiar to Latin America and best described in the fiction of Gabriel García Márquez or Alejo Carpentier.

The Commander British Forces, another 'tied' appointment, is a brigadier. Should the Guatemalans ever attempt to reassert their sporadic claims to the territory by force, he can call upon the destroyer or frigate acting as the West Indies guardship, and use his RAF Harriers, a British battalion group, and the Belize Defence Force to hold off an attack until reinforcements arrived by air. (In exercises, the enemy is diplomatically designated the 'Petenian' armed forces.) For aerial reconnaissance and transport, he has an Army Air Corps flight with three Gazelle helicopters, in addition to an RAF flight of Puma helicopters.

The Belize Defence Force, raised in 1979, has an establishment of 1,200, of whom 500 are part-timers and twenty-five are women. Their headquarters is near Airport Camp. The first Belizean commanding officer took over in June 1990. The unit is subsidized equally by the British and the American governments. (Sir John Nott, in 1981 when Secretary of State for Defence, wanted to withdraw the British Army from Belize, but the Reagan administration, heavily involved in the Salvadorean and Nicaraguan civil wars, pushed very hard for the British to retain a presence in the region. The United States government wanted an Allied international police force to work with them. And that, said Nott, 'puts an extraordinarily heavy moral pressure on a British prime minister'.)

The infantry battalion headquarters, with one rifle company, is based at Airport Camp, near Belize City on the Caribbean. The rest of the battalion is split between Battle Group North and Battle Group South, each supported by an armoured recce troop of Scimitars and Scorpions and a troop of 105mm light guns. Battle Group North is based at Airport Camp, with its main detachment at Holdfast Camp, beyond the new capital of Belmopan and near the Guatemalan border on the western side of the country. Battle Group South is close to the southern border, part at Salamanca Camp, the rest at Rideau, close to the sea and the insalubrious town of Punta Gorda. From these bases, the infantry carry out week-long patrols and, resupplied by helicopter, man border observation posts with members of the Belize Defence Force.

Helicopters are vital since so much of the country defies modern transport. Rivers are accessible with the Royal Engineers' Rigid Raider boats, but the few roads, described as 'probably the worst in Central America' by the most authoritative guidebook to the region, reduce the life expectancy of four-tonners and Land Rovers dramatically. The recovery vehicles of twenty-four Squadron RCT, who call themselves the Caribbean Truckers, are seldom idle.

An independent squadron from the Royal Engineers, or Queen's Gurkha Engineers, on a six-month roulement tour is always busy, improving defensive positions, rebuilding observation posts along the border or constructing blast walls to protect the Harriers on the ground. During the tour, workload permitting, they will take on community tasks, such as building bridges and improving roads, and also 'hearts and minds' jobs for the local population. Sappers from one field squadron recently rebuilt an orphanage, another repaired the roof of Belize City's cathedral, and 16 Field Workshop REME mended the Baptist church's organ.[2]

Apart from the satisfaction of learning how to survive in the jungle – another good source of stories for back home – soldiers can see more of the region during their week or so of leave. Most take the opportunity to travel into Mexico, while some fly up to the United States and visit New Orleans. The distances covered during such a brief period can be amazing. One or two are always bound to get into some sort of trouble somewhere, not always of their own making (the Army seems to attract rather more than its share of disaster-prone individuals). British consuls will ring up, or a signal will arrive from London, and an exasperated commanding officer has to deal with the culprit on return. He, depending on character, will either accept his punishment with a maddening stolidity, or will protest with the most genuine sense of injured innocence, however damning the circumstances.

The other disciplinary problems are usually associated with the dubious and highly unhygienic pleasures offered by Belize City. A brothel such as Raoul's Rose Garden is princely in comparison to what is on offer in some parts of the town. Most eating places are also proscribed by the Army's medical authorities, but a far greater danger for a drunken soldier is to find himself cornered on his own in one of the rougher areas. As a result, they are only allowed out in pairs. Soldiers claim, and some officers support this, that Military Police NCOs patrolling Belize City have always been particularly officious and heavy-handed, often triggering a serious fight instead of defusing the situation.

A healthier side to a six-month tour in Belize is the week spent by almost all soldiers at the adventure training base on St George's Cay, close to where the Royal Navy defeated the Spanish in 1798. Ferried to this Caribbean paradise by one of the RCT's small landing craft, they can windsurf, dive along the coral reef, or simply fish and swim. It offers a much more relaxed regime than most of the Army's adventure training courses.

Belize is just as important to the Army as the Army is to Belize. A touch of the exotic, whether collecting parrots, baby alligators, and tarantulas as pets, or sending locally painted coconut shells home as postcards (causing chaos to the postal system in the process), is what counts. As Sir John Nott acknowledged, senior officers are bound to want to keep such postings in order to recruit and retain their men. On the other hand, it would be hard to see the Falklands in the same light.

To the dismay of the Falkland Islands Tourist Board, the arrival of the twice-weekly RAF Tristar from Brize Norton is an uncompromisingly military affair. Photography is forbidden and all passengers, servicemen and civilians alike, receive a ponderous lecture on the dangers of minefields, a welcome likely to appeal only to those visitors who have come on one of Major Holt's Battlefield Tours. Outside, the windsock is liable to be horizontal, such is the force of the wind.

Mount Pleasant Airport, opened in May 1985 at a cost of £395 million, was described four years later by Robert Kee as the 'the most unequivocal and unabashed of all the monuments which can be seen to commemorate ten years of Mrs Thatcher's rule'.[3] To appreciate the whole complex in its setting, it needs to be viewed from afar, across the wilderness of peat-bog and hills the colour of dry moss, a mirror image of the west coast of Scotland. The huge cathedral hangar in matt green industrial cladding dominates the artificial town below, part industrial estate roofed in the same material, the rest a maze of several score accommodation blocks linked by what is said to be the longest corridor in the world.

This military capital, thirty-five miles from the civilian capital of Port Stanley, is the seat of the Commander British Forces Falkland Islands, usually known as C Biffi. This 'fully purple' appointment is rotated between the Services, a major general followed by an air vice marshal, and then a rear admiral. But Mount Pleasant itself is primarily an air force base, and the RAF predominates.

The task of British Forces is 'to deter aggression so that the Falkland Islanders can pursue a lifestyle of their choice'. The cost of this, estimated at around £105 million a year in 1990, is already extremely heavy, so in the increasingly unlikely event of another full-scale invasion the defence of the islands would depend on the rapid reinforcement of resident troops. This was practised in Exercise Fire Focus in March 1988, when the 3rd Battalion of the Light Infantry and the 3rd Battalion of the Parachute Regiment flew out from England, triggering off protests from the Argentine government and the Organization of American States.

Yet even at the time of the Argentine elections in 1989, when the belligerent statements of Carlos Menem had to be taken seriously, British Forces headquarters did not expect another invasion, only a maverick attack or calculated provocation. Since then, Argentina's need for financial assistance from Europe has drawn off most of the venom. But, until told to stand down by the politicians, the forces maintain their 'state of military vigilance'. One officer was prompted to complain that the Falklands had become 'the forgotten theatre', as if they were XIV Army in Burma. His colleagues, however, were less sensitive to issues of public image.

Nevertheless, a theatre such as the Falklands has some advantages. Bureaucracy is relatively reduced, and the headquarters, just one long corridor of offices, is comparatively economical in manpower. Almost everyone is there on a six-month tour from a parent unit. 'I have no indigenous assets,' explained the Commander British Forces. 'Everything is culled from other Services. They are really bits of Lego in and out.'

The RAF operations wing includes the Phantom fighters and helicopters, both Chinooks and Sea King. During the squid season, fishing fleets offshore keep the Sea Kings busy with requests to evacuate casualties to the hospital in Port Stanley. The more mundane work has been contracted out: Bristow helicopters drop off the infantry patrols and do the milk-run round the outlying detachments and mountain-top radar sites. Meanwhile, the RAF Regiment mans the air defence missile batteries which guard the key installations.

The largest units in the Falklands are from the Army. The first priority of the Royal Engineers field squadron is airfield damage repair, so as to ensure that, in the event of an enemy air strike, reinforcements can always land. They are also responsible for emergency repairs to essential services, whether water, electricity or fuel. And they can, of course, be deployed as an infantry reserve. In practice, much of the squadron's time is spent rebuilding or reinforcing installations.

In addition there is a separate Royal Engineer EOD detachment in Port Stanley responsible for the remaining 16,000 plastic mines. The immediate concern is to keep people away from them. Most do, but expatriate construction workers from Stanley have been known in drunken sport to lob cans of beer into the minefields, then take turns to retrieve them. Miraculously, nobody has yet been killed.

The task of the infantry, meanwhile, is to patrol the islands, guard the installations at Mare Harbour and RAF Mount Pleasant, and provide a quick reaction force. Kit to hand and ready to move, they kill time watching videos.

The week-long patrols cover from ten to twenty kilometres a day, each man carrying sixty-five pounds of equipment as well as his personal weapon. One company commander described the going as 'pretty ankle-biting stuff': 'Every two hundred metres the ground changes. It's wonderful and fascinating, but bloody difficult countryside.' In 1991 a company from the Grenadier Guards acquired horses locally, and sent out mounted infantry patrols with pack animals. They managed to cover at least forty kilometres a day.

The landscape there is marred only by the odd khaki Portakabin, sold off by the Army, or a rusty shipping container converted into a shepherd's refuge. The settlements are widely scattered, with less than half of the islands' 2,000 civilians spread around the Camp, as the countryside is called. The Falklands are often described as 'a village the size of Wales'. Everyone knows everything about everyone, just by listening in to the islander radio net, although the new telephone system is changing that.

Company commanders find that the Falklands offer good

professional training. A subaltern learns to command his platoon properly, and the opportunites for live firing are excellent. Onion Range to the north of Mount Pleasant has few restrictions, except the danger of setting the peat alight in summer, and the parts used for air attack exercises with 1,000 lb bombs, naval gunfire support and the 105mm light gun have to be designated as 'no troop movement areas'.

The garrison on South Georgia, 800 miles away, comes from the same battalion. Commanded by a major who is automatically appointed magistrate, harbour-master, and customs and immigration officer, the soldiers are quartered next to the Grytviken whaling base. Their existence is isolated and arduous, and the Army extracts full training value from it. A mountain and arctic warfare instructor from the Royal Marines is attached to each detachment during their tour. (One of them, to the delight of the soldiers, was called Sergeant Barnacle.) Once a month a ship arrives to resupply them, and every fortnight a Hercules drops fresh rations and mail into Cumberland Bay, where a Rigid Raider boat waits to retrieve them.

The only other body of infantry in the South Atlantic is the part-time Falklands Islands Defence Force, based in Port Stanley. Its enthusiasm and strength tend to fluctuate, mainly according to the threat from Argentina. The weather does not affect attendance in the way someone fresh to the islands might expect. 'If the weather's good,' explained the full-time adjutant, 'they dig their peat. If it's filthy, they go soldiering.'

British Forces Falkland Islands are perhaps of greatest interest because they represented the first real attempt to put 'jointery' into routine practice. The theory of jointery demands official enthusiasm, whatever the private feelings of the speaker. 'We like to see ourselves as a sort of fourth Service,' said an officer on the operations side. 'We've had hiccups and a lack of understanding,' said a senior officer, 'but never any problems at the coalface.' He then went on to acknowledge that there was a certain unevenness in commitment to 'purple' principles amongst the Services. 'The Navy is the most reluctant to give command of its ships to an outsider.' And 'the Army is the only one prepared to give full command, because it's used to units and sub-units being transferred back and forth.'

But inter-service feelings are deeply instinctual, almost atavistic. RAF dominance in the Falklands is resented. 'The joke down there', a naval officer had said, 'is that the people who did nothing in the war have taken it over.' RAF officers tacitly acknowledge their exclusion from the band of brothers on this latterday feast of Crispin. 'The Falklands conflict', said an air marshal, 'brought together the Army and Navy – who rarely meet – in mutual respect.' Yet the RAF somehow manages to provoke a degree of dislike amongst the other two Services which, for an outsider, is often hard to comprehend.

Whatever their capbadge, and in spite of a widespread professional respect for RAF pilots, Army officers object most to sharing a mess with the RAF. 'RAF officers', said a sapper, 'are merely officers by virtue of the job they do. They have no idea of command.' The Army is horrified when RAF, and especially WRAF, officers, try to get on first-name terms with soldiers. 'The boys don't like it. They don't know where they are.' A captain, a former warrant officer, agreed. And, along with virtually all his Army colleagues, he felt the RAF-managed officers' mess was as characterless as a waiting-room. 'We've got a dining-in night coming up,' he said with a grimace, 'and I dread to think what that'll be like.'

On duty, these feelings are very properly repressed. 'Mismatch' is caused more by the different way of doing things. A REME captain commands the transport workshop (hard pressed because everyone flogs the life out of their Land Rovers) with both soldiers and RAF personnel. One found the RAF 'totally different'. Their senior NCOs, on average much older, were set in their ways, refused to delegate and went entirely by 'their magic book' with a checklist on every job. The result

291

was that everyone was working at different rhythms and speeds.

The Joint Communications Unit Falklands Islands, on the other hand, appears to work well, largely because its personnel have clearly defined tasks. Operating mostly within Service groups, they are all highly qualified and thus require little of the detailed supervision which causes inter-service tension. The only disagreement seems to be on the subject of radio voice procedure: the Army is clearly offended by the abuses of the other Services.

JCUFI, the most closely balanced of all tri-service organizations, with the Army just the largest, is commanded by an officer from the Royal Signals. He has automatic jurisdiction over his RAF personnel, because the Army's and the RAF's legal systems are virtually identical. The Navy's is so different that a naval officer has to be present when he awards punishment.

The different attitudes to discipline can be a major source of ill-feeling, as members of the Joint Service Provost and Security Unit soon find out. 'The law may be the same,' said a Royal Military Police warrant officer, 'but the interpretation is completely different.' A sapper captain who had served in the Falklands was still angry that one of his best NCOs 'was busted for doing a Moonie in front of a barmaid' and promptly left the Army. 'They [the RAF]', he explained, 'have remarkably well-behaved boys who aren't going to do that sort of thing.' Army officers, on the other hand, feel the very best they can hope for is 'no damage and no fighting'. A sapper major who served down there on a subsequent occasion also said: 'The RAF is totally inexperienced in dealing with soldiers . . . The RAF's a different animal because they don't have to fight the enemy.'

A truly 'purple' organization is impossible to envisage, even in non-combat areas. The amalgamation of the three medical services has been discussed for a number of years. 'But I honestly don't believe it'll ever happen,' said a major in the Royal Army Medical Corps. 'If you worked here and experienced the difference between the way the RAF does things and the way we do things, you'd be certain it'd never happen. They could never even decide what colour the uniform would be.' Amalgamation had been tried in the Canadian forces 'and morale went rock bottom'.

And yet, as everyone agrees, when decks are cleared for action, the three Services generally work well together. 'If only', said the air marshal, 'we had the administrative and support programmes to go with it.' But his wish is unlikely to be granted in the immediate future. As a staff officer remarked, to persuade the three Services to co-ordinate their systems would be far more difficult than getting the British to drive on the other side of the road.

Off-duty life in the Falklands is limited in time as well as choice. Everyone works a six-day week during the tour. When work finishes at five, servicemen trudge back to the accommodation complex, which early on was dubbed the Death Star. Once they've eaten and 'done their dhobi' for the next day, they can write a bluey (a free forces aerogramme) home, or telephone via satellite if the need to speak to their wife or girlfriend seems greater than the considerable cost.

The recreational facilities are as good as can be expected, especially for sports. The 'beasties', the fitness fanatics, have all they need in the gyms. But for many the lethargy of video and bar is easy to slip into. Warnings from the senior medical officer seem to have little effect. Beer alone is consumed at the rate of over 4,000 cans a night in what passes for a social life.

Not surprisingly, the sixty-odd servicewomen find themselves very popular. They 'get spoilt rotten', invited on ships and helicopter rides, whenever there are spare places. But in the confines of Mount Pleasant they have to learn quickly to back out rapidly at the first sign of trouble. Trouble is inevitable in such an artificial environment, and short of posting down many times more servicewomen it is hard to see jealousies not flaring.

Relations between servicemen and the wives or daughters of Falkland Islanders, rare enough in any event, can prove even more problematical.

At one stage, when the Mount Pleasant complex was nearing completion, a consortium of Hong Kong Chinese investigated the possibility of floating brothels moored off the coast. One officer recounted with amused amazement how he had been invited out to dinner in Hong Kong by one of these millionaires, then offered a large 'commission' if he put them in touch with the general who could guarantee that servicemen would always be allowed access. As politely as possible, and trying not to sound too pompous, he explained that really the British Army didn't work that way, and generals simply couldn't be bought.

In accordance with the bracing formula of the cold shower, the only real satisfaction to be had in the Falklands is to escape the atmosphere of 'the open prison' for the brilliant clean air outside. 'You mustn't let them fester in this place,' said one officer. 'You've got to get them out into the country in their free time, even if it means making yourself unpopular.' For those who do make the effort to 'bimble' (hike) with their 'bimble-box' (packed lunch), there is superb fishing, and a fascinating variety of wildlife. (The Rockhopper penguins look just like a Scarfe cartoon of Denis Healey.) For the festerers, there is only the 'chuff-chart', ticking off 'days to do' until the farewell round of 'gozome' parties, and finally the glorious moment when Timmy the Tristar takes off and a cheer goes up like on the last morning of term.

The roulement system on which the Ministry of Defence has come to depend to garrison these faraway places now dominates Army life. Originally an emergency procedure for the reinforcement of Northern Ireland, it became institutionalized almost without anyone noticing. (The British seem to turn improvisation into a habit faster than most nations.)

The roulement system has not only endured, it has

even proliferated owing to its advantages. It saves the considerable expense of moving and housing families overseas. In certain cases, such as armoured regiments taking turns in Cyprus, it provides a much-needed break from routine in Germany. And troops passing through Belize give the impression that the Army can still offer some exotic postings.

The increase in the length of roulement tours from just over four months to six months has been more economical in time – Northern Ireland training is better amortized – and has reduced disruption, since fewer battalions and field squadrons will need to move in a year. Yet the burden of the extended time away will be borne by service wives, not by the Army.

That this change coincided with suggestions from the money men in Whitehall that soldiers in Northern Ireland and the Falklands should pay messing and accommodation charges, hitherto exempted in operational theatres, was unfortunate to say the least. Officers were angry and baffled at such a lack of imagination when the Army was facing a manpower crisis. 'By all means increase the tours to six months,' said an infantry colonel, 'but you've got to sell it.' Already senior NCOs on the logistic side have to be tempted to accept Falklands postings by 'carrot-dangling with accelerated promotion'. But there was nothing to tempt soldiers or officers.

Hong Kong, the last British-owned military base in the Far East, will be evacuated by 1997. (The possibility of serious unrest towards the end may of course demand the sudden reinforcement of the garrison on a temporary basis.) Even in the western hemisphere, not all the four commands have a certain future. The sovereign bases in Cyprus will be maintained, and some form of military presence will be kept in the Falklands. But now that the United States government has at last discovered that Nicaragua was never a Soviet beach-head, there is less pressure to maintain the Belize garrison at its present strength. And Gibraltar ceased to be a British Army garrison when the 3rd Battalion, the Royal Green Jackets left on 18 March 1991, handing over to the locally raised Gibraltar Regiment, which was little more than two hundred strong. This last decade of the century will see the final extinction of that empire over which the sun never set.

Part Four

ARMS AND THE CORPS

CHAPTER 19

The Regiment's Tribal System

Unless he is a fanatic, a man facing death in battle needs more than an abstract cause to defend. His own family is far away, so the regiment takes on its emotional focus. And a soldier's fear of shaming himself in its eyes can balance his fear of the enemy. This tribal instinct has always been the basis of the regimental system. 'On a number of occasions,' said General Sir John Chapple, 'it has proved to be a rather stronger bond, dare I say it, that King and Country, God and the Cause, creed and caste.'[1]

The regimental system has come to seem so quintessentially British that its Continental origins are easily forgotten. The word regiment, meaning a command of troops, was French, but the British version owed more to German, Dutch and Swedish models: the Emperor Maximilian's *Landsknechts*, the Dutch forces of Maurice of Nassau and the Swedish army of Gustavus Adolphus. The Scots adopted the organization for service at home long before the English, and the oldest regiment in the Army today, the Royal Scots, had been one of many bands of licensed Scottish mercenaries on the Continent. Pride in their longevity led to the nickname of 'Pontius Pilate's bodyguard'.

Regiments first came into being in England during the Civil War. Leaders such as Skippon, Astley and Goring, veterans of the Dutch wars and the Thirty Years War, formed their own units with distinctive uniforms. But, paradoxically or predictably, this revolution in military organization soon acquired some distinctly feudal characteristics after the restoration of 1660.

The Blues received their name because they wore the blue livery of their colonel, the Earl of Oxford. The

Green Howards had a similar origin. In a peculiarly British phenomenon, such traditions have endured into modern times. The capbadge of the Duke of Wellington's Regiment – 'a demi-lion rampant holding a forked pennon' – is the crest of the Iron Duke and of his descendant, their present colonel-in-chief. And the 24th Air Mobile Brigade, descended from the wartime 24th Guards Brigade, retains the phoenix of General 'Boy' Browning's family crest as its badge.

The tradition of the powerful patron still holds good. In Victorian times, regiments began to acquire a royal colonel-in-chief, which gave them influence at court. But, after the death of George V, the Palace intervened little in serious military affairs, and the colonel-in-chief retained only a symbolic value. Now, the principal lobbyist is the colonel of the regiment or, in the case of large regiments and corps, the colonel commandant. 'When something goes wrong,' said a senior infantry general, 'he goes in to bat for the regiment.' Whether a retired or serving officer, he will either work through the relevant arms director (the Director of Infantry or the Director Royal Armoured Corps) or speak to senior generals if he has the right contacts. The patronage principle even extends to sport. Field Marshal Lord Carver records in his memoirs that 'I was asked to assume two honorary posts, admiral of the Army Sailing Association and president of the Army Lawn Tennis Association. I did not feel qualified for either, but realized that both associations wanted influence in high places, and was delighted to accept.'[2]

The colonel of the regiment is often the most senior serving officer the regiment has produced, or a distinguished one who has recently retired. A small corps, unable to produce an officer higher than a brigadier from its own ranks, will often ask a general with the promise of four-star rank to become its colonel commandant. 'It is a very important protection', said a senior officer in one small corps, 'to have an influential colonel commandant who believes in what you do.' Small corps seem to feel particularly vulnerable now that, under the new budgetary system, a theatre headquarters has much more control over their resources. And the control of funds, as the Army has finally discovered, is the control of power.

The colonel commandant determined to be more than a figurehead will take on the job with gusto. Before he retired, General Sir Michael Gow had a reputation for fighting the Intelligence Corps' corner even more energetically than that of his old regiment, the Scots Guards, and his lobbying helped them achieve the status of a combat arm in 1985. For a serving colonel commandant, a conscientious attention to regimental matters can take up a large amount of his time, particularly if his regiment has three battalions.

The colonel of an infantry or cavalry regiment presides over a semi-official voluntary organization: a typically British hybrid which encompasses most of the responsibilities which a conscientious landowner would have fulfilled on behalf of his tenantry and the local community. In the military world that means heading the regimental association's fund-raising drives, either to help old comrades fallen on hard times or improve amenities within the regiment, presiding at dinners, the old comrades' reunion and the regiment's open day, which is usually on the anniversary of their major battle honour. (Luckily, campaigning in the eighteenth and nineteenth centuries was restricted to the summer months.) Details, such as ensuring that a wreath is sent on the regiment's behalf to the funeral of a former or serving member, fall to the regiment's home headquarters. Most of the colonel's figurehead duties are mainly retrospective by nature, but one responsibility, to interview and select young officer applicants, is vital for the future.

In spite of the genesis of the regiment and its hierarchical nature under a powerful patron, the conservatism of the system is as much psychological in origin as political. War, the epitome of unpredictability, with chaos restrained beneath the mask of discipline, inspires a profound yearning for permanence and order. Uniformity therefore provides reassurance. Regimental ritual can be both soothing and, in the aftermath of death or disaster, cathartic. No ceremony handles emotion more effectively than a military funeral. Even if it cannot make loss seem worthwhile, it at least bestows a value on it. Army psychiatrists are the first to recognize its importance in helping soldiers suffering from 'survivor guilt' come to terms with the death of comrades. All shared experience of this sort strengthens the collective identity, even if it is that of the group *contra mundum*.

The hierarchy of the British Army fully grasped the potency of tribal emblems only after the Battle of Waterloo. Badges, ciphers and insignia proliferated, at first engraved on the regimental silver, and later reproduced on everything from an officer's hunt buttons to enamel and diamond brooches for his wife, and then, in more modern times, on car badges, ties, wall-plaques and cufflinks. (The practice of having the regimental badge tattooed on an arm is not exclusively limited to the barrack room: one duke has the capbadge of his old regiment tattooed on his wrist under his watch.) The regimental crest was borrowed for brands of cigarettes, and the success of even its most meretricious imitation, the designer emblem, is an indication of a badge's appeal as a symbol of belonging.

The sense of belonging is not only the basis of the regiment's strength, but can shape the attitudes, behaviour and even dress of those who join. 'Nobody has laid down rules for brain-washing,' said a recently retired colonel, 'but it still happens. You're brainwashed from day one.' This form of brain-washing is mainly self-induced. Anyone who joins a regiment, and wants to be accepted, will mould himself to it. (In a way, this constitutes a reinforced reflection, since his choice of regiment is probably guided by his own image of himself.) Even when a regimental flag of non-conformity is waved, this is often misleading. 'In my regiment,' joked a colonel, 'if two officers were dressed the same, the junior would go home to change.' The very idea of being different bolsters a sense of common identity.

'I never realized', said a Guards general, 'quite how different regiments were until I became a brigade commander. I don't just mean the difference between an infantry regiment and a cavalry regiment, but the difference between two cavalry regiments.'

The contrasts are still noticeable, even if they are a lot less pronounced than in the past, when an officer with a good eye could often spot the regiment of a stranger out of uniform. Some regiments even seemed to produce a physical stereotype – willowy cavalry officers with flopping hair, slim Green Jackets with saturnine good looks, and large, fair-haired and ruddy-faced officers in the Scots Guards – but the exceptions almost certainly outnumbered such a thumbnail rule.

Clothes were a better guide. A waisted, full-skirted hacking jacket 'cut in the cavalry style with ticket pocket' was hard to miss, but to specify the regiment required a mass of minor clues, ranging from the jacket's state of repair to the visibility of a polka-dot handkerchief; while a Coldstreamer who had the cuff buttons of his grey suit arranged in two pairs, like those on his uniform, presented no challenge, and if a gunner could not be spotted by his dapper pinstripe his Labrador would give the game away.

In a more professional and homogeneous world, such anthropological amusements are almost, but not entirely, out of date. Yet some officers, and even some senior NCOs, still cling to the old idea that a regiment capable of organizing a good party is a regiment capable of performing well in the field. To claim that this is the basis on which horse gunners are considered the élite of the whole Royal Regiment of Artillery may be an exaggeration, but it is not that wide of the mark.

The social life of a regiment has long assumed great importance. And, as if to mark its family character, Christmas

Day is accorded the greatest ritual importance of all, and never more so than when the regiment is far from home.

All regiments have their own traditions. A fairly common one is for the officers and sergeants to bring the soldiers their morning tea in bed, and later on to serve them their Christmas dinner. But the most 'serious socializing' takes place between the officers' and sergeants' messes, usually after a football match between them. 'As always,' recorded the sergeants' mess notes in one regimental magazine, 'the officers' sports kit gave rise to much hilarity.'

When the sergeants come over to the officers' mess for drinks, the atmosphere may at first be a little self-conscious, but this seldom lasts long. One such invitation cost the officers of a Foot Guard battalion seventy-nine bottles of champagne. That was just the start of the proceedings. The officers were then invited back to the sergeants' mess for 'hanging the brick', a Household Division custom dear to the sergeants' mess. This ritual celebration was born when an RSM once gave permission for the bar to stay open so long as one of the sergeants held up a brick, at which he fastened it to a rafter.

The officers' mess sets the tone of a regiment; at least, that has always been the theory. Sergeants have privately disputed this, and they may well be justified, so much has life in the officers' mess changed. Younger officers show little enthusiasm for formal occasions, and the half-dozen dinner nights a year are greeted with groans. Yet ceremonial entertainment in the mess is still minutely laid down, especially if the commanding officer is a 'stickler for form'. Mess rules, set out in a booklet in each bedroom, proscribe and prescribe behaviour. There are strict limits on gambling, no 'treating' to drinks, no women in bedrooms, no track suits or combat kit to be worn in the mess after seven in the evening. They also define the ritual for dining-in nights, ladies' guest nights and regimental dinner nights.

Guest nights can form a useful part of a regiment's public

relations. Hospitality can be paid back – cavalry regiments who hunt locally will invite farmers and the master of the local hunt. Diplomacy can be exerted on local worthies such as the assistant chief constable, or influential staff officers at headquarters who have been helpful or need buttering up.

In some regiments, the mess rules govern every aspect and moment of the evening from the manner in which the colours are to be unfurled and displayed in the dining room to the duties of the buglers – Half-Hour Dress Call, Quarter-Hour Dress Call, Officers on Parade and Dinner Call – to the regimental band's selection of tunes – 'Roast Beef of Old England' is usually played on taking places for dinner – to the protocol for passing the port and toasting the Queen. In Guards and cavalry regiments such codification, particularly the need to remind officers of the direction in which port should be passed, is considered unnecessary, if not *infra dig*. Perhaps even more than the rest of the Army, the cavalry has relished the richness of its traditions without taking them too seriously.

There is a host of different customs and petty snobberies surrounding the loyal toast. Some regiments have been permitted by a sovereign to drink the loyal toast sitting down, usually through some maritime connection, because if officers staggered to their feet at the end of dinner on a ship of the line they risked striking their heads on beams and rendering themselves even more insensible. (The officers of one regiment managed to convince many people that their tradition was to drink it with one foot on the table.) Others have been absolved from the practice altogether because of royal favour in the past, in several cases for having proved their loyalty to the Hanoverian cause. In some, the right to add 'God bless her' was established, rather pompously, as the prerogative of field officers.

Although such dinners are much less frequent than in the past, junior officers begrudge the cost, which will be added to their monthly mess bill. They would much prefer to spend the money on a dance. Their other *bête noire*, although for different reasons, is the curry lunch.

To foster community life, many headquarters and regiments, above all in Germany, organize a curry lunch one Sunday a month, often after a church parade. This rather stilted attempt to bring together the 'married patch' and those who live in the mess often results in younger officers discovering that they have something terribly important to do that day. They much prefer their own version of informal entertainment, which in Germany usually consists of a *Kellerbar* evening during the week. The *Kellerbar* is a converted room in the basement of the mess incongruously decorated with Tudor beams and horse brasses – in fact very like their own soldiers' company or squadron bars. There they can invite a girlfriend for a fork supper – probably curry again, perhaps even the leftovers of the one avoided on Sunday – and relax in an evening of banter and beer drinking. Apart from a greater discussion of 'shop', particularly technical advances, the level of conversation and sense of humour seems to have progressed little over the years: 'sex, sex, and more sex', as a female assistant adjutant put it with the resigned good humour essential to her position.

It is in England that the change in mess life is most apparent. A university careers adviser visiting the regular commissions board at Leighton House, Westbury, looked round in wonder at the fine Regency rooms. Although blighted by the colour fixations of the Property Services Agency, it remains a handsome place. He remarked that it was amazing how officers still managed to live in the country-house style of an earlier generation. The officer with him tried to explain in a rather defensive manner how so much had in fact changed. Nowadays they did their own washing, and all that, and in any case they needed somewhere pleasant to come back to from exercises – and, after all, there had to be a few perks to compensate for the low pay. Instead, he should have pointed out that to have such a grand mess was now extremely rare.

Whatever the style of building, whether the Edwardian red-brick variety with high ceilings, the Hore-Belisha neo-Georgian block of the 1930s or the Poulson concrete box, the decoration and furniture inside have been standardized. Pale wood veneers, modernist chandeliers, orange carpets and loose-woven curtains make them look like badly modernized hotels of twenty-five years ago. Only a mess lucky enough to have some of its own furniture or wise enough to hang on to the old pattern can escape its dismal mediocrity.

Pale-framed paintings of tanks and helicopters by artists such as Terence Cuneo and David Shepheard and a corridor lined with group photographs of departed faces only accentuate the impression of anonymity. In comparison with the older regiments with their portraits and battle scenes with richly coloured uniforms, many ante-rooms, especially those of headquarters and depot messes, seem more like military versions of a Midlands country club. After meals there is little sound save the clink of coffee spoons as the older officers leaf through magazines and military reviews. The young ones are probably watching a lunch-time soap opera, such as *Neighbours*, in the television room, which in the old days housed a billiard table.

Comparisons with the Edwardian nursery are no longer apt now that the children want to flee the nest as soon as their commanding officer will allow them to live out. Some of their rooms, ironically, have been taken by middle-aged majors who live in during the week and commute home to their wives and families on Friday afternoon. At weekends, the orderly officer will probably be on his own. Rather than dine in solitary grandeur, he will take his plate through and watch television.

The generation gap which has opened up does not only apply to the mess. At one point during a discussion, a cavalry colonel confidently asserted that one of the great advantages of the regimental system was that 'a disgruntled officer would remain in his regiment out of loyalty to it'. Two captains, one cavalry, one Royal Tank

Regiment, replied with equal conviction that, although almost certainly true in the past, this was no longer the case. The colonel and the other senior officers present were clearly surprised. Everyone, however, agreed on one thing. The regimental system was 'a very positive factor in recruitment'.

Senior officers from the combat arms are often the first to depict their organizations in tribal terms. 'The Army is a collection of semi-nomadic tribes,' said a gunner brigadier. A cavalry general spoke of the different combat arms as collections of wigwams round a totem pole which they spent their time polishing.

Few see any chance of the system of tribes and confederations of tribes changing, for the moment at least. 'You can't change the history of the British Army,' said a gunner commanding officer, 'and therefore you can't change its federal structure.' Later the same day, he returned to this subject, which seems to fascinate officers more than any other: 'There's no such thing as the British Army . . . That's why there could never be a coup in this country. Can you imagine the Grenadier Guards and the Royal Corps of Transport going in together?'

The anti-traditionalist professionals feel that the regimental system cannot retain its grip for much longer. It will disappear, or change out of recognition once their generation has worked its way to the top. Some feel even this may be too long for the Army's good.

'We live on tradition,' said a REME officer. 'If we don't curb it the Army will fall apart.' Many argue that the obsession with capbadges and regiments is a peacetime luxury and that 'a war soon shakes all that up'. In the Second World War, a sapper colonel pointed out, replacements were allocated at random. A colonel in the ordnance believed that 'jointery is hastening the end of the regimental system, because the Army just cannot form a common front' against the Navy and RAF. A sapper major said that the regimental system was 'too concerned with self-preservation and internal bickering'. Since 1945, a senior infantry general pointed out, there had been 'a retreating perimeter, but the bastions have been the capbadges'. Although devoted to the welfare of his own regiment, he felt things had to change. 'It's been a nice system up to now,' he said, 'but it's not the only system.'

The vast majority of combat arm officers think that the regiment itself remains as valid for counter-revolutionary warfare and the land/air battle as it was in the days when the Gatling jammed and the colonel was dead. They only curse the paralysing effect of regimental loyalty at higher levels, its tentacles fastened on to almost every decision-making process, with rivalry, compromise and trade-offs maintaining the status quo.

The part played by the directors of the major combat arms as standard-bearers and lobbyists prompts some officers to argue that their influence must be neutralized. The appointment should be downgraded from major general to brigadier, and they would have responsibility only for technical training so they do not feel obliged 'to fight their corner'. Above all, they must be kept out of any dispute over resources, doctrine or operational requirements.

The director of one arm said that they must have two stars to be able to speak to their American counterparts on an equal basis – a brigadier would not get the same attention. But, perhaps more revealingly, another said that 'below two stars you don't have the clout to influence things'. He then admitted that 'when you're on the General Staff, arms directors are a bit of an embuggerance'. During his tenure as Commander-in-Chief UK Land Forces, General Sir Frank Kitson swept the arms directors out of Wilton, an event depicted almost in terms of Christ chasing the money lenders from the temple. But little seemed to change as a result.

The most acute threat to the system has not come from any Options for Change or Defence Review proposals, but from the manning crisis which sapped the morale of many regiments and from the change in social attitudes.

The infantry's difficulties are made worse by different roles requiring different sizes of battalion – establishments can vary from 50 officers and 700 men down to 34 officers and 600 men. But for most regiments such figures became purely theoretical by 1990, particularly when those away on courses or on leave were taken into account. Northern Ireland has always been an obvious priority, and the humiliation of having to borrow platoons, or even companies, to get anywhere near establishment strength became fairly routine. Whether in Northen Ireland or the Gulf, this unsatisfactory and supposedly temporary solution of the 'patchwork regiment' creates an enormous administrative burden. It also dilutes a regiment's identity still further without resolving the essential inflexibility of the system.

The cavalry, although not racked by changing commitments, is vulnerable in a different way. The Nato-assigned armoured regiment with an establishment of about 50 officers and 400 soldiers is smaller than an infantry battalion, but a shortfall of 75 men, an insignificant figure by present infantry standards, basically means the equivalent of a sabre squadron unmanned. Any extra commitments only overtax a weakened base, and a downward spiral begins. If decisions on Options for Change are delayed or fudged, and 'overstretch' continues, then infantry and armour will have to change their system of manning and deployment. Otherwise a number of regiments will be irreparably damaged.

The obvious course of cutting or amalgamating regiments to bring the survivors up to strength may have an arithmetical logic, and work in the short term, but it will not resolve the more complex problems.

In almost every respect, the regimental system is a reactionary force when change is most needed. And, however much one sympathizes with the reluctance to become a fully owned (a regimental loyalist would say fully cloned) subsidiary of British Army plc, a tribal patriarchy cannot keep step either with the needs of the organization as a whole or with contemporary civilian society. 'If the regimental system does not adjust to change,' said Colonel Gaffney, the author of the report on Army wives, 'then it will destroy itself.'

The regiment was bound to come under severe strain once officers and soldiers began to accord civilian priorities to family life. And when certain vital aspects have gone, such as the myths and the traditions, and, most important of all, the taste for such things, then it all begins to unravel.

The regimental system 'is a priceless asset', said General Sir John Chapple, 'and not one to be lightly cast aside.'[3] But the threats to it have little to do with operational considerations. They are administrative, economic and, above all, social. So great has been the change in attitudes over the last few years that the system is unlikely to survive in its present form. This stems not so much from the greatly decreased respect for tradition as from a soldier's growing reluctance to put his wife and children second. The real family has at last become more important than its military substitute.

CHAPTER 20

Queen and Army

The Queen's position as head of the armed forces is peculiar, if not ambiguous. While 'effective command, control and deployment are exercised ultimately by the Ministry of Defence . . . the loyalty of the armed forces is owed to the Monarch'.[1]

Many might dismiss this formula as one of those polite constitutional fictions so dear to the heart of traditional Britain, but such scepticism greatly underestimates its importance. Of all the institutions of British government, the Foreign Office and the three Services are the most conscious of the royal seal of legitimacy. The police, whose genesis was political, rather than royal, has never been imbued with class mystique. This may in part explain why attempts to create an office corps along military lines have always been resisted.

Of the three Services, the Army takes its links with the royal family the most seriously. It is a feeling which certainly seems to be reciprocated.

Most British regiments have a member of the royal family as their colonel-in-chief, thus reconfirming the monarchy as the pinnacle of the regimental system.[2] The only non-royal to hold such an appointment is the present Duke of Wellington, colonel-in-chief of the Duke of Wellington's Regiment. Several regiments have foreign monarchs. Queen Margarethe of Denmark and Princess Juliana of the Netherlands are allied colonels-in-chief of the Queen's Regiment, the Grand Duke of Luxembourg is colonel of the Irish Guards and the late King Olav of Norway, colonel-in-chief of the Green Howards, presented his regiment with new colours on its tercentenary in 1989.

In the days of Queen Victoria's genetic hegemony, the appointment was often conferred on members of the 'cousinage'. The Kaiser was colonel-in-chief of the Royal Dragoons, the Tsar of the Royal Scots Greys, and the vulpine features of his son, 'Little Willie', remained instantly recognizable in spite of an 11th Hussar uniform. King Alfonso XIII of Spain became colonel-in-chief of the 16th Lancers and officers from that regiment helped rescue him and Queen Ena after a bomb blasted their coach during his coronation in 1906. His influence still lingers in one of those morsels of tradition which the British so adore. On his first visit, someone spotted in advance that the cross-strap of his Sam Browne was on back to front, and rushed ahead to warn the regiment drawn up on parade. The commanding officer promptly ordered all officers to reverse theirs quickly, and to this day officers in the 16th/5th Lancers wear the cross-strap back to front.

Since the Second World War, the links have continued in a rather different way, with foreign royalty, mostly of the exiled variety, in British uniforms as subalterns, not colonels-in-chief. In the latter part of the 1960s Crown Prince Alexander of Yugoslavia served with the 16th/5th Lancers and Prince Nicholas of Prussia with the Royal Scots Greys. (The influx of officers bearing such un-Scottish titles as Preussen, Frankenstein and Westenholz led to the regiment being dubbed the Royal Central European Greys.) More recent years have seen Prince Paul of Greece in the Royal Scots Dragoon Guards (the amalgamation of the 3rd Carbineers and the Greys) and, in the Coldstream, Prince Alois of Liechtenstein – whose word of command in a strong German accent sounded so strange to the guardsmen.

British princes abstaining from the Royal Navy have joined line cavalry regiments. And, out of uniform, there are other, usually equestrian, connections between the royal family and the Army. For a number of years the Prince of Wales, like his father and Lord Mountbatten, has played polo at Windsor with the Guards Polo Club. The Princess Royal, who married an officer from the Queen's Dragoon Guards and became colonel-in-chief of the 14th/20th Hussars, enjoys good cavalry sports such as eventing. Like her brother, the Prince of Wales, she even rode in the Grand Military Gold Cup at Sandown, the cavalry's favourite social event. But it is hard to see these links continuing in the same way. The younger members of the royal family have different tastes. They mix and live with a much wider group of contemporaries, preferring London to country pursuits. They too are part of the new civilian generation.

Although not officially prescribed, the duties of a colonel-in-chief are predictable. Whenever possible, he or she will receive a new commanding officer or colonel of the regiment; he will visit the regiment at fairly regular intervals, often to take the salute on the day of its foremost battle-honour; and every twenty-odd years, when the time comes round, he will present a new colour, standard or, in the case of cavalry, guidon.

The time the regiment spends in preparation for such visits might well be regarded as excessive. Never is there more truth in the old barrack joke 'If it moves, salute it; if it doesn't, whitewash it.' But the Army is loath to drop its perfectionism in such matters. Whether the visitor is to be greeted by quarter guards, lance guards, guards of honour or the whole regiment drawn up in review order, everything will be 'four-square' and immaculate. Only the families, craning to see as much as they can from the sidelines, are liable to spoil the RSM's geometrical precision.

The wives of officers and senior NCOs will have dressed up for the occasion, and their excitement is discreetly manifest. But amongst the young wives of junior ranks there is more often an air of curiosity, as if they were about to see a celebrity from the tabloids rather than the regiment's colonel-in-chief.

A royal visitor is at some point requested to sign the

visitors' book and join an immaculately aligned group photograph, first with members of the officers' mess and then of the sergeants' mess. A slight variation occurred on the visit of the Prince and Princess of Wales to the Special Air Service at Hereford. After witnessing a demonstration of close-quarters combat in the stage-set interior of 'the killing house', a formal group photograph was taken with the royal couple surrounded by the SAS teams in full gear.

A colonel-in-chief may also wish to be present on more sombre occasions. For example, the Duke of Kent, as Colonel-in-Chief of the Royal Regiment of Fusiliers, was at Brize Norton when the bodies of soldiers killed in the Gulf returned.

While the most senior regiments of cavalry and infantry provide ceremonial guards, the corps provide services to the royal family. On almost every great occasion, some part of the Army is involved, from a warrant officer from the Army Catering Corps making a wedding cake to a band playing background music at a royal garden party.

The Royal Corps of Transport, an indirect descendant of the royal wagon train, provides the Queen's Baggage Train in the highly polished vehicles of 20 Squadron RCT. And the Royal Signals provides the Queen's despatch-rider, a lance corporal based at Chelsea Barracks and part of 10 Signal Regiment. His busiest time comes during the visit of a head of state, when he is at the disposal of the Master of the Household, delivering letters, parcels and invitations between the Palace and embassies. The last despatch-rider left in the British Army, he is usually a former member of the White Helmets display team.[3]

The infantry too provides extracurricular services. The Queen's Guard at Balmoral, a company from the public duties battalion at Edinburgh Castle, helps exercise the deerstalking ponies and has been known to act as beaters for grouse drives. There are colourful, but no doubt dated, stories of platoons marking time in the heather

315

as a sergeant major tried to execute a right wheel with perfect dressing.

The royal institutions and ceremonial bodyguards dominated by former Army officers are firmly based in historical tradition. They include the Military Knights of Windsor (instituted in 1348), the Queen's Body Guard of the Yeomen of the Guard (1485) and Her Majesty's Body Guard of the Honourable Corps of Gentlemen at Arms (established 1509). The Queen's Body Guard for Scotland, the Royal Company of Archers (organized 1676, reconstituted 1703), might better be described as an annual gathering of grandees, since military service would appear incidental more than essential. Rank in the strict sense of the term plays little part: George Younger, even when Secretary of State for Defence, was one of its most junior members.

Army appointments to the Royal Household range from the purely honorary to the more active. Amongst the former are Aide de Camp General to the Queen, an additional honour for a four-star general; honorary chaplains, including the Chaplain-General; honorary physicians and surgeons from the most senior ranks of the Army's medical services; and even an honorary veterinary surgeon to the Queen. The more active appointments, such as equerries of varying degree, are held by retired and serving officers, usually from the Household Division.

The oldest military posts – Gold Stick and Silver Stick in Waiting – date back to the reign of Charles II and Titus Oates's spurious allegations of Catholic plots. Today, the office of Gold Stick in Waiting alternates between the Colonel of the Life Guards and the Colonel of the Blues – now the Blues and Royals. These two colonelcies are honorary appointments and not restricted to former members of the regiment. Lord Mountbatten, in his days as 'Colonel Dicky', so adored his full dress Life Guards uniform that he took every opportunity 'to wear it in'.

There is only one Silver Stick: the commander of the Household Cavalry, a full colonel who occupies an office in Horse Guards just beneath that of the GOC London District. He enjoys a curious position in constitutional terms. He is a member of the Household, in theory at least he has direct access to the Queen, and one of his duties is to be on the balcony of St James's Palace for the proclamation of a new sovereign. Yet, as a serving officer, he is part of a chain of command which stretches up via the GOC to headquarters UK Land Forces and ultimately the Secretary of State for Defence.

Silver Stick's infantry counterpart is known as the Colonel Foot Guards (the former Field Officer in Brigade Waiting). Like most Foot Guards who have to appear mounted on the Queen's Birthday Parade, he is liable to be haunted by the fear of joining the empty saddle club, a distinction awarded to those exceptional unfortunates who 'unintentionally dismount' in front of the crowds and the television cameras.

The Earl Marshal, the Duke of Norfolk, is responsible for state funerals, coronations and the state opening of Parliament. All other occasions, such as state visits and the Garter ceremony, are organized by the Lord Chamberlain's office, which requests the relevant escorts and guards of honour from Silver Stick or the Colonel Foot Guards. Their ceremonial bible for such events is *Her Majesty's Regulations for the Household Division*.

The Household Division consists of the two regiments of Household Cavalry – the Life Guards and the Blues and Royals – and the five regiments of Foot Guards. Its motto set in a Garter Star is *Septem Juncta in Uno* – seven joined in one. (With masonic undertones, this insignia is known as 'the ever open eye'. Freemasonry has a long tradition in the Guards, the only part of the Army to have two lodges: the Household Division Lodge for officers, and the Comrades' Lodge for senior NCOs and warrant officers.)

The Household Cavalry enjoys many advantages, of which the first is a considerable degree of independence. As part of the Household Division, it does not belong to the Royal Armoured Corps, although its soldiers are trained at Catterick after Pirbright, while its officers go to Bovington. And unlike line cavalry regiments (dragoon guards, hussars and lancers) which face very long tours in Germany, the Life Guards and the Blues and Royals change round every five years. Not only do they change places, they also change roles. For example, in the spring of 1990 the Blues and Royals became the armoured recce regiment at Windsor and the Life Guards took over their Challenger tanks in Germany (as well as the Weser Vale Hunt, an idiosyncratic export reminiscent of the Peninsular War).

Further variety is provided by the Household Cavalry Mounted Regiment based at Knightsbridge Barracks. This offers the chance of judicious trickle-posting when required: a soldier with family problems in Germany can always be sent back to London.

Most troopers who pass out of Pirbright start with the mounted regiment. The riding master, with the 1937 edition of *The Army Manual of Horsemastership* as his bible, will make sure that they can handle and look after their Irish blacks better than any driver and vehicle. The training is far more arduous than imagined by sceptics in other parts of the Army. After twenty weeks, a young soldier who has never sat on a horse before will be ready for the Queen's Life Guard at Whitehall.

The Household Cavalry Mounted Regiment consists of a headquarters and a sabre squadron from each of the two parent regiments. For a trooper, life at Knightsbridge consists of long hours and few free weekends, because 'horses can't look after themselves'. Preparing horse, tack and uniform for Queen's Life Guard takes at least four hours. (Unlike the Foot Guards, the Household Cavalry has appreciated that the new generation is not prepared to put up with hours of bull, and that plastic alternatives must be found.) When soldiers do have time off, they supplement their pay with a wide variety of moonlighting jobs, such as serving at private parties. London produces its own black economy subculture.

Life in the armoured recce regiment at Windsor could hardly be more different. As part of the 5th Airborne Brigade it is tasked for out-of-area operations; it was in this role that two troops of the Blues and Royals saw action in the Falklands. At least forty members of the regiment are para-trained, and one troop is permanently allocated as air-droppable. (They wear the maroon beret in the field but revert to regimental headgear on returning to barracks, a detail typical of the Household Division). Like armoured corps regiments, a squadron is sent off to the UN Force in Cyprus every other year for a six-month tour and a pair of troops do a tour of similar length in Belize.

All officer applicants for the Household Cavalry are first interviewed by Silver Stick at Horse Guards. They are then sent down to Windsor for a whole day to whichever regiment is there.

A generation or so ago Household Cavalry officers had a reputation as the richest in the Army without many redeeming features. In the early 1960s, my eldest brother, meeting a freshly commissioned young officer of the Blues whom he knew a little, asked how he was enjoying the Army, only to receive the reply: 'Er, Household Cavalry, actually.' As one of their senior officers acknowledged, 'It wasn't very attractive.' Things started to change, he believed, when the Blues, the Royal Horse Guards, amalgamated with the Royal Dragoons. Although the Royals inevitably lost their identity, changing from line cavalry to the Household Division they brought in fresh attitudes and a good dose of professionalism.

The selection system is far more meritocratic than before: a Welbexian (normally destined only for the technical corps) was accepted, an event hard to imagine twenty years ago. No longer is a private income essential, at least not for the armoured and armoured recce regiments. From half to two-thirds now live on their pay. Life in London with the Mounted Regiment is much more expensive, and officers with a penchant for polo and other equestrian sports inevitably gravitate towards mounted duties.

Because of its very considerable advantages, the Household Cavalry is in a position to turn away applicants. (They claim with nonchalant satisfaction that most of their rejects then join the Foot Guards, but the Foot Guards deny this hotly.) With around sixty subalterns all told, more than a full complement, they can 'spare enough to send them off to the SAS and on loan service'.

The eight battalions of Foot Guards were designated the Guards Division in the reorganization of 1968. The five regiments are fiercely conscious of their identities and traditions, yet theirs is the most cohesive infantry organization in the Army. This, it might be said, is not hard, considering that some of the others are very artificial groupings. But with the Guards Division's strong identity and *esprit de corps* comes a marked sense of difference, and also an introspective, and occasionally touchy, reaction to the way others see them. They convince themselves that the rest of the Army is jealous of their role as the sovereign's personal troops, and only with great reluctance will they admit that their hauteur and periodic attempts at empire-building might well be seen as provocative.

In an unashamedly patriarchal fashion, they are proud of being family regiments, both in the officers' and sergeants' messes. The Welsh Guards, with more justification than most, pride themselves on the numbers of sons, brothers and nephews in the regiment. As in other Welsh regiments, so many soldiers have the same name that they operate a number system where the last two digits of their service number become prefixed like a double-barrelled name, 71 Williams, 84 Jones, 97 Evans. There are said to be enough to be used in an improvised radio code for grid references, for example: 'Move to grid: Williams the provo sergeant, Jones the storeman, Evans the driver.'

The Guards are rigid in many ways and surprisingly

pragmatic in others. They demonstrate a curious combination of commercial enterprise and paternalism. They augment Household Division funds by selling books by mail order, as well as records of their bands and souvenirs; there is even a Guards wine club. Former soldiers can apply to the Household Division Employment Agency. In his report, Colonel Gaffney praised the Coldstream for their positive attitude to soldiers' families in Hong Kong, and underlined the advantage of the Guards having a home base area. As 'the most effective in-fighters' in the whole confederation of 'warring tribes', the Guards also lobby for their men, both by regular means and shameless string-pulling. (According to Sir James Spooner, a former managing director of the Naafi, the Guards and the gunners were the best at obtaining extra facilities for their men.) But whether the Guards system will thrive or buckle in a recruiting climate which could hardly appear more unfavourable to their beliefs in discipline and turn-out is a subject for emotive debate. Household Division conservatism is rooted in the sergeants' mess and reflected in the officers' mess. 'Our system has got more chance of surviving because we are moulded and steeped in tradition,' said a regimental sergeant major. 'If we forget our past, and progress too quickly, then we are lost.'

Officers argue that things have moved. 'We shift gently,' said one commanding officer. 'When I was a subaltern we never walked out of that gate [Wellington Barracks] without a stiff collar and bowler hat . . . We'd never think of having a dinner party unless it was black tie.' Shocked by the recent decline in ethics in society at large, and fearing that the Army was beginning to be contaminated by careerism and dishonesty, he believed very strongly that the Guards must hold on to their moral values as a beacon for those outside to look up to.

Appearance is all-important to the Household Division's geometrical eye. Guards recruiting sergeants try to divert tall soldiers to the Household Division – one cannot help thinking of the agents of King Frederick William of Prussia scouring the countryside for his Potsdam regiment. In the Grenadiers the tallest are posted to the Queen's Company in the 1st Battalion – all the men are over six foot two and the officers over six foot – while in the Welsh Guards they go to the Prince of Wales's Company. Such giants look very impressive on parade when 'soldiering in scarlet', but the system does not adapt well to 'soldiering in green'. The sight of a section of the Queen's Company crammed into the back of an infantry fighting vehicle in Germany inspires more pity than admiration. Applicants who wear glasses are not accepted, nor are any with visible tattoos. And the reluctance of officers to accept black recruits had more to do with breaking a line of white faces on parade than with racial prejudice. Ironically, when negro servants were fashionable in Regency times, the Household regiments employed black kettledrummers.

An RSM remarked, with Jesuitical implications, that if a guardsman 'gets through his first year we can do something with him'. Guardsmen themselves say that those who had 'joined straight out of school and known nothing else' are more likely to become 'regimental' and stay. Anyone who has had a taste of adult life in the outside world is liable to find the existence too claustrophobic and petty to take.

The discipline is harsher because Guards warrant officers suffer no hint of doubt about the rightness of their approach. 'We have a cut-and-dried easy solution,' said a company sergeant major. 'Black is black and white is white. If someone in another corps like the engineers or the pay corps gets drunk and smashes the place up, they sit the guy down and ask him about his problems. We don't. We slam him straight in jail.'

An image of arbitrary oppression would, however, be exaggerated. Much of the yelling and stamping and hair-raising threats while defaulters are lined up in the corridor for 'orders' forms no more than a ritual, and is viewed as such by all, except perhaps the terrorized recruit. The quick smirks or jokes when the company sergeant major turns his back do not suggest a downtrodden soldiery. But such performances, more reminiscent of a Victorian day school, hardly seem the best way to encourage responsibility. Even such incentives as a half-day off for three 'recommends' only reinforce the impression that a guardsman is not really considered an adult.

Officers say that anyone joining the Guards who doesn't like public duties has made a mistake. But a number of guardsmen claim that their first choice had been another capbadge. More surprisingly, officers claim that the guardsmen are of 'much higher quality and much more committed than ten years ago', yet almost in the next breath they admit that they are losing about a third of them every year. Battalions on public duties probably have the highest turnover in the Army. As fewer and fewer recruits come in, this rate of attrition puts the whole of the Guards system at risk.

A guardsman's only way out of such a restrictive life is upwards through promotion. 'I keep telling the younger ones,' said the same company sergeant major, 'you don't wait to be promoted, you go for it. It's the only way to get a pay rise.' The crude proposition – you won't be on the receiving end any more, you'll be the one dishing it out – seems to be an effective stimulus.

It is indeed a tough and unforgiving world, but that alone cannot explain why the Foot Guards represent the best NCO factory in the Army. (Although the best factory, they do not necessarily produce the best NCOs. An RSM from the Parachute Regiment argued convincingly that the system gave them tunnel-vision.)

Once a guardsman makes it to lance corporal, he will be scrutinized even more closely by warrant officers. The jump to lance sergeant is significant for all concerned. Although the equivalent of corporal in the rest of the Army, a lance sergeant joins the sergeants' mess. This weakens the corporals' mess considerably, but the Guards regard this early initiation into the sergeants' mess as a

323

great advantage. 'Their attitude to life changes,' said an RSM, 'and they mature a lot quicker as a result.' But he acknowledged that, with only a corporal's pay, the expense of sergeants' mess life is difficult for them and their families.

'A sergeants' mess in the Household Division', he went on to explain, 'would appear to be much more rigid than in other regiments. We never relax rank. Warrant officers are always called "sir". . . But everything is kept within the four walls. Any misbehaviour or indiscretion is never talked about outside. That would not happen in a line regiment.'

In other ways he thought a Guards mess more relaxed. Unlike some line regiments, extra duties were not handed out to sergeants who came in improperly dressed or who passed the port the wrong way. They were usually fined a round of drinks instead. Social life was very important. The highlight of the year, the Troop Ball, took place on the night of the Queen's Birthday Parade. More day-to-day events were organized on a company roster. For example they had games nights – darts and snooker matches – with the Metropolitan Police. (Throughout the Army these get-togethers provide a good opportunity to sort out any little disciplinary problems on an informal basis.) And each year a dinner is held for the Sergeants Past and Present Association: once a member of the Household Division, always a member.

Such fierce devotion to the regiment and its history is remarkable today, even in the British Army. Its outward display takes the form of every piece of Household Division paraphernalia that the regimental shop can provide: ties, cufflinks, wall plaques, ashtrays, keyrings and car badges. The other favourite memento is the group photograph. In an organization keen on this ritual, the Foot Guards stand out as obsessive. Every major event and course is commemorated, the officers seated in the centre of the front row flanked by warrant officers and senior NCOs, heads erect to see under the peak of their forage caps, knees apart in a regulation manner, and pace sticks held upright against the inside of the thigh. In scarlet tunics, they have to be photographed bare-headed. Nobody would be recognizable in bearskins, which would in any case obscure the faces of the row behind.

The sergeants' mess continues to see itself as the 'engine room of the battalion . . . it's where all the spadework and the organization is done, and it's where all the experience is'. The idea of officers as little more than elegant figureheads, only there to give the right order at the right moment, still seems to persist. Until only a few years ago commanding officers on most days would turn up at battalion headquarters at ten, hold orders, see some officers and the RSM, wander round and then disappear after lunch. The presence of officers in the afternoon was regarded as unnecessary, if not undesirable.

A major in the Royal Engineers who once had a Guards sergeant major as his CSM at a training regiment discovered this to his astonishment. He described how after a few weeks, this CSM marched into his office wearing his hat, a sign that something was wrong. The company sergeant major requested permission to speak his mind. 'I would very much like to know, sir, why you find fault with the way I'm running the company.' The major, taken aback, replied that he thought he did his job admirably. 'Then, why don't you trust me, sir?' The sapper major assured him that he trusted him completely. What on earth did he mean? 'Well, sir, you keep coming back to the company office in the afternoons.'

Today, few officers are allowed to slope off in the afternoons for polo or any other form of diversion. But, according to the adjutant of one battalion, the new approach makes senior NCOs uneasy because it represents 'a switch of power away from the sergeants' mess'.

The outward confidence, however, continues unabated. There is far greater glory in their eyes 'to be the regimental sergeant major of a Guards battalion than go off to be an officer elsewhere'. But the Household Division's self-importance does not always go down well with NCOs in the rest of the Army. The Foot Guard domination of the sergeants' mess at Sandhurst, and their cheerful disdain for the sensibilities of other regiments on the all-arms drill course at Pirbright, mean that whenever the Household Division slips on a banana skin a good deal of chortling can be heard elsewhere.

To an outsider, the Guards seem to have a slightly unreal quality. Whether justified or not, you get a strong sensation of having suddenly stepped backwards in time. In reply to a quivering salute of the sort rarely seen in the rest of the Army, a subaltern returns the compliment in absent-minded slow motion, saying 'Thank you very much.' And back at the mess he sprawls diagonally across a club armchair, ignoring the mass misbehaviour of terriers and spaniels. (At Pirbright, they created such chaos in depot headquarters as well as the mess that I wondered whether one was supposed to measure the discipline of a regiment in inverse proportion to that of its officer's dogs.)

To judge the validity of general opinion about different regiments is hard. The Grenadiers are often thought the most formal and stand-offish, yet they are one of the few left in the Army to harbour eccentrics. The Scots Guards appear a curious mixture of lairdery and meritocracy. The Irish Guards – the Micks – are known for having the wildest officers, and being the least stuffy regiment in the Household Division. (The Irish Guards, although one of the most undermanned battalions in the British Army, partly because it takes up to six months to clear each applicant, whether from the Irish Republic or the north, are rich in officers, so subalterns are sometimes loaned out.) Yet no sooner has one identified a characteristic than an exception to the rule appears. After a large, bovine and numbingly incurious officer has bored you with crashing banalities, you meet another whose intelligence makes it hard to imagine that they can inhabit the same world; after meeting a languid creature who would appear at a complete loss anywhere else, you encounter a type who has clearly served in the SAS. So by the time you realized that many of the subalterns drive Golf GTIs and have flats in Fulham, the temptation to stereotype has receded considerably. Once the complex variety beneath the uniform surface is understood, the success of the Foot Guards in a number of fields and the quality of many Household Division generals becomes much less surprising.

There are usually five public duties battalions stationed in and around London at Wellington Barracks, Chelsea Barracks, Hounslow, Pirbright and Caterham. This may seem a great deal but other commitments – a six-month unaccompanied tour in Northern Ireland or Belize, training in Kenya, or stand-by as Spearhead battalion – may take the figure down to three or even, on rare occasions, two battalions. Other 'green' commitments also intrude, such as Operation Tonnage, the anti-terrorist stand-by force for Heathrow. In spite of bleepers and platoons on instant stand-by to move, this is known in typical Foot Guard fashion as the Heathrow Picket, as if it were little more than a replacement for the Bank Picket (the Bank of England Guard, discontinued nearly twenty years ago).

If military commitments elsewhere have reduced the number of Foot Guard battalions available to two, then the General Officer Commanding London District will obtain a gunner regiment or line infantry battalion to share the guard-mounting roster. The Guards welcome the idea of other regiments on Queen's Guard, if only to convince the rest of the Army that 'public duties are not a swan, but *very* hard work'.

In Guards parlance, 'the Major General' can only mean one person: the General Officer Commanding London District and the Household Division. When not out inspecting his troops, he works at the Iron Duke's oval desk in the old levée room of Horse Guards, with a magnificent view over St James's Park. The Major General's Parade in April, the only occasion when the Household Cavalry canters past, officially opens the 'ceremonial season', but the Foot Guards will have already been practising for the Queen's Birthday Parade; it is a four-month programme. The other event which requires enormous preparation is known as 'Major General's', a terse phrase for the full-dress inspection of each regiment. It is the public duties version of the annual review of the unit. Every single soldier is inspected individually, including the small REME detachment whose members have probably not bulled boots since basic training. 'You can imagine that goes down like a lead balloon,' said a guardsman.

Undermanning has become serious. A battalion, already a company down on full establishment and with the equivalent of another half a company away on courses, finds it a 'permanent struggle to get the manpower' for all the guards and pickets.

Each rifle company is reinforced with a platoon from support company to make a duty team of just under 120 men and at least four officers. The duty team would then man Queen's Guard – Buckingham Palace and St James's Palace (known as Jimmy's) – and Tower Guard. But if the battalion is also responsible for Windsor Guard – one officer and thirty men if the Queen is present – and is on stand-by for Heathrow on top of providing its own barrack guard, then the roster rapidly becomes 'a snake-charmer's nightmare'. Guardsmen might be coming off duty in one place – two days' worth of two hours on, four hours off – and then go straight on to another. In theory they should do no more than three 24-hour guards in a week, but there are always unexpected extra duties.

In the spring, during the preparation for 'the Troop', senior NCOs with houses far from London may not see their wives for two or three months, while a married NCO in a London quarter gets up at a quarter to five, and is not home before eight at night. A subaltern acknowledged that in London 'the officers have a super time, but it's a killer for the soldiers'. (Officers have their uniform prepared for them by orderlies, and apart from parades they have to turn out only once in the night.)

'Nobody likes public duties,' a guardsman will say, except for the odd 'drill nut'. A recruit's romantic notions do not survive more than a few Queen's Guards. Guardsmen usually have to devote at least two or three hours each time to get their kit ready, working mostly on their boots 'to get them diamond'.

Officers, however, say that things have 'changed very subtly' and that 'unthinking discipline' has been reduced along with unnecessary bull. But sergeant majors vigorously deny that change has taken place. And any suggestion that the Household Division's manpower problems might be eased with plastic belts instead of buff is considered a contemptible compromise. 'If you start cutting back on standards for inspection,' a company sergeant major said forcefully, 'you start cheating.'

Whatever the pressures in London, soldiering in scarlet must not interfere with soldiering in green. Normal training with range days, and refresher courses for the mortar and anti-tank platoons, have to be kept up and basic fitness tests must be run. Battalions in London have only to remember 1982 and the shock when two battalions on public duties were chosen for the Falklands' task force.

It is also easy to forget the battalions serving elsewhere, whether on a six-month tour in Northern Ireland or the two battalions in Germany. But the Guards still strive to maintain a certain style amidst the roar and fumes of their Warrior infantry fighting vehicles. The 1st Battalion of the Grenadiers was honoured to be the first unit in the Army to receive them, and when the Queen's Company decided to name their Warriors after racehorses (a predecent established by the Guards Armoured Division in 1944) the commanding officer, Lieutenant Colonel Evelyn Webb-Carter, applied to Lord Carnarvon, the Queen's racing manager, for a list of appropriate names.

329

The Grenadiers, having blazed the way with Warrior, were deeply dismayed to find that when the 7th Armoured Brigade and then the 4th were detailed for the Gulf they were required to split up to supplement other armoured infantry battalions. In fact, there were no Household Division battalions or regiments in the 1st Armoured Division, only large fragments from the Grenadiers, a sabre squadron in Challenger tanks from the Life Guards, the 1st Battalion of the Coldstream guarding Iraqi prisoners and bandsmen from several Household Divisions bands in their medical role. For the Lord Mayor's Banquet in 1990, which proved to be Mrs Thatcher's swansong, there were no State trumpeters available because they were all away on a stretcher bearers' course.

Virtually the equivalent of a company of Grenadiers had reinforced the Staffords in 7th Armoured Brigade, the whole of the Queen's Company was attached en bloc to the Royal Scots and No. 2 Company to 3rd Battalion of the Royal Regiment of Fusiliers. To emphasize their identity, No. 2 Company flew their company flag with its crown and Tudor rose from company headquarters in the desert. One Grenadier recounted that for a visit by Mr Major before the war began in earnest the Grenadier company received orders to parade in helmets, not berets. But, when they arrived at the designated spot, they found to their intense resentment that, while they looked like anonymous infantrymen, the Fusiliers were wearing berets with their red and white hackles to ensure that the media focused on them. The Grenadiers, of course, allege that their khaki berets with the Household Division patch of blue, maroon, blue behind the flaming grenade would have attracted camera lenses away from the 'budgies'.

Although rivalry in the face of the world's press was without quarter, co-operation in the face of the enemy was assured. In the second of 7th Armoured Brigade's engagements, an Iraqi anti-tank grenade from

330

an RPG7 killed a private in the Staffords and went on to strike a Warrior, setting it on fire. Guardsman Darren Chant, a Grenadier in the vehicle, managed to drag out the commander and driver, and then to put out the flames.

CHAPTER 21

Infantry at the Double

The term 'line infantry' to denote regiments outside the Foot Guards gives a misleading impression of uniformity. The Parachute Regiment clearly stands apart in attitude as much as role, while the Light Infantry and Green Jackets, whose original purpose as scouts and skirmishers vanished long ago, still see themselves as different from county regiments. Over the last twenty-five years, however, many of the more idiosyncratic characteristics of different regiments have diminished greatly as a result of professional standardization. Yet nothing has had a greater effect on some regiments in the last few years than the depressing effect of manpower shortages. The infantry, representing just over a quarter of the Army's strength, suffered 35 per cent of the total outflow in 1990. This state of affairs produced the 'patchwork' battalion – a unit destined for a priority task such as Northern Ireland which had to be brought up to strength with men borrowed from all over the place.

The reorganization following the Healey Defence Review of 1968 reduced the infantry to fifty British and five Gurkha battalions. The Cameronians and the York and Lancaster Regiment were disbanded, and many others were amalgamated, or reformed in large regiments of three battalions. For example, the Northumberland Fusiliers, the Warwickshire Fusiliers, the Royal Fusiliers and the Lancashire Fusiliers were distilled down into the 1st, 2nd and 3rd Battalions of the Royal Regiment of Fusiliers.

To rationalize training, uniforms and administration even further, the infantry (with the exception of the Parachute Regiment and the Brigade of Gurkhas) was also regrouped in administrative divisions: the Guards

Division, the Scottish Division, the Queen's Division, the King's Division, the Prince of Wales's Division and the Light Division.

Fears of 'rationalization', a word which made the Army feel instinctively ill at ease, in fact proved justified. Regiments which lost their county identity have in general suffered the most. The Queen's Division found itself at a double disadvantage. Consisting of three reprocessed regiments of three battalions deprived of individual identities, its home areas cover the eastern side of the country, including East Anglia and the south-east, where recruiting has suffered the most over the last ten years. The Queen's Division's shortage of manpower represents over 40 per cent of the total for the whole infantry.

The Scottish Division, still the best recruited in the British Army, consists of three regular Lowland regiments and four Highland. Scottish regiments are notable for the way their character is defined not so much by the officers' or the sergeants' mess but by the Jocks themselves. Officers and sergeants alike always talk in terms of the Jocks' reaction to something. 'If the Jocks are bellyaching the whole time', said a major in the Royal Scots, 'then it's normal. If they're silent then I'm worried.' Dour they may be, when soaked to the skin and sitting around, but the old stories about a sudden transformation when there's the chance of a battle are true. Unfortunately, the Jock's other mark of fame remains his compulsive consumption of alcohol.

The Royal Scots, the third armoured infantry battalion to convert to the Warrior and part of 4th Armoured Brigade deployed in the Gulf, is the oldest regiment, as the First of Foot. This led to the unfair nickname of the Fleet of Foot after the surrender of Hong Kong in 1941. Less ancient Highland regiments call them the First and Worst. The soldiers prefer to call themselves the Royal Jocks. The Royal Scots are basically an Edinburgh and Lothian battalion, but, like the rest of the division, they are topped up with Glaswegians. In the Gulf, their commanding officer, Lieutenant Colonel Iain Johnstone, prepared them for war in Covenanter style with hymns and a stirring speech about their 358 years of history. His Jocks meanwhile had stocked up with St Andrew and Lion Rampant flags ready to place on captured enemy berms. A corporal asked about Iraq's 'élite' Republican Guard remarked, 'They won't feel so bloody élite when they hear the Royal Jocks are on their way.'[1]

The Royal Highland Fusiliers are Lowlanders in spite of their name, coming entirely from Glasgow and Ayrshire. They were created in the 1959 amalgamation of the Royal Scots Fusiliers and the Highland Light Infantry, one of the most controversial of its day. The HLI, known as Hell's Last Issue, were the Glaswegian half, and, perhaps predictably, they pride themselves on their street-fighting expertise. The King's Own Scottish Borderers, the third Lowland regiment, traditionally recruits from the whole width of the Borders. They and the Royal Highland Fusiliers served in the Gulf guarding 1st Armoured Division's prisoners.

The Black Watch, a Dundee and Tayside regiment, is still suspect in the eyes of its fellow Highland regiments. As a Hanoverian militia it was given seniority over them, and to this day it is known, perhaps unfairly, as a regiment for the sons of rather un-Scottish lairds, 'doing three years before taking over Daddy's estate', as a Lowland officer remarked. Highland battalions call it 'that fine old English regiment spoilt by a few Scotsmen'.

The Queen's Own Highlanders, the amalgamation of the Seaforths and Camerons, is the Black Watch's great rival and social equal. One Seaforth tradition they inherited is that of 'The 78th Walkaround' (the Seaforths were the 78th Highlanders), at which the most junior officer gets up after dinner and walks around the table followed by the next and the next and so on, in a dignified version of the conga. This practice was invented to free a commanding officer trapped at table by an unspeakably boring guest. The Queen's Own Highlanders also maintain the custom of an

officers' dancing parade before breakfast under the tuition
of the pipe major. The Jocks and NCOs, on the other hand,
are proud of the regiment's poacher reputation, which is
the best training for fieldcraft. Two-thirds of them come
from the Highlands, about a tenth, including a handful
of Gaelic-speakers, from the Islands, and nearly a fifth
from Glasgow. The 'Wegians' are a minority shamelessly
discriminated against. 'A Wegian'll never make RSM', say
senior NCOs with matter-of-fact good humour.

The Gordons appear the epitome of a solid and utterly
reliable Highland regiment. They have an engaging lack of
pretension at all levels. One young Jock described public
duties at Edinburgh Castle as 'two hours at a time of trying
to keep a straight face'. They too have their 'Wegians', but
spread them about: 'every platoon has a couple or so, so
you get no ghetto.' Over half the battalion comes from
within their Grampian recruiting area, and less than a dozen
from Shetland. The Gordons, centred on Aberdeen, were
inevitably the worst hit by the oil boom and, according to
the other Scottish regiments, never quite recovered from
it. But they insist that, contrary to mistaken reports in the
press in 1989, they are one of the best recruited.

The Argyll and Sutherland Highlanders, known by English regiments as the Agile and Bolton Wanderers, come
from the Campbell country of Strathclyde, which also gives
them the highest proportion of Glaswegians in a Highland
regiment. Their great enemies are the Queen's Own Highlanders, a vendetta which started after the death of an
Argyll in a fight. They are said never to have recovered from
the time they were reduced to company strength in 1968
and then reformed following a well-orchestrated campaign.

For the next Defence Review, Scottish regiments were
thought to be in a strong position. As well as having
the best recruited infantry battalions in the Army, the
large Scottish contingent in 1st Armoured Division and
the strength of national feeling was considered enough
to deter any politician.

*

The Queen's Division is, theoretically, one of the biggest in the Army, with three large regiments of three battalions each, but at the time of the Gulf war it was so under-strength that out of nine battalions it was virtually the equivalent of two battalions short. This made it the most vulnerable of all infantry divisions when regiments for amalgamation were chosen.

Recruits come to its depot at Bassingbourn in Hert-fordshire from as far apart as Eastbourne and Berwick-on-Tweed. More than any other division, its recruiting has suffered disastrously. This is partly because its main catchment areas covers the most prosperous parts of the country, London, the South-east and East Anglia, and partly because the 1968 reorganization pushed together some very dissimilar regiments and made them appear amorphous.

The Queen's Regiment is senior to the Fusiliers and Royal Anglians, because its three battalions are descended from the Queen's Royal Regiment (West Surrey), the old Second of Foot, and the Buffs, the Third of Foot, as well as all the other Surrey, Kent, Sussex and Middlesex regiments. The officers of the 2nd Battalion of the Queen's, descendants of the Buffs, still drink the loyal toast sitting down, a legacy from the regiment's days as marines on board ships of the line.

The Royal Regiment of Fusiliers brought together a variety of regiments which only really had the name 'fusilier' in common. The regional contrasts could hardly have been greater – Northumberland, Warwickshire, London and Lancashire. The red and white feather hackle in their beret – giving rise to their nickname, 'the Budgies' – was that of the Royal Northumberland Fusiliers, the senior regiment. The 3rd Battalion, which was part of 4th Armoured Brigade in the Gulf, was so short of men that it had to be brought up to war strength with a company of Grenadiers and reinforcements from nearly twenty different capbadges. Tragically, it attracted most attention because of the attack on two of its Warriors by an American A10 warplane which killed six young soldiers from the battalion and three reinforcements from the Queen's Own Highlanders.

The Royal Anglian Regiment is a slight misnomer, since it also encompasses the old Lincolns, Leicesters and Northamptons. The rest of the Army knows them collectively as the 'angle-irons', but each battalion has its own nickname. The first are the Vikings, the second the Poachers, and the third the Pompadours. The Anglians, inheriting an old affiliation, provide instructors for the Royal Bermuda Regiment; and they also have a close link with the Gibraltar Regiment, which in March 1991 took over sole charge for the defence of the Rock.

The King's Division, which covers the north-east, Yorkshire and Northern Ireland, is much better recruited because most of its regiments have retained separate identities and its recruiting areas are traditionally amongst the strongest. After the Scottish regiments, its battalions are on average the closest to strength in the six infantry divisions.

The senior regiment, the King's Own Royal Border Regiment, has its regimental headquarters in Carlisle Castle but extends down into northern Lancashire. The King's Regiment has always recruited from Liverpool and Manchester. The Prince of Wales's Own Regiment of Yorkshire (rather predictably known as the Yorkies) and the Green Howards, just to the north, enjoy some solid pockets of loyalty. The Prince of Wales's Own Regiment provided guards for Iraqi prisoners and a defence platoon for the headquarters of 1st Armoured Division.

The Royal Irish Rangers, on the other hand, have a much more difficult time. Their two battalions result from the 1968 amalgamation of the Inniskilling Fusiliers, the Ulster Rifles and the Irish Fusiliers. They wear a dark green caubeen (a rather large Irish beret with a hackle) and trousers to match, their pipers have plain, saffron-coloured kilts, and their officers carry black knobkerries. Like all

337

Irish regiments, their recruiting is profoundly effected by the troubles. Because of IRA attempts to infiltrate the Army, applicants have to been screened carefully, a process which can take up to six months. Those who join know that their families may become targets. Only their closest friends are told that they are joining the Army; they tell everyone else that they are off to find work in England. The 1st Battalion, of whom about a third are Catholic, completed their first roulement tour in the winter of 1988. After five and a half years in Germany, they now form the demonstration battalion at the School of Infantry. The 2nd Battalion of the Royal Irish Rangers serving in Northern Ireland in the autumn of 1990 were the object of Mrs Thatcher's last visit to the province shortly before her resignation.

The last two members of the division, the Queen's Lancashire Regiment and the Duke of Wellington's Regiment, are solidly based, the Queen's Lancs around Preston, Burnley and Blackburn, and 'the Dukes' up the Pennine strip of west Yorkshire. The British Tommy, and today's Tom, comes from Thomas Atkins, who was a member of the Duke's old regiment, the 33rd Foot, and chosen by the Iron Duke himself to represent the archetypal infantryman.

Although they do not benefit from the recruiting strongholds of the north, the regiments of the Prince of Wales's Division have in most cases managed to hold on to their county names. No less than four bear the name of a single county.

The Devonshire and Dorset Regiment is known both as the 'Janners' (the West Country version of John) and also as the 'armoured farmers', from when they were mechanized during the Second World War. The regiment has produced some widely respected officers. Indeed, such a burst of talent coincided at one point that Colonel 'H' Jones, who was awarded a posthumous Victoria Cross in the Falklands, had transferred to the Parachute Regiment.

The Cheshire Regiment returned to Chester Castle to celebrate its tercentenary in 1989, with a tattoo and the presentation of new colours. The Royal Welch Fusiliers, another regiment to celebrate its tercentenary in 1989, are perhaps best known for the black ribbons attached to the back of their uniform collar commemorating the fact that they were the last regiment to give up the wig. The Royal Regiment of Wales, which includes the old South Wales Borderers of Rorke's Drift fame, has a museum full of memorabilia visited by the present Zulu king.

The Gloucestershire Regiment's name is still most closely associated with the Battle of the Imjin in Korea. It too produced a well-known paratrooper in the form of General Sir Anthony Farrar-Hockley. The Worcesters and Sherwood Foresters, a regiment whose recruiting areas are separated by the great Birmingham conurbation, are called the 'Woofers' from their military abbreviation of WFR. The Hampshires, known as the 'Tigers', a nickname for once bestowed by a monarch (in the corpulent form of George IV), are proud of their marksmanship and of their colonel-in-chief, the Princess of Wales. As a former airborne regiment, the Staffords are among the few to get on well with members of the Parachute Regiment, who tend to be contemptuous of anyone without a maroon beret. They were the second armoured infantry battalion to convert to Warrior, and the first to deploy with it in the Gulf. Lastly, the Duke of Edinburgh's Royal Regiment (Berkshire and Wiltshire), recently returned from Hong Kong, is another to be known by its initials.

The Light Division, the smallest division at six battalions, comprises the Light Infantry and the Royal Green Jackets. The four former regiments of Light Infantry – the Somerset and Cornwall, King's Own Yorkshire, King's Shropshire and the Durhams – merged into three regular battalions without county names. The three Royal Green Jackets battalions were originally the old 'Ox and Bucks' Light Infantry, the King's Royal Rifle Corps (the 60th Rifles), and the Rifle Brigade. In the years following this re-organization, training was consolidated on the Rifle Depot in Winchester, where it remained until the 1988 move to new barracks outside the city at Flowerdown (an unmartial name which some officers wanted to change).

The Light Infantry has always been renowned for its rapid drill and marching speeds, both on parade, where it causes major problems at events like the Queen's Birthday Parade in Berlin, and across country. In 1988 Lieutenant Richard Fullerton and Sergeant Paul Corcoran of the 2nd Battalion marched a hundred miles non-stop in under twenty-four hours.

Despite its small size, the Light Division has had, in the words of its officer recruiting material, 'a decisive influence on British military thinking'. Few within the Army consider this an exaggerated boast, although they might have a number of other things to say on the subject. The Green Jackets, whose three battalions represent just over 5 per cent of the infantry, produce far more senior generals than any other part of the Army. This phenomenon led to the dark hints and nickname of the 'black mafia'. At the time of the Gulf war in 1991, two out of the four military members of the Army Board were Green Jackets – the Adjutant General, General Sir David Ramsbotham (his three predecessors were all Green Jackets), and the Quarter Master General, General Sir Edward Jones. And the Chief of the General Staff, General Sir John Chapple, although a 2nd Gurkha, had also started as a Green Jacket in the form of the 60th Rifles.

The success of Green Jacket officers is not entirely a recent phenomenon. Rifle regiments were the most fashionable of English line infantry. The 60th Rifles recruited many of its officers from Eton, and the old Rifle Brigade had a close association with Winchester. They prided themselves on having more imagination and a less restricted outlook than the Guards. With a tradition of semi-independent action dating back to the eighteenth century, their soldiers were always considered brighter than average, and officers were picked as much for their intellect as for their social connections.

The Green Jackets went for graduates long before it became Army policy in the 1970s, and they also ascribe their success to good officer selection and training. Certainly, their senior officers and colonel commandants take great trouble, interviewing their large number of applicants individually. Once their candidates are through Sandhurst and into the regiment, Green Jacket generals make sure that commanding officers get the right jobs for likely high-flyers to give them the right 'ticks' for selection boards in the future. In an army which used to pride itself on eschewing vulgar ambition, such practices were almost considered sharp practice. Now, of course, other regiments have been forced to adopt similar practices, but the rigorously unsentimental approach of Green Jacket officers, perhaps best typified by General Sir Frank Kitson, has not made them loved by other regiments.

The Navy takes a particular pleasure in teasing the Army about the internal rivalry and suspicions provoked by Green Jacket successes. Admiral Sir Henry Leach is said to have asked a group of senior officers: 'Are you all Green Jackets, or are you just Army?' In Gibraltar, another admiral visiting in hospital a Green Jacket major who had fractured his skull after falling off a human pyramid one boisterous night in the mess, joked: 'As you're a Green Jacket, I can hardly say I'm surprised you were scrambling over other people's backs to get to the top. And I am equally unsurprised that when you tumbled nobody made an effort to break your fall.' Not surprisingly, perhaps, Green Jacket officers have become slightly exasperated by some of the stories which persist, such as the impression amongst officers in other arms that they and the Guards have a different promotion system from the rest of the Army. Yet although there are still rising Green Jacket stars entering the upper reaches of the officer corps, the future for their regiment became much less secure with the Light Division under-officered and undermanned.

While most of the infantry has suffered a sharp drop both in quality and quantity of recruits, the Parachute Regiment still attracts more than enough applicants to choose from. (With the same number of battalions as the Green Jackets, it has nearly 30 per cent more officers).

The range of backgrounds can sometimes be surprising. Admittedly, exceptional cases, such as a fully qualified doctor forming up to join as a private, make one think of a domestic version of the Foreign Legion. The common factor amongst recruits appears to be their desire to prove something to themselves, or perhaps to other people. 'They all want to be little Rambos,' said one officer from the regiment.

The rigours of the Parachute Regiment depot at Aldershot provide an even less forgiving version of basic training than in the rest of the infantry. All the time the symbol of the maroon beret for those who make it is held before their eyes. 'They're brainwashed into believing that they're the best,' said a regimental sergeant major, 'and they come out believing it.' He acknowledged that he was not sure whether this approach produced the most responsible sort of soldier.

After completing their common military syllabus, including the week of 'basic Wales', sweating up and down the Brecon Beacons, recruits embark on the real test – the pre-parachute selection course. Pre-para selection starts on a Friday with a warm-up. In the morning there is a steeplechase and then a log race, followed in the afternoon by 'milling', a form of boxing in which nobody is 'too interested in the rules'. A veteran para major described it as more 'a test in what we call controlled aggression'. During this one minute of 'flailing without flinching', anyone who cowers is deemed unsuitable for the paras.

On the Monday they go to Brecon for four days of endurance tests, with speed marches, stretcher races and assault courses. The failures are bussed back to Aldershot for discharge from the Army or transfer to another regiment. Those who survive stay on for three weeks' field training known as 'advanced Wales'. This next stage in the selection system – by this stage only injury is liable to make a candidate fail – consists of a week's practice in defence – digging and filling in trenches – a week's patrolling and ambush training, and a week's field firing. After Wales comes the climax of their training.

The Parachute Training School at RAF Brize Norton is run by PJIs – parachute jump instructors. The four-week course starts with a fortnight's concentration on drills and landing technique, working up to jumps from an enclosed platform, the 'knacker-cracker', and then from a tower. The first proper jump is from a balloon at the end of the second week. Most find it the most unnerving of all. 'It's dead quiet, just the noise of the wind, and then you fall straight down.' During the last week they 'go out of the Herc'.

'The worst part's the waiting, staring at each other across the aircraft. Then the red light's on and the door's open – the wind's rushing in – the adrenalin's pumping. There's no time to think. You're so shocked, you just run up to the door.' Once the parachute opens, 'You're totally amazed. And when you get down on the ground, you can't stop talking about it. But the instructors quickly get a grip of you.' After a total of eight jumps, including a night drop, they receive their wings. 'I was on cloud nine when I got them.'

There are occasions when at the last moment a man refuses to jump. He is asked three times. If he still refuses he is taken up to the cockpit out of sight: fear is infectious. Once the aircraft lands he is 'got rid of quickly . . . By the time we got back to the block, he'd gone.' His bed space was empty, the locker cleared.

For a dedicated para, life outside has little meaning. Some of those who leave come back in because they are hooked on the notion of belonging to an élite. This tribal identity extends even to the extraordinary extent of missing

Aldershot. When one battalion was posted up to Tern Hill in Shropshire, officers found that most of the unmarried soldiers were returning to 'the Shot' for the weekend.

Aldershot's appeal for groups of young single men may seem hard to fathom, unless it is the prospect of battle. From military police accounts – the paras' principal enemy – it almost sounds as though more blood has flowed on the streets of Aldershot than in the Falklands.

The paras are conspicuously proud of being unlike other regiments. 'This fundamental difference', said the RSM of one of their battalions, 'stems from the fact that everyone from the Colonel down to the private soldier goes out of the door of the aircraft, and when they reach the ground they have to carry their own kit. That is the great leveller.' In such a muscular and meritocratic society, it was curious to hear officers regretting the 'roughness' of newly commissioned companions and expressing a desire to have a much higher proportion from public schools.

One company sergeant major described their recipe as 'pure arrogance and big-headedness. If we didn't have it, we probably wouldn't do what we do . . . The thing that binds us together is physical standards.' In good airborne forces style, he despised the idea of armoured infantry: 'The paras in mech? It just wouldn't work.'

Such attitudes do not make them loved by the rest of the Army. Junior NCOs complain that the directing staff at Brecon take it out on them just because they are paras. But as a regiment they are not at loggerheads with everyone. They get on with the Guards, and the Junior Parachute Company at Pirbright works well. And they have stayed in close touch with the Queen's Own Highlanders ever since the Warrenpoint disaster, when both regiments suffered casualties. But for some reason they cannot abide the Green Jackets.

In spite or because of its pride over the Falklands, the regiment can be touchy about its public image. One commanding officer said he was staggered at a recent officer selection board when applicants were asked to name well-known para operations. Apparently most of them just cited Bloody Sunday; only one mentioned Suez and the Falklands. He felt the paras' reputation in Northern Ireland was distorted within the Army as well as outside. As a staff officer he had seen other regiments operate in a much more aggressive way: 'We're seen as aggressive, because if we're given a task we don't dilly-dally.'

There can be no doubt that the Falklands conflict represents the Parachute Regiment's most intense and emotive experience since the Second World War. The impression of a St Crispin's Day, dividing those who were there from those who weren't, still lingers. None suffered so much as the 1st Battalion – 1 Para – who, although based in Edinburgh, were serving in Northern Ireland on a four-month roulement tour when the Task Force was designated. Their commanding officer flew to London to plead they should be sent instead of the Gurkhas, and soldiers in the regiment, contrary to all military regulations, inundated Downing Street with letters to the Prime Minister. They all believed that the operation was theirs by right. To think they could jump the queue, and expect a fresh infantry battalion to replace them in Northern Ireland at a moment's notice, was absolutely typical of para arrogance in the eyes of other regiments.

Outsiders might well think that the two battalions who served there are still obsessed with the Falklands. The Sergeants' Mess of 2 Para recently organized a 'Goose Green Night'. Army tents represented each place of significance and, for example, lamb stew was served in mess tins in the tent marked Fitzroy. The sergeants dressed in clean para smocks, preferably those they had on when the *Norland* sailed; wives were supposed to wear what they had seen their husband off in – or what they wore to welcome him back, a category which provoked a good deal of ribald amusement.

On a more serious note, the annual drumhead service, in which 2 Para commemorates the Falklands conflict, will probably continue to mean more than any other anniversary. For the new recruits, Arnhem is too long ago. 'Goose Green they can understand,' said the commanding officer. 'Their corporal was there.' He added that there were still over 100 members of the battalion who had served with it in the South Atlantic. 'This means that if you sent us on operations tomorrow we would be far more measured, far more steady under fire.'

When the Gulf crisis developed towards war, para-troopers were predictably resentful that none of their battalions were sent against the Iraqis when the US Army deployed both the 82nd and 101st Airborne Divisions. Only the Parachute Regiment's Pegasus Band was sent. To have maroon berets at the head of 1st Armoured Division – those of Major General Rupert Smith and his chief of staff, Colonel John Reith – offered little consolation. Only officers relished the significance of paras commanding a heavy army formation.

Suspicions of some sort of freemasonry in rifle green was perhaps hardly surprising when the Gurkha lobby appeared almost as ubiquitous as Green Jacket generals. Two Chiefs of the General Staff in the last eight years, Bramall and Chapple, were from the 2nd Gurkhas and, to cap it all, so was John Nott, the Secretary of State. The 2nd Gurkhas, or Goorkhas as they prefer to spell it in the old-fashioned way, do not have colours but the Queen's Truncheon, a huge silver-headed mace, which is saluted even by their colonel-in-chief, the Prince of Wales. Their close relationship with the 60th Rifles during the Indian Mutiny gave them their rifle regiment style, including light infantry drill, and their uniform with its black buttons and cross-belts.

The Gurkhas, the most threatened of all infantry groups, currently consist of five battalions – two from the 2nd Gurkha Rifles, and one each from the 6th, the 7th (the one sent to the Falklands) and the 10th. In addition there are the Queen's Gurkha Engineers, the Queen's Gurkha Signals and the Gurkha Transport Regiment.

On 22 May 1989, George Younger, then Secretary of State for Defence, announced that the brigade was to be reduced from five to four battalions of 700 men each, instead of 900 as before. Two years later, in June 1991, reports appeared that General Sir John Chapple accepted that Gurkha battalions had to go before British Army regiments. Even after the announcements in the White Paper later in the year, some uncertainty still remained. Rumours persisted that another battalion might be taken on by the Sultan of Brunei (the agreement on the present arrangement must be renegotiated before its expiry) and there was even talk of a battalion going to Oman, although this was mostly wishful thinking.

These possibilities would not, however, solve the basic problem of deployment. To station a Gurkha battalion permanently in Belize would deprive British battalions of one of its few warm-weather breaks. For political and practical reasons, service in Northern Ireland is out of the question. And diplomats are still uneasy about Germany. Gurkha officers see the Foreign Office as their main enemy in Whitehall, but there is also a lack of enthusiasm for the idea amongst their counterparts in British regiments.

Gurkhas have long aroused protective emotions in some British military breasts – Field Marshal Lord Bramall, during his time in office, apparently tried to obtain a commitment that they would never be touched – but all this rather exasperates officers in other regiments, who talk of the 'infatuation for little Johnny Gurkha' as a romantic nostalgia for imperial days, pillbox hats and all. The Gurkhas may be superb, they say, in their specialist role of jungle warfare (some dispute even this), but put them in Osnabrück for five or six years and they are liable to go to pieces. Some middle-ranking officers suspect that one or two generals wanted to hang on to them at all costs because they long for a continued British presence on the Pacific rim.

Nostalgia runs deep in almost any officer who has served with them. A sapper colonel described the experience as 'like the old Army', with officers caring more for their men than for their own ambitions. As a further sign of a passing era, the Gurkha depot at the Dharan Cantonment closed down in 1989. From 1990 the annual selection parade will be carried out at the Gurkha transit camp in Kathmandu.

British soldiers tend to react to the Gurkhas with a fascination tinged with fear, particularly among those who have provoked their anger. A sapper major who had also served with the Gurkha Engineers recounted how the cheerful custom of British squaddies – welcoming a newly arrived unit 'by doing over their accommodation and kit' – can backfire. Personal possessions are sacrosanct to the Gurkhas and they look after their equipment better than any British regiment. Their reaction is to go straight after the miscreants: 'You've never seen anybody run so fast as British soldiers chased by angry little men with drawn kukris.'

In the Gulf, the only Gurkha presence was the 28th Gurkha Ambulance Group – 200 men serving as part of 5th Armoured Field Ambulance.

Despite the pride in their differences, British infantry regiments have a go-anywhere, do-anything image of themselves unequalled in any other army. This developed during the withdrawal from empire, when they were called upon to perform riot control, rural counter-insurgency, street fighting, cordon and search, and anti-guerrilla operations in mountainous country. Then, at the end of the 1960s, just as it seemed that the British Army could at last concentrate on conventional soldiering in Nato, Northern Ireland exploded, and a dozen years later Argentina invaded the Falklands. The British infantry, which has always disliked 'mech', was able to justify its preference for serving on its feet.

The infantry obsession that it should be 'all-singing-all-dancing' affects the whole Army. One general (ironically an infantryman himself), wrestling with the problem of over-instruction, pointed to the absurdity of trying 'to

348

teach cooks how to mount guard at Buckingham Palace'. Many staff officers go further. They argue that in the interests of economy some regiments should sing and some should dance, just like the armoured corps, the artillery and everyone else. Two roles, Northern Ireland and one other, is all that any battalion should train for.

A combination of factors now points clearly towards a very different approach. Traditionalists have successfully argued that the rash of amalgamations in 1968, and the consequent establishment of large anonymous regiments without a specific territorial identity, has proved disastrous for recruiting. Others point to the lack of a military presence in the infantry heartlands of northern England and Scotland. And the Gaffney Report on Army wives emphasized the importance of a 'home base concept' to offer a focus for stability and an end to the semi-nomadic tribe.

The infantry battalion is increasingly split between the interests of the single and the married man. While the go-anywhere, do-anything image appeals most to the young single soldier, those with families soon want to put down roots. Their wives in particular find the long-term unpredictability hard to take. With a home base for each regiment, families would be encouraged to look for a house nearby and become part of a local community, instead of – as at present – buying near one of their parents. The Guards, with London as well as Pirbright and Caterham, and the Parachute Regiment, with two battalions in Aldershot, already have a home base area with which families can identify. The only problem is the prohibitive cost of housing in the south-east.

The current argument on deployment and permanent specialist roles for battalions began in the summer 1986 edition of the *Guards Magazine* with 'a thought-provoking article' by Lieutenant Colonel Craster of the Grenadier Guards. 'If we wish the Guards Division to survive as we know it,' he wrote, 'we must be ahead of the game; to be reactive is to go under.' He proposed that the Guards Division should have two composite infantry battalions in Germany, drawn from all regiments, like the wartime Guards Armoured Division, and an air-transportable infantry battalion for overseas and Northern Ireland resident postings. Meanwhile, the first battalions of each regiment would remain on public duties in London. Although this article aroused a few long-standing suspicions amongst the rest of the infantry that the Guards were once again engaged on a little empire-building on the side, the basic idea attracted a lot of support. Reactions from the Ministry of Defence, however, were a good deal less enthusiastic.

The Parachute Regiment provides perhaps the best example of what more and more officers argue must be the model for the future, assuming that the Options for Change estimate of two Nato divisions is maintained. The reorganization of the line infantry into its administrative divisions was a mistake. Wherever possible, regiments should have back their original identities, and reform in three battalion brigades. These could either trickle-post or rotate from a home-base barracks in one of their recruiting areas (preferably the most northerly, to reduce the excessive proportion of the Army based in the very expensive southeast). The three would consist of a home-base battalion which, like the Ulster Defence Regiment, would have a regular cadre and at least one regular company, with the remainder made up of reservists and territorials; a United Kingdom battalion, which would be co-located with the home-base battalion; and an 'overseas' battalion, which could mean service either as armoured infantry in Germany or as a resident battalion in Northern Ireland. In some ways it is a return to the old two-battalion system for service in the empire, but the addition of the home-base battalion offers the only chance of hanging on to NCOs and officers whose families no longer want to move.

The administrative side could, on the other hand, be centralized still further under the control of the Director of Infantry. Advanced training is already the responsibility of the School of Infantry based at Warminster, and under his eye. There, and at the Support Weapons Wing at

Netheravon, the instructors belong to the Small Arms School Corps. This body, some 135-strong, dates from 1853, when attempts were being made to improve the standards of British musketry. Now they teach every infantry weapon, from the SA80 rifle to the Milan anti-tank missile launcher.

The School of Infantry's other outpost, at Brecon in Wales, is the most firmly imprinted in the memories of NCOs. Formerly the Parachute Regiment Battle School, Brecon's main purpose is to train section commanders and platoon sergeants in rigorous exercises on the Sennybridge training area, a stretch of countryside famous in the Army for filthy weather and steep hills rather than for its bleak beauty. A company of Gurkhas from the battalion at Church Crookham in Hampshire provides a convincingly foreign enemy.

Apart from what might be termed these communal facilities, the infantry is just another federation, albeit a more structured one than the cavalry. To an accountant, a battalion of infantry represents about £12 million a year; to a staff officer on the manning side, it represents so many hundred men, depending on role; but to its sergeants' mess each battalion is unique. Senior NCOs in the Staffordshire Regiment, for example, claim that there is still a definite hint of the differences in character between the old South Staffords and the North Staffords, a distinction which ceased to exist in 1959, long before most of them joined the regiment. Yet in an age of amalgamated regiments and increased cross-posting an outsider, particularly a younger officer, would regard such nuances as little more than a curiosity.

CHAPTER 22

Land/Air Battles: The Royal Armoured Corps and the Army Air Corps

The Royal Armoured Corps is split in two ways, historically and operationally. The historical division is between the thirteen cavalry regiments and the four regiments of the Royal Tank Regiment. Operationally, it is divided between armoured regiments with Challenger or Chieftain tanks, and armoured reconnaissance regiments, with Scimitar and Scorpion, the light tracked vehicles which replaced armoured cars.

In the past, regiments alternated between reconnaissance and tanks, but 're-roling' each time with a training programme was expensive and time-consuming. When the permanent division between the two roles came in the early 1970s, regiments were given the choice. The Royal Tank Regiment opted en bloc for tanks, as did most cavalry regiments, including several which were in a reconnaissance role at the time. They wanted to be part of the mainstream, the backbone of the 'heavy army'. Reconnaissance, although fast-moving and more fun, did not help officers' careers.

Differences between the cavalry and the Royal Tank Regiment, though greatly reduced, still manifest themselves today. Cavalry subalterns tend to regard their RTR contemporaries as rather too serious – 'clank, clank, I'm a tank' – while they in turn are seen as rather too unserious.

The mortification and jealousy in the Royal Tank Regiment during the deployment to the Gulf was intense. The armoured reconnaissance regiment and the three armoured regiments in the 1st Armoured Division were all cavalry, and about the only Royal Tank Regiment black beret to be seen on television screens was that of Brigadier Christopher Hammerbeck, the commander of the 4th Armoured Brigade.

A computer was used to choose the name Operation Granby at random, yet the commander who lost his wig charging at full gallop (his exposed pate is shown in several portraits by Reynolds and on countless pub signs) could hardly have been more appropriate for what the rest of the British Army soon regarded as a largely cavalry show. By the opening of hostilities, the Royal Scots Dragoon Guards, the Queen's Royal Irish Hussars, the 14th/20th King's Hussars (whose guidon bears the battle honour Baghdad from an engagement against the Turks in 1917) and the 16th/5th Queen's Royal Lancers had been deployed in the Saudi Arabian desert with reinforcements including squadrons of the Life Guards and the 17th/21st Lancers and a squadron of the Queen's Dragoon Guards.

The differences between cavalry and the Royal Tank Regiment are military as well as social. In the field the cavalry still prides itself on its élan, while the Royal Tank Regiment prides itself on discipline and solid professionalism. Although these perhaps oversimplified differences remain most marked between junior officers, they are reflected to a lesser extent at other levels.

The cavalry trooper is best known for his friendliness. Relaxed and unaggressive, very seldom in a fight, he could hardly be less like his counterpart in the infantry. Cavalry RSMs talk with smug amazement of the disciplinary problems of other arms. Soldiers in the Royal Tank Regiment, on the other hand, often like to see themselves as an armoured corps version of the paras, with black berets instead of maroon. And yet it was an RTR officer who, when describing house-search training for Northern Ireland, remarked that 'the trouble is our boys are too nice'. When a servicewoman, playing the part of a Catholic housewife, began to scream abuse at them, 'they couldn't stop apologizing', whereas a marine, carried away by the spirit of things, 'laid her out with a socking great slap'.

These differences between cavalry and tanks even extend to sport; cavalry regiments prefer football, while the RTR, mainly because of officer interest, concentrates on rugby. And the cavalry, with predictable disdain, shows little taste for running, so the Royal Tank Regiment usually wins armoured corps competitions with ease.

Although the most consciously professional part of the armoured corps, the Royal Tank Regiment's four regiments – they were termed battalions before the war – are not automatically the best, as even their own officers will acknowledge. Cavalry regiments have their peaks and troughs. Sometimes, to slight surprise, a particular regiment will suddenly improve, often thanks to a sequence of good commanding officers, and prove itself outstanding, while a traditionally good regiment, showing the effects of overlong years in Germany, declines.

The vastly different characters of its regiments make the armoured corps an even more heterogeneous federation than the infantry. To summarize some thoroughly superficial thumbnail-sketches by officers from other regiments: the Royal Scots Dragoon Guards have 'still got a lot of rich officers', the 4th/7th Dragoon Guards are seen as 'very heavy cavalry', the 'Skins' are ambitious, the Queen's Royal Irish Hussars are considered 'very formal for a cavalry regiment' and 'almost Guards-like', the 13th/18th Hussars are said to have improved dramatically in the last ten years, the 14th/20th are greatly liked, and the 17th/21st Lancers appear to be admired in every way, having just the right 'work hard, play hard' balance.

Contrary to the belief of many cavalrymen, the Royal Tank Regiment is far from monolithic. Each regiment has its own identity, largely influenced by its recruiting area. For example, 3 RTR from the West Country, 'the armoured farmers', could hardly be more different from 4 RTR, which recruits in Scotland. Troopers and NCOs tend to stay where they are, while officers move around. A major observed that he 'had to adjust a great deal' when changing from one regiment to another within the Royal Tank Regiment.

There is far more inter-arm co-operation today, and it starts earlier in an officer's career. Each year up to a dozen armoured corps subalterns serve with infantry battalions in Northern Ireland as platoon commanders. Necessity thus provided an introduction to the scheme – started by General Sir Nigel Bagnall – of sending armoured corps majors to command rifle companies, and infantry majors to command sabre squadrons. In all cases the candidates 'must be on the Pink List [for promotion to lieutenant colonel] so the move is not seen as a career foul'.

Attitudes to other arms and corps have changed greatly. Bovington is now the centre for all heavy tracked vehicle training and armoured gunnery, and infanteers, gunners and sappers are constantly passing through. The often arrogant insularity of the past is now rare. Yet even in those days, whatever the disobliging remarks made about 'hatmen', 'dropshorts' or 'jam-stealers', you never heard a word against 'nut-stranglers', because cavalrymen knew that, without the REME, they would literally grind to a halt. And having seen fitters work through the night in freezing rain to get a tank moving again, the respect was genuine. During the Gulf war, cavalry admiration for the REME, which maintained an astonishingly high rate of vehicle serviceability in the desert, increased still further.

Cavalry regiments vary greatly in their numbers of officers. Some are rich in subalterns and short on captains, others are weak at all levels, and several have a glut of majors, who may thus find themselves deprived of a regimental command. In 1989, the Royal Armoured Corps appointed a senior staff officer to deal specifically with the problem of recruiting young officers and smoothing out the very uneven distribution between regiments. But, if the colonel of a regiment has introduced a candidate, 'then clearly, that's his horse from the outset'.

Unlike the RTR, or infantry regiments with three different battalions, the cavalry is completely fragmented. There are not even links between dragoon guard regiments, hussars and lancers. The reluctance to cross-post in an organization devoted to the individualism of the regiment means that it is seen as abnormal and therefore suspect. But cross-posting to command can work well. In spite of widespread misgivings, officers from the Royal Tank Regiment have, on a couple of occasions, commanded cavalry regiments very successfully. But too much depends on the character of the individual chosen, and of the recipient regiment. Often the process causes deep unhappiness, since the regiment feels humiliated by the decision not to appoint one of their own. In 1989, lieutenant colonels from the 4th/7th Dragoon Guards were commanding three regiments – their own and two others. (With a tradition of producing a high proportion of senior officers, it might be tempting to portray the 4th/7th as a cavalry version of the black mafia, but that would be over-fanciful.)

Armoured recce regiments have a different problem. They may offer 'much more job satisfaction' on the way up, both as troop and then squadron leader, but it does not help an officer's career in the long run, because the specialized task of reconnaissance takes place away from the basic fighting unit of the 'heavy army' – the battle group. One cavalry general felt that coming from armoured recce should not hold anyone back: 'top horses go on any going', he said. But another pointed out that, in the last ten years, the four armoured recce regiments have produced only one brigadier between them. Their commanding officers get no experience of commanding a battle group, that most vital of 'ticks' for advancement in an Army obsessed with formation command.

Armoured corps generals are already thinner on the ground than even ten years ago, and they are liable to become thinner still in a reduced Army. Many, not just within the armoured corps, regard this as a pity. Generals, such as Bagnall and Swinburn, have a reputation for original tactical thinking. Bagnall, an old 4th/7th Dragoon Guard, won the admiration of his Secretary of State for Defence, John Nott, when he managed to persuade General von Senger of the Bundeswehr to abandon the idea of forward defence – 'a thin red line up near the border' – in favour of defence in depth, something the Allies had been advocating for years. But the armoured corps' presence in senior positions will almost certainly diminish further by the turn of the century. They have lost too many good officers in the monotony of the north German plain, and, despite their high profile in the Gulf war, both the lack of training areas and Army thinking is against them.

Reconnaissance regiments feel much less threatened than those with tanks. In addition to the Blues and Royals at Windsor, there are four line cavalry armoured recce regiments, two in Germany – at present the 13th/18th Hussars and the 16th/5th Lancers, which was 1st Armoured Division's recce regiment in the Gulf – and two in England. The regiment at Tidworth in Hampshire, at present the Queen's Dragoon Guards, one of whose squadrons served with the 16th/5th in the Gulf, is part of the UK Mobile Force, while the regiment at Wimbish in Essex, for the moment still the 9th/12th Lancers, will continue to be tasked to the 3rd Armoured Division in Germany until the Rhine Army is reorganized.

Armoured recce has considerable appeal. It is fast-moving and independent. Half-troops (a Scimitar and a Scorpion) commanded by the troop sergeant or subaltern act as mobile observation posts, screening the division's front. Each regiment has three gun squadrons of Scimitars and Scorpions and a guided weapon squadron of Strikers.

At full strength, but without the REME light aid detachment, an armoured regiment with just over fifty tanks should have nearly 50 officers and 480 men. It consists of regimental headquarters, a headquarters squadron, and usually four sabre squadrons. Each sabre squadron has four troops of three tanks, an admin troop and a section from the light aid detachment. The British have fourteen-tank squadrons because it is uneconomical to provide REME support for anything smaller, and three tanks to each troop. 'The French have five-tank troops', said a cavalry colonel, 'but that means that every lieutenant thinks he's a Napoleon.'

In spite of the Gulf war, armoured regiments face a very uncertain future. In disarmament talks, as the same cavalry colonel put it, 'people count tanks'. There are also the pacifist and environmental movements which object to major exercises. 'If you don't put your armour in Germany, where do you put it?' said his general. In 1991, out of fourteen armoured regiments, twelve were stationed in Germany.

Most of the demoralization before the Gulf war came from the lack of training opportunities and the state of the vehicles. The tank fleet was in a bad way, mainly due to a shortage of spares, particularly of the famously unreliable 'black boxes' – the junction boxes all round the inside of the turret. A fairly typical regiment had only a minority of its tanks fully operational. Most could make their way out of camp, but more than half could not fire their guns with any accuracy. A troop leader from the Royal Tank Regiment said with feeling: 'The public may think we've got six hundred tanks rocking on their sprockets, revving and ready to go, but they're not.' The stripping of the armoured corps in Germany to scrape together enough serviceable tanks for three regiments reduced the remainder to virtual immobility.

One of the most difficult and politically complex issues which the Defence Staff and the Government must face is the question of a new tank to replace Chieftain and Challenger. Even before the Gulf war, a general on the Procurement Executive acknowledged that it was 'a very real worry as to how we are going to handle the tank problem'.

Should the ageing tank fleet be renewed, or would that be a disproportionately expensive stop-gap? What is the point of buying new heavy tanks unless they can be used on training areas? Should all the available money instead be devoted to the next generation of small one- or two-man tanks, or even robot armoured vehicles? Until the tank flies – a phenomenon not expected much before 2040 – will it not be vulnerable to new minelaying techniques? Surely the British Army's priority is to catch up on the air-mobile route with its own version of the US Army's Air Cavalry? And, if the attack helicopter is the intermediate step to the flying tank, may not the flying tank of the future, electromagnetic guns and all, be based on the attack helicopter instead? And won't all these systems be prohibitively expensive just when budgets are being cut?

In an army streaked to the core with capbadge loyalty, every one of these questions is liable to be loaded. Almost all of them are aimed against the heavy tank's central role. To find anyone outside the armoured corps convinced of its future is hard, particularly when the 'heavy army' is so clearly threatened. Some officers in other arms say that the armoured corps has been blind to the shift of military opinion against heavy armoured formations and in favour of air-mobile (helicopter-borne) brigades – a shift which was under way by 1987, well before the collapse of Russia's outer empire in 1989. But accusations of blindness against the armoured corps are not entirely fair. Many of its brightest officers have been looking to the future. Unfortunately, the British Army has still not entirely escaped its preoccupation with heavy tanks, which probably dates back to an armoured inferiority complex against panzers in the Second World War. This continued into the Cold War – that useless iron hulk, the Conqueror tank, was hurriedly introduced to counter an even more useless hulk, the Josef Stalin III. This developed a special subdivision of the arms race with the Russians. In a rhinoceros version of scissors-paper-stone, armour was thickened, spaced, laminated, and finally made reactive (by exploding outwards when hit by a shell or missile). But the 'wash-up' reports on the Gulf war will probably confirm that the day of the heavy tank is over.

The Challenger tank did not perform badly. Fears about its reliability proved greatly exaggerated, and there was euphoria after the battle. Much was made of a gunner in the Royal Scots Dragoon Guards who laid on to an Iraqi tank at 5,100 metres range and knocked it out with his first round. And the devastating overkill of the Challenger's 120mm gun was lauded. Curiously, but significantly, much less was said of the four decisive factors in the ground offensive: air power, artillery, night vision and speed of advance.

In the era of sophisticated weapons, with laser-guided bombs launched from aircraft and smart bomblets from multi-launch rocket systems, a heavy tank becomes vulnerable from above since it cannot be armoured as thickly on top as in front. Air power, night vision and speed enabled the Allied armoured formations in Iraq to close with the enemy on far more favourable terms than any advantage offered by the weight of their armour or the power of their guns.

In the new era of air-mobility, Challenger tanks cannot be lifted over minefields or other obstacles by helicopters. In the new era of rapid reaction forces, which the British Army passionately wants to be part of, Challenger tanks are far too heavy to be air-transportable: they can only reach their destination on railway flats and transporters and by ship. In short, if domestic politics, or deeply rutted thinking, directs the British Army into accepting another generation of heavy tank, the Royal Armoured Corps' future is as bleak as a latterday dinosaur's.

To give the armoured corps its due, it became interested in air-mobile warfare very early on, and studied the idea of air cavalry twenty years ago. The 13th/18th Hussars was even suggested as a prototype regiment, but the idea never attracted support at the top. In those days, most British officers were convinced that the American performance in Vietnam provided the classic example of how not to fight a war, and they tended to see the US Army's Air Cavalry as a brainchild which owed more to John Wayne movies than to adult military thinking. In any case, the aviation experts argued that a single cavalry regiment could never produce enough helicopter pilots of the required standard: 'the idea of re-roling a whole regiment was a complete non-starter.'

Yet the suggestion still lingers, if only as a pipe-dream. To this day some generals, remembering the early 1960s, when helicopters formed air troops within armoured regiments, remark that the Army Air Corps should have been kept as an armoured corps subsidiary and never allowed to develop separately. 'We missed a trick there,' said one general. Yet at the Royal Armoured Corps Centre at Bovington they acknowledge that such a plan would never have been practicable. The training alone would have been far too much for one corps to handle satisfactorily.

Resistance to the independent development of the Army Air Corps has never come from armoured corps generals alone. Several senior infantry and artillery officers utter similar sentiments of regret at a lost opportunity to suppress an upstart rival. The prospect of another full combat arm, and one which will expect to sit at the top table, does not appeal to its elder and much larger brothers. 'There'll be blood on the floor,' said one general.

The Army Air Corps was reformed in 1957 out of artillery observer and light liaison flights. In 1962 the first air troop was established in an armoured regiment, and soon the nickname of 'Teeny Weeny Airways' spread. In 1973 it became a combat arm, and today its manpower represents a little over 1 per cent of total Regular Army male strength. In other words, it is only one-sixth the size of the Royal Armoured Corps, and less than a twentieth the size of the infantry.

This relatively fledgling organization has another much larger rival, even a potential predator, in the form of the

Royal Air Force. The RAF never regarded the Army Air Corps as a threat in the early days when it could still be dismissed as a taxi service for generals. But once the importance of air-mobile operations began to become clearer in the early 1980s, empire-building, and empire-defending, became the biggest obstacle to progress.

According to most versions of the story, the first serious attempt to create an air-mobile formation occurred when the Navy insisted on replacing their Wessex helicopters with the new Sea Kings. The Secretary of State, John Nott, advised the Chief of the General Staff at the time, General Sir Edwin Bramall, to get the Wessex cheap off the Navy and set up an air-mobile brigade. 'The only trouble then', Nott recalled, 'was that the RAF wanted to get in on the act.'[1]

The Army allowed the RAF in mainly for budgetary reasons. It lacked the money at the time, and to have the support helicopters paid for out of someone else's vote proved irresistible. This decision has been regretted by the Army Air Corps and all believers in air mobility ever since.[2] The RAF would not let go their monopoly of transport helicopters. And once the specifications for an attack helicopter were discussed, including the capability to engage the latest Soviet models, the RAF said that this constituted aerial combat, which had always been acknowledged as their preserve. The Army Air Corps countered with the argument that it was only one of only several capabilities: the fundamental task remained close support to ground troops, which was acknowledged to be their preserve. They felt tempted to extend the close support argument and suggest the transfer of Harrier squadrons to the Army Air Corps; after all, the US Marine Corps had its own Harriers. But this they knew would provoke war to the knife in the corridors of the Ministry of Defence.

The rivalry simmers. RAF officers describe the Army Air Corps as 'cowboys'. And in Northern Ireland where they work alongside each other – the RAF in Wessex and

Chinook transport helicopters, and the Army in Gazelle and Lynx helicopters – a certain amount of needling occurs from time to time. An RAF flight lieutenant, flying an old warhorse of a Wessex, and displeased to see an Army Air Corps NCO at the controls of the much more impressive Lynx, may then have salt rubbed into the wound by the knowledge that in the Army he would be only a sergeant.

To make matters worse, the infantry do not conceal their feelings that they have a good deal more confidence in the Army Air Corps on 'troop extraction missions' than in the RAF. This distrust seems to have deep roots. Explaining why 'the last thing we want is to be seen as the RAF in khaki', an Army Air Corps officer attributed it to the 'Dunkirk syndrome' and the cry of 'Where the fuck are the Spitfires?'

To the RAF's horrified disbelief, the Navy and, above all, the Army began in the mid-1980s to question its future as an independent service. In the words of one general, 'The fixed-wing aircraft is dated. Its roles are basically rocket roles.' The debate came into the open in 1988 when Field Marshal Lord Carver expressed his doubts 'whether it will be right to maintain a separate air force', since most air defence will be unmanned. Operational support to land and naval forces should then come under Army and Navy control.[3] He again raised the subject in the House of Lords in the July 1989 debate on the Defence Estimates.

Then, to the Army Air Corps' alarm, the RAF assembled economic and organizational arguments, backed by a tactical doctrine, to the effect that all combat helicopters and close support aircraft should be integrated in a 'hellcat' concept under RAF command. Hellcat – essentially the joint application of firepower by helicopters and fighters – may look very impressive on a firepower demonstration, Army officers contend, but it would be far too difficult to co-ordinate in war.

The outcome of this argument is far from settled, and may well not be settled by Options for Change. The Gulf war, while greatly strengthening the RAF's public image through the bravery and skill of the pilots, left open a number of questions about command and control. Criticism of senior RAF officers has been strong within both Army and RAF messes. Nevertheless, the RAF is a devastatingly effective organization in Whitehall close-quarters battle, as the fragmented Army and rather unworldly Navy know only too well. The Army Air Corps fear that if the RAF wins they might be knocked back to their old 'Teeny Weeny Airways' size.

'Air-mobility is a bad word,' said a senior infantry general. 'It's not just picking up troops and plonking them down again.' He preferred to define it as 'the application of force by helicopters on the orders of a ground force commander'.

The first step in air-mobility, the re-roling of 6th Brigade in the Rhine Army in 1983, consisted of little more than picking up and plonking down. In 1988, 24th Air Mobile Brigade took up the torch when it was set up round Catterick as part of 2nd Infantry Division tasked to Germany as part of 1st (British) Corps. Its first major demonstration was Exercise Key Flight in September 1989. This experimental formation, consisting of three infantry battalions, an engineer squadron and the newly formed 9th Regiment, Army Air Corps, may have its drawbacks, but it is a foot in the water rather than just a toe. 'It's token, but at least it's there,' said an Army Air Corps major.

The drawbacks consist of the continuing RAF control of transport helicopters (Pumas and Chinooks) and the lack of a proper attack helicopter. The Lynx is a good multi-purpose aircraft, but, as the Army Air Corps says, it is an armed helicopter, not an attack helicopter. In aerial combat and tank engagement the Lynx cannot compete with the Apache, even less can it compare with the next generation known as 'son of Apache'.[4] Similarly, the Puma should be replaced by the larger EH 101 in the next few years. But the sharp rise in the cost of sophisticated helicopters is daunting.

The next stage, although this again may be symbolic rather than practical, is the establishment of a Nato air-mobile, or *Luftland*, division. Exercise Certain Shield in September 1991, the first test involving 24th Air Mobile Brigade, the German 27th Luftland Brigade and the Belgian para commandos, was planned long in advance of the announcement of the new air-mobile division in the rapid reaction corps. Much of course depends on Options for Change, although almost everyone agrees that a real attack helicopter is needed to make air-mobility credible.

In the Gulf war, the 4th Regiment Army Air Corps deployed in support of the 1st Armoured Division, with eighteen Gazelle helicopters and eighteen Lynx Mark 7 armed with TOW missiles. Although the Lynx seems to have performed well up to standard in the few engagements in which it was used, Army Air Corps pilots cast longing glances at their American counterparts in the Apache attack helicopter. The American Apache is the obvious choice for the British Army on military grounds, especially after its performance against Iraqi armoured vehicles, but there is a European contender. For the Army Air Corps, the attack helicopter represents far more than just a new toy. Infantry, armour and artillery will not accept them as a full combat arm until they have the firepower.

A recruit or junior leader joining the Army Air Corps should know that, even if he is one of the few to make it to pilot, 'he is a soldier first and a pilot second'. He has to serve at least three years as ground crew, by which time he should be a corporal, before he receives an aptitude test. The carrot of pilot training is what brings most of them in, and to fail an aptitude test then can be a cruel disappointment. (It is not, of course, in the Army Air Corps' interests to let them find out before, since it is nearly 10 per cent under strength.)

In 1987 the Army Air Corps started to phase out observers, nicknamed 'talking baggage', and replace them with a second pilot. This is a deliberate step towards treating the helicopter as a flying weapons platform rather than just a means of conveyance. The P1 pilot is the aircraft commander. His co-pilot, the P2, is there to take over the controls when he needs all his attention to command the aircraft during an attack or complicated manoeuvres. To become a P1 pilot, or aircraft commander, the corporal has to pass a senior NCO cadre course. If he has the potential 'he can do air trooper to officers' mess in thirteen years'.

Selecting officers for the Army Air Corps is inevitably more difficult than for most capbadges. As well as the Regular Commissions Board and Sandhurst, its officers have to pass a flying aptitude test, a much stiffer medical and eventually pilot training. For some inexplicable reason, public schoolboys seem far more likely to fail the aptitude test than those from state schools. Out of 500 applicants each year, maybe fifteen subalterns 'get their wings'. After Sandhurst, young officers are sent off as platoon commanders or troop leaders to give them 'teeth arm experience' before they begin flying training.

The Army Air Corps has about 40 non-aircrew officers, mostly commissioned warrant officers, and 250 aircrew officers. So far there are only about sixty P2 pilots. (Senior officers are very keen to fly whenever possible 'to keep their hand in', but this provokes mutterings lower down that the practice is dangerous and that they should be grounded.) About 30 per cent of the Army Air Corps' pilot strength should come from subalterns and captains attached from other capbadges. But, owing to the general shortage, the commanding officer of their regiment may often try to dissuade them from volunteering. Some of the shortfall has been made up from the logistic corps, but not enough. To make matters worse, civilian pilots are still in short supply, and service personnel remain the favourite recruitment target for aviation companies.

The only other possible source of pilots would be to train women, a move which the RAF announced in 1989. The Army Air Corps admits that women, with their more sensitive touch on the controls, are liable to make better pilots than men, but all their aircraft are defined as combat, and even under the revised deployment rules women are still excluded. They also argue that the cost of training – over £1,000 an hour – represents too high a gamble so long as women receive an automatic discharge from the Army on pregnancy.

The Army Air Corps feels trapped in a circle of wilful inertia. It does not have the officers in sufficiently senior appointments to influence events, and its junior officers sense that they are at a career disadvantage. Other arms reply that their protests are exaggerated. The promotion stakes are bound to be loaded against those who never command a battle group, and in that they are no different from officers from armoured recce regiments, gunners and sappers. But the Army Air Corps is objecting precisely to this virtually sealed circuit. 'We want brigade commanders in the mainstream Army,' they still insist, because they will have as much, if not more experience of the land/air battle as anyone else. Nonetheless, they acknowledge that the breakthrough may take as much as ten years. Again the conviction is reiterated: 'Attitudes will only change once we get the right kit.'

CHAPTER 23

Rival Siblings and Adam's Rib: Gunners, Sappers and Signallers

The Royal Artillery and the Royal Engineers constitute the Army's best example of sibling rivalry. The Engineers and the Artillery parted company during the early eighteenth century, though the exact circumstances are obscured by the fog of historical dispute. Both arms have kept the same motto: *Ubique*. The sappers say that while in their case it means 'everywhere', for the gunners it means 'all over the place' – and the gunners, needless to say, return the compliment reversed. The ritual battle is continued in the annual rugby match between them, the most important and most ferocious event in their sporting calendars.

More relevant similarities between these very dissimilar organizations persist to this day. For both gunners and sappers, the regiment is a relatively artificial grouping in comparison with the battery or squadron. Until 1938, the basic artillery unit was the battery, and even today they retain their individuality – often they bear the name of a battle honour – and are sometimes switched round between regiments. The sappers have always preferred to work as a squadron, partly because of their different specializations, and the independent field squadron frequently lives up to its name.

The Royal Signals, the last of the large combat arms, was a rib from an existing body, since it was born from the Royal Engineer Signals Branch in 1920. Sappers like to add that the RAF was also one of their offspring, since the Royal Flying Corps began as the Royal Engineer Air Battalion.

★

The Royal Regiment of Artillery – traditionalist gunners like to call it the Royal Regiment *tout court* – is the largest regiment in the British Army. It also has the largest superstructure. After the Queen as Captain-General comes the Master-Gunner of Saint James's Park, a title dating from 1678. The present Master-Gunner, General Sir Martin Farndale, took over on relinquishing command of the Rhine Army. There are also about a dozen colonels commandant, and now colonels of regiments have been introduced. All of this signifies a good many visits and tours of inspection, but the gunners are very paternalistic in this way.

They also have more tied appointments and commands than any other capbadge. There is, for the moment at least, a Major General Royal Artillery at corps headquarters in Germany, and a Commander Royal Artillery (a brigadier) at every divisional headquarters. Infantry and cavalry officers argue that these appointments could easily go as part of an economy measure; gunners reply that other arms merely want to split up the field artillery, permanently allocating a regiment to each brigade. This would be wasteful. 'They cannot grasp that artillery is a divisional weapon,' complained a gunner general.

Even before the Gulf war, the introduction of the multi-launch rocket system (MLRS) greatly boosted the Royal Artillery's self-confidence, particularly in the domestic all-arms battle. They argue that they are no longer just a support arm, but an arm in their own right. Tanks will still be needed in certain tactical situations, but direct fire is almost becoming obsolete. They can now hit a vastly superior enemy over thirty kilometres away. This, in the words of one commander of divisional artillery, means that 'by the time the players arrive on the field, they've got dirty kit'.

The power of the MLRS, as keen viewers of the Gulf war will remember, is rather repetitively (but accurately) described as 'awesome'. The 39th Heavy Regiment, who used it in action for the first time six days before the ground offensive started, had already nicknamed it the 'grid square removal service' since a salvo of twelve rockets from each of four launchers is said to destroy anything within a square kilometre. This single salvo is reputedly 400 times more destructive than the firepower of an eight-gun battery.

Until the collapse of the Warsaw Pact in 1990, gunners were particularly keen to highlight the Soviet emphasis on artillery forces, which represented 28 per cent of the Red Army. This prompted them to hark back wistfully to the end of the Second World War, when the Royal Artillery, at over a million strong, was larger than the Royal Navy. At just under 9 per cent of the Army, they are now slightly smaller than the Royal Engineers.

The gunners have most of their weight in the 'heavy army', and are therefore almost as vulnerable to the changes in Europe as the Royal Armoured Corps. Two-thirds of the Royal Artillery is in Germany: eight field regiments, three heavy regiments, one regiment with Lance missiles, and three air defence regiments with Rapier missiles. There are five regiments and a headquarters in Dortmund alone – a home from home which makes it seem like Woolwich-am-Ruhr. Other arms call it the 'gunner ghetto'. Senior NCOs in the Royal Artillery are probably the most 'Europeanized' of all soldiers: most of them have been even longer in Germany than their counterparts in the Royal Armoured Corps.

Most of the artillery based in the United Kingdom is also allocated to Germany. The rest is for home defence and the various intervention forces, such as 26th Field Regiment with the UK Mobile Force, the 7th Royal Horse Artillery with the 5th Airborne Brigade and 29 Commando Regiment RA with the 3rd Commando Brigade. The two 'coloured beret' regiments have the 105mm light gun. Officers, NCOs and soldiers who apply to serve with them have to pass the appropriate physical endurance tests before being accepted – the all-arms P Company course and parachute training in the case of 7th Royal Horse Artillery and the commando course in the case of 29 Commando RA. The green or the maroon beret and 'putting up your dagger' or your wings are the outward declarations of their difference. Few soldiers in either regiment want to return to conventional gunner life. A gunner general commented on the 'great difficulty in moving NCOs out of coloured beret regiments'. Many of them went 'from gunner to troop sergeant major in the same regiment . . . It's the officers that move.'

The battery of a typical field regiment consists of two troops of four 155mm self-propelled guns. Each gun has a crew of seven. In the field, the guns are commanded by the battery captain (known as the BK) and the gun position officer, who carry out the instructions radioed back from the battery commander (BC) and the forward observation officers. A battery commander and forward observation officer (FOO) are attached to a particular battle group headquarters, based on either an infantry or an armoured regiment. The FOO in the British Army is usually a captain. He will order fire, unlike Bundeswehr or US Army NCOs, who can only request fire.

There is one field regiment per armoured brigade, and each armoured brigade has three battle groups. They remain with their battle group even if all artillery fire is diverted elsewhere on orders from brigade or division. The battery does not belong to the battle group. If things are quiet to its front, fire will be redirected elsewhere. 'Guns are never in reserve,' is the great gunner cry.

The Royal Artillery, which became rather homogeneous after its basic denominator of the battery had to be subsumed into regiments, is clearly a little envious of the diversity of the infantry and cavalry. 'In a sense there's a certain ordinariness about us,' said a gunner general. At times the yearning for distinct regimental identities produces a slightly artificial, or at least exaggerated, emphasis. The 22nd Air Defence is described as Welsh, 16th Air Defence as Scottish and 40th Field as the Lowland Gunners. In the case of 40th Field, the regiment which served with 7th Armoured Brigade in the

Gulf, little more than a third of the soldiers come from Scotland, and if a Scottish officer is posted in it is only by chance. So the unofficial establishment of a commanding officer's piper and the liberal use of tartan in regimental headquarters is a little contrived. It is perhaps significant that the nicknames of gunner regiments are no more than a play on their title: 'Fifty Miserable' for 50 Missile and 'Nine Fornicating' for 94 Locating.

Their 'coloured beret' regiments, on the other hand, have very distinct characters – but they come mainly from their parent brigades, whether parachute or commando. Despite the horse artillery cachet in gunner circles, members of 7th Regiment, Royal Horse Artillery, see themselves as paras first of all; 29 Commando RA, which provided 3rd Commando Brigade's close support in the Falklands, has a similar independence. Commando gunners adopt naval language with a certain relish, because it distinguishes them from the rest of the Royal Artillery. 'Excuse my rig,' said one of their officers when turning up unchanged for dinner at Larkhill.

The only part of the Royal Artillery which can lay claim to a regimental identity are the horse gunners. In practice this now means the 1st and 3rd Regiments Royal Horse Artillery and the King's Troop, since those who wear maroon berets are no longer seen as proper horse gunners. All officers are expected to ride – apparently a recent Commandant of the Staff College was nearly kicked out as a subaltern because of his lack of horsemanship – and para gunners and horses don't spring to mind as a natural combination.

The RHA has traditionally been something of a self-regarding élite, lending a certain panache to the rest of the Royal Artillery. Any snobbery is one of attitude far more than background. Of those I met, the *beau idéal* of a horse gunner was best portrayed by a young captain, the son of a former sergeant major: he had charm, good looks, and an amusing cavalry insouciance as he tapped the side of his leg with a well-worn cutting whip.

Officers who have served in an RHA regiment have the right to keep the ball buttons on their mess kit for the rest of their career, thus giving them a club badge. They refer to their less fortunate colleagues as 'our flat-buttoned friends' or simply 'the flatties'. This, along with talk about the privilege of commanding the King's Troop, or Chestnut Troop – almost akin in horse gunner terms to commanding the Queen's Company of the Grenadiers – can provoke a certain amount of irritation in officers who have followed the air defence route in missile regiments.

Until very recently, the RHA was considered a command élite. Its members 'got all the plum jobs' and the best regimental commands throughout the whole Royal Regiment. But things have changed. A gunner general described the RHA as no more than 'supposedly the centre of excellence from which we spread officers and NCOs throughout the Royal Regiment: in the old days you had to earn your jacket, but now we also take first-tour subalterns'. They are sent to the RHA either 'as a pace-setter or as a benefiter – one who would gain from going to the regiment'. This essentially means to 'learn the niceties', because the RHA produces 'more polished personalities' among both officers and senior NCOs.

Senior members of the Royal Artillery seemed to have been the most shaken in the late 1980s by the change in attitudes of most young officers. They, perhaps more than any other part of the Army, were most appalled by their disregard for just about every sacred cow in sight – custom, the opinions of their seniors, and conventional morality.

The artillery needs at least eighty officers from Sandhurst a year. For a couple of years it dropped to around fifty. This coupled with the high rate of departure of captains caused serious worry. The gunners benefited from the general upturn in 1990, but they are still suffering the most serious officer shortage in the whole Army.

Little more than a handful of officer entrants now come from public schools. 'We are very conscious', said the same general, 'of not getting the right young men from the right schools.' Efforts are made to 'smooth off the rough edges' during the young officers' course at Larkhill. Evenings of wine-tasting are organized, as well as dinners to put into practice the Sandhurst etiquette classes, and they are encouraged to go out with the Royal Artillery Foxhounds, the last Army pack.

A gunner subaltern is only deemed to have joined the Royal Regiment once he has been dined-in at Woolwich, which is traditionally described as the 'heart of the regiment' – as opposed to Larkhill, which is its 'brain'. Woolwich was much more of a home before the Second World War, when gunner officers were trained there at the Royal Military Academy, founded in 1741 and known to generations as 'the Shop'.

In those days 'gentlemen cadets' destined for the infantry and cavalry went on to Sandhurst. The two establishments were amalgamated in 1946 and concentrated on Sandhurst. Now, the Royal Artillery Barracks at Woolwich house the 17th Training Regiment (the gunner depot for adult recruits), the Director Royal Artillery and his staff, Territorial Army headquarters and various regimental associations. The imposing mess, with its ceiling-high display-cases of gigantic silver centrepieces, has an institutional air, like that of a museum with an uncertain future.

The subaltern's military life varies according to the sort of regiment he joins. 'Air defence', said a senior officer, 'is a super job for subalterns' because they have a command and 'it is not so structured'. Those going straight to a field regiment soon find that it is a captain-heavy organization. An extreme case is 148 (Meiktila) Battery in the commando gunners, which needs six captains as forward observation officers for directing naval gunfire. Apart from gun position officer, there are few jobs for a newly arrived lieutenant, and no independent field command, because the battery operates in a body. Only in barracks will he be responsible for a section of two gun crews. On the other hand, if he is any good he will be pushed on to a captain's job, because the black hole shortage is so acute.

Out of all arms, the gunners are the shortest on officers. There is a standing joke amongst junior captains in the officers' mess at Larkhill that as soon as they see anyone above them in the Royal Artillery promotion list looking morose at a party or in the bar they go up to them and say: 'Yes, things are so bad that I'm thinking of leaving too.' For senior officers, the shortage is worrying, and also deeply frustrating at a time when the gunners have at last 'started to get the kit'.

For some reason gunner officers baffle their colleagues in other parts of the Army. In return, gunners feel misunderstood. They try hard to get their message across. The generous distribution of their magazine and journal around the Army, free of charge, prompted one gunner colonel to write: 'Could such a preponderance of Gunner mumbo-jumbo be one of the reasons why others treat us with suspicion?'[1]

Their *frères ennemis*, the sappers, treat them not with suspicion but with compulsive disparagement. A caricature lingers of characters who are slightly bumptious in a self-conscious way, perhaps trying to escape their own general's description of 'a certain ordinariness'. Their 'officer-issue' black Labradors, much rarer today because of the jokes on all-arms courses, were always considered a faintly preposterous attempt to look county.

Gunners are very sociable amongst themselves. They always seem to be off to some reunion dinner, and the masonic lodge, the largest in the Army, thrives. They are extremely hospitable, and their critics admit that they always mean well, albeit in a hail-fellow-well-met sort of way. Yet even the gunner general thought they were 'desperately introverted' and should mix more outside.

More important, he felt that the Royal Artillery was underrated by officers in the rest of the Army because artillery fire cannot be properly replicated on exercises;

people often forget that it won wars, and need to be reminded of General Menéndez's words when he surrendered in Port Stanley and spoke of the demoralizing effects of naval gunfire support and battery fire: 'It was the artillery which beat us.' Iraqi officers, deep in their bunkers, were hardly in a position to distinguish between aerial and ground bombardment, but the sympathy for the enemy expressed by British soldiers, as they watched the softening-up by guns and MLRS just before 1st Armoured Division attacked, was probably just as eloquent.

While gunners somehow seem to attract pigeon-holing, sappers, as befits a corps responsible for a wide variety of tasks, seem to defy it. Yet, although the Corps of Royal Engineers forms a church as broad in social background as in attitude, it has several common denominators. More of its officers have degrees than any other major capbadge.

Sapper officers are self-confident, yet seldom brash. And despite the civilian impression given by engineering skills such as surveyor draughtsman, construction materials technician and plant operator mechanic, they are far more military than the other arms seem to realize. In sporting terms, they are an active lot, with rugby and skiing, especially in Rhine Army regiments, sailing, scuba-diving, and mountaineering – Colonel Everest was a Royal Engineer. There is, however, one sporting field in which they are noticeably absent: a sapper on a horse is a rare sight.

The engineers probably deserve the motto of *Ubique* more than the artillery, if only because they are spread more widely. This dispersal camouflages their numbers – about 13,000 strong. Over half their strength is nonetheless devoted to the Rhine Army, where they have been losing as many NCOs and soldiers as the Royal Artillery.

Traditional military engineering tasks, such as survey, road-building, bridging, demolition and trench-digging (to 'sap' was to dig trenches to attack enemy fortifications), have been vastly extended. For example, another responsibility is airfield damage repair – the rapid filling of bomb craters to make the runway operational. In 1982, as part of Operation Corporate, the Royal Engineers laid a 3 1/2 mile pipeline to Wide-awake airfield on Ascension Island and built a bulk fuel installation to provide 300,000 gallons per day for the RAF, all in just over a week. Nine years later, the Engineers began to prepare for a far larger deployment.

One of the first construction tasks of Operation Granby – 39th Engineer Regiment's – was to prepare accommodation for the troops at the port of Al Jubail on the Saudi Arabian coast. A huge dockside warehouse known as Shed 4 was adapted. Then Tent City (later rechristened 'Baldrick Lines') was constructed to house 2,000 soldiers on a container park with kitchens, showers and lavatories.

The Engineers' most visible role in preparation for the ground offensive into Iraq was the rather euphemistically termed 'route development'. As practised by 32nd Armoured Engineer Regiment, this meant bulldozing breaches in berms for the tanks to go through, blasting a way through minefields with Giant Vipers, flailing the ground with Aardvark armoured vehicles, and demolishing any other obstacles with the stubby 165mm gun on their AVREs (armoured vehicle Royal Engineers).

When the fighting was over, the sappers' skills were still needed for repairing roads, clearing minefields and, in the case of 49 Explosive Ordnance Disposal Squadron, removing charges from the Kuwaiti oil wells. The British sappers alone had dealt with over 600,000 mines, unexploded ordnance and other devices by mid-March.

For the sappers, Germany means mainly combat engineering in support of the armoured divisions there. To their exasperation, the armoured battle groups who charge ahead on exercise in their Challengers and Warriors complain that the bridge-layers and other sapper vehicles are never there when they need them: this is because engineer regiments are still equipped with superannuated vehicles, many of them over twenty years old, and cannot keep up with the Challengers. In the Gulf the odd thirty-year-old Centurion with dozer blade and 165mm demolition gun earned nicknames such as 'the Antique Road Show' and 'Arthur Negus's Own'.

In addition to the close support regiment, each division also has a general support regiment. Equipped with much more plant, this larger unit concentrates on major defence construction projects and reinforces the mine laying or mine-clearing of the close support regiment. In addition there are the Corps units, including the amphibious engineer regiment for major river crossings, based at Hameln, the Hamelin of Pied Piper fame.

Sappers appear to like Hameln better than anywhere else in Germany. Few seem fond of any of their other bases and find service in the Rhine Army restrictive – a former commanding officer observed that the Royal Engineers were 'much more rigid' in Germany. Most sappers prefer to be in some isolated place, far from paperwork and chains of command. They like the challenge of an unusual task, whether advising the Afghans on mine clearance or 'a hearts and minds job' for villagers in Belize.

For the sappers, as for the rest of the Army, the end of the Gulf war means that Northern Ireland is once again the main operational commitment. There they have two major tasks: defence construction and searching for bombs and booby-traps – but not disarming them, which is the responsibility of the Royal Army Ordnance Corps. A third Royal Engineer speciality, boats and divers, is also important in such a land of loughs and inlets; 33 Independent Field Squadron, based on the shore of Lough Neagh, operates the high-speed Rigid Raider patrol boats used to intercept suspect craft.

Defence construction is the work of a resident field squadron nearly 300 strong. They build and repair security force bases, ranging from a corrugated-iron version of a US Cavalry fort to the new generation of super-sangars, whose wire-mesh rocket screens make them look like a modernistic aviary. Existing bases always appear to be undergoing repairs or improvements with blast walls and special roofs to counter mortar attacks. 'Rapid assembly protective wall' – military industrial cladding – is replacing the old cover-from-view screens in corrugated iron, or 'wriggly tin' as the soldiers call it.

The Royal Engineer workload has grown considerably as a result of Provisional IRA threats and attacks against civilian contractors. Sappers at work are vulnerable to sniper fire and have to be covered by infantry. If the border is ever wired off – the option has been studied – the engineers would be the only ones able to carry out such an immense and hazardous task.

The search teams attached to each of the three brigades come from a reinforced squadron on a six-month roulement tour. Each team of six men is commanded by a RESA – a Royal Engineer Search Adviser – who is usually a sergeant. He is called in when a suspected bomb is discovered, or if a hidden secondary device is feared after a single explosion. Once the RESA has made his search plan, the team begin their meticulous work with detector equipment to establish a safe path for the Royal Army Ordnance Corps bomb-disposal team. The main problems are caused by Semtex and the lack of metal parts in the detonating device. Sniffer dogs can be called in to help, but they are not always successful. An experienced RESA has been known to sniff out an explosive device himself in a drystone wall after a dog has failed to do so.

The line between Royal Engineer responsibilities for explosive ordnance disposal (EOD) and those of the Royal Army Ordnance Corps is complex. In general terms, the sappers are responsible for mine-clearance, range-clearance and unexploded aerial bombs (during the Falklands conflict they had to tackle those lodged in the unfamiliar depths of warships), while the ordnance corps concentrates on defective munitions and terrorist devices.

This division has created a rivalry between the two

corps so intense as to cause great amusement to other capbadges. The sappers say that the ordnance corps was only brought into the business to give it something sexier to do than counting blankets, while the ordnance corps claims that whenever a rusty old Luftwaffe bomb is dug up the sappers turn the whole performance into a drama by calling in the press.

Until the announcement of September 1989, which heralded an increase in the number of servicewomen employed, neither corps allowed women officers or NCOs to train in bomb disposal. Although women can now officially train in bomb disposal, they will not be used by the ordnance corps for tackling terrorist bombs, on the grounds that considerable strength is required to work in the 'heavy suit'.

The Royal Engineers have a number of less well known subsidiaries. The Military Survey Department is vital, given the Army's voracious consumption of maps. For the Falklands conflict, three-quarters of a million were printed. In Germany, the 14th Topographical Squadron (14 Topo) at Ratingen near Dusseldorf has twelve million maps in its store. With each map valued at about a pound, cartography is an expensive operation. But, however meticulous their work, military map-makers know they can never please. If a wood has not been cut down since the last edition – the usual excuse for mistaking one's position – the exercise is bound to take place just where four sheets join. For Operation Granby, the squadron's obsolescent print train – a huge tractor-towed vehicle for printing maps *in situ* – was shipped from Rattingen to Al Jubail, then moved northwards where the squadron began production for 1st Armoured Division and the US Marines.

The Postal and Courier Section is almost like a small corps in its own right with a page to itself in the Army List. From its depot at Mill Hill in north London, it runs the whole network of British Forces' Post Offices around the world. But the depot is due to move so that Inglis

Barracks, which was bombed in 1988 by the PIRA, can be sold off for redevelopment.

The sappers have a 'coloured beret' side too, with 59 Independent Commando Squadron and 9 Para Squadron, both of which served in the Falklands conflict. Whether jumping from a Hercules or landing 'over the beach', they are initially hampered by the restricted range of equipment, especially plant, they can take with them. The field squadron with the 24th Air Mobile Brigade is in a much better position. They can ride to work in a large Chinook helicopter.

Another alternative to mainstream sappering is service with the Queen's Gurkha Engineers in Hong Kong, although 69 Independent Field Squadron based at Chatham goes to the Falklands and Belize on roulement tours just like the others.

With detachments all over the world, the Royal Corps of Signals is perhaps even more widespread than the engineers. Signallers are unhampered by regimental tradition and take great pride in their technical professionalism, though this combination only seems to confirm the old gut feeling at the top table that the scientifically minded seldom make natural formation commanders.

This may be the outward expression of another prejudice. The Royal Signals has the highest proportion of Welbexians in the Army, in that just over half its regular officers came in that way; and a stereotype of 'the Welbexian clone' is deeply embedded in the officer consciousness of the combat arms. Welbexians are thought colourless and conformist, archetypal products of 'the chameleon process' at Sandhurst. Some suspect that the Welbeck system attracts a certain type of earnest boy who, pushed on by parents, is especially susceptible to moulding. A sapper colonel, on the other hand, pointed out that there were interesting exceptions. He had come across a number who, perhaps reacting against their education, had become positively eccentric.

The Royal Signals are slightly smaller than the Royal Artillery. Unlike the gunners, under half their strength is in Germany, yet by early in 1991 they had become the worst-recruited arm of all for soldiers and the second worst-recruited after the gunners for officers. Around half of their officers in 1990 were commissioned from the sergeants' mess, by far the highest proportion of all the combat arms.

The Rhine Army has a wide variety of signals units: 16th Signal Regiment for rear areas communications, 21st for liaison with the RAF and 28th for Northern Army Group. In addition, 1st (British) Corps has a signals brigade of two corps communications regiments, 7th and 22nd, and 14th (Electronic Warfare) Regiment. There is also, for the moment, 29th Signal Regiment in Berlin.

Each armoured division – like 1st Armoured Division in the Gulf – has its own headquarters and signals regiment, which provides each brigade with a headquarters and signal squadron. One of their main tasks is to operate Ptarmigan, which is basically the battlefield answer to the car telephone. Ptarmigan is a secure system, and thus saves an enormous amount of encoding and decoding. The Royal Signals operate it with 'trunk node troops', spread out in small detachments and acting as rebroadcast and scrambling stations.

The Royal Signals is 'a corps of detachments'. Almost everything depends on a small group commanded by a corporal, such as a rebroadcast crew on a hill. 'It's the most important rank we've got,' said a squadron commander. 'As an OC you've got to trust him or sack him.' Some come to enjoy lonely spots. One corporal has volunteered for five tours on the same mountain top in the Falklands, with a shift system of eight hours on, sixteen hours off, and only one break in four and a half months.

In the United Kingdom, the Royal Signals has a large training organization, with the Apprentices' College at Harrogate, the School of Signals at Blandford, and 8th and 11th Training Regiment at Catterick. Blandford is also the base for 30th Signal Regiment, which provides satellite communications (SATCOM) detachments for intervention formations such as 5th Airborne Brigade and mobile forces. Alpha Troop is attached to ACE Mobile Force and Bravo Troop to the United Kingdom Mobile Force. The other SATCOM specialists are 264 Signal Squadron, permanently attached to the SAS.

Signallers are not often in the public eye, but when attention focused on them in Namibia in 1989 the elements of 30th Signal Regiment loaned to the UN Transition Assistance Group could hardly have done better amidst the sorry chaos. Their commanding officer, Lieutenant Colonel Neil Donaldson, became something of a media hero, although mercifully not in the Mad Mitch mould. The way he and the Australians faced up to South African officers even managed to restore some credibility to the UN operation. This in itself was a considerable achievement. The regiment again attracted press attention in August 1990 when it was the first ground force detachment sent to the Gulf as part of Operation Granby to establish satellite communications with London and High Wycombe.

Other groups liable to move at short notice include 244 Signal Squadron at Brize Norton, which provides the communications between the RAF and the Army. Apart from 9th Signal Regiment in Cyprus, which forms part of the GCHQ listening network, most of the rest of the world is dotted with independent squadrons and even troops. There are trickle-posted signal troops in Belize and Hong Kong and with the UN Force in Cyprus; the Falklands, on the other hand, has a tri-service Joint Communications Unit. Hong Kong is also the base for the Queen's Gurkha Signals.

In this age of specialization and rationalization, almost every corps has a rival in at least one field. For the Royal Signals the field is information technology, and their rival is the Royal Army Pay Corps, which started from a stronger position because it has the Army's mainframe at its depot in Hampshire. The tri-service Defence Automatic Data Processing Training Centre is now established with the School of Signals at Blandford in Dorset, but the reorganization of the Army's various computer systems is not a task to be envied.

The Army has vast stocks of data and statistics, but often cannot use them, because they can only be extracted manually. No commercial organization would tolerate such a state of affairs because, unlike the Services, their accounting procedures cost in the time of their executives. In 1989, the Commander UK Field Army at Wilton had a chart made with all the different systems in use. It ran round two walls of his office. There was hardly a system capable of talking to another. One senior officer faced with the problem described the situation as 'an absolute horror story'. The whole area of information technology in the Army was 'an absolute morass'. That the Pentagon has suffered just as badly can be of little consolation. With ADA (All Defense Applications) it had to reconcile around a hundred different languages.

Another major difficulty will continue to be recruiting and, above all, holding those with any talent. The Army is losing programmers fast just when it needs many more. The Royal Signals may be very stretched in their existing fields, but they have one advantage over other combat arms. They can employ many more women.

CHAPTER 24

Special Intelligence and Special Forces

Allied intelligence did not have a good war in the Gulf. In fact this was one of the few occasions when intelligencers have been held responsible for something of an anticlimax rather than a nasty shock. Part of the trouble seems to have been that estimates of enemy strength were given margins of added caution at each stage in the system, rather like value added tax. The Allies were so conscious of the dangers that they made the opposite mistake to the famous failures, such as Arnhem and the Ardennes offensive, when the enemy threat was discounted because the commander did not want to believe in it.

If anything illustrated how much the United States had to catch up in the intelligence field during the Second World War it was the famous statement by Henry Stimson, a former Secretary of State, that 'gentlemen do not read other people's mail'. For once ahead of the game, the British were very interested in the cryptanalysis of other people's radio messages. Although this did not win the war, it certainly helped to save us from losing it. In the Cold War years, the Americans, perhaps compensating for their inauspicious start, took intelligence gathering to excess. In Vietnam, their processing system became clogged and the bureaucratic machinery worked directly against Patton's dictum that intelligence should be 'like eggs, the fresher the better'.[1] The British plugged away in their shadow. They certainly made mistakes and lacked resources, but they seem to have remembered the basic lessons better.

Intelligence work should not be a haphazard series of one-offs, but a continual cycle: direction, collection, processing, dissemination. It is a chicken-and-egg process, because direction, which consists of defining the problem and working out how to tackle it, will be largely determined by previous experience and information. 'Commanders', said a senior officer, 'tend to regard intelligence like logistics, but it is crucial that they give the direction. Unless the intelligence system gets that direction at the start, there's a tendency to go off and collect almost anything.'

Once the objective and means have been decided, the collection agencies are tasked and they in turn task the relevant sources. A source can include anything from satellite intelligence (SATINT) to signals intelligence (SIGINT), stand-off radar in fixed-wing aircraft, RAF photo reconnaissance or Army Air Corps 'heli-tele' to armoured recce units, field intelligence or front-line infantry. The collection agency chain in the field army – 'overt intelligence as opposed to sneaky-beaky' – runs from unit Intelligence Officer (the IO) to the 'int cell' at brigade headquarters and on up to theatre headquarters.

Processing consists of three stages: collation, evaluation and interpretation. The problem of sorting the wheat from the chaff is immeasurably reduced by computers, provided of course that they are correctly programmed. Computers can identify enemy formations from their component elements, but first the photographic interpreters have to give them the right information. As a standard safeguard, confirmation is required from a separate source to eliminate error. All work should also be subjected to continuous review, so that the task in hand is not forgotten and the temptation to chase hares resisted.

The greatest danger is to lose objectivity. An analyst has to guard against the instinct to eliminate evidence which conflicts with a favoured theory or pattern. And, because 'deception is a fairly big deal, he must check that material is not being deliberately fed'. Clever deceptions pander first to existing suspicions.

Finally, the last segment of the circle, dissemination, is as vital as all the others. There is no point collecting intelligence if the right elements of information do not reach the right people in time for them to take a decision. A further aspect should also be added: the best intelligence is no good unless the commander is prepared to believe it. History is littered with examples of commanders rejecting intelligence which conflicted with their own wishful certainty.

In the Gulf war, signals intelligence gave the number of headquarters, while satellite intelligence provided the basis of calculation of the ratio of manpower to observed vehicles. But with Iraqi units, especially in the front line, up to 50 per cent under strength, and with the Iraqi use of decoy tanks and guns to disperse the effect of air attack, estimates of enemy strength ranged up to around 600,000 when the true figure may have been as low as 300,000. Confirmation of these estimates could come only from human intelligence on the ground (HUMINT). In southern Iraq and occupied Kuwait, the main source of battlefield intelligence came from the teams of special forces swanning around at night. Ironically, their reports of under-strength and demoralized Iraqi units were taken with a strong pinch of salt, on the assumption that their overconfident teams, running rings round their enemies, would naturally tend to scorn their fighting potential.

One of the most important post-war reforms has been the establishment of the Defence Intelligence Staff. This development was inevitable, but 'jointery' seems to work more effectively in the intelligence world than in other areas of tri-service co-operation. 'It's so much better than it used to be,' said a senior Intelligence Corps officer. 'If you try to do it on your own you only get part of the picture. The vast bulk of the intelligence business is joint nowadays.'

The Chief of Defence Intelligence is a three-star appointment which rotates between the three Services. A lieutenant general recently relinquished the post, so a soldier will not be in the chair again for a few years. The CDI is not an 'intelligencer' by profession, but he must have had high-level purple experience. One of the best preparations for the post is to have been Commander British Forces –

Falklands, Cyprus, or Hong Kong – or Commander Land Forces Northern Ireland.

In general terms, defence intelligence work is split between Nato-relevant and ROW, 'rest of the world'. The CDI reports direct to the Permanent Secretary, but probably has more 'dotted lines' of liaison than almost any other three-star appointment. One of the most important of these is his link to the Deputy Chief of the Defence Staff (Commitments) responsible for the Joint Operations Centre, whose subordinates include the Director Special Forces. (The Director SAS, a one-star appointment on the General Staff who reports to the Assistant Chief of the General Staff, has been double-hatted as Director Special Forces since 1987.)

The Defence Intelligence Staff also report to the Joint Intelligence Committee, the umbrella organization of which the CDI is a member, along with the director-generals of the Security Service and the Secret Intelligence Service. The Joint Intelligence Committee, in theory both the fuse and junction box of the whole British intelligence community, tries to ensure that duplication of activity is kept to a minimum, and, most important of all, that the different agencies don't bump into each other in the dark. 'But nonsenses will still happen,' said the same senior officer philosophically. The classic example occurred during the Vietnam War, and is taught as a warning. A US Army commando force mounted an attack to rescue some American prisoners held near the Ho Chi Minh Trail, but they arrived to find the camp waterlogged and deserted. The North Vietnamese had been forced to move the prisoners because the CIA had just organized a sabotage operation to flood the supply route.

Wherever possible, 'jointery' begins in training. The Joint School of Photographic Interpretation is at RAF Wyton, and the Defence Intelligence and Security School and the Joint Services Interrogation Wing are co-located with the headquarters of the Intelligence Corps and its depot at Ashford in Kent.

The Intelligence Corps' first incarnation from 1914 to 1919 was a typically British example of improvisation for war, followed by its demise through lack of official interest as soon as peace came. One of its major tasks was, and remains, the interrogation of prisoners. In July 1940, the Corps was resurrected, and survived beyond the Second World War because of the Cold War and the Malayan Emergency. But its position was not securely established until 1958, when it was finally allowed a permanent cadre of regular officers. 'Borneo really was the start of everything,' said one of their colonels, 'because it was an intelligence war.' Twenty-seven years later, largely as a result of active service in Northern Ireland and the Falklands, the Intelligence Corps became the seventh (and smallest) combat arm. In the Gulf war, Intelligence Corps officers worked closely with US Army divisional headquarters, and their cypress-green berets stood out as much as the maroon berets in the headquarters of 1st Armoured Division.

The Intelligence Corps has to be different. For a start it is a 'closed corps'. Every member undergoes positive vetting by the Army's Directorate of Security. And every soldier who passes out from the depot automatically becomes a lance corporal. (In a rank-conscious organization, briefings from a private would not carry weight.) Most have the equivalent of four O levels, quite a number have three or four A levels, though the myth – still current within the Army – that many of them have degrees is a great exaggeration; usually there is no more than one per intake. From time to time, however, an unusual and brilliant former public schoolboy, searching for something different, insists on joining the corps as a soldier, rather than as an officer.

Applicants are sent from the recruiting office to Ashford before signing up. Liaison with recruiting offices is important since so few people in the Army know much about the Intelligence Corps. At Ashford, they do a modern languages aptitude test, and are given an idea of what a career in the corps involves.

Their first part of basic training is the same as for every other arm. During the second part they begin on the basic skills of the main Intelligence Corps trade, as an operator in intelligence and security (Op Int & Sy). They learn map-marking, presentation and briefing – they will be virtually the only NCOs in the Army to brief generals. Other subjects include basic German, the Warsaw Pact, photographic interpretation, still photography and an introduction to computers. Every soldier has to pass a driving test before going on to Leconfield in north Humberside for Land Rover training, since the Intelligence Corps operates in small self-contained groups. Finally, eight months after arriving, and qualified as an A3 Op Int & Sy, they march off the parade ground as lance corporals, having already received their posting order.

Roughly a third of all NCOs, those with the right skills and aptitudes, follow a different path as an operator in special intelligence, usually known as an Opsi. But whichever branch they join, there will always be another exam to pass or qualification needed to receive promotion. The Intelligence Corps NCO enjoys one of the fastest promotion rates in the Army, mainly because 'intelligence is a growth industry', as everyone keeps saying. The only complication is that growth comes in the senior ranks and there are not enough NCOs coming through quickly enough to keep up the momentum.

The enviable rate of promotion and specialist pay, particularly for an Opsi, are hard-earned. In Northern Ireland – 'essentially an intelligence war' – the strain of work inevitably produces its own form of casualty from time to time. Responsibility for an NCO comes early, whatever his special qualifications. The FINCO (field intelligence NCO) lives off his wits and out of touch with higher command. In Borneo they worked on their own from kampongs in the jungle for months at a time.

With such a high calibre of NCO, it is no handicap to have over 40 per cent of officers promoted from the ranks. The vast majority are commissioned warrant officers, but each year two or three of the most promising young NCOs – they have to be under twenty-three – go to Sandhurst as Army entrants.

The Intelligence Corps also differs in its selection process for young officers. Most potential candidates are put in touch by university liaison officers. Some write direct, but they are redirected back into the system. 'I'm always slightly suspicious of people who just want to come into the Int Corps,' said the officer in charge of officer recruiting. The attraction to fantasists is obvious. Candidates have to be good officer material first; special aptitudes come second. A brilliant linguist who cannot organize a platoon attack will never get through Sandhurst.

The Intelligence Corps organizes 'familiarization visits' to Ashford for up to 140 prospective officers a year. Most are at university. 'We aren't too fussed as to what they read, although a good analytical subject is useful, and of course a language.' Those keen to continue are interviewed either before or after they have attended the Regular Commissions Board. Around a dozen are accepted. The Intelligence Corps is not very interested in short-service commission officers unless they are very good and liable to stay on. This is because 'they are really of no use to us until they've done four years or so'.

After passing out from Sandhurst, a subaltern spends a month at Ashford on 'corps briefing and orientation' before he is sent off to an infantry battalion. This attachment ensures that he acquires an experience and an understanding of the mainstream Army, and also provides him with useful employment, since there are so few jobs for inexperienced lieutenants. Ideally, he will serve with a battalion in Northern Ireland. The arrangement is popular with infantry commanding officers, who are often desperately short of platoon commanders. For reasons of personal security, the young subaltern will not wear the cypress-green beret of the Intelligence Corps, but the headgear of his host regiment.

After at least nine months with the infantry, he returns to Ashford for three months' special-to-arm training. Depending on his specialization, he will then go on to language training – German, Russian and Arabic are the main languages – or to his first job with an intelligence section at a headquarters in the United Kingdom, or to Northern Ireland. After between one and three years' experience, most officers will command a security section. There, the main job is to advise the rest of the Army on security and check on their measures. From then on careers can follow any one of a number of paths, but all are subject to the regulated steps of courses and exams on the road to Staff College.

Some young officers switch to the Intelligence Corps from other parts of the Army. Transferees must be under twenty-eight, and they should have 'some form of intelligence training, either as an IO [unit intelligence officer] and SO 3 G2 [staff captain intelligence] or in special duties in Northern Ireland'.

Mainly for security reasons, the Intelligence Corps directorate is involved in all officer postings. The Military Secretary's branch has to be guided, because it cannot know why a particular officer must never be sent back to a particular place. The directorate also has to root for its officers on selection boards because the rest of the Army does not really understand their work, and therefore cannot judge an officer's performance. The old assumption that they are backroom boys with little field experience still militates against them. But partly thanks to the combat arm tag, and the years of close work with the infantry in Northern Ireland, the Intelligence Corps is increasingly accepted as mainstream, and seen less and less as a 'funny'.

At higher levels, however, the trend is if anything in the other direction. Intelligence has become such a specialized business that a recent Military Secretary, General Sir Patrick Palmer, decreed with the Army Board's approval that certain senior appointments should be Intelligence-Corps-tied. (In 1989, 40 per cent of their colonels were in tied posts, and three-quarters of their lieutenant colonels.) This was more remarkable than may appear on the surface. The Army in general does not like the idea of tied appointments: above all, it is deeply suspicious of 'black arts', such as intelligence and information technology, which exclude the non-specialist. Inter-arm suspicion of backroom boys dates back to the Second World War when the Intelligence Corps badge, a rose set in a laurel wreath, was described as 'a pansy resting on its laurels'.

During the Second World War women constituted an essential part of the intelligence community. When given the chance, they proved how effective their contribution could be. In some areas, such as photographic interpretation, they are recognized to be better than men, while those sent into the field by SOE were no less courageous than their male colleagues.

A peacetime army is incomparably more cautious. Women are not allowed in a full field intelligence role, even though the deployment rules have now been eased. Yet a general closely involved in the field said that he saw 'no reason why a woman should not become director of the Intelligence Corps'. Senior officers in the Corps agreed, with reservations – 'given the right woman', which meant clearly exceptional. 'Women can't do the sharp end stuff,' said one, 'which may be a disadvantage, but they can make it up if they're very intelligent.' On present levels – just under 5 per cent of the Intelligence Corps officer strength is female – a woman would indeed have to be outstanding.

That such a paragon should eventually appear is not impossible. The young women officers 'are invariably of much higher quality'. But their careers may be limited, if not by marriage, by the required resignation on pregnancy. So far no woman officer has gone beyond a major commanding an intelligence and security company in Germany. But, since the number of women will more than double over the next few years, so should the opportunities.

A small corps, especially one working in the world of intelligence, could easily produce an introverted, even paranoid mentality, but the Intelligence Corps is spread around in small detachments working closely with the field army so the risk is reduced. And although it is different from the rest of the Army in many ways, the Intelligence Corps is not as eccentric or unmilitary as outsiders might imagine. First names may be used in operational circumstances for reasons of personal security, but they are 'not as informal as special forces, who tend to be very informal in certain situations'.

The Army's position on the subject of the Special Air Service is not entirely consistent. It maintains an air of disdain for the fascination the SAS arouses in the press, yet rather relishes it. 'Much of the publicity surrounding the alleged activities and roles of the SAS is at best guesswork,' runs the Military Secretary's advice to potential volunteers; then it adds: 'that there is an air of mystique surrounding such a unit is undeniably true.'

Based just outside Hereford, at Stirling Lines, 22 SAS Regiment has a predictably unusual organization. Regimental headquarters controls the back-up and training side as well as directing the four sabre squadrons, A, B, D and G Squadron. (That a regiment co-founded by a Foot Guard – David Stirling during the North African campaign – should have taken on the cavalry nomenclature of sabre squadrons is indeed curious.) G Squadron was so named because it was supposed to be based on the former Guards Independent Parachute Company, but the wholesale transplant of such a different organization never worked. R Squadron, an additional patrol squadron, can be added in time of emergency from ex-SAS reservists.

Each squadron has four troops, usually a captain and fifteen men, and a signal troop or eight-man satellite communications detachment from 264 Squadron Royal Signals, whose members will accompany them wherever they go. Each of the four troops has a different specialization: mountain, amphibious, mobility (vehicles) and an air troop trained in tactical free-fall parachuting, including HALO – high altitude low opening – an activity described by one Army pamphlet as 'swift, silent and exciting'. The sabre troop divides into four-man teams. The four-man 'brick', later fire-team, or team, became the basic operational infantry unit in Northern Ireland, partly as a result of SAS experience of working in pairs.

The troops rotate on a squadron basis between overseas training (the SAS goes on small-scale exercises, by squadron or half-squadron, in most parts of the world), Northern Ireland, leave periods, skills upgrading, and periods of stand-by: both military and the anti-terrorist special project teams waiting for a MACP (military aid to the civil power) call-out.

Training and contingency planning is carried out and continually revised by a permanent cadre of some half a dozen officers and over 150 NCOs. Specialist skills, amphibious, sub-aqua, and both static line and free-fall parachuting are taught at the relevant establishment, courses for which the training wing merely acts 'as booking clerks'. The training wing concentrates on basic skills – entry and exfiltration, demolition and combat medical. The operations and intelligence wing has a CRW (counter-revolutionary warfare) department to teach anti-terrorist techniques, including close-quarters combat and hostage rescue, taught in what is known as 'the killing house'. Language skills are taught with unconventional techniques, such as learning during sleep. The intelligence and operational research departments are well staffed and, above all, well equipped with computer systems which have on file the detailed plans of every make of commercial aircraft and most of the key buildings in the country. Other attachments include an integrated RAMC medical team and an Army Air Corps flight in direct support.

Nobody can go straight into the SAS. Troopers come from all arms and services, usually having served at least three years. Most are from the infantry, but the determination of 'loggies' – those from the logistic corps – to prove themselves as good if not better than the combat arms is striking. A soldier becomes a trooper on qualifying for the SAS even though he may have been a corporal, but although he does not carry on in his 'green army' rank he does not lose out on his former rate of pay. He will also receive SAS additional pay. (In the 1991 pay award this came to a maximum of £2,562 extra a year for corporals and below, £5,856 for WO2s and below, and up to £6,822 for all officers and WO1s.)

In theory, an officer applicant for the SAS must have his commanding officer's recommendation as being 'particularly suitable' for Special Forces marked in the box provided in Section 3 of his confidential report, but the headquarters at Hereford takes little notice of this. They tend to find that those most warmly recommended are frequently the least suitable. Four potential officers' briefing courses a year are held at Hereford and one in Germany, each lasting just under two days. Attendance is obligatory before a volunteer goes forward for the SAS's euphemistically entitled 'aptitude course'.

Five weeks of muscular masochism 'through the pain barrier' – anything up to sixty miles in twenty-four hours over the Brecon Beacons with heavy Bergen packs – and mental stress, including resistance to interrogation, has become progressively more intensive. At any moment an instructor may appear from nowhere to assess determination, murmuring like Mephistopheles to the candidate that he only has to say the word and he can return to dry clothes, warmth and food. To consider the temptation even for an instant means immediate failure. Psychological screening has been brought in, but for officers the most daunting form of test comes during the final selection, known as 'first sight': their introduction to 'the regiment'.

During 'first sight', which takes place in the training-wing theatre, those officers who have made it through the endurance tests have to stand up and address the assembled company, including the commanding officer and the Director Special Forces, as well as a select group of outsiders defined as 'friends of the regiment'. Afterwards comes very tough and disrespectful questioning from the soldiers, demanding why somebody with a posh accent thinks he is capable of commanding them. A vote is then taken on whether or not he is to be accepted into the regiment. Everyone has a single vote, yes or no. Pure democracy is, however, diminished by the overriding vote of the commanding officer or the Director Special Forces, although they will use it as little as possible.

The aptitude course is followed by continuation training in parachuting, combat survival and a stint at the jungle warfare school in Brunei, which produces its own rash of casualties, albeit of a rather more exotic kind. Although there is a WRAC detachment at Hereford, servicewomen are barred from an operational role. At the moment, the closest they get to the dramatic part is on training exercises, playing the part of hostages or hijacked passengers on a grounded airliner. But the possibility that women could be used in certain circumstances has certainly not been ruled out.

In Northern Ireland, rumours about the SAS can be both an advantage and a disadvantage. Tremendous confusion exists about the different intelligence organizations and agencies involved in the province. (Some officers joke that things seem just as confusing on the inside.) The unclear dividing lines between the responsibilities of the Army, the Security Service and the RUC Special Branch have led to a good deal of exasperation.

Even within what might best be described as the 'un-green army', the volunteers on 'special duties' attached to what used to be called 14 Intelligence and Security Company have frequently been thought to be members of the SAS. But the SAS is not used in Northern Ireland for the sort of 'sneaky-beaky' intelligence work in which the special duties boys are engaged. They would be wasted in random gathering or speculative ambushes. Their speciality is to 'act on hard intelligence', which means to ambush the ambushers, such as their operations at Loughall in May 1987, Gibraltar in March 1988, Omagh five months later, and Coagh in East Tyrone in June 1991. Imitating their enemy, they too play a waiting game.

In more conventional military operations – the Falklands conflict provided an opportunity only surpassed in the Gulf – the SAS can play as important a part in intelligence gathering as in attack. Standing patrols from G Squadron, having been landed by helicopter three weeks before the main landing, lay hidden very close to Argentinian positions for extremely long periods. Their information provided a very accurate picture of the state of Argentinian morale and capabilities, and they pinpointed targets for naval gunfire missions and Harrier strikes.

D Squadron, on the other hand, performed a classic sabotage mission against the airstrip on Pebble Island when, with hand-placed charges, they destroyed eleven aircraft and a quantity of munitions. It could almost have been one of the early SAS exploits in the Western Desert. The greatest danger in the Falklands came from overconfidence, not so much through underestimating the enemy but underestimating the weather and disregarding Murphy's Law that everything that can go wrong will go wrong.

When Iraq invaded Kuwait, SAS deployment to the Gulf was very rapid because of the desperate need for reliable human intelligence (HUMINT) obtained on the ground. The SATINT and SIGINT pictures of the situation could be interpreted in two ways. One group, as is usually the case, was already in the region on training.

A far higher proportion of the regiment was committed than during the Falklands conflict. The equivalent of only a squadron was left behind in England to guard against terrorist emergencies. Most of the regular sabre squadrons, followed by R Squadron of reservists, and reinforced by some Territorials from 21 and 23 SAS, deployed in the late summer and autumn of 1990.

The desert war was the ideal opportunity for the SAS to test their new Longline LSVs (light strike vehicles). Six of these vehicles were acquired at the beginning of 1989 and, on proving satisfactory, a further twenty were ordered shortly before the Iraqi invasion of Kuwait. An LSV can be parachuted along with its crew, who can then camouflage it – virtually burying it and themselves by day – and range freely in the hours of darkness using night vision aids and satellite navigation at speeds over rough ground at up to 100 kilometres per hour. Armament can be mounted from a single general-purpose machine gun up to a 40mm grenade launcher and even a Milan anti-tank missile launcher. The Longline is much lighter than the US special forces' dune buggy, which looks more like something out of a Mad Max movie.

The Longline teams, usually a pair of vehicles, were mainly used in the first few weeks as hounds to track the mobile Scud launchers. Deep into Iraq, they identified aircraft bunkers and Scud and Frog missile sites for laser target acquisition equipment. They also seized Iraqi prisoners, who were 'exfiltrated' at night by helicopter for interrogation. Once the battle started, the biggest danger was from 'friendly fire', but there were two clashes with the enemy which were not on terms chosen by the regiment. Once again, the problem appears to have stemmed from overconfidence. Casualties comprised four killed (a sergeant from the Royal Army Ordnance Corps, two corporals from the Royal Engineers and a private from the Parachute Regiment); and two captured (a captain from the Royal Anglians and a senior NCO from the Parachute Regiment). Later in the battle, once the ground offensive was under way, they were able to revert to their role in Western Desert days as raiding forces.

*

It is not just the operational professionalism of the SAS which intrigues people, both within the Army and outside, but the motives and character of men prepared to devote themselves so exclusively to military perfectionism. With slogans such as 'we walk alone' and the quotation on their memorial clocktower at Hereford –

> We are the pilgrims, Master, we shall go
> Always a little further. It may be
> Beyond that last blue mountain buried with snow,
> Across that angry or glimmering sea.

– the SAS conveyed an impression of quasi-oriental mysticism, a sort of transcendental suffering of strength through pain. This used to prompt officers, quite content to forgo such ordeals, to remark that one really did have to be a bit peculiar to want to do that sort of thing. But ever since the Falklands conflict, which produced something of a 'tabbing' cult of carrying heavy loads across country, the emphasis at Hereford has become rather less spiritual and rather more physical. This, and a Parachute Regiment major in charge of the training wing, led to an influx of 'punchy paras'. The Parachute Regiment has been in a position to fill a higher proportion of the officer vacancies than any of the infantry divisions, because it is one of the very few capbadges with a surplus of extremely fit subalterns and captains. There are of course bound to be fluctuations. Not long ago, two out of four squadron commanders were cavalrymen.

For the SAS, as for other regiments, stereotypes are misleading. You can meet some perfectly relaxed and well-balanced characters whose personalities certainly do not seem to have been warped. On the other hand, one also hears rather disturbing accounts of an introverted society with distinctly illiberal views. They are almost bound to acquire a view of the world that cannot allow for shades of grey. Their professionalism, a relentlessness of training and testing to prevent the slightest slide into complacency, leads to a single-mindedness akin to that of a Wimbledon champion. In addition there is the unplanned brainwashing of a kill-or-be-killed training environment, and the inevitable addiction to danger.

Soldiers and NCOs are more likely to be affected than officers. Most officers serve only one or two tours, because progress in their career requires experience on the Staff and a return to the mainstream. Soldiers, meanwhile, stay much longer with the Regiment – often for ten years or more – and service with it becomes the only thing in their life which means anything. This makes it very difficult for them to come to terms with leaving – usually into the outside world, for few can face the prospect of a return to conventional soldiering. And, as many members of special forces have found ever since the Second World War, it is very hard to adjust to civilian life. Coming off an addiction to tension and danger can produce as bad a form of 'cold turkey' as giving up drugs. It can also be an embittering experience and foster a sense of betrayal.

Unable to face the claustrophobia of anything like an office, some try to freelance, perhaps running a survival school. Financial problems lead many into accepting the large salaries offered by firms with often disturbing reputations who offer bodyguard services and various 'security packages' to individuals, companies and governments. These organizations seem to be viewed with unease in the 'green army'. One major recounted how representatives of two well-known companies in the field, lecturing on terrorism at Staff College, received 'a rough ride' when it came to question time.

The regiment at Hereford comes directly under the Director SAS, a brigadier, who reports to the Assistant Chief of the General Staff. Wearing his other hat, he is also Director Special Forces on the Defence Staff. This provides a general counter-terrorism command for both SAS and the SBS, the Royal Marines' Special Boat Section, responsible for off-shore operations whether along a coast, on a ship or on an oil rig. There is a perhaps a predictable tendency amongst members of the SAS to regard the SBS as 'a bit of a poor cousin'.

The SAS is far better placed in Whitehall battles than any other capbadge, and not just because it is incomparably better represented in the hierarchy than ever before: in 1991 one four-star general, two three-star generals and a two-star general had spent significant parts of their careers with the regiment and all had served as Director SAS. General Sir Peter de la Billière, as has already been mentioned, owed his appointment as Commander British Forces Middle East to Mrs Thatcher's admiration of his handling of the Iranian Embassy siege when in that post.

Admiring the regiment's single-mindedness and pursuit of excellence, Mrs Thatcher viewed the SAS with something akin to maternal pride and showed herself ready to defend them like a lioness. She was certainly not the first prime minister to be fascinated by special forces, nor will she be the last. And, even though Mr Major's temperament is unlikely to produce a similar pitch of enthusiasm, the SAS is the least likely unit to be threatened by disbandment or amalgamation or even budgetary restrictions after the Defence Review.

Every effort is taken to shield the SAS from hostile, or even curious, gaze. Great care clearly has to be taken to protect personal and operational security: the Provisional IRA's longing for revenge cannot be doubted. The names of SAS personnel are never divulged for 'operational reasons', and regimental occasions have to be guarded most vigilantly. With remarkable coincidence, less than two hours after the mortar attack on 10 Downing Street which took place on 7 February 1991, the memorial service for Colonel Sir David Stirling, the regiment's founder, started in the Guards' Chapel. With armed teams from the regiment in position, security was considerably better round Wellington Barracks than Downing Street. The regiment's 50th anniversary celebrations required similar precautions.

Nevertheless, the all-embracing blackout applied to the

SAS has gone beyond normal security measures. In 1989 the page listing the regiment's title, motto, battle honours and regimental march was removed from the Army List. One cannot help sensing the development of another of those official fictions that an organization does not exist.

CHAPTER 25

The Three Qs and Other Corps

The three 'Q Services', as they used to be called, today comprise the Royal Corps of Transport, the Royal Army Ordnance Corps and the Royal Electrical and Mechanical Engineers. Together they account for over a fifth of the Army's strength.

The old term, Q or Q Branch, was a reference to the Quartermaster General's empire. Their history over the last century or so provides several examples of that old Army party game of about-turn and as-you-were. Supply and transport services were split and later merged and then 'ordnance' and 'commissariat and transport' were separated again. Between the two world wars, the Royal Army Ordnance Corps was basically responsible for stores and repair, and the Royal Army Service Corps for commissariat and transport. The most important development occurred in 1942, when the whole system came under severe strain in the Western Desert. Repair was given to a new corps, the Royal Electrical and Mechanical Engineers. The process was finally taken to its logical conclusion in 1965 when the Royal Army Service Corps surrendered its remaining supply functions to the ordnance corps, and concentrated on transport and movements in its new guise of the Royal Corps of Transport.

Fortunately, the capbadge rivalries between the logistic corps are much less intense than those between the combat arms. On the other hand, to the amusement of the combat arms, some of the 'loggies' – the ordnance and the RCT and, above all, the Royal Pioneer Corps – often try to be more combat than the infantry. The Directorate of Army Training discovered to its amazement that, out of the entire

Army, the ordnance corps packed the most drill into recruit training.

One area where the logistic corps can be as 'tactical as the teeth' is when serving with the 'coloured beret' brigades and the ACE (Allied Command Europe) or UK Mobile Force. Each has its logistic support battalion, the first two manned by green- and maroon-bereted 'loggies' who have passed the same commando or para course as the gunners and engineers.

Members of the Royal Corps of Transport are, not surprisingly, rather fond of quoting Churchill's dictum: 'If victory is a brightly coloured flower, transport is the stem without which it could never have blossomed.' The RCT's first task is the delivery of stores, munitions and fuel to the fighting troops, and their performance in the Gulf more than played its part in Churchill's quasi-Confucian aphorism.

After the Yom Kippur War, Nato armies realized that their estimates of tank and artillery ammunition expenditure were woefully low, and war stocks were doubled. A corresponding increase in cross-country delivery was needed. Just in time for the test which really counted, a revolutionary new delivery lorry known as DROPS (demountable rack and off-load pick-up system) was introduced in 1990. DROPS increased delivery potential fivefold mainly because no fork-lift trucks are needed: the driver on his own can offload a flat-rack of ten 1-ton standard Nato pallets in ninety seconds. This highly versatile vehicle was used in the Gulf war for delivering ammunition, fuel, stores, water tanks and even armoured vehicles.

Each armoured division in Germany has its own regular transport regiment, and the British Corps in Germany has other general transport regiments in support. For the Gulf, one of the most important was the tank transporter regiment. The transporter squadrons are rather predictably known as 'the heavies', since a Scammell Commander loaded with a Challenger tank weighs over 100 tons. In the Gulf, 7th Tank Transporter Regiment moved the armoured regiments up to the Kuwaiti border.

Resupplying the field army in Germany from England was the RCT's chief priority, until the Gulf crisis occurred. The network between the major ordnance centres in England at Bicester, Donnington and Kineton via the military port at Marchwood to Ostend and Antwerp, and then on to the central distribution points in Germany, was converted and extended to northern Saudi Arabia via Al Jubail on the Persian Gulf coast.

10th Regiment RCT using 14-tonne lorries and DROPS shifted the bulk ammunition from the port squadron operating the Jubail dockfront to two Anglo-American ammunition supply points in the wilderness. Known as Moonbase 1 and Moonbase 2 because of their desolate aspect, they consisted of a huge area of bulldozed desert surrounded by heaped banks of sand known as 'bunds'.

Most of the fuel was moved north up the 'main supply route' from Al Jubail in civilian tankers run by 66 (Phoenix) Squadron, which shuttled loads of up to 50,000 litres at a time forward from bulk fuel installations run by the Royal Army Ordnance Corps. Water was also brought up on DROPS in 'bean can' tanks containing 14,000 litres each.

The Royal Corps of Transport is headed by the Director General of Transport and Movements, who presides over an international transport operation by road, rail, sea and air. The RCT has no aircraft of its own, but it works closely with the RAF; 47 Air Despatch Squadron loads and ejects freight by parachute from Hercules, a task which included dropping famine relief in Ethiopia. And there are joint helicopter support units, nicknamed 'the hookers' because they attach the underslung loads to RAF Chinook and Puma helicopters. Movement controllers from the RCT also organize the departure overseas of specialized deployment forces such as 5th Airborne Brigade. An air-mounting centre near Cirencester is run by 29th Transport and Movements Regiment for the deployment of units. Meanwhile, individual servicemen and their families flying by RAF Transport Command from Brize Norton are marshalled by RCT as well as by RAF movement controllers.

The centre of the RCT's seaborne operations is near Southampton at Marchwood military port, which it shares with the Royal Fleet Auxiliary after a modernization programme costing £21 million. The RCT's 17th Port and Maritime Regiment, which is based there, also has detachments in Cyprus, Belize, the Hebrides (for the artillery missile ranges) and the Falklands. For a young captain, running Mare Harbour in the Falklands is a command of unusual independence because 'no-one else knows how to do it, so nobody can tell you what to do'. The sailors, the only members of the Army to wear navy blue, man small vessels such as the LCL (landing craft logistics), eight RCLs (ramped craft logistics) and the ingenious Mexeflote powered rafts, a sort of Meccano set 120 feet long for landing stores and vehicles in over-the-beach operations.

In a more domestic setting, another major task of the RCT is to train drivers from the whole Army on all sorts of wheeled military vehicles. (The armoured corps at Bovington is responsible for tracked vehicles.) Land Rover training takes place at the school of mechanical transport near Leconfield in Yorkshire, while heavy goods vehicle drivers are taught by civilians at Blackdown. The RCT's great recruiting pull is the chance of obtaining an HGV licence at the age of eighteen – three years earlier than for civilians. Altogether the Army trains nearly 20,000 drivers a year, some of them from the other Services.

The first posting for subalterns and soldiers alike is known as a 'rubber wheels tour' because it is usually with a conventional transport unit in Germany. A tour in Germany could also involve a six-month tour in Northern Ireland, as part of a roulement squadron which supplements the resident 21 Transport and Movements Regiment. Apart from usual duties, drivers have to be provided for the the ancient Humber armoured personnel vehicles (unaffectionately known as 'Pigs') which are based at Moscow Camp in Belfast. For drivers, the most popular breaks from Germany include an attachment to the UN Force in Cyprus or six weeks in Canada assisting a battle group on field training.

Historically minded officers in the Royal Army Ordnance Corps trace its line back to the first Master General of the Ordnance in 1414, but a far more solid and perfectly respectable ancestor can be found in the Military Store Department of 1857, set up to correct the shambles of the Crimea. Renamed the Army Ordnance Department and Corps in 1893, it then took over the responsibility for clothing and the central depot at Pimlico during the Boer War, finally becoming the Royal Army Ordnance Corps in 1918.[1] War, especially a disastrous one, produces the only true energy for reform.

Today, the Director General of Ordnance Services is part of the Quartermaster General's Staff, and has five directorates under him, ranging from clothing and textiles to land services ammunition and the supply of computer services. The ordnance empire is certainly varied. It includes everything from the Army Fire Service to bakeries, laundry, ammunition technology, petroleum, printing and the mobile bath unit. The chief task, however, is the resupply of the field army, whether in the Gulf or in Germany, from three major complexes – the ammunition depot at Kineton, and the central ordnance depots at Bicester and Donnington.

Donnington, near Birmingham, sadly famous for its two fires of 1983 and 1985, has some 40,000 stock items in ten huge sheds covering 17 acres. The most unusual piece is the chunk of bronze Crimean cannon from which Victoria Crosses are cast. Urgently required spare parts are despatched by priority issue teams, but the bulk items leave each day by container lorries, known as the

Donnington or Bicester Express, according to their point of departure. These go to one of the four distribution points in Germany, such as the forward ordnance depot at Dulmen. The National Audit Office, in its report of April 1989, was clearly unconvinced by Ministry of Defence arguments that this service should not be privatized.[2]

The resupply of British forces in Germany comes through 'the tube', the line of communications from Ostend or Antwerp, where there is a large base, to the depots of the rear combat zone in the Ruhr. These are controlled from a logistics headquarters in an old Luftwaffe barracks on the edge of Dusseldorf. This infrastructure comprises around a hundred major and minor units. Some operate on a huge scale: for example, ammunition which comes from Kineton via Marchwood goes to 3rd Base Ammunition Depot at Bracht, where nearly 50,000 tons of rounds from .22in to 175mm shells are stored, while the Forward Vehicle Depot at Recklinghausen stores over 2,000 vehicles, still waiting for UK-based units to reinforce the Rhine Army.

In addition, each armoured division has an ordnance battalion, in theory about 400-strong. A considerable proportion of the ordnance corps also serves in small detachments. There are stores sections of up to ten men within REME light aid detachments. And aviation is such a complex business – the main aircraft support unit at Middle Wallop has over 20,000 items listed – that they have first-aid aircraft outfits, manned by ordnance personnel in the sky-blue berets of the Army Air Corps, to get the most frequently needed parts to the REME in aviation regiments. Parts for all three services come from the RAF, which, to the Army Air Corps' exasperation, has the monopoly of helicopter supply.

The greatest challenge for all 'loggies', but especially the Royal Army Ordnance Corps and the Royal Corps of Transport, came in the Gulf; and the system certainly seemed to work.

From the beginning the task in Saudi Arabia was enormous. US Marines fed and housed the advance parties in Al Jubail until Tent City was built. Bulk fuel installations based on TFCs (tank, fabric, collapsible, in quartermaster-speak) were established and run by the RAOC, using Saudi production direct from their refineries. A Port Squadron of the Royal Corps of Transport organized the arrival and landing of the armoured vehicles shipped from Germany; the 'movers' of RCT movement squadrons took over the landing of British transport aircraft. Containers full of stores, spare parts, modification kits for tanks – one even arrived with fifty Christmas trees – were stacked by 6th Ordnance Battalion on another asphalt expanse which became known as 'Iso City'. Joint Anglo-American ammunition supply points received the bulk ammunition before it was moved forward by the RCT. Departments of every imaginable sort began to set up shop – a Royal Engineers postal and courier squadron, a field hospital in a sprung steel bubble tent, a medical equipment depot, a 'local resources section' from the RAOC responsible for the daily purchase and distribution of fresh food and water in plastic bottles, even a mobile bakery from 91 Ordnance Company.

The Royal Army Ordnance Corps' best-known activity in an age of terrorism is also one of its most recent skills. In the 1965 reorganization, it was given a responsibility for 'explosives ordnance disposal'. Bomb disposal officers (a term which includes NCOs) are called ATOs, or ammunition technical officers, because their basic job is to accept ammunition and explosives into service, store it, test it and dispose of it at the end of its shelf life. One ATO who deservedly received attention recently, was WO1 Barry Johnson, formerly of 321 EOD Company in Northern Ireland, who in 1990 received the George Cross for dismantling a bank of six IRA mortars. Johnson, to reduce the danger to a nearby hospital, decided to tackle them in person without using the Wheelbarrow. The very last missile to be rendered safe exploded, blinding him in one eye and causing other serious injuries.

A candidate spends six months at Shrivenham studying ballistics and chemistry, then just over seven months at the school of ammunition at Kineton, which is the centre of what is perhaps the most admired of 'black arts'. The selection process has to be meticulous. Like volunteers for the SAS, special duties, and now Royal Military Police close protection teams, candidates are subjected to psychometric tests to check their emotional suitability for the work. Kineton offers courses for officers from the other services and members of the Metropolitan Police, a number of whom previously served with the ordnance. The culmination of their training, a final assessment exercise in 'render safe procedures', takes place in the Longmoor FIBUA (fighting in built-up areas) training area, an abandoned Army housing estate, where they do their 'practicals' on improvised explosive devices, the Army's term for terrorist bombs. The exercise is organized by the unit which specializes in bomb disposal, 11th Ordnance Battalion, which has companies in Yorkshire, Middlesex and Herefordshire. After qualifying, ATOs are retested every six months, and before going to Northern Ireland they do a 'special-to-theatre' course to update them on the latest developments.

Since their formation in 1942, the Royal Electrical and Mechanical Engineers have grown along with the Army's mechanical sophistication. Today virtually every field army regiment has a detachment and, together with second-line repair and base workshops, the REME is the largest single capbadge in the Army, with more men than either the sappers or gunners. As part of Michael Heseltine's 'tail to teeth' reforms reducing the proportion of logistic support to combat arm strength, its maximum size was set at 10 per cent of the Army's total strength.

The home of the REME is at Arborfield near Reading, the largest training centre in the country. It has its own apprentice college, the Princess Marina College, the training battalion, the school of electronic engineering and the REME officers' school.

REME support to the Army consists of three lines of repair. The first line of repair is the light aid detachment which, depending on the unit it is attached to, can range from less than a dozen men to over a hundred in an aviation regiment. The second line, for the Rhine Army, is the armoured workshop, which varies in size. Third-line repair in this country, beyond which lies only the scrapheap, is carried out by four base workshops, one central workshop and three vehicle depot workshops. (The Royal Navy is responsible for all helicopter third-line repair.) But the rest of the Army sees and knows little of this considerable substructure: to the average soldier or junior officer, the REME means no more than the fitters and armourers in the regiment's light aid detachment, or LAD.

The REME's working relationship with the combat arms varies mostly according to their interest in their machinery. In the view of several captains commanding an LAD, only armoured corps regiments try to treat their vehicles properly. The average infantry soldier dislikes 'mech', while the artillery 'are only keen on the gun side, not on the automotive'.

The importance of the REME in army aviation is perhaps best demonstrated by the fact that there are about 3,000 members of the Army Air Corps and 1,500 members of REME wearing its sky-blue beret; so, if the Army invests in the number of helicopters needed for true air-mobility, REME will once more have to be allowed beyond its 10 per cent limit. But to hold on to trained craftsmen is a major problem. The civil aviation industry is prepared to buy them out of the Army and double their salaries. The Army's unintentional contribution to British industry, by providing it with skilled and reliable labour, has been seriously underestimated. This may be bad for both sides: many companies have so depended on poaching service personnel that they have not bothered to invest in training schemes of their own.

Some members of REME feel vulnerable on the question of capbadge. There is a certain superficial logic in a distinctive arm like the Army Air Corps having its own technical support, to say nothing of the inevitable temptation to empire-build. But that does not take account of avionic work outside the Army Air Corps – mainly on pilotless aircraft for the Royal Artillery. REME officers are also worried that without the existing separation there may be pressure from aviation commanders to declare an aircraft serviceable in an emergency. A separate capbadge and chain of command protects them. The RAF derides this argument, saying that any technician who allowed an unserviceable airframe to take off should be fired anyway, but that reflects a cut-and-dried world of peacetime rule books, not the grey areas arising from operational necessity.

It has even been suggested in the armoured corps that first-line REME should become an integral part of the unit – the result of the 'Endurer' exercises, which vividly demonstrated that, under intense operational conditions, tank crews rapidly became too tired to service their own vehicles and that 'pit-stop' teams of combat mechanics were needed.

Looking after armoured vehicles, above all tanks, can be extremely frustrating and depressing. It is very hard for a captain commanding a light aid detachment to come up with convincing arguments to persuade good craftsmen to stay in. A particular nightmare concerns the electrical black boxes on which nearly all a tank's functions depend – and above all its fire control equipment. Annual firing will knock out eight tanks' worth of black boxes, but for reasons of economy the 'repair loop' can take up to a year on some items. 'The ebb and flow of spares is completely unpredictable,' said one captain, 'and yet you only need to prime the pump by bringing in a reserve of six tanks' worth of black boxes, but that means investing a little money.'

413

Light aid detachments consequently resort to discreet 'cannibalization', even though it was strictly forbidden until Operation Granby prompted a rapid defenestration of such hypocrisy. In a few cases spare parts are simply not available: one item used to be improvised out of the tin lids from compo rations. Finally, to add insult to injury, REME officers have to fill in an efficiency return, charting the savings achieved each month.

Both NCOs and officers feel very strongly that the moral cowardice of staff officers who dare not tell those above them how bad things are could lead to the Army's disintegration. Some senior officers have fought hard, such as the cavalry general commanding a division who insisted that the statistics on unserviceable vehicles should not be fudged any longer; but even less is likely to be done now, given the Rhine Army's very uncertain future.

Working conditions are so bad in a number of vehicle parks, particularly the older ones, that, according to more than one REME captain, their workshops would undoubtedly be closed down on health and safety grounds if the Army were a civilian firm. The inadequate facilities extend beyond personal discomfort – warmth, washrooms and light – to items vital for business efficiency, such as telephones. In one armoured regiment, for example, the REME light aid detachment, an organization with two officers and two senior warrant officers supervising 90 mechanics and technicians in a dozen different departments, had just one extension. 'I'm losing all my most qualified men to civvy street,' was a fairly common complaint. 'They're off the moment their time comes up. You just can't expect them to carry on working in these conditions.' Some impressive new vehicle sheds and workshops have been built, but the modernization programme is severely slowed by financial restrictions, and it is hard now to envisage heavy expenditure on barracks in Germany, the future is so uncertain.

The Army Catering Corps enjoys the appropriate and memorable motto of 'We Sustain'. Making up just over

3 per cent of the Army, it is either the largest of the small corps or the smallest of the large corps. In common with the REME, its members are attached to field army units, and go almost everywhere with them. Cooks on exercise or in Northern Ireland share most of the discomfort and sometimes the same dangers for little recognition. But sometimes, especially in Northern Ireland, where they will turn out at almost any hour to prepare a fry-up for a returning patrol, their efforts are for once more than grudgingly appreciated. Nobody calls them 'slop-jockeys' then.

The cookhouse or canteen in each regiment is run by a warrant officer with up to thirty NCOs and cooks. Most make great efforts to provide healthier and more imaginative dishes, but the gastronomic conservatism of the British soldier (above all in northern regiments) and a general addiction to junk food means that attempts to wean them off a chip-based diet can be rather demoralizing. Such philistine ingratitude makes the photographs in *Soldier* magazine of trainee chefs at their training centre in Aldershot slaving over delicate confections all the more poignant.

Officers and NCOs leaving the corps seldom have trouble finding a job outside: Trust House Forte is said to be run at almost every level by former members of the Army Catering Corps.

Members of the Royal Pioneer Corps may be nicknamed the 'chunkies' by the combat arms, who joke about their 'seriously military' posture, but when called upon to open fire in earnest they have proved that they can shoot straight. Perhaps a measure of their rather macho image of themselves is that they resisted the employment of women the longest.

Their headquarters and training centre is at Wootton in Northamptonshire, where they learn everything from infantry tactics and security procedures to basic engineering skills. One traditional Pioneer Corps responsibility, certainly the most gruesome, is dealing with the dead. In 1982 a graves registration team worked hard after the Falklands conflict, exhuming, identifying and reburying remains. Nine years later in the Gulf, the bodies that needed urgent burial were Iraqi. A French journalist described a Pioneer Corps team led by Captain Paul Messenger at work on 'the traffic jam', the wrecked Iraqi convoy from Kuwait City which was caught in the open on the Basra road by American air power. A fortnight after the slaughter, the masks he and his men wore did little to stem the stench. The carbonized bodies fell apart as they tried to lift them into body bags. Although Messenger felt the job should be done by Iraqi prisoners of war, he said: 'They deserve a decent burial. They were soldiers just like I am. I hope they would do the same for me.'[3] Clearly, he and his men did not earn their extra £10 a day – 'For work of an objectionable nature (exceptional)' – with any relish.

In the Gulf, as elsewhere, the Pioneers' main work is 'military logistic support', which basically means loading and unloading stores, and headquarter guard duties. The main RPC contingent in Saudi Arabia was 518 Company. It assisted the Royal Engineers and REME and provided guards.

The basic unit of the Royal Pioneer Corps is the company. Each has anything up to eight platoons, which in theory should consist of an officer and twenty-four NCOs and soldiers. In the United Kingdom there are five companies altogether, including one at the Central Ordnance Depot at Bicester and another at the Central Ammunition Depot, Kineton.

In Germany, as in Northern Ireland, they are responsible for defending all major headquarters, including Rhine Army headquarters at Rheindahlen. One of their most welcomes breaks from guard duty is to act as enemy in Bavaria for the long-range reconnaissance patrol school.

As a sort of equine and canine REME, one might have expected to find the Royal Army Veterinary Corps on the Q side as well but, conforming to the instincts of an animal-loving nation, the British Army evidently classifies its 600 horses and 1,300 dogs as personnel. The head of the RAVC, the Director of Army Veterinary and Remount Services, reports not to the Quartermaster General but to the Adjutant General along with the head of the Army's medical services.

The Royal Army Veterinary Corps centre, and the home of Army equitation with both the Long Riding Course and the Army School of Farriery, is appropriately located at Melton Mowbray – the regimental march is an arrangement of 'A Hunting We Will Go'. The vast majority of its work on the equine side is devoted to the Household Cavalry and the King's Troop Royal Horse Artillery. In its report, the National Audit Office strongly suggested that civilian vets would be much cheaper in London. This dismayed the Household Cavalry who, apart from reasons of loyalty to the RAVC, are worried that the 400 horses in London District would not receive such good treatment if only because of the shortage of civilian vets.[4]

While aspects of its work with horses may be under threat, the RAVC's work with 'defence animals', both guard and sniffer dogs, has grown rapidly over the last fifteen years. Arms explosive search dogs and their handlers are trained in the deserted hamlet of Rype next to the centre, and the Army dog-training school procures dogs for all the services worldwide and gives them initial training and veterinary care at its animal hospital. The main training centre for dog handlers, however, is the Defence Animal Support Unit, a tri-service organization run by the RAVC at Sennelager.

The three main logistic corps, together with the Pioneer Corps, the Army Catering Corps, and the Postal and Courier Services of the Royal Engineers, all come under the Quartermaster General, who automatically has a seat on the Army Board.

For the combat arms, the Quartermaster General's

department and the logistic executive is a completely foreign world. This ignorance was vividly illustrated by the story of a young infantry officer whose father had just been appointed Quartermaster General. He was tackled on the subject by a couple of his soldiers during a company 'smoker' or get-together, and the conversation apparently went as follows: 'Here, sir. Is it true that your old man's a general? The *Quartermaster* General?' The young officer admitted that he was. 'Cor,' came the reply. 'That must be a fucking big quartermaster's store.'

The Quartermaster General has three 'bricks' of departments under him, two military and a civil service secretariat of 'number-crunchers' under an assistant under-secretary, which deals mainly with finance and contracts.

The Director General of Logistic Policy (Army), a two-star appointment, heads six logistic executive directorates – logistic operations, support planning, logistic communications and informations systems, engineer services, postal and courier services and pioneers and labour. The third brick consists of the three Q directorates-general (Transport and Movement, Ordnance Services, and Electrical and Mechanical Engineering), the Directorate of Army Quartering, now only a one-star appointment in spite of its responsibility for one of the largest budgets in the Ministry of Defence, and the Directorate of Army Catering. Nothing, however, is permanent, least of all in the Army. There are persistant neo-Heseltinian mutterings that the Army's 'tail' must be cut further, that the Qs should be merged again or amalgamated with those of the other services.

If desert war is a tactician's dream and a quartermaster's nightmare, then the Whitehall war is a theoretician's dream and an administrator's nightmare. The nightmare of a tri-service Q branch might best be illustrated as a logistic version of a nationalized industry in a state of concealed civil war.

CHAPTER 26

Military Police and Military Law

The Royal Military Police, little more than 2,000-strong, has an even wider range of duties than its civilian counterpart. In peacetime these vary from community policing to providing bodyguards for the Foreign and Commonwealth Office abroad, from the detective work of the Special Investigation Branch to weapons intelligence in Northern Ireland. The corps' wartime responsibilities now include checking that routes are safe after nuclear or chemical attack in addition to its traditional duties of traffic control, rounding up stragglers and the prevention of looting. The Special Investigation Branch was set up in 1940 because of British looting in France early in the Second World War.

The senior officer in the Royal Military Police is the Provost Marshal (Army), a brigadier who reports to the Adjutant General. The Provost Marshal's headquarters are housed in the same building of the Ministry of Defence as the Directorate General of Personal Services, whose PS2 branch deals with military law and courts martial. The home of the Military Police, however, is at Roussillon Barracks on the outskirts of Chichester. Built during the Napoleonic Wars to house French prisoners, the barracks later became the depot of the Royal Sussex Regiment until 1960. In the last century – a detail to sharpen a drill sergeant's wit – a gallows stood where the parade ground now is. More recently, the infamous Captain Alfredo Astiz was held under guard there in 1982 after his capture on South Georgia.

Military policemen join from three sources: junior leaders trained at Bovington; adult entrants, including those

reallocated from other capbadges; and voluntary transferees from other parts of the Army.

Once the junior leaders and adult entrants have done
their common military syllabus at Chichester, they are
joined for the sixteen-and-a-half-week basic provost course
by the voluntary transferees, some of whom may be full
corporals or even sergeants, and the young women who
come from the WRAC Centre at Guildford on permanent
attachment. (Overall, women make up some 12 per cent
of the RMP's strength. This may rise to 14 or 15 per cent
with the increasing proportion of women in the Army, but
no further since the vast majority of the RMP's clients are,
of course, male.)

The first phase, military enhancement, concentrates on
map-reading, nuclear, biological and chemical warfare,
first aid and signals, and other aspects of corps work
in support of the field army. Male and female recruits
receive further skill-at-arms training, using both pistol and
sub-machine-gun. The second phase, police duties, covers
military law, taking statements, and PACE (the Police and
Criminal Evidence Act), which the military police also
follow. The third phase consists of driver training and
environmental testing, which means playing everything
they have learnt 'for real', or as close to real as can be
simulated in a single building.

A large house has been converted into mock-up training
areas. Almost every room provides a different set – a fully
equipped RMP duty room, an interview room, a bedroom
in a married quarter for 'scene of serious crime', a barrack
room to practise searching for drugs or stolen property. All
are covered by closed-circuit television cameras connected
to a control room at the top of the house. With other
students or permanent staff playing the part of corpses,
drunken soldiers, or distressed wives, this part of the
course prepares them as far as possible for the shock of
their first job.

'The girls' who make up just over a fifth of each course are completely integrated except for fitness tests and some field training. They share an accommodation block with the men and, although they have the top floor to reduce access by window, 'extracurricular activity' is hard to prevent. The officers and senior NCOs of the permanent staff become more concerned when at least one couple per course announce towards the end that they intend to marry. Often they are little more than eighteen or nineteen years old.

Marriage is common within the Royal Military Police, with men and women working so closely together. Husband-and-wife teams can often arrange joint, or at least compatible, postings for several tours in succession. Few marry outside the corps because a clannish, professional attitude extends into their off-duty life, and the rest of the Army regards them with reserve. The RMP usually have their own little bar, because in a garrison 'we can't go drinking with the soldiers; they'd feel we were spying on them'. In the opinion of some NCOs, their rather introverted existence can be unhealthy. 'We lack the camaraderie of the infantry,' said a woman corporal. 'We have cliques.'

On passing out from Chichester, both men and women recruits become lance corporals Class III on general police duties. They will be posted to provost companies around the world, and to Northern Ireland if over eighteen. Whenever a two-man patrol is tasked, a full corporal will always accompany a novice. Uniformed patrols in Land Rovers or white Cavaliers, known as 'jam sandwiches' because of the stripe along the middle, investigate minor incidents (known as 'level one'), such as drunkenness and petty barrack-room theft. Like the civilian police, they are not keen to become embroiled in 'domestics' and, providing no crime has been committed, they will call in the orderly officer from the regiment concerned to make him sort it out. But a young subaltern straight out of Sandhurst will probably turn back to them or to his orderly sergeant for advice.

A 'level-two' investigation into an assault or serious theft is the province of the unit investigative element in each provost company. This usually consists of a sergeant and six corporals, who operate mostly in civilian clothes. Level three – major theft or fraud, breaches of security, grievous bodily harm, murder, rape or child abuse – is automatically the responsibility of the Special Investigation Branch.

The 'helmets', those on general police duties, inevitably attract the animosity of soldiers. Among some capbadges, Scottish regiments and the paras above all, hatred for the 'monkeys' can be intense. There are, of course, two dramatically different sides to every story.

A sergeant in a Highland regiment ascribed the problem entirely to the heavy-handedness of the military police: 'The Jocks say these guys aren't human, they're robots.' He felt that they resorted too quickly to formal discipline – 'When you've got a couple of Jocks drunk out of their brain-box, they should just be helped to their bed, but if you try and lock them up, you get trouble.' He did not, however, mention how provocative drunken Jocks can be. As well as calling a military policeman 'monkey' to his face, groups of them put on monkey impressions, scratching their armpits and gibbering in simian glee. A Green Jacket major illustrated how much military police patrols have to put up with on occasions. In Gibraltar, after a series of fights with taxi-drivers, the local provost company offered to give some drunken soldiers from another infantry regiment lifts back to barracks in their Land Rovers, yet some of those who climbed in behind could not resist spitting at the necks of the RMP corporals running them home.

Members of the Parachute Regiment, with unconcealed pride, can make Aldershot sound like a battlefield. 'The MPs hate the Para Reg,' said a private, describing the vendetta between redcaps and maroon berets. (It is revealing that the only military policemen they respect are the parachute-trained members of 160 Provost Company, attached to the 5th Airborne Brigade.) Parachute Regiment officers, while conceding that 'some of the boys are not very clever when they're performing down-town', go on to say that the RMPs 'lay themselves open to it'. The military police describe things differently. 'Quite a lot of us', said a woman corporal, 'have had to pick up the pieces after they've been on the rampage and, to put it mildly, it's always ended in tears. I have every respect for the paras as soldiers. It's their social habits I can't stand. As a woman you'll be told to get down on the floor with your legs apart because that's where you belong.'

There are, however, those within the RMP who admit that all too often situations which could have been defused flare up because 'the new unwrapped lance corporal' coming out of Chichester is a different product. They are often far too arrogant and do not try to understand soldiers. 'The biggest problem', said a corporal with seven years' experience, 'is their lack of common sense and lack of imagination. They've also got no character.' An SIB warrant officer agreed strongly. He said that only voluntary transferees should be taken. School-leavers knew little of life and even less of the Army. 'It took a long time before I was army-wise. It should be an absolute minimum of two years in another corps.'

In Saudi Arabia, military police work followed the wartime role, with a special attention to the threat of chemical attack. The huge convoys rolling northwards up the main supply route from Al Jubail towards the Kuwaiti border needed directing, and the routes had to be patrolled. This was the task of 174 Provost Group. Meanwhile, 203 Provost Company with the first Armoured Division formed part of the euphemistically termed 'route development battle group' with the armoured engineers who were going to blast a way through the Iraqi defences. The military police task was to mark the route through the minefield with chemical lightsticks. Once the armoured units were through, the Royal Engineers constructed some 400 kilometres of 'main supply routes', which the military police signposted with traditional tactical signs. As soon as the fighting was over, the Royal Military Police established anti-looting patrols to control the souvenir hunters on the Basra road.

Roughly in line with the Army as a whole, just under half of all provost strength is devoted to north-west Europe. But the era of 'real policing' in Berlin with its 'great job satisfaction' is over. Berlin was generally considered the best posting of all until the Four-Power agreement, which gave the RMP precedence over the civil police, ended in 1990. Six months before the opening of the Wall, one young captain explained with unrestrained enthusiasm: 'You are it. You are the law.' But those days, Checkpoint Charlie and all, are now gone.

The Provost Marshal for the whole theatre, like his counterpart at United Kingdom Land Forces, is a full colonel. Based in the joint headquarters at Rheindahlen, his responsibilities stretch from the Danish border to Göttingen, and from Antwerp in the rear communication zone to Berlin.

The end of the Cold War has brought another favourite RMP activity to an end. Within West Germany, RMP personnel used to engage in 'white mice', the task – or sport, depending on attitude – of tailing members of the Soviet Military Mission, Soxmis. This was an operation demanding advanced driver skills. Like the British and American Military Missions on the other side of the wire, the Russians had the right under the Four-Power agreement to move around within the old British and American Zones. Since certain areas are forbidden on both sides, it was always a point of honour among military missions to try to shake off those who were tailing them: when finally surrounded, the military mission would give in as gracefully as possible and be escorted home.

At the other end of the scale of excitement, the Rhine Army was the first to try community policing in its garrisons. This began in 1972, not as a social experiment but because the Northern Ireland theatre at that time needed every man available. An experienced and carefully

424

selected corporal or sergeant – 'more your plodder, a family man' – will police the community from his married quarter with only a telephone and a sign outside. In true Army fashion, his wife – who acts a message-taker, supplementary diplomat and general helper – receives nothing for the considerable effort she contributes.

'Most of our work', said one warrant officer who knew the job well, 'is picking up the pieces.' With only 'two or three mobiles' to cover a considerable area, they cannot count on much back-up. They are on duty seven days a week and can sometimes be called out several times in a night, but most of them 'love the job – they're on their own and not being buggered about by anyone else'.

After two tours of general police duties – senior instructors feel that one in Germany followed by one in Northern Ireland is the ideal – the young military policeman should be a full corporal and ready for specialization. He can, for example, apply for para provost with 5th Airborne Brigade or to join Nato's ACE Mobile Force military police unit. Service in this multinational group of US and Canadian MPs, Feldjager, Gendarmes and Carabinieri will take him to the Nato flanks – Denmark and northern Norway for Arctic warfare, and Greece, Italy and Turkey for southern flank exercises. Much importance is placed on maintaining good relations with Allied military and civil police forces through exchange visits and training as well as sporting events. RMP teams take part in the international police rally and 'cop shoot' at Hohne, a friendly competition with other Nato military police forces and the German civil police, all of whom try out each others' weapons.

A more unusual attachment is to the mounted troop. The bread-and-butter work of the mounted troop is to patrol the ranges and training areas around Aldershot. As well as leading this relatively isolated existence, they form the most conspicuous part of the corps. On ceremonial duties and performances at the Royal Tournament and the Edinburgh Tattoo, they wear No. 1 dress with cross-belts and carry lances. The two best-known specializations, however, are the SIB and close protection.

The Special Investigation Branch requires particular talents, and, until close protection became such an important priority, it used to have the pick of the corps. Potential members are talent-spotted as early as the initial investigation course, which they do after about three years of service. If they show promise, they are subsequently steered into the unit investigation element, and will be encouraged along the right route until they have passed the qualification course and are potential sergeants, the SIB's minimum rank. They only join the SIB on passing the intermediate special investigation course. By then they will have seen at least six years' service.

The SIB is in many ways closer to the civil police than the Army. It follows all techniques and developments, whether advances in forensic science or the introduction of taped interviews, which they welcome. Senior NCOs operate in civilian clothes, their training is little different from CID officers and they cannot rely on any superiority in rank when interviewing soldier suspects. Their reputation for integrity, however, owes much more to the Army than the police. A senior SIB officer pointed out that the opportunity for corruption was, of course, much smaller: they did not spend their time rubbing shoulders with organized crime. Real villains are thin on the ground in the Army, if only because they are dumped back on civilian society as quickly as possible.

Military policemen also admit that the relative lack of real problem families in comparison to the inner cities – 'at least none of them are on the dole' – allows them to devote more time to each case, particularly the preparation of evidence for a court martial.

The SIB's training was put to other uses in February 1991 when a team was flown into Kuwait City following its liberation. Its task, in co-operation with other Allied teams, was to interrogate Iraqi personnel suspected of war crimes during the seven-month occupation. The best prepared were those who had done the course at the Joint Services Interrogation Wing at Ashford.

Although the military police have provided bodyguards to members of the royal family and other dignitaries visiting the Army since just before the Second World War, their specialization in close protection began when a section guarded the British Embassy in Saigon during the Vietnam War. And, after a period when embassy guards were hired from companies with rather controversial reputations, the RMP were given much wider responsibilities.

Close protection requires very different skills from general police duties. Everything from close-quarters battle to tactical driving is taught, yet those in charge of the CP course insist that 'We're not looking for SAS style, we're not looking for para style', only for the qualities of 'a good military policeman'. Candidates are not expected to march sixty miles a day with heavy packs over the Brecon Beacons, but they must be capable of bursts of furious activity.

Fitness training includes an orienteering log race in which each team of eight carries half a telegraph pole across country from point to point over a six-mile course, map-reading their way. The directing staff who accompany them just watch. There is no 'bogey [qualifying] time', although instructors do little to discourage the idea. They are looking for guts, and a sense of humour when things go wrong, rather than sheer physical stamina, and to see 'who's a leader and who's a sheep'. Above all, each candidate must show that he can work effectively in a small, closely-knit team – that he can 'dovetail'.

The main physical requirement is for 'upper body strength' – close protection team members must be able to shoot accurately when tired and encumbered, even when carrying somebody, so wherever possible range work is preceded by strenuous exertion.

A high standard of marksmanship has to be achieved with a wide variety of weapons, including non-standard makes such as Kalashnikovs and Uzis. Close-quarters battle techniques evolved by the SAS are also taught, should part of the team need to engage in hot pursuit. Standard close-quarter battle weapons include the 9mm Browning pistol, the Heckler & Koch MP5 sub-machine-gun, and the Remington 870P pump-action shotgun, all of which can be concealed in shoulder holsters with varying degrees of indiscreet bulge.

Apart from the obvious rules of safety, there are firm standing operational procedures which govern the use of firearms, but at times team leaders have to use their initiative. In Beirut, where warring factions carried their weapons openly, if not ostentatiously, an ambassador's bodyguard would have been most unwise to give an impression of being unarmed. Heckler & Kochs remained in view, on the grounds that 'prevention is better than cure'. A team guarding a general in Northern Ireland would be acting in a 'green army', or uniformed, role, and would carry unconcealed weapons as a matter of course. But in close protection work demanding a low profile, firearms must stay under cover.

Close protection team members have to be subtle. The last thing their principals want is bodyguards liable to leap about, sprouting guns at the slightest movement. Yet, as their chief instructor emphasized, 'If they overreact, they cause embarrassment, but if they underreact, they've got a catastrophe on their hands.'

An important part of the seven-week course covers tactical driving, including anti-ambush drills. Using the Army's FIBUA (fighting in built-up areas) training grounds, every eventuality is rehearsed in realistic environments. There are drills for embussing and debussing a principal, or party of principals, for walkabouts and other public appearances.

Peripheral skills are varied. They include such subjects as anti-surveillance techniques, and searching for explosives as well as for bugs, but in a curious way one of the most important of all is protocol. Not only do the selected soldiers have to blend into the background of official residences and receptions, but they need to get on well with their principals and their families, with whom they will live for twenty-four hours a day, because 'you can only protect your principal as far as he will allow you to'. This is even more essential when teams attached to the Foreign and Commonwealth Office are on Isodet (isolated detachment) in an embassy in Africa or the Middle East. The youngest of those to qualify from the course are normally kept on 'green army' duties for their first tour before being sent to out-stations.

The Royal Military Police course is highly respected because of the corps' reputation and field experience. The medals won in Kampala (when a team saved the lives of diplomatic families during the Ugandan civil war) and other actions which are talked about on the security circuit tend to make them victims of their own success. Retaining experienced NCOs is a problem because, however much a young sergeant on £15,000 a year may enjoy the work, the £25,000 offered by private security companies for a 25-week year becomes hard to resist after a time.

Instructors emphasize how much a corporal in his early twenties can develop. He has 'to grow up very quickly' and adapt to unfamiliar situations. He soon becomes self-assured, both socially and professionally. Many of them find the prospect of returning to a slot within the conventional military hierarchy rather irksome.

Apart from his position as head of the Royal Military Police, the Provost Marshal is also head of the Military Provost Staff Corps, one of the smallest corps in the Army. All members of the MPSC are voluntary transferees. There are seven officers and about a hundred senior NCOs. The minimum rank is sergeant, and all the officers are late-entry commissioned. This unusual organization has provided the Army's own prison service since the end of the Boer War, and now holds Royal Navy and Royal Air Force personnel as well. Its base and sole peacetime establishment is the Military Corrective Training Centre at Colchester. The commandant is, however, appointed from outside the Corps. The last three have come from the Household Division.

Berechurch Hall Camp, Colchester, had, until fairly recently, changed little in appearance from its wartime origins as a prisoner-of-war camp, but only one of the original Nissen huts now remains, earmarked as a museum. If this nostalgia seems curious, the officers' mess has a scale model Nissen hut in solid silver as a centrepiece. Even in an army prepared to reproduce the most unlikely objects as table decorations, this would surely win a prize for the most bizarre item.

The camp at Colchester – long known unaffectionately as 'Collie' – holds just over 200 inmates. They include servicemen under sentence (those who will return to duty at the end of their sentence), those awaiting court martial or confirmation of sentence (it is much better from every point of view to hold them at Colchester than in regimental guardrooms), and finally those to be dismissed the service. Prisoners to be dismissed the service are held in A and D Wings. Some respond to resettlement advice and education, but there are clearly some hard cases amongst the rest who look back on their time at Colchester with a perverse nostalgia. A sporadic correspondence is received from 'what seems to be a Battalion of ex-D Wing in the French Foreign Legion'. Two deserters were even brought to Colchester after contracting malaria with the Foreign Legion in Africa.

For the 800-odd servicemen under sentence who pass each year through A Wing, the regime is of the short sharp shock variety, but in military rather than prison terms: it is hard to imagine weapon training carried out at Dartmoor or Parkhurst. The Army's approach to training loses none of its thoroughness at Colchester. There is even an introductory briefing on prison survival and recovery. In a symbolic turning over of a new leaf, servicemen under sentence are made to start again at the beginning with the common military syllabus. Education and counselling programmes are also designed to return them to their units as better soldiers, and not to humiliate them. The Provost Marshal stated the belief that 'Soldiers who find themselves in the MCTC are not criminals in the accepted sense. They are often immature and weak-willed young men who get into trouble because of such reasons as broken homes, lack of parental guidance, or inadequacies of character which can be improved or put right with leadership.' The average age of servicemen under sentence is usually between twenty-one and twenty-two.

To judge by the reaction of many adjutants, the system now seems to work as well as it possibly could. Colchester is proud of the fact that of the 500 men returned to their units around half performed satisfactorily or well, and nearly 5 per cent were promoted within a year. The MCTC's attitudes seem to be uncensorious and down-to-earth. They also demonstrate a refreshing lack of self-deception about the causes of most crime. Commenting on the preponderance of absence without leave as an offence in the Army, the commandant remarked: 'Apart from the usual domestic upsets, the majority go absent from reasons of boredom, especially in BAOR; this is also the most common reason given for experimenting with drugs.'

The reason for the high proportion of former junior soldiers – 22 per cent of D Wing – is also attributed to 'boredom and dissatisfaction with adult service'. Adjutants in Germany confirm this diagnosis. In their experience, calculated crime is rare. They reckon that drink plays a large part in 80 to 90 per cent of cases, and describe the commonest chain of events leading to a spell at Colchester as boredom, drink, some stupid or violent action when drunk, followed by panic leading to absence without leave. So, although between 40 and 50 per cent of soldiers at Colchester are there for absence or desertion, few ever planned it in advance.

The charter of the Military Provost Staff Corps requires it to 'hold in safe custody any persons subject to Military Law as may be required at the time by the Secretary of State'. The full scope of this definition was demonstrated in

431

January 1988 when 'a Women's Royal Army Corps private and a female dependant' were admitted for the first time. Senior NCOs from the WRAC had to be brought in to act as guards. Others outside the Regular Army to be held at the Military Corrective Training Centre during 1987 included a Territorial Army soldier and two male civilian dependants. In Germany, civilian dependants are subject to military law, and can therefore be tried by court martial.

In 1991, a completely new responsibility was given to the RSM at Colchester. He flew out to Saudi Arabia before the ground war started to advise the Coldstream Guards and the other battalions detailed to guard Iraqi prisoners of war on procedure.

Along with several other small corps, the independent existences of the Royal Military Police, the Military Provost Staff Corps and the Army Legal Corps will shortly be coming to an end. A decision was taken in principle in May 1990 to amalgamate them into an Adjutant General's Corps along with the Royal Army Pay Corps, the Royal Army Educational Corps and the Royal Army Chaplain's Department. This new corps will also take on strength all clerical staff at present badged to the Royal Army Ordnance Corps and the Women's Royal Army Corps.

In a normal year, formation or garrison commanders convene a total of about 700 courts martial. On average the whole process, including the SIB's investigation, takes around seven months.

General courts martial, of which there are about seventy a year, deal with serious offences and any committed by officers or warrant officers. They can award any sentence up to life imprisonment. The president, a full colonel or brigadier, is assisted by four other officers, usually captains or majors. A judge advocate must be present to advise the president and members on all legal matters. A field general court martial can take place only in an operational theatre during a state of hostilities, and because of the gravity of the circumstances it still has the power, at least in theory, to pass the death sentence. None has been held for a long time since Northern Ireland does not count as a state of hostilities, and no soldiers were tried on sufficiently serious charges either in the South Atlantic during the Falklands conflict or nine years later during the Gulf war.

A district court martial is the commonest form of trial. The accused, as in all forms of court martial, is automatically given a defending officer and may also request a civilian lawyer. The president is generally a major who specializes as a permanent president of courts martial. He sits with at least two other officers, and the maximum sentence they can award is two years' imprisonment. A judge advocate is usually present to advise them on the law, precedent or guidelines; he must take no part in the verdict or in the sentencing, which is decided by the president and members. His advisory role can best be compared to that of the clerk in a magistrates' court. Judge advocates come under the Judge Advocate General, usually a former county court judge; and, to ensure the absolute independence of his branch, its budget comes from the Lord Chancellor, not the Ministry of Defence. They are civilians. The Army Legal Corps, on the other hand, is a body of some fifty qualified barristers and solicitors commissioned as officers and ranging in rank from lieutenant up to major general, which gives legal advice to the Army on all matters and to individual soldiers.

The procedure for appeals against sentence is scrupulously exhaustive. Appeals can be made to the convening officer before he confirms the sentence, then to the theatre commander at Rhine Army headquarters or his counterpart at UK Land Forces, then to the Director of Army Service Conditions in the Ministry of Defence, then to the Army Board (in effect just two members) and finally to the courts martial appeal court, which is really the High Court sitting under another name. About fifty appeals a year reach the DASC, and five or six reach the courts martial appeal court.

Lesser offences are dealt with by commanding officers

under the heading of Summary Disposal. For example, most cases of absence without leave are dealt with in this way, while desertion is usually a court martial offence.

The commanding officer can award a maximum of twenty-eight days' loss of pay and twenty-eight days' detention. This limit may be extended up to sixty days if he seeks extra powers from his brigadier. For any offence involving the loss of pay, he must offer the alternative of a court martial. In civilian terms, this is the equivalent of a magistrates' court offering the option of trial by jury at a crown court.

The misdeeds of soldiers arouse a fascinated, atavistic fear in civilians, as the tabloids have found to their profit. Any story is exploited to a lurid maximum, which makes it all the more important to see the question in proportion.

Staff officers emphasize that the number of crimes committed by soldiers must be seen in the context of an army at the moment nearly 140,000 strong. Regimental officers say, quite genuinely, that they are always surprised how little crime soldiers commit, given their profession. 'We are not paid to be nice people,' remarked a brigadier at Rhine Army headquarters. Yet, in spite of these pleas in mitigation, the drunken brawls of British regiments, although greatly exaggerated on occasions, still appear to be worse than those of other European armies.

A regular army overseas is always liable to outbursts of indiscipline, as Wellington found. But many of the British Army's current recruits come from a generation that is suffering from the disintegration of traditional working-class communities and values. Imbued with a street tribalism, British football fans horrify the rest of Europe. The most depressing characteristic of young civilians and soldiers is the need to bolster their confidence with alcohol. This machismo of the beer-can seems to indicate a sense of desolation that we have not yet fully comprehended.

CHAPTER 27

'Female Manpower'

Few combinations have caused more unease in the male psyche than women and war. The ancient myth of the Amazons is riddled with illuminating contradictions, while Homeric legends of the siege of Troy involving goddesses, above the fray yet partisan, were the inspiration for later patriotic symbols in time of war. A female figure of purity, an ethereal vision in armour, came to represent the nation and its ideals. Like the heroine of an adolescent dream, she had to be distant and unreal.

At the time when draftees were being shipped out to Vietnam, such symbolism became an easy target for mockery. The growth of the women's movement alongside the anti-war protest was no coincidence. Yet sexual equality soon led to an unprecedented enlistment of women volunteers when conscription ceased and the US Army needed to make up numbers.

In 1978 the Pentagon, influenced by equal rights legislation, decided to disband the Women's Army Corps – 'the typewriter soldiers' – and move towards a large measure of integration. But within a few years the process had been partially reversed, because women 'disturbed the male bonding process'. The Israeli Defence Force's about-turn was even more marked. They found that the performance of men in battle deteriorated if women were with them. Their instinct was to protect the women, rather than fight the enemy.

The British Army, one of the most socially conservative in Nato, was deeply sceptical of integration at the time. A general taken round an encampment of US troops on exercise in Germany was amazed to see male and female personnel sharing tents. He asked one of the women soldiers what effect this proximity had on their day-to-day life. 'Well, I guess it means we get laid more often,' she replied, leaving him scarlet-faced and speechless.

The Army only began to re-examine its views when infantry battalions became overstretched during the latter part of the 1980s. A general from the Light Division recalled how his outlook had changed in south Armagh. Visiting a Royal Marine commando based at Bessbrook Mill, he found the place virtually run by Wrens. They were doing most of the jobs performed by the headquarters company in an infantry battalion, which enabled the marines to deploy far more men on the ground than previous units.

A rather curious revelation had already prepared the way for such a change in attitude. In 1976, a year after the US Army decreed that weapon training was mandatory for female personnel, a number of British senior officers were startled by a report on the future employment of servicewomen, which pointed out that nowhere in the Geneva Convention of 1906, nor in its amendments of 1925 and 1949, were women defined as non-combatants. If women were to be 'an integral part of the Army', then they should be able to defend themselves and not have to rely on male guards. The report 'even foresaw women being considered for special duties with the Special Air Service or the Intelligence Corps'.[1]

The Army Board's reaction to such recommendations was cautious, to say the least. Five years later, it approved a measure to allow women weapons for self-defence, but weapons were not issued systematically for another seven years. Conservative ministers, no doubt keen to reassure backbenchers that traditional roles would not be subverted, stuck to the deployment rules keeping women out of combat zones and combat jobs. But both definitions, territorial and functional, were unclear. There was never a suggestion that women should join rifle companies or sabre squadrons, but in modern warfare the rear echelon and formation headquarters are all in the combat zone. The Army took very seriously the threat of Spetsnaz attacks on

436

headquarters and communication centres well behind the lines and in the United Kingdom itself. Virtually all servicemen and servicewomen were thus by definition at risk, yet deployment rules stayed the same: servicewomen were still not supposed to serve in Germany 'forward of corps rear boundary'. The fact that WRAC provost (military policewomen) and searchers had already run considerably more risks in Northern Ireland was ignored.

In the British Army, necessity is the mother of change; often, it seems, the only one. With the manning crisis, necessity has grown so clamorous that previously unthinkable developments have become possible. In September 1989, the main recommendations of a study into the wider employment of women in the Army were published. Some of the more publicized steps, such as women training for bomb disposal, are little more than a tentative foot in the water – the ordnance corps will not allow women to serve as ATOs in Northern Ireland, because of the physical strength needed to work in the 'heavy suit' worn by bomb-disposal experts. The military police, like their civilian counterparts, now train and arm women for close protection work, where they may be required to fire, not in self-defence, but to protect their principals.[2] In the case of the military police, the rules governing their deployment are so far uncertain. The Army Air Corps, on the other hand, has not followed the RAF's step towards allowing women pilots. All its helicopters are defined as combat but, perhaps more pertinently, senior officers insist that the training is too expensive given that women are still allowed to leave when they marry, and are forced to leave when they become pregnant.

In September 1989 Lord Arran, the Under Secretary of State for the Armed Forces, announced the relaxation of deployment rules so that 'women should be allowed to be employed in peace and war in all posts except where the primary role is direct combat'. The Adjutant General, General Sir Robert Pascoe, explained the shift thus: 'We are not saying keep them [servicewomen] out of danger, we are saying keep them out of combat.'[3]

Servicewomen were bound to become embroiled in combat. In the US invasion of Panama approximately a tenth of the 26,000-strong force were women, and in one episode, initially over-dramatized by Pentagon public relations officers, Captain Linda Bray, commanding the 988th Military Police Company, became the first woman in the US Army to lead troops in action. Technically, she infringed the regulation limiting a servicewoman's use of weapons to self-defence 'on a gender-neutral basis'.[4]

In 1991, the deployment of many thousands of servicewomen into an operational theatre shocked the conservative Saudis. And the recall of married reservists with children caused considerable disquiet at home. The whole question became very emotive when, in the confused fighting round Khafji, Melissa Rathbun-Nealy became the first US servicewoman since the Second World War to be captured by the enemy. But in spite of intense fears for her fate at the hands of the Iraqis she was well treated. Her captors apparently acclaimed her, saying she was 'as brave as [Sylvester] Stallone and as beautiful as Brooke Shields'.[5]

The British deployed relatively few servicewomen. Apart from doctors, such as Captain Vanessa England of the Royal Army Medical Corps, who served in the 1st Armoured Field Ambulance with her husband, Captain Mike England, the closest to the fighting were with A2 echelon – such as Lieutenant Sharon O'Connell, with the Royal Scots, and Lieutenant Karen Cord, the assistant adjutant of 39th Heavy Regiment.

The widening of job opportunities and the changes in the deployment rules were accompanied by the decision to double the number of servicewomen over the next ten years. In the spring of 1991 there were nearly 650 women officers spread through the non-medical side of the Army, and about 5,000 servicewomen and NCOs.

438

The Women's Royal Army Corps was formed in 1949 and became a regular corps of the British Army. The jobs open to servicewomen were strictly limited, roughly those that the Auxiliary Territorial Service had performed during the war. Very gradually, a few other lines of work opened to them when the need arose, but an improvement in male recruiting might then reverse the advance a couple of years later. In the 1970s, when the manpower demands of Northern Ireland created a strain and female searchers were needed, servicewomen were employed in relatively dangerous work.

In the 1980s, the Army found itself employing more and more highly qualified women who were clearly not averse to the challenge of working in a male-defined world. The shortages of male officers grew more serious during the decade with 'Black Hole' and 'Son of Black Hole'. This opened up specialist jobs outside the Women's Royal Army Corps. In addition to WRAC officers already working with the Royal Army Educational Corps, female officers began to be directly employed by the Royal Engineers, the Royal Signals, the Royal Corps of Transport, the Royal Army Ordnance Corps, the Royal Electrical and Mechanical Engineers, the Royal Military Police, the Royal Army Pay Corps, the Intelligence Corps and the Army Catering Corps. Other women joined the Medical, Veterinary, Dental, Legal and Nursing Corps directly.

By the end of the decade, the WRAC's position bore a superficial resemblance to that of the Habsburg Empire: it had a main body, and then widespread groups of subjects over whom it was losing sway. The vast majority of these subjects, both servicewomen or permanently employed officers in nearly a dozen different corps, wanted to become part of those with whom they worked, and whose trade they practised. Their natural loyalties and sense of identification were usually directed to that capbadge rather than to the lovat green of the WRAC, and the majority were impatient with the old system. 'We should have been RMP years ago,' said a woman corporal with the military police. Young female officers felt just as strongly.

This wish was first granted for officers. On 1 October 1990, 194 female officers officially transferred from the Women's Royal Army Corps to the corps with which they were permanently employed. And on all subsequent Sandhurst courses women officer cadets and probationary second lieutenants would be commissioned directly into their employing corps. A similar opportunity for servicewomen and NCOs will not be long in coming.

The WRAC will also take part in a sort of Equal Opportunities Commission within the Ministry of Defence to ensure that women do receive a fair chance to compete within their employing corps. These corps had tended to say, 'We can't really offer real careers to women until they really become part of us.' Now that they are, the theory of career opportunity will be tested.

The WRAC 'main stream', the Ministry of Defence said in 1990, will continue for 'the foreseeable future'. But in fact it will be affected by another proposed development, the formation of an Adjutant-General's Corps, which, apart from a main disciplinary and educational body (an amalgamation of the Royal Military Police, the Military Provost Staff Corps, the Royal Army Educational Corps and the Army Legal Corps), will have a subsidiary clerical and financial corps including the present Royal Army Pay Corps, and all staff clerks from the Royal Army Ordnance Corps and the Women's Royal Army Corps.

The days of the mainstream WRAC as an independent entity are also limited. On 18 December 1990, Archie Hamilton, Minister of State for the Armed Forces, stated: 'Those members of the WRAC who do not elect to join existing corps under our plans for the wider employment of women will also become members of this new corps.' The Ministry of Defence sees the WRAC continuing its key role 'in the recruitment, selection and training of female manpower' until its absorption into the Adjutant-General's Corps on 1 April 1992.

At the moment, girls wanting to join the Army apply at recruiting offices just like boys. (Fewer have come from areas such as the north-east, where masculine values held firm, but this has started to change.) Depending on the trade they choose – clerk, driver and military policewoman are the three favourites – they are called forward for selection at the WRAC Centre at Guildford. Mainly eighteen-year-olds, they are given a good chance to see something of the life at first hand and to talk to privates and corporals little older than themselves so as to find out more. This undoubtedly contributes to the low fall-out rate at Guildford during basic training. An unimaginative Poulson-style barracks with one of the largest parade grounds in the country, the WRAC Centre at least has plenty of trees and grass. And, despite the squirm-inducing assurance that the permanent staff 'share in the joys of birthdays and weddings to foster a family atmosphere', the place has an incomparably more relaxed and friendly air than an infantry depot. Perhaps it is easier between women, but the WRAC seems better able to deal with welfare problems.

Over the last four years NCO instructors have noticed a change in the new recruits which parallels that remarked upon with such feeling in the rest of the Army. Many of the girls have never learned to look after themselves: their mothers have done everything for them, and few know how to cook, wash their clothes or sew on a button. Quite a few cannot even wash themselves properly, so NCO instructors have to start with lessons in basic hygiene.

This general lack of awareness baffles women NCO instructors as much as permanent staff at male depots, and they too date the dramatic decline from around 1987. 'They'll ask you the first thing that comes into their heads,' said one sergeant. 'It's not that they're stupid. But they've got no idea about anything. To get them to understand that in the Army they've got to do what they're told is really hard . . . they just don't seem to understand about rank.'

At Guildford, the recruits do their common military syllabus along the same lines as male recruits. The basic fitness test is proportionately easier, and the lack of road-running in boots and stamping on the drill square meant that the WRAC suffered far fewer casualties from lower limb injuries. WRAC drill movements are generally less frenetic – for example, arms are swung only to waist height. For men who loathe drill, the satisfaction which women recruits and officer cadets claim to get out of it is hard to believe at first. (When I expressed scepticism at Sandhurst, I was put firmly in my place. 'Not only do they take it very seriously,' said a WRAC colonel emphatically, 'they thoroughly enjoy it.' Subsequent talks with WRAC officer cadets and recruits proved how right she was.) This, and the genuine enthusiasm for weapon training with the 9mm sub-machine-gun, suggest the piquancy of the challenge which military professionalism offers them.

It has been suggested that women are far too scrupulous of human life to use a gun. This may well be true of attack – little reliable evidence is available – but self-defence is a very different matter. If any differences exist, they are almost certainly cultural rather than innate. In any case, US Army research, albeit slightly discredited, has shown that a large proportion of male soldiers cannot bring themselves to fire their weapons at the enemy even when under attack.

After basic training, the intakes divide, or rather fragment. Some mainstream WRAC soldiers, such as bandswomen and administrative assistants, receive their training at Guildford, but others, such as medical assistants, stewardesses and physical training instructors, go to the centre relevant to their trade.

Those who opted on joining for trades with other capbadges will depart for their corps training depot: the military policewomen to Chichester, those destined for the Intelligence Corps to Ashford, the cooks to Aldershot, supply controllers and specialists for the Ordnance Corps to Deepcut, data telegraphists and switchboard operators to the Royal Signals at Catterick, 'posties' to the Royal

Engineers at Mill Hill, military accountants to the Pay Corps at Worthy Down, and movement controllers to the Royal Corps of Transport at Aldershot. Although for the time being they remain on WRAC strength, and are dealt with by the WRAC records office, most of them return to Guildford only for promotion courses or for administrative reasons. Attempts to foster a WRAC *esprit de corps* outside the mainstream WRAC proved an almost impossible task.

Although fated to become part of the Adjutant General's Corps, the WRAC mainstream has begun to expand strongly to help ease the gaps in combat arm units. Providing headquarters platoons for battalions in Northern Ireland, women have become a recognizable part of the field army.

After the Falklands War, the Minister of State for Defence announced that 'the services should also seek to post reasonable numbers of women in uniform' down there.[6] The first contingent left in July of the following year. They and their successors came from a mixture of trades and were therefore not employed together, which made life difficult for the female officer responsible for their welfare.

In such an isolated and masculine society, a service-woman's life has its advantages and disadvantages. Much depends on outlook, and much on circumstance. Those who joined for 'the social life' – in both the literal and euphemistic sense – are seldom disappointed by the male to female ratio. And while they may enjoy being 'spoilt rotten', invited to sea by the Navy or taken on helicopter rides with the RAF, the risk of rape back at base cannot be ignored, mainly because of the men's heavy drinking.

Servicewomen, finding themselves in a sex-obsessed environment, have to learn very early on to 'bite their lip'. The soldiers' slang term for a 'Wrac' – a Cadbury's Snack – gives an indication of what they have to put up with. Harassment takes many forms, but the threat of being labelled a lesbian is one of the most common.

(Some certainly are. The WRAC, like the female branches of armed forces all over the world, tends to attract a higher proportion of lesbians than most civilian jobs, probably not so much because of the sexual opportunities, as male soldiers allege, but because an institution of female solidarity appeals to them.) A servicewoman's problems are certainly not solved by consenting to a soldier's advances. She can seldom rely on him to show any sense of responsibility; too many still regard the idea of taking precautions as a joke.

Pregnancy has always been one of the commonest reasons for servicewomen leaving the Army. Whether single or married, 'women must be discharged by their sixteenth week of pregnancy'. A few years ago, a former Director of the WRAC, Brigadier Helen Meechie, explained the policy on the grounds of military necessity: 'We need to be a hundred per cent manned and therefore we discharge a girl when she is pregnant.'[7] But now manning requirements have a different perspective, and there is 'nothing to stop [servicewomen] applying to re-enlist after their confinement'. The situation, already a semantic quagmire, was further confused by an announcement that 'servicewomen who are pregnant or fall [sic] pregnant during 1991 may be entitled to claim Statutory Maternity Pay'. Clearly, the position is being quietly eased in certain cases to keep highly trained women during the manpower crisis.

The male assumption that expensive training is wasted on women began to look very shaky in the later 1980s when highly qualified men started to leave the Army in unprecedented numbers. And a US Department of Defense Study in 1977 showed that their servicewomen (who do not have to leave on pregnancy) lost less time off work, even when having a baby, than the average serviceman did through sickness, absence without leave, or drug and alcohol problems. Leaving aside the maternity issue, British servicewomen are generally thought to have a much lower absentee rate than their male colleagues. 'For a start,' said a WRAC sergeant, 'they don't have hangovers every morning.'

When the Army decided to recommence advertising for WRAC officers in the late 1980s, its advertising agency carried out some attitudinal research amongst male and female students. The results rather took them aback. On the whole the young men interviewed had a positive image, but many of the young women produced the most terrible stereotypes, not far removed from that of the bull dyke with a moustache. As a result, the agency placed considerable emphasis on femininity. A beautiful officer, immaculate both in make-up and combat kit, marched across the page at the head of a squad of male soldiers under the headline 'Behind every successful woman'. The copy continued: 'When you meet a bunch of WRAC officers the first thing that strikes you is how feminine they are. No jolly hockey sticks. No Barbara Woodhouse voices suitable for barking orders. And not a pair of brogues in sight. They like dancing, candle-lit dinners with friends and good movies.'

The account director admitted he had felt very uneasy about the reaction this advertisement would cause. He thought it 'frankly sexist', and expected an outburst of feminist protest. To his surprise, the average response rate was over three times that for male officer advertisements.

Recruiting has been successful over the last few years. The standard of female applicant has been noticeably higher than that of the male, as the Regular Commissions Board and Sandhurst are the first to acknowledge. They should be better, say the WRAC, because there are many more girls applying for each place, and at twenty they are much more mature than their male equivalents. One RCB president, a brigadier from the Welsh Guards, found them so articulate and confident that he almost felt they were interviewing him.

From their first day at Sandhurst, 'the girls' rise with gusto to the task of disproving male prejudice. Several have abandoned other careers, as teachers, secretaries or sales representatives, in search of a greater challenge and a different, more satisfying form of professionalism. Slightly fewer than in the past have service connections, but they still represent a sizeable minority; quite a number have a brother serving. The educational profile has changed the most. Only about 10 per cent were at a private sector school, and almost three-quarters of each intake at Sandhurst are graduates. The graduates, like their male equivalents, are probationary second lieutenants, and will receive two and a half years' seniority.

Out of an intake of forty, only around half join the WRAC mainstream. The largest batch destined to a corps, usually around nine, join the Royal Army Educational Corps. A couple each will go to the engineers, signals, REME or the Royal Corps of Transport, and one each to small corps such as the Royal Military Police, the Intelligence Corps, the Royal Army Pay Corps and the Army Catering Corps. Also in the WRAC wing at Sandhurst will be one or two officer cadets who will become non-nursing officers in the QAs – Queen Alexandra's Royal Army Nursing Corps.

The first few weeks are spent largely on PT and drill. As the course progresses, the favourite subjects seem to be communication studies and weapons training and fieldcraft. They mainly practise patrols under the instruction of male officers and NCOs, but they do not dig in or do platoon attacks. They also carry out a number of command post exercises. Overall, the women's course at Sandhurst is roughly similar to that of the graduates, except for a good deal more military law, records and service writing, and much less range-firing and field training.

The maturity and university background of most of the young women at Sandhurst lead them to associate more with the standard graduate course – both are housed in Victory College – than with the officer cadets on the standard military course, a preference which causes a certain amount of friction. They also find that the male graduates, no doubt influenced by the experience of civilian student life, do not attempt to put them down so much, while infantry officer cadets on the standard military course, above all those bound for the Parachute Regiment, apparently try to exert their machismo with a conspicuous display of contempt.

The most frequent loser is the civilian boyfriend. He will find it hard to cope with her new life. In a short space of time she has far more in common with people he does not know, while the idea of her being surrounded by hundreds of physical young men can only foment jealousy. Any attempt to tie her down will only make things worse. Marriage tends to be pushed to the back of her mind at that stage, although there is a saying amongst female officer cadets at Sandhurst that the girl who is most determined to stay with her career is usually the first one up the aisle.

At Sandhurst, the young women, like their male contemporaries, receive lessons on dress and behaviour. This includes both a warning against outspoken feminism, which might provoke the men – the WRAC motto, *Suaviter in modo, fortiter in re* (gentle in manner, resolute in deed), was carefully chosen – and a strong caution to be discreet in their private life.

They look forward to the commissioning ball as much as the men. Until 1989, however, the WRAC mess dress was enough to spoil their pleasure: made of gold brocade, with a lovat green plaid over one shoulder, it conjured up images of Highland dancing in the 1930s. Indeed, it was hard to find members of any of the women's services who like their evening wear. 'They never date,' remarked one officer; 'they will always be out of fashion.'[8] But now senior women officers have listened to complaints and brought in the bolero jacket and cummerbund which young officers wanted.

The newly commissioned mainstream officer is often as ambitious as her male contemporary. She too cultivates a professional image, and like him she looks forward to her first command appointment: the true test of leadership, as they have so often been told. But the WRAC has had ιεw commands to offer their subalterns. The majority of mainstream lieutenants are destined to become assistant adjutants. Since few adjutants allow them much responsibility, and male subalterns despise the job, many feel with a good deal of resentment that they are treated as 'niff-naff' fodder – in other words, given all of the petty details to sort out. 'Sandhurst is good training for the Army,' said one woman captain, 'but it's not good for their expectations. All this Wilco enthusiasm gets turned off.'

Many of the commanding officers and adjutants for whom they work feel that it is wrong to send them newly commissioned WRAC lieutenants. The assistant adjutant's job always used to be performed by a senior subaltern. A young woman, who is a double outsider, lacks the experience and authority to sort out orderly officers or chase up the companies or squadrons. They have to resort to charm, and the best they can hope for from the 'subbies', as they call the male subalterns, is to be treated as a younger sister.

Usually the only female in a mess full of young subalterns, the assistant adjutant has other problems to cope with. (There are exceptions now. The Royal Regiment of Wales recently had three women officers, the paymaster and the regimental medical officer as well as the assistant adjutant.)[9] First of all, she has to learn to be a good sport and treat the endless jokes and innuendo with a long-suffering smile. At Sandhurst she was warned about the danger of sleeping around, that 'once you lose your reputation you'll never get it back', and 'you'll become a bad joke in the mess'. She may not have been warned, however, that in a number of regiments the subalterns make a communal bet of a case of champagne to the first officer to get her into bed. One assistant adjutant acknowledged that hearing about the custom from a fatherly sergeant had made it hard to relax from then on. She could never know whether a subaltern was genuinely friendly or just trying to win the bet.

A mess full of over-sexed young men can easily lead to

rivalries, especially when away from home. For that reason, one piece of standard advice before leaving Sandhurst is to 'get yourself attached to someone outside the unit pretty pronto'. One or two, on the other hand – usually the most good-looking – are spoilt shamelessly and enjoy being the centre of attention. They seem to be sent to infantry and cavalry regiments in particular. An especially glamorous one, in a good example of Army humour, received the acronym MUSK: major unit sex kitten. In a slightly paradoxical way, their lives are easier, because they have more confidence when they need to fend off young officers. As the life and soul of the party, their livers are probably in more danger than their virtue; at worst they may have to lock their door against a drunken, lovesick bore. Fortunately, a Zuleika Dobson has not yet appeared, producing a lemming-like disaster of infatuated subalterns.

But more depressing than the often infantile sexuality which the Army seems to engender in men is the day-to-day professional prejudice with which both servicewomen and officers have to contend. Many men feel threatened when working alongside women. To have a woman promoted over them is seen as a humiliation. The infantry and armoured corps, which women cannot join even with the new rules on badging, have no need to feel threatened – but that does not make them less patronizing.

Like other women officers, assistant adjutants will continue to be at a disadvantage until they are seen to have 'proper jobs', which means a command. 'In the Army credibility is everything,' said a brigadier about the career problems facing women in his organization. However pleasant the officers and senior NCOs may be to an assistant adjutant, she can never really feel part of things so long as she is 'just blistered on'. A senior woman officer described this double discrimination as a 'catch-44'. Another said that because everyone expected women officers to get married and have children they were seldom sent on the important courses or appointments. This stopped them from 'getting the ticks for the A1 jobs'.

Senior women officers were always dubious about the longer-term effects of women being split up amongst different capbadges, and the eventual hiving-off of the WRAC. No doubt partly influenced by loyalty to the WRAC itself, they strongly believe that women in an alien, even hostile, environment such as the Army – one described them as fish in a desert – need their own pool of water in order to survive. They feared that career opportunities in the different corps would prove a disappointment, because 'permanent employment leads you to hardware rather than command'. The only exceptions had been one woman major commanding a provost company at Aldershot and another commanding an intelligence and security company, yet in theory everyone should have the opportunity to reach lieutenant colonel. Most of the younger officers, full of self-confidence, considered that the worries of senior women officers were unnecessarily defensive in a fast-changing world.

A potentially significant breakthrough came, ironically, with the WRAC mainstream, not the hiving-off process. In a sudden move in the spring of 1989, the GOC Northern Ireland requested WRAC support platoons for all resident infantry battalions in the province. Deployment began in July, with the first platoon sent to the 3rd Battalion, the Queen's Regiment at Aldergrove.

Bubbling with enthusiasm at this breakthrough, the WRAC Centre immediately revised its training schedules to ensure that a total of 180 administrative assistants, drivers, clerks and medics would be ready on time. The vision of Wrens running the headquarters at Bessbrook Mill – log-keepers, stores assistants, map-markers and all – had at last become a lovat-green reality. 'They're all our career-controlled beings,' said a senior WRAC officer, proud that such a coup belonged exclusively to the WRAC mainstream.

A senior member of the General Staff said that the experiment's overall success could be judged properly only once it had been tried in battalions elsewhere. There certainly does not appear to be any resistance to the idea from the infantry. Even the paras, who are not renowned for enlightened views on the subject of women in uniform, welcome the prospect. No longer would their soldiers be wasted on undignified jobs as clerks or storemen. But it is hard to imagine the Parachute Regiment allowing women to wear the maroon beret.

The great advantage for young women officers is that they will have a support platoon to command instead of the hated post of assistant adjutant. There should also be a knock-on effect. The brigadier who said that credibility was all, also added: 'If women are to be taken seriously in the Army, then they must be alongside the men.' Deployment rules have now been eased, but some edges remain conveniently blurred. Whether in the next few years there will be support platoons with armoured infantry battalions, or whether women will be allowed to serve at 'the sharp end' of field intelligence, and how far career prospects will improve, is impossible to foretell.

Women in the Army have been very conscious of every first: the first women lieutenant colonels to the Joint Services Staff College, or Brigadier Helen Meechie attending the Royal College of Defence Studies in 1986 and then becoming the first woman to hold a senior staff appointment. But a greater measure of change will occur only when female captains, majors and lieutenant colonels fill more staff appointments. The Army's need, as recent years have shown, is their opportunity.

CHAPTER 28

The Other Army: The Territorials

During the nineteenth century, Militia and volunteer forces were quite separate from the Regular Army. Their fortunes were at the mercy of popular mood and jingoism. The invasion scare of 1859 brought 119,000 men flocking to join volunteer forces to repel the French, Britain's ally of only four years earlier. Enthusiasm waned again soon afterwards.

The basis of the modern second-line force evolved over the next fifty years. In 1871 control of the Militia was removed from the lords lieutenant of counties. (Their successors still play a part, however, as presidents of the regional Territorial Auxiliary and Volunteer Reserve Associations.) Yet the volunteer, and hence amateur, essence of the system has continued, partly because it was the British way of doing things, and partly because we abhor peacetime conscription, the only other source of trained reserves. Even so, the Prussian Landwehr's contribution to the German victory of 1870 over the French led to the decision to bring volunteer units closer to the Regular Army. In 1908, the title of Militia disappeared, and today the doyen of the Territorial Army, the Royal Monmouthshire (Royal Engineers) Militia, is the only British regiment to retain it.

The modern belief in a greater measure of integration, and the notion of the Territorial Army as part of the 'mobilized order of battle', as opposed to a follow-on force, was reaffirmed with 'the one Army concept', which dates from 1967. On a more routine basis, the link between the two consists of a handful of key figures in each unit from the parent regiment in the Regular Army – often the commanding officer (although ideally a TA officer

452

should be found), the training major, the adjutant, the quartermaster, the RSM, the chief clerk, and several other senior NCOs. Some of the permanent staff posts are held by ex-regulars, perhaps a late-entry captain, and several senior NCOs.

'The TA', said a senior general, 'suffers from both a Dad's Army and a Rambo image.' Many members are teased by workmates who cannot imagine a normal person wanting to give up spare time in order to submit to another discipline.

There are numerous reasons for serving, and few people join for just one of them. The image of action and physical challenge clearly appeals to many of those locked into a monotonous job. To some it appeals as 'an escape from the wife'; others are attracted by the social side, so giving the TA the reputation of a drinking club. Some are ex-regulars who find after a year or so that they miss the comradeship of the Army: 'It's your mates that keep you going.' Out of a company of about seventy, as many as fifteen may be ex-regulars.

Others are what might be called frustrated regulars. These may include a handful of 'gun freaks'. A corporal, differentiating himself from the perpetrator of the Hungerford massacre, said rather unreassuringly that 'Discipline stops me from doing what he did.' (His commanding officer's comment on the subject earlier that day had been: 'The TA could be said to provide a useful safety-valve.')

Except in regions of high unemployment, few join for the pay, but it certainly acts as an added incentive and, perhaps more important, offers a useful justification when informing a wife. Since wives often resent being abandoned at weekends, commanding officers try to ensure that TA social life is not exclusively male and that they are brought in. Grass widows often form their own little groups, and sometimes today husband-and-wife teams join together.

Another problem facing commanding officers is the

dispersal of their men. The 4th Battalion of the Queen's Lancashire Regiment, for example, has its headquarters in Preston, and a company each in Burnley, Blackpool, Bolton and Blackburn. But they are comparatively fortunate. Some units are scattered over anything up to fifteen locations, while the Royal Yeomanry has one squadron in Northern Ireland, one in Nottingham, another in Wiltshire and the rest in and around London.

Drill nights take place on a single night around the middle of the week. Senior ranks and officers should turn up by 7.30 and the rest arrive at about eight. Some of the time is given over to administration, but they should also have two forty-minute lessons of training, whether in skill-at-arms, first aid or map-reading, or a briefing for an exercise. Afterwards they adjourn to the bar, which generally stays open until about ten. Some sort of activity – whether an exercise, range-firing or adventure training – usually takes place on one weekend in three. To qualify for their 'bounty' or bonus, members need to go on six designated weekends a year and the two-week annual camp. They must also pass the personal weapons test and the basic fitness test, as well as tests in first aid and nuclear, biological and chemical warfare.

The attitude of employers towards the Territorial Army has greatly changed. Small firms are the least sympathetic to anyone wanting extra time off for annual camp. Large companies are better, and the Civil Service the most sympathetic of all. But there are hardly any managers left who did National Service, and the only ones with any knowledge of the Army are those who held short-service commissions – a tiny minority. As a result, commanding officers have to devote much of their time to local diplomacy, giving dinners for employers in the officers' mess – usually a bar and a dining-room above the drill hall – so as to persuade them to allow their workers or managers more time off for training. The National Employers' Liaison Committee, an MoD backed organization, has the prime task in persuading

British industry that service in the reserve forces is good for industry as well as for the country.

The Territorial Army is seldom short of middle-ranking and middle-aged officers, mainly those with a taste for it who have stayed on. Recruiting young officers, particularly in northern areas, has not been easy. 'If he's any good,' said a commanding officer, 'then he's already under pressure in his civilian job.' Great efforts are made to attract them, such as the 'fast track' scheme to accelerate their training and get them on to the short Sandhurst course for Territorial Army officers as quickly as possible. There is also a public relations exercise known as 'Executive Stretch', which offers leadership training to civilian companies. The 4th Royal Green Jackets, for example, ran the scheme for London District in 1989; the idea of yuppies sleeping on a drill hall floor in Mayfair before a 'beasting' on the assault course at Pirbright the next morning had a certain piquancy.[1] But even if young men with the right qualifications do come in the problem is not solved. 'We mustn't demand too much,' said the same commanding officer, 'otherwise they just leave.'

The situation is very similar with the ordinary TA member. NCOs from the professional permanent cadre can easily criticize too much. They have to realize that 'the TA is a hobby, and when that hobby ceases being fun, then he votes with his feet'. Fun means providing the right mix of field training, which should be realistic enough to interest the part-timers. But resources are very limited: blank rounds are rationed on economy grounds, and Regular Army soldiers are not keen on spending their weekends acting as the enemy for a bunch of amateurs.

The oversell indulged in by TA advertising campaigns – some cinema commercials were shamelessly glamorized – is, in the view of many officers, counter-productive. 'When was the last time we had helicopters on exercise?' They also feel it makes for 'a real come-down when a prospective recruit takes his first look at the drill hall'.

With training areas and ranges heavily booked, especially

in the south, and travel restricted by tight fuel budgets, Territorial units are hardly in a position to spend every weekend doing platoon attacks across the Sennybridge or Stanford training areas or Salisbury Plain, even if their members wanted to. Proper field training exercises are limited to the two-week summer camp. 'Nato-roled' units should have trained in Germany at least once every three years, but the change in mood against military exercises of any sort has virtually put an end to this; now they may well alternate between Sennybridge and Otterburn, where the support platoon can fire its Milan anti-tank missiles. Overseas training, whether dry-training in Cyprus or four or five exercises in the United States with the National Guard, provides the best boost to morale. But surprisingly small things can have an effect, particularly in the way of equipment. When Territorial units were issued with the same new helmet as the Regular Army they could 'walk tall'. They no longer looked like Dad's Army, with the old tin hats bouncing around.

The Territorial Army is almost as varied and as tribal in its nature as the Regular Army. Perhaps its best-known regiment is the second senior, the Honourable Artillery Company. (A long-standing dispute over precedence with the Royal Monmouthshire Militia was revived by the HAC's rather provocative application to have the Armada added to its battle honours.)

The Honourable Artillery Company exists in a sort of splendid isolation at Armoury House in the City of London. It is famous for providing guards of honour on state visits and for firing salutes with its old 25-pounder field guns, yet its wartime role is both highly specialized and secret. Reflecting these two aspects of its nature, the Regular Army members of its permanent staff come from both the Foot Guards and the gunners. Recruited from the City – the HAC freemasonry of contacts in City institutions provides a strong incentive for joining – it has some of the best-educated and certainly some of the richest soldiers in the Army. There is a standing joke that they go on exercise in Range Rovers.

Yeomanry regiments were originally defined as 'provisional cavalry'. From a murderous rabble at Peterloo, they developed into an effective part of Allenby's victorious army in Palestine. A large number of regiments were mechanized in 1941 and 1942 to serve as armoured regiments in the Western Desert. Since the war most have been disbanded, or amalgamated with the local infantry battalion – the Pembrokeshire Yeomanry, for example, joined the 4th (Volunteer) Battalion, the Royal Regiment of Wales – or turned into signal or transport units. (Some yeomanry regiments had already opted to become artillery between the wars, as this offered the only way at the time to hang on to their horses.) The only survivors are the two allocated to the Rhine Army, the Royal Yeomanry Regiment and the Queen's Own Yeomanry, and three home defence regiments, the Royal Wessex Yeomanry, the Queen's Own Mercian Yeomanry and the Duke of Lancaster's Own Yeomanry.

Of the infantry, the Guards Division alone has no territorial units. (Spared this responsibility, their wealth in senior NCOs has helped to maintain their stranglehold on Sandhurst.) The Scottish Division, with 52nd Lowland Volunteers and 51st Highland Volunteers, has five battalions, with a good balance between officers and soldiers. With one or two marked exceptions, southern English battalions generally have plenty of officers and few soldiers, while northern battalions suffer from the opposite problem. The Queen's Division, most of whose seven battalions recruit in the south-east, and the King's Division, whose eight battalions are spread over Yorkshire, the north-east and Northern Ireland, provide a distinct contrast in this way. The Prince of Wales's Division has eight battalions, varying widely in strength, while the Light Division has six battalions, four Light Infantry and two Green Jacket.

Like their parent regiments, Territorial infantry battalions are convinced of the importance of resurrecting titles with strong local associations lost in the 1968 reorganization. Profiting from the tradition of the local King's Own Yorkshire Light Infantry, the recently raised 8th Battalion of the Light Infantry recruited from scratch to the strength of some of the weaker battalions in under two years. But, to give an idea of the future difficulties, one in every seventy-two men in the 15–29 age group will have to be recruited in the Wakefield–Pontefract area over the next five years if the battalion is to be fully manned.[2]

The three volunteer battalions of the Parachute Regiment – 4 Para recruiting from Yorkshire and Lancashire, 10 Para in London and 15 Para centred on Glasgow – do not have to appeal to local loyalties: they need only rely on the regiment's image and the attractions of a good ration of weekend aggression-venting. A major, who in civilian life managed a sweet factory, said of his men: 'They are definitely more physically fit and more aggressive than other TA units, and the whole experience of serving with the Parachute Regiment adds a new dimension to their lives.'

The part-time SAS, the 21st (the Artists' Rifles) and the 23rd SAS Regiment, have seldom been short of applicants in the past. (Whether they were of the right standard was another matter.) But now, in order to boost recruiting, the regiment has taken to advertising in *Soldier* magazine. As with the paras, they join to add a new dimension to life, although their aggressive instincts tend to be vented with more subtlety. They are always in great demand as the enemy for home defence exercises. The defenders love to claim afterwards how they fought off 'the Sass', implying that they were from the Regular Army version.

The specialist units of the Territorial Army are remarkable. Many have a flavour both of the 'pals' battalions' of the First World War and of a busman's holiday, because their members take their civilian skills into the Army, often in a group. Most of 135 Topographic

Squadron Royal Engineers come from the Ordnance Survey in Southampton, while AA patrolmen account for much of the strength of 174 Provost Company Royal Military Police. The job of 126 Reclamation Workshop REME (V), most of whose members come from the car industry round Coventry, is to recover anything worthwhile from wrecked or shot-up vehicles. British Rail employees provide the core of 275 Railway Squadron, Royal Corps of Transport, and stevedores from Liverpool and Southampton docks belong to port-operating squadrons at Marchwood. The RCT looks to volunteers for about half its wartime strength. Nearly 10,000 strong, they form the largest volunteer organization after the infantry.

As the Gulf crisis demonstrated, the Army depends heavily on TA members of the Royal Army Medical Corps and the Queen Alexandra's Royal Army Nursing Corps: they represent half of all medical support. Surgeons, doctors, nursing sisters, and managers, nearly all from the National Health Service, help constitute an officer strength alone of over 1,500.

The sappers also have officers so highly qualified in their related fields that in the Army List their entries often run to two lines because of all the letters after their names. The Intelligence Corps, on the other hand, has no real civilian equivalent, except perhaps the Security Service, which would hardly accept the loss of its personnel on transition to war. About 500 strong, of whom nearly a quarter are officers, the Intelligence Corps Territorials represent, in the words of one of their Regular Army colonels, an 'amazing range of qualifications and professions . . . Lawyers and BBC producers are very happy as lance corporals. The Int Corps,' he added, 'is one area where the one-Army concept is a reality.'

Although not strictly part of the Territorial Army, the nineteen University Officer Training Corps are organized on similar lines. Male and female students are encouraged

459

to join at the freshers' fair and become officer cadets. (Future Sandhurst entrants on cadetships or bursaries are certainly expected to join.) The formal commitment is minimal, and the main objective is to stimulate attitudes favourable to the Army amongst future managers rather than create a reserve officer corps. Of course the Ministry of Defence hopes that some of them will get a taste for it and join the Territorial Army, or even the Regular Army. The OTC often has a reputation for attracting the more boisterous and physical members of the university. They elect an entertainments committee, and the Army's glossy pamphlet, as well as extolling its character-building advantages, claims rather racily that 'some OTC parties have become legends in their own time'.

According to the old Cold War scenario, the Territorial Army was there to increase regular forces by some 60 per cent, most of it to reinforce the Rhine Army. The rest, including the Home Service Force, are responsible for home defence. The Home Service Force, raised as an adjunct to the Territorial Army, is now about 3,000 strong. Mainly made up of slightly older ex-regulars intended primarily for guard duties, the Home Service Force Company is sponsored by a parent TA unit. In practice, this means it often becomes the fifth company – usually E Company – of the local battalion.

In the event of war, all volunteer units would be called up by the Queen's Order under the Reserve Forces Act – 'either for permanent service in any part of the world when war-like operations are in preparation or progress. Or if it appears to Her Majesty that national danger is imminent or that a great emergency has arisen.'

No Queen's Order was used to call up the reserves en bloc. The Government felt during the Gulf crisis that discretion was the better part of political controversy. (The 13th/18th Hussars might well have found it rather tricky calling up one of their reserve officers – HRH Prince Hussein of the Hashemite Kingdom of Jordan.)

Instead of using their own reservists, regiments were brought up to strength with the accustomed practice of blistering on sub-units and individuals. The number required varied enormously between arms. An armoured regiment depends on reservists for just over 5 per cent of its war strength, while gunner regiments, requiring a large manpower reserve of 'ammo-bashers', depend on reservists for up to 40 per cent.

The whole question of reservists is extremely relevant to the current discussion about 'cadreization' – the degree to which regiments can operate with a smaller full-time cadre and a larger proportion of reservists. Like all reserve forces, the theory is fine when war is expected, as it was in 1939. But no regiment forming part of a rapid reaction force can wait for reservists to be called up, processed and transported to the unit. Cadreization, not surprisingly, raises suspicions of yet another formula to fudge the figures.

In 1990, during the build-up in Saudi Arabia, the Government tried to achieve its targets for medical personnel by calling for volunteers. Of the 1,200 reservists who served in the Gulf, at least 90 per cent were from the Royal Army Medical Corps or Queen Alexandra's Royal Army Nursing Corps. Nearly 500 of them were called up under Section 10 of the Reserve Forces Act. Another volunteer group was 711 Laundry Platoon RAOC, serving the two field hospitals and the two general hospitals in the Gulf, 22 and 32 Field Hospital and 33 and 205 General Hospital. The 205 (Scottish) General Hospital RAMC (Volunteers) was a 600-bed hospital on the edge of Riyadh. One volunteer who understandably attracted a good deal of attention was Captain Charles Goodson-Wickes, the Conservative MP for Wimbledon, a former member of the Life Guards who, as a physician, became the first sitting member of the House of Commons to serve on operations since the Second World War.

The first member of the TA to reach the Gulf was Lieutenant G. J. Moore, who happened to be on an attachment to 40th Field Regiment, the gunner regiment deployed with 7th Armoured Brigade in October 1990. A very close second were the TAPIOs, or Territorial Army press and information officers, each one of whom acted as 'minder' to a mixed group of journalists and radio and television reporters. These six-strong groups were known as 'media response teams' – a title presumably designed to appeal to journalists with a taste for the trappings of combat. The TAPIO and a driver conducted their six clients around in long-wheelbase Land Rovers.

The Territorial Army officers who belong to the All-Arms Watchkeepers and Liaison Officers Pool organized by the Royal Artillery at Woolwich could have provided a much larger reinforcement for harassed headquarters. The plan is that, together with Royal Army Educational Corps officers, they supplement divisional and corps staffs to release regular officers for regimental duty.

The Territorial Army, runs the official line, represents 'an economical addition to our regular forces', and the figures quoted would certainly appear to support that view. With pay and bounty coming to £142 million a year and other costs over £200 million, the TA is bound to seem inexpensive compared with the Regular Army, in which a single armoured division in Germany costs nearly £400 million a year in personnel alone, while the capital cost of its armament, vehicles and equipment is nearly £2 billion. 'The Government', states the National Audit Office report of 1989, 'are committed to making more use of reservists, particularly volunteer reserves, which they believe is the most cost-effective way of enhancing the front-line capability of regular forces.'[3] But many in the Regular Army would say that this merely means that the emphasis is being placed on cost rather than on effectiveness.

Some of the Territorial Army, particularly the specialist units, are clearly excellent value. But one cannot help suspecting that the attraction of 'the numbers game' has proved too strong when figures combining Regular and TA strengths are bandied about as if the troops involved were of equal quality. *The British Military Doctrine* provides a circumspectly phrased warning on the subject: 'Experience has shown that reserve forces will require time and further training before committal to complex tasks in war.'[4] In reality, this means that they should not be counted as front-line troops on transition to war.

The targets for the TA and the Home Service Force (86,000 and 4,750 by 1990) were not met. (With the diminishing reservoir of manpower, regular officers regarded them as unrealistic from the start.) More important, the official statistics never provide a true indication of operational strength. A senior general admitted that the high turnover means that 'at least one third at any one time are untrained'. The commanding officer of a BAOR-assigned battalion estimated that to bring his men anywhere near the standard of regular soldiers for operations in the central region would require six weeks' intensive training, an opportunity which they would never get in the circumstances. And although he thought half of his men could 'give as good a performance as Regulars, within the limitations of their training', the other half did not inspire confidence. 'But at the end of the day,' he said with a slight shrug, 'if that's what you've got, then that's what you use.'

The real problem is the rapid turnover. 'They join to give it a whirl,' said a staff officer. The average length of service was only 2.7 years, with about a third leaving in their first year and another third in their second. 'We're in a down-trend situation,' said the same staff officer. 'Once they've seen the same programme the second time round, they want out. Variety is what's needed.' The bounty incentive to stay on – £200 after the first year, rising to £400 after the second and £600 after the third – does not seem to make much difference. The high turnover is extremely expensive when recruiting and induction costs are running at over £2,000 per head.

Yet the motives for leaving, or not joining in the first place, are complex. Some are personal and perennial – falling in love, marriage, the birth of children, moving to another district – while others reflect the social environment. A young person's spare time now is often devoted to moonlighting in order to accumulate the deposit for a flat, or pay the mortgage. Pressure at work is much greater, particularly for managers. More young fathers than in previous generations regard their spare time with the family as precious, if not sacrosanct. And the ideal of part-time voluntary service has declined, largely because in an anti-amateur age people prefer to believe that things should be left to the professionals.

The new generation which grew up in the 1980s lacks patience and has a far lower attention span. A flicker of boredom leads them to reach for the channel-changing gadget. And the prospect of not learning or doing anything new at the drill hall, or going somewhere different on exercise, means that they lose interest more rapidly than ever before. Never has familiarity bred boredom so quickly.

Paradoxically, or perhaps with a curious logic, the greatest growth in this rather macho organization has been in women volunteers. Between 1984 and 1990, the number of women increased from nearly 6,000 to nearly 9,000.

With the whole Army entering on a period of self-examination about the future, it is clearly a good time for the Territorial Army to do the same. Its former Inspector-General, the dual-hatted Commander UK Field Army, said that he would like to see it moving much more towards a disaster-relief role. In several recent disasters, informal groups from the local TA unit have often been amongst the first on the scene to help. If this were possible, the Territorial Army could take some of the load of Military Aid to the Civil Community off the back of the Regular Army and earn a considerable amount of respect with new skills. The Ministry of Defence, on the other hand, feels that the whole idea 'is not feasible'. Legislative complications are cited, but the reluctance seems to lie elsewhere.

The future of the Territorial Army is bound to be uncertain at the end of the age of mass mobilized warfare. As a force that needs to be called up by Queen's Order, it is also less relevant to the new age of smaller, highly trained rapid-raction forces. (The Gulf war was exceptional in the way that the stand-off allowed time for a progressive build-up and even intensive training before going into battle.) There is talk of cutting the Territorial Army from 73,000 to 50,000, perhaps even less. But even regular officers who resent the dishonest arguments advanced in favour of relying on reservist manpower would not dismiss the vital importance of specialist volunteers. The idea of the 'Ever-readies', a concept from the 1960s, is greatly favoured. The cost of around £3,000 per man is high, so it would have to be limited to key specialists only. Perhaps the final answer will be a two-tier structure, with specialists who deploy abroad with the Regular Army and an exclusively home-based Territorial Army ready to help with the responsibility for national defence.

Part Five

CONCLUSION

CHAPTER 29

Public Perception and Political Masters

The Army's reaction to public controversy and criticism is not always easy to predict. Sometimes it consists of a tight-lipped reserve, sometimes it is acutely self-conscious, sometimes the Army overreacts and sometimes, particularly in the face of tabloid excesses, it is phlegmatic. Like armies everywhere, but mercifully much less than most, the British Army from time to time feels undervalued and wilfully misunderstood by politicians as well as by the press.

A senior general, well known for his articulate presentation of issues, recounted the five benchmarks which he had used during his time as the Army's Director of Public Relations. 'First,' he said, 'the Army must be seen as vital for national defence. Secondly, it must be militarily efficient, and for that it needs to exercise. Thirdly, it must be cost-effective, because the armed forces have to be accepted by the public at large. Fourthly, the Army must be a good employer. And lastly, the Army must be responsible in its attitude to national affairs; i.e. it mustn't be organizing coups or anything like that.'

The public's perception of the Army 'as vital to national defence' probably went through more ups and downs in the course of 1990 and 1991 than at any time since the end of the First World War. Gorbachev's barb that the worst thing he had done to the West was to have 'taken away your enemy' felt uncomfortably accurate in the ears of the professional soldier, even if the reverse proved far more devastating for the Soviet empire. But when Glasnost reached its peak with the signing of the Treaty on Conventional Armed Forces in Europe on 19

November 1990, the build-up of forces in the Gulf was proceeding rapidly.

From a mixture of instinct and self-preservation, and because it is their job to remain on guard, most senior officers do not believe that, even though the Soviet Union has lost its 'launch-pad' in Eastern Europe, the Russian leopard has changed his spots. One Russian defector who lectures to officers on the threat from the East expounds a curiously intriguing theory that Soviet leaders alternate between bald reformers and hairy atavists. The bald – such as Lenin, Khruschev and Gorbachev – are pragmatists prepared to work with the West when it suits them, whereas the hirsute – Stalin and Brezhnev – revert to the Muscovite xenophobia of the Middle Ages. After Gorbachev, according to this theory, we are due for another paranoid Muscovite with bushy eyebrows and the full ideological baggage. This Esau–Jacob expression of the old Slavophile–Westerner conflict in the Russian soul is supposed to provide a Kremlinologist's guide to dangerous dark horses during the next power struggle. Younger officers, on the other hand, are much less concerned about the old enemy. They point with satisfaction to the way Red Army generals were 'shaken rigid' by the almost effortless destruction of Soviet military hardware in Iraq.

These ups and downs have thrown long-term planning into total disarray. 'If the main variable', said a general on the weapons staff, the longest of long-term planners, 'is the very thing you're trying to design for, then you're lost. But this is the way the world's going.' But the key question now for the British Army is not so much the dangers inherent in the collapse of the Soviet empire but whether the Germans are prepared to keep more than a single British armoured division on their soil.

A senior officer at Staff College voiced the Army's more personal concern. The end of the Cold War with a partial withdrawal from Germany must lose them priority in government spending, and they would 'not get decent kit'. Many officers felt that the total effect might induce the vicious circle described in the oft-quoted passage of Alexis de Tocqueville: 'The best part of the nation shuns the military profession because the profession is not honoured, and the profession is not honoured because the best part of the nation has ceased to follow it.'[1] To the dismay of many, the threat still remains, even after the astonishing success of the Gulf war. A failure of political will with fudged or postponed decisions could have an equally devastating effect, since most of the best people will leave.

Whether or not the Army was seen as 'militarily efficient' by the public was confused by sitcom clichés based on National Service days with twittish officers and booming sergeants. These vied in people's memories with other television footage such as the storming of the Iranian Embassy, foot patrols in Belfast, or British troops marching on Port Stanley. Now, the sustained televisual bombardment from the Gulf, with Challenger tanks and multi-launch rocket systems in the desert, may have finally banished the old sitcom image from the popular mind.

As the Gulf war proved, even to lingering doubters in the City, the British Army has become a very professional organization when it counts. (This was perhaps reinforced by the knowledge that a drawn-out war in the Gulf would have caused a recession far worse than anything seen since the 1930s.) But whether this professionalism has created its own problems, such as careerism, bureaucracy and the occasionally stifling effect of a systems approach to everything, is a separate issue. The most difficult part of an army to assess in the field has always been its commanders and staff. But the very latest generation of computer war games for testing commanders and staff in large-scale manoeuvres have become extremely realistic – certainly enough to put the decision-making of participants under relentless pressure.

There were very few criticisms of formation commanders or staffwork in the Gulf. But the whole infantry-dominated promotion structure is still not above reproach. Most commanders are very intelligent and capable but there are still said to be a few brigadiers and even major generals 'who are astonishingly thick'. It is a question which affects morale as well as efficiency.

At any rate, modern generals probably suffer much less from the disabilities analysed by Norman Dixon, the author of *On the Psychology of Military Incompetence*, who argues that mental blockages stemming from an emotionally crippled childhood were responsible for the worst of our military disasters. His theory about the link between the potty-training of embryo generals and their subsequent performance on the battlefield is compulsive reading.[2]

It seemed ironic, to say the least, that the breakthrough in computer simulation – 'attrition-smart' and representing the clash of Western army group against Eastern operational manoeuvre group – should have finally occurred in 1989, coinciding with the apparent fulfilment of the prophecy made by a number of writers that the 'heavy army' would become as unusable as the nuclear deterrent. Yet within a year the same computer war games, rapidly adapted to the Gulf region, proved invaluable. But, whatever the military sophistication displayed in 1991, the possibility remains that the true test of an army will be a corporal's war.

Whether the British Army is 'cost-effective' or not is a far more vexed and emotive question, particularly when the Government is desperate to save money for other purposes. Senior officers are deeply concerned that, at least until after an election, the military side of the equation has been dropped from consideration. 'The whole thing is Treasury-driven,' said one. 'How on earth', demanded one brigadier, 'do you define productivity in a non-commercial organization?'

The privatization of a very wide range of support services – contracting out the Royal Military College of Science at Shrivenham, driver training, mess catering and service, and the security of some barracks – has provoked very uneven feelings. Some cases have worked very well: Shrivenham is an outstanding example, and the change in mess catering has been widely welcomed. Others have led to a disastrous decline in quality and reliability, mainly because of the high turnover of staff in the contracting companies, which constitutes a security risk in itself. The feeling amongst most officers and NCOs is that each case should be examined on its merits, and thought through with regard to the state of local employment. Many camps in the south-east of England lost their establishment of Army clerical staff in civilianization programmes, then, because they could not find replacements at the salaries offered, the remaining military staff had to shoulder the extra load. The impression of a blanket policy to save money at any price has caused great resentment.

Military bureaucracy can also be as self-generating as civil bureaucracy. General Westmoreland's headquarters in the Vietnam War demonstrated the full counter-productive potential of an overcentralized systems approach to warfare. Body counts, kill ratios and efficiency reports often degenerated into a surreal black comedy. The compulsive accumulation of data proved how well statistics could keep decision-makers out of touch with reality. To imply that the Ministry of Defence and major headquarters are following this route would be a gross exaggeration. Nonetheless, there seems to be a recognizable tendency, largely caused by the sales-chart view of the world imposed upon the Army, to slip into some of the same mistakes. Martin van Creveld wrote of Westmoreland's administration: 'The men who designed the system and tried to run it were as bright a group of managers as has been produced by the defense establishment of any country at any time, yet their attempts to achieve cost-effectiveness led to one of the least cost-effective wars known to history.'[3]

The Army has been suffering badly from the imbalance between resources and commitments, and the constant pressure of economy measures. Generals say somewhat defensively that commitments are closely and continually re-examined, but the field army does not find that this reduces the burden. 'The politicians have got to decide what their commitments are,' said the same brigadier. 'Only when resources and commitments are balanced will you get any confidence.' The trouble is that generals cannot be seen to criticize the Government. 'The word "over-committed"', said a senior staff officer at United Kingdom Land Forces, 'has been deleted from the official vocabulary. It's a bit Orwellian, really.' Field Marshal Sir Nigel Bagnall wrote in the wake of the Gulf war of the Options for Change document that 'it is difficult to to see how any claim to have identified "an adequate defence capability" can be justified. The proposed force levels have not been designed to meet defined commitments but to reflect an imposed financial ceiling.'[4] His article was pinned on a lot of noticeboards.

Most officers date this state of affairs back to the doctrine of 'no spare capacity' implicit in the Heseltine reforms. This is a perfectly good management strategy for an organization which does not have to face emergencies and which can always recruit and retain the necessary personnel. But as soon as an organization falls below strength, especially when morale is a vital factor in its success, and then has to take on extra duties and cancel leave, a crisis in confidence and a vicious circle of overwork develop as more and more people decide to leave. This is precisely what has happened to the Army over the last few years. The doctrine's most serious flaw was to have left no margin for increased security on barracks, a potentially enormous drain on manpower resources. Whether the pay increases from April 1991 and the military success of the Gulf war have been enough to halt the spiral is most uncertain: the Ministry of Defence can only bank on the recession and unemployment outside in civilian life.

'The best measure of overstretch', said a senior civil servant with the Ministry of Defence, 'is that we've got fewer people than even the Treasury admits we need, and that's pretty alarming.' He went on to describe the development of a 'catastrophe model', in which the work pressure increases to a critical threshold where 'a comparatively minor event can trigger a catastrophe' – in this case, an exodus of unmanageable proportions. But to lay the responsibility entirely on the generals would be unfair. As one senior general said in a slightly different context, 'It's a fact of Whitehall life that you only face up to a problem when you really have to.' And, for the moment at least, the Government is keen to postpone a Defence Review until after the next general election.

Overwork is not the only problem. Even with the pay rise announced during the Gulf war, military salaries at the bottom end have slipped behind over the last five years, and the relentless salami-slicing of budgets has inevitably had a serious effect on morale. The drive for savings has often led to illogical decisions which take no account of the long-term effect. 'Spend-to-save measures' – projects requiring capital expenditure which could save considerable sums in the longer term – are all too often vetoed in a system geared to annual budgets. 'False economy rules our system,' said one commanding officer. 'The Army is doomed to spend nineteen pounds trying to save nineteen pence.' But once again the Army is also the victim of its own tribal nature. Imbued with loyalty to existing structures, and hobbled by the power of its internal lobby system, it has only been able to spread the load of suffering by cutting a little everywhere.

The Army, with a certain amount of justification, has an instinctive distrust of performance indicators fixed by civil servants. But an RAF group captain pointed out the weakness of the armed forces at the moment: while there are still areas of waste, and he felt there were, the Government can use them as an excuse for continuing down the same road. Michael Heseltine, for example, set a target of reducing the number of major office buildings in London from eleven to five, but little progress has been made in over five years. And a senior officer who had looked at the wide variety of appointments in the Ministry of Defence remarked, 'We think we've been cut and cut and cut, yet it's astonishing how many non-jobs there still are.'

The subject of whether the Army, or in this case the Government, were 'good employers' came up during the Lords debate on the Defence Estimates in July 1989. Field Marshal Lord Bramall, using lightly veiled speech, articulated the Army's sense of betrayal. He found it sad that 'this Government, having done so much for defence – and for whom incidentally the Services themselves had done so much – seem to have lost interest in taking on the Treasury to achieve the comparatively small amount of resources that are needed to establish their position as good employers'. He referred to 'the considerable number of service people who find themselves homeless at the end of their service and yet cannot be accommodated by local authorities. Such homelessness at the end of faithful service is hardly an incentive to stay in the Service in the first place.'[5] Field Marshal Lord Carver helped press home the attack, but there was little reaction.

Some generals, however, were not entirely blameless during the development of the manpower crisis. They underestimated the strength of feeling in the Army, and pushed through measures – such as the reform of allowances in October 1988 – which provoked considerable ill-feeling. Even as late as the winter of 1988–9 some members of the hierarchy tended to take up the 'ostrich position' on the subject of manning. A staff officer, accompanying me to one interview, observed with an apologetic grin that it might be better if I avoided the subject, because it upset senior officers. His warning proved accurate. The character in question came out with an angry and preposterous rationalization of why it was a very good thing to have a high turnover of soldiers. Another staff officer in another theatre reaffirmed the point. 'Generals,' he said, 'always take these things very personally.'

The emotional confusion must have something to do with

476

a sense of frustration at their powerlessness. 'Generals', said a former Army wife actively involved in welfare, 'cannot admit that problems are caused by [a lack of] money because they cannot be seen criticizing the Treasury and therefore the Government.'

Fortunately, some generals on the other side of the 'brass curtain' do not lose touch, and do not attempt to suppress problems. They are a great deal more impressive as a result. Not surprisingly, they also prove to be the most widely respected in other ways. But there is only so much that even the best of generals can do, short of the 'kamikaze option' of resigning.

On the general's fifth and last point – that 'the Army must be responsible in national affairs' – the tradition of steering clear of politics still holds good on this side of the Channel. If the British soldier ever harboured the illusion that military solutions can be imposed on national problems, the Falklands conflict, where the enemy was a country ruined by its armed forces, should certainly have helped to cure it.

The British Army is usually relaxed and good-humoured about the domestic political scene but, if it feels threatened or besieged, illiberal views of varying degrees can emerge. This should hardly be a surprise. A somewhat Manichaean view of the world is bound to exist in any organization which is authoritarian and a relatively enclosed order, particularly in one which has suffered considerable casualties at the hands of terrorists.

Much of the British public, press and politicians still fail to appreciate that the Army is at war with the IRA, while they are not. In 1988, when the row escalated over the SAS killing of 'the Gib three', a feeling of angry disbelief developed. 'Don't they realize we've got a war on our hands?' was a widespread reaction in regimental circles. The difference of perspective between the two sides of the khaki curtain was in a way more important than the exact circumstances of the shooting.

Following the Gibraltar shootings, when unexpected disasters, riots and bomb attacks mounted during 'Mad March', a brigade commander in Northern Ireland recalled that 'We felt, "Come on, God, who's writing the script?"' By the end of the summer, with the assassination of servicemen on the Continent, the 'fun-run bomb' at Lisburn, and the Ballygawley coach bomb bringing the death toll to twenty-seven soldiers in just over six months, the IRA appeared close to provoking the British Army into a dirty war. Field Marshal Lord Bramall warned that 'A majority of officers are now strongly backing a shoot-to-kill policy as the principal method of defeating the IRA.'[6] The temptation was an appalling irony, when one remembered where that particular road had led to in Argentina's 'dirty war'. Mercifully, the strength of feeling passed, and political primacy was never in question. The Army soldiered on.

On issues other than security, the Army's attitudes to democratic politics are on the whole close to those of the public at large. The military view of politicians is often sceptical and sometimes unprintable – the Army has a quick nose for self-interest – yet there is very little of that gut contempt for civil institutions inherent in so many of its counterparts around the world. Some senior officers, in expansive mood, love to philosophize on the subject of the Army and politics. 'Democracy is like a raft,' said a brigadier in the Rhine Army. 'It never sinks but you've always got your feet wet.'

Sir Frank Cooper, a former Permanent Secretary at the Ministry of Defence, once said that personal chemistry was all-important in Mrs Thatcher's choice of people. It is just as important in the reaction of Army officers, the only difference being that their chemistry has a wider range. To assume that the Army automatically reacts according to a minister's political views is to grasp the stick very firmly by the wrong end. Much, of course, depends on whether the politician in question likes them or not, and whether he has 'sound views' on defence. But character and trustworthiness play a considerable part.

Manny Shinwell, Labour's War Minister in 1947, was regarded with great affection, particularly by the Guards because he vigorously supported their return to full ceremonial dress.[7] Army officers also took to Denis Healey with his war record and his air of an amiable bully (his opposition to the Gulf war rather surprised them), yet the greatest contrast was between two Conservative Secretaries of State: John Nott was trusted and liked, but Michael Heseltine was not.

A Secretary of State has to ride roughshod over departmental and individual sensibilities in order to make an impression on an organization like the Ministry of Defence, but Heseltine's manner could only intensify resistance to his ideas. A suspicion rapidly arose that Heseltine was interested only in vaunting Heseltinian solutions, not in the long-term effect of his measures, however sound they they might be. Some of the opposition to him could be seen as reactionary. The way he wore a Guards tie for the television cameras irritated the Household Division, who had not accepted him as a National Service officer when he went through Brigade Squad. (A senior Foot Guard officer is said to have remarked: 'I'm afraid we must consider Michael Heseltine one of our failures. We didn't manage to make either an officer or a gentleman out of him.') But even the most unsnobbish younger officers from regiments and corps with utterly different outlooks and a genuine desire for an organizational shake-up seem to have taken against him after a single address at Staff College or some other defence gathering.

After the upheavals of Nott's departure and Heseltine's resignation over Westland, George Younger's time as Secretary of State was bound to be 'a non-period', as one of his former colleagues remarked; Mrs Thatcher did not want any more upsets. At first, the Services felt at ease with Younger. Then, especially at lower levels, disquiet increased at the steady-as-you-go approach while the manning crisis escalated. Many feared that nothing was being done on purpose. His successor, Tom King, was generally respected for his calmness and firmness in Northern Ireland – a notable achievement in a post known as a graveyard for political careers. His strongly supportive, if not combative, stance during the Gulf war was also appreciated, but the Government's continuing reluctance to address itself to problems decisively has caused very deep unease.

The Army's feelings about Mrs Thatcher herself were much more complex. During her time as prime minister, respect for her leadership, determination and courage was quite genuine, as befitted such an incarnation of military virtues. Despite a reference to 'Her with the handbag', a general made it clear that she was about the only politician the Army trusted not to shilly-shally should the nightmare uncertainties of transition to war ever come about. They were not disappointed during the Gulf crisis.

At an all-arms establishment, a major in the Royal Corps of Transport made a mildly disrespectful remark about 'Maggie' during lunch. His brigadier replied, with a reproof that was both measured and dry, 'Mrs Thatcher, it must be remembered, is a *very* good commanding officer.' Yet Thatcherism, the Army discovered to its dismay in the late 1980s, was utterly inimical to traditional values of public service and collective ideals.

Officers were dismayed at the changes in society, and the effect that they had on the Army itself. 'In the old days you were part of a team,' said a major in the Parachute Regiment. 'Now, everyone's out for themselves.' Middle-aged officers particularly disapproved of the climate of *enrichissez-vous*, and the pervasive attitude that cutting corners, even outright dishonesty, was acceptable, if not admirable, provided that you could get away with it.

In the national change of mood surrounding Mrs Thatcher's departure, officers prayed that the 'one nation' spirit of public service, which had provided the Army's ethical basis, stood a chance of reviving before it was too late.

CHAPTER 30

Setting Suns and the Future

The Army has not been lucky. In the course of only a few years, changes in society, attitudes, population and, above all, international politics have coincided with devastating effect. And the Gulf war, far from staving off the Army's dilemmas, in fact accelerated the need for radical restructuring. Some of the problems had been building up for some time, but the end of the 1980s will be remembered as the beginning of the end of the Army in its traditional form.

In July 1990, Tom King made his statement to the House of Commons on the discussion document, Options for Change. He gave the main outlines of the plan: a basic Nato contribution of two divisions with one armoured division stationed in Germany, the other 'a strategic reserve division' based in Britain; a sufficient infantry reserve to 'sustain our contribution in support of the police in Northern Ireland'; and 'forces for our dependent territories and other overseas responsibilities'. These outlines were clarified in his statement of 4 June 1991, which announced a reduction of the Army to 116,000 officers and soldiers and a probable loss of 19 infantry battalions out of 55.

The strategic reserve division, said a senior officer from the Defence Staff, 'makes total politico-military sense'. In the general terms in which it has been outlined, it would consist of three brigades: the 3rd Commando Brigade, the 5th Airborne Brigade and an armoured infantry brigade. It is really more of a strategic reserve than a division since all of the three component elements are unlikely to be deployed together as a single formation. Meanwhile, the 24th Air Mobile Brigade will form part of a Nato multi-national air mobile division.

The most complicated part of the whole scheme was bound to be the reduction of the Rhine Army. At the moment our Nato forces consist of three armoured divisions in Germany and an infantry division in Britain. The Ministry of Defence wanted to keep two armoured divisions, one in Germany and one at home. But even a single armoured brigade for the new Strategic Reserve Division will cause massive problems. Salisbury Plain is not really big enough to train a single armoured regiment realistically, and the quarterers at HQ UK Land Forces usually have only two spare barracks. In the end, the Nato plan announced at the end of May 1991 allowed for only a single armoured division. The main consolation for the British Army is the rapid reaction corps which will be under British command and contain a substantial British contribution. This would provide an action-packed image for recruiting purposes, and offset the impression of the British Army making its final withdrawal.

The last time Britain's commitments were studied was in 1981, with John Nott's Defence Review. Then the main objective was relatively modest: to clarify priorities between the Rhine Army and the eastern Atlantic. Nott even asked whether the Brussels Treaty was inviolable. After discussions with Sir Frank Cooper, the Permanent Under Secretary and Sir Michael Quinlan, Nott came to the conclusion that 'although by subterfuge we could reduce our numbers, the Nato commitment had to be maintained'.[1] The only major change was that the 2nd Infantry Division, while remaining part of the Rhine Army, was pulled back to the United Kingdom.

Nott asked the service chiefs for initial suggestions on restructuring. His note, 'a beautifully drafted memo by Quinlan' – then second Permanent Under Secretary – became known as the Bermudagram, because Nott and Quinlan were at a conference there at the time. 'But the service chiefs came back with another salami-slice approach – all the easy things. The whole thing was a farce. Nobody had begun to think what they were supposed to do.'[2] The question was then rephrased: 'If you were building your Service from the bottom up with your current commitments, how would you do it?' The Army was able to evade such radical thinking on the grounds that its prime commitment to Nato's central region was sacrosanct, and the infantry had to be kept up to strength for Northern Ireland. Attention focused on the Navy instead. The battle of their eastern Atlantic commitment turned into the war for Nott's head, which the Navy won in the end when the Falklands conflict allowed the original question to lapse. The key decisions were then evaded because the Government fixed a 3 per cent per annum increase in real terms to the defence budget.

Little more happened over the next ten years, until the certainties of the Cold War suddenly crumbled. The British Government, more than its allies in Nato, wanted to wait until things became much clearer before coming to any decisions. But some six months before the signature of the Conventional Forces in Europe treaty in Paris in September 1990, a senior team in the Ministry of Defence went through a speedy exercise which more or less amounted to a pro forma Defence Review. One important advantage which Heseltine's restructuring of the Ministry of Defence had achieved since Nott's unhappy experience was to improve the decision-making process in such instances. The possibility of fractiousness was greatly reduced by keeping decisions in the Centre and sidelining the individual service staffs.

The first stage for the senior Options for Change team in the spring of 1990 was to attempt to define commitments by consultation within Whitehall. Whatever government is in power, the subject of overseas commitments always seems to provoke a triangular argument. The Foreign Office usually wants every commitment to be maintained, the Ministry of Defence agrees on condition that it has the money to do the job properly, while the Treasury wants a drastic pruning. Even if intervention abroad is very seldom

483

required, the outstanding guarantees to Commonwealth and friendly governments represent potentially huge commitments. Only when this insurance risk assessment had been made could the question of restructuring the single Services be addressed.

In the Army, all eyes, or certainly thoughts, were fixed on the Defence Staff during the spring and early summer of 1990. The first stage of Options for Change was carried out in great secrecy, which was probably just as well since there is no rumour factory like the armed forces. But the veto imposed on consultations with anyone outside a very narrow range, including the Army's General Staff, created great resentment in the Directorate of Military Operations and the Directorate of Army Staff Duties. The apparent machinations of a small group of faceless bureaucrats behind firmly closed doors created a great deal of suspicion and distrust. But there should have been no lack of confidence in the abilities or attitudes of those saddled with the task. The team contained officers from the field army with distinguished careers, and the senior civil servants involved were liked and respected by those who had worked with them.

The architect of the whole exercise was Richard Mottram, the Deputy Under Secretary of State (Policy), who reported to the Vice Chief of the Defence Staff, General Sir Richard Vincent. Below Mottram was Roger Jackling, the Assistant Under Secretary (Programmes), working in tandem with the Assistant Chief of the Defence Staff (Programmes), Major General Thomas Boyd-Carpenter, a former Scots Guards officer described by one officer who had worked with him as 'very, very clever'. Boyd-Carpenter, a brother of Sarah Hogg, the head of John Major's think tank, had been chief of staff of the Rhine Army. The Director of Army Plans was a very impressive sapper, Brigadier Peter Sheppard. Under him was another Scots Guards officer, Colonel John Kiszely. Kiszely had won an MC in the battle for Tumbledown, commanded a battalion of his regiment in

484

Germany, instructed at Staff College and then done the Higher Command and Staff Course. Their team consisted of 'the brightest and best' Staff College graduates from a range of arms.

Officers who had a good idea of what was at stake still did not envy them their job, whatever its fascination and importance. One described it as 'trying to build a castle on sand'. Another compared it to 'three-dimensional chess', and a third likened it to 'magnetic spillikins' because the Army's fibrous structure made it impossible to separate issues and address them individually.

By the time Tom King made his 'Options for Change' statement to the House of Commons on 25 July 1990, speculation of dramatic cuts had reached such fearful levels in the Army that when the outlines were finally revealed they provoked a partial sigh of relief. But, as one senior officer pointed out, the proposals were deliberately vague. 'People took things at face value, yet there's a lot of room for manoeuvre.'

Eight days after the Secretary of State's speech, Iraq invaded Kuwait, and within a couple of months British armoured formations were deploying in the Gulf. Not surprisingly, attention turned away from the programmes directorates, and reverted only when the Gulf war was over.

Once the team studying the implications of the conflict had delivered its report to put into the decision-making mix, the next stage was a revised outline and detailed decisions on the degree and nature of cuts to be made. But it was not the job of the Directorate of Army Plans to say which regiments or battalions were to be cut. That decision was left to the Army itself. For example, the Director of Infantry at Warminster, after 'consultations' with the colonel commandants and colonels of the different infantry divisions (which were bound to consist more of listening to passionate lobbying), then had to make a recommendation to the Executive Committe of the Army Board. This set off an even more energetic round of lobbying. Similarly, the

Director of the Royal Armoured Corps had consultations with all the regimental colonels of cavalry regiments and the three colonels commandant of the Royal Tank Regiment, before passing on his recommendations to the Army Board. Of course, the Army Board's decision, to judge by past occasions, will not be the end of the matter. As one senior officer commented, 'this time it will be a "Save the Argylls" many times over'.

However genuine the original intentions of Options for Change to create 'smaller forces, better equipped, properly trained and housed, and well motivated', one cannot help suspecting that the whole exercise rapidly turned into a compromise solution on the basis of dwindling resources. And Government concern, and therefore money, may well move even further away from defence if the economy does not improve.

Army officers fear that the 'pot of gold' for restructuring forces effectively is shrinking rapidly before their eyes for other reasons as well. The Gulf war (like the Falklands conflict in its time) complicated budgetary forecasting, but the unforeseen factor which threw the long-term costings into turmoil was the Government's assumption that inflation would drop in 1990 and thereafter. The recession coupled with high interest rates has created other complications – for example, contracting companies deliver ahead of schedule and demand payment more rapidly.

After the Gulf war, with its decisive demonstration of air power, the Royal Air Force is in a very strong position to demand a bigger slice of a diminished defence budget. The problem is further exacerbated by the almost exponential growth in the cost of sophisticated equipment, and the success of smart weaponry in the Gulf is bound to increase the pressure on budgets. Already in the later 1980s Nato planners were making black jokes to the effect that, by the next century, the arms budget of most countries will run to one super-fighter, and no more. The battle between the Services will also have a knock-on effect, exacerbating the Army's own inter-arm rivalry. The armoured corps needs new tanks, the gunners after the Gulf will want more multi-launch rocket systems, and so on.

There is a broad measure of agreement on certain changes: it is hard to find anyone who does not think air mobility is vital for the future, but hopes for a significant shift in this direction depend on buying an expensive attack helicopter such as the Apache, and the implications of defining Army Air Corps and RAF responsibilities go well beyond budgetary concerns. In the early days of air mobility, the Army accepted the poisoned apple of budgetary advantage when the RAF took over the transport helicopters. And there is no doubt that the RAF wants to take over the Army Air Corps, and especially the responsibility for attack helicopters, which it covets for itself. But, this time, things should be organized rather more rationally.

One of the most welcome appointments for many years was the surprise promotion of General Sir Richard Vincent from Vice Chief to Chief of the Defence Staff in the spring of 1991. One senior Army officer from the Centre, expressing his pleasure and relief, said: 'It's not just the Army that thinks that. My peers in the other two Services were delighted.'

In an ironic way, Vincent's appointment was 'one in the eye for the Army', which, with 'its promotion on command bullshit', had decided that he could not be Chief of the General Staff because he had not commanded a field army division. As a result nobody imagined that he would turn out to be the first Vice Chief of the Defence Staff to be chosen for the top job, instead of one of the three service Chiefs of Staff.

Vincent is thought to be 'utterly purple' and capable of taking tough decisions on behalf of all three Services. His leadership at this time is especially fortunate for the Army, which has always found it very difficult to step outside itself for a fresh look at things. The Army remains an organization of emotional loyalty to the past, and therefore

487

has trouble in defining its true priorities for the future. It is significant, although not necessarily wrong, that in its military doctrine the British Army should be the only one to give the 'moral component' equal prominence with the 'physical component' in the production of 'fighting power'.[3]

Over the last couple of years, the regimental system, the pride of both the infantry and cavalry, has been at more immediate risk from the strain of manpower imbalances than from social anachronism, although the two are partially linked. Damage to the system increases with every month the Army's structural problems and future uncertainties are left unresolved. In crude terms, three 'patchwork' battalions cannot match two fully manned.

Even to accept that a given number of regiments will disappear is not enough. If the Army is to continue to improve standards of professionalism, it must force the infantry to drop its 'Jack of all trades' credo. The constant re-roling of battalions is unnecessarily expensive, wasting both time and expertise. The armoured corps was forced to specialize either in tanks or in armoured reconnaissance; now the infantry must finally follow the same route. Their battalions should be trained for Northern Ireland and one other role, whether armoured infantry, air-transportable, airborne or overseas. In the case of armoured infantry in Germany or overseas battalions, they would be rotated and could establish a system of partial trickle-posting as some infantry divisions have done in Germany. Specialization would reduce the upheavals for families, by enabling them to settle round a regimental home base in Britain, as the Parachute Regiment has round Aldershot. Infantry officers, on the other hand, argue that to introduce specialization with a reduced number of battalions would drastically reduce flexibility. They ask whether an armoured infantry battalion could be thrown straight into a Falklands-style campaign, an example which also highlights the contrast between their most detested form of soldiering and their ideal.

Defence planners have an understandable desire 'to budget against the unpredictable'. Rather like putting away winter clothes on the first day of spring, to stand down on a particular front seems to risk provoking the bloody-mindedness of fate. Yet to maintain armed forces at an unnecessarily high level is a more than burdensome insurance policy, as Britain has found for a considerable time. 'The divergence', wrote Professor Paul Kennedy, 'between Britain's shrunken economic state and its overextended strategical posture is probably more extensive than that affecting any of the larger powers except Russia itself.'[4] Britain's per capita expenditure on defence has for some time been a third higher than that of West Germany.[5]

This state of affairs will almost certainly change soon, partly through a natural reduction of commitments, both within Nato and for the rest of the world, and even more from a lack of funds. Yet the British Army's enthusiasm to take on responsibility for the ACE rapid-reaction force remains unconcealed. Several generals who have spent more of their careers in post-colonial soldiering than in Nato still believe passionately in the British Army's aptitude for the role of an international police force. The British soldier has often displayed a knack for defusing potentially explosive situations, whether in Cyprus or Namibia, and Britain, they feel, still has an important part to play far beyond Europe.

Britain still has some well-placed and unsinkable aircraft carriers around the world – the Falklands for Antarctica and Cape Horn, the sovereign bases in Cyprus for the eastern Mediterranean, and Ascension Island for Africa – to say nothing of friendly successor states elsewhere prepared to offer facilities in an emergency. Yet the French retain an even more extensive neo-colonial network, particularly in Africa and the Pacific. After the Allied success in the Gulf, the combination of a British strategic reserve and the French army's Force d'Intervention might provide the basis of that increasingly advocated institution, a distinctly European rapid-response force for out-of-area deployment.

This possibility suddenly regained momentum after the Gulf war, with the idea for a real European force, based on the Western European Union initially, and then coming under the direction of the European Community in Brussels. The Americans are not enthusiastic since they prefer to keep control of developments through Nato; and to Thatcherite anti-Europeans in this country the proposal is anathema. Senior British Army officers, on the other hand, feel that if the idea is to become flesh then Britain should be in there from the beginning. They regard it as virtually inevitable in the long run. 'The EC cannot possibly aspire to statehood', said one, 'if it does not take on a responsibility for defence.'

The prospect certainly does not dismay them. They get on well with US Army officers, but the relationship is no more special than it is with Bundeswehr officers, for whom most British officers express a good deal more respect. There is also a new regard for the French army after its division's dash across southern Iraq. Many feel that within ten or twenty years some sort of Euroforce, either under or outside a Nato umbrella, will be the natural order of the day.

Whatever national grouping is decided upon, there can be no doubt that joint rather than unilateral action is clearly safer in a world of complex interests. Multinational forces, as the Gulf crisis showed, are less likely to become rashly embroiled, and they carry far more moral conviction, and clout, within the United Nations.

The prospect of fighting in the Gulf may have brought thousands of applicants to recruiting offices, but in January 1991, the month the war started, only fifteen infantry and two armoured corps reservists rejoined. The shortage of men had already forced some units to close down a company or squadron. So, with or without the collapse of the Warsaw Pact, regiments would have had to have been cut to ensure that the rest were up to strength.

The whole question of cutting regiments is especially painful and emotionally charged for the Army. In Washington DC, the United States Marine Corps is known as 'the third rail of American politics – touch it and you're dead'. The British Army no longer has anything with quite the same degree of lobby muscle (the Household Division's representation in Parliament and the Cabinet has declined significantly over the last twenty years), but regiments with strong local associations and powerful contacts are still capable of mounting enough of a rearguard action to worry government business managers.

Unfortunately, clear criteria for reprieving or sentencing regiments were hard to establish. To maintain the old system of historical precedence in which the junior regiment or battalion in a particular group was cut regardless of its quality would be inexcusable. Yet nobody dares openly advocate the quasi-Darwinian alternative of deciding according to recruitment.

The final recommendations on the fate of regiments put to the Secretary of State by the Army Board are unlikely to prove entirely final. There was always a risk that the decision on the fate of individual units might not be seen as entirely objective. Many, for example, felt that with the Green Jackets forming part of the second worst recruited division in the infantry, yet with representatives in the most senior positions on the Army Board, the Defence Staff should have chosen the regiments to stay or go; but this would have been regarded as an outrage to the military constitution.

A disbandment and amalgamation of regiments is not the only result of a change of era. A large number of officers and NCOs were saying well before Options for Change that this was 'the end of the Army as we've known it'. A captain in the Parachute Regiment announced rather brutally in January 1989: 'I see the Army in more or less the same position as the coal industry in the seventies.'

491

One subaltern just out of Sandhurst, whose commission in the family regiment represented the achievement of a childhood dream, found that virtually everything for which he had joined was rapidly disappearing. 'It's very, very sad,' he kept saying, shaking his head in dejected disbelief. Many, on the other hand, hope that the force for change will be a healthy one: that it will give the British Army the opportunity to decide which of its traditions are relevant to the future, and which have outlived their usefulness. Others fear that, with the British Army facing the prospect of a final withdrawal to an increasingly home-bound, semi-suburban, bar-charted future, it will provide the final triumph of the bureaucrat over the fighting man. But the pessimists have been proved wrong before. And, if the idea of rapid reaction force enables the British Army to grab back its traditional talisman of foreign adventure, perhaps they will be proved wrong again.

Much, however, depends on the adventure. Will it be swift and glorious? Or will it take place on the far side of a line of Dannert wire holding back refugees who have vainly attempted to flee famine and civil war? Soldiers are not heartless in the face of misery. The way they spontaneously gave their own rations to starving Iraqis in the spring of 1991 was proof of that. But compassion, when overwhelmed by numbers, is exhausted more rapidly than courage.

APPENDICES

Glossary of Army Jargon and Slang

Aggro   rioting (Northern Ireland).

Alternative Command Structure   Wives' Club.

Agile and Bolton Wanderers   Argyll and Sutherland Highlanders.

Angle-irons   members of the Royal Anglian Regiment.

Anglo-Banglo   Anglo-German, particularly joint social events (BAOR).

Argie, an   a short tour in the Falklands (Joint Service Falklands).

Bean cans   140,000-litre water tanks.

Beasties   fitness freaks.

Beasting   similar to *Rifting*, intensive drill on the square or PT, either to lick recruits into shape or as a form of collective punishment.

Berm   not a trench, but a moat dug by the Iraqis, usually in series, to delay an advance. Can be filled with burning oil.

Birthday Cake   the Victoria Memorial in front of Buckingham Palace (Guards).

Bimble   to hike for pleasure or go on an outing in the Falklands. Also noun, a *bimble*.

Bimble-box   a packed lunch in the Falklands.

Bin-liners   Arab women dressed from head to toe in black (Gulf).

Birdshit   nickname for Paras. Also known as *Danglers*.

Bird table   tabletop map spread for both operations and war games in HQs, Staff College and battle group trainers, etc.

Black arts   specialist skills at senior level such as intelligence or advanced data processing which exclude the non-specialist and lead to appointments 'tied' to a particular capbadge.

Black bag job first staff appointment of a Staff College graduate.

Black bag process allocation of staff appointments by Staff College and the Military Secretary's Branch at the end of the course.

Black economy driver, batman or mess steward working for a general kept on strength of parent regiment.

Black mafia Royal Green Jackets, a combined reference to their black buttons and crossbelts and to the way so many of their officers have occupied the top jobs in the Army.

Blade runner an ambitious Sandhurst cadet determined to win the Sword of Honour.

Blanket Cove to visit Blanket Cove when in the Falklands is to spend the afternoon on one's bed instead of going out to look at wildlife.

Blanket pressing sleep achieved during the day. See also *Egyptian PT*.

Blanket stacker member of the Royal Army Ordnance Corps.

Bleeps members of the Royal Signals. See also *Scaley-backs*.

Bloody assizes commanding officer's orders, when punishment is meted out.

Blue-on-blue accidental clash between one's own forces, which are marked in blue on maps. See also *friendly fire*.

Bluey Forces' aerogramme letter.

Bog-standard common or garden.

Booties commandos.

Boys, the SAS, or *the Sass*. Not to be confused with *the Boyos*: the IRA.

Brown jobs Army personnel as opposed to Navy or RAF.

Buckshee free, spare, especially in buckshee kit unclaimed or 'liberated' (from Indian Army).

Budgies Fusiliers because of their feather hackle worn with their beret capbadge.

Bullet doctor Ammunition technician. Also called a *missile mechanic*.

Bund sand rampart.

Bundook weapon, from Arabic.

Bundu the wilderness, implying alone and a long way from anywhere. See also *ulu*.

Bust to demote, to strip of rank, e.g. so-and-so was busted from corporal.

Buy your ticket to purchase your discharge from the Army.

Buzzard Airways helicopter operations in and out of Bessbrook Mill (Northern Ireland).

Cadbury's Snack rhyming slang for a Wrac (Women's Royal Army Corps).

Capbadge a regiment, arm or corps with a separate capbadge and therefore identity.

Capbadge job an example of favouritism, preference or advancement based on regimental or Corps patronage.

Centre, the the Defence Staff, which is tri-service, or *'purple'*. It includes the Defence Intelligence Staff and the Office of Management and Budget, but excludes the Defence Scientific Staff and the Procurement Executive.

Chain of contempt in inverse direction to the chain of command, the invective increases against the Ministry of Defence the further away from it you get.

Chameleon effect the gradual, mainly subconscious change in an officer's appearance, accent, behaviour or opinions to achieve group acceptance and accord with military orthodoxy.

Chuff-chart a chart for ticking off 'days to do' before returning home or discharge from the Army.

Chummery a triangular defensive for a troop of tanks in the desert inside ramparts of bulldozed sand.

Chunkies Members of the Royal Pioneer Corps.

Coloured berets   a collective term for Paras and Royal Marine Commandos.

Come-as-you-are war   an unexpected out-of-area operation like the Falklands conflict or the Gulf war in which training and equipment designed for Central Region has to be used virtually without adaptation.

Corky   Corps Commander (BAOR).

Corner shop, the   the guardroom.

Crab, a   a member of the RAF.

Crabair   RAF Transport Command (as in 'Time to spare? Travel CRABAIR!')

DS Pink or **DS solution**   the Pink is the Directing Staff's approved manner of carrying out a manoeuvre or operation. Traditionally, the Directing Staff solution to a posed problem was always printed on pink paper.

Dagger   as in so-and-so has 'got his dagger' means that he has received the shoulder badge (worn on opposite shoulder to Para wings) which denotes service in a Marine Commando. (Can also mean an officer, Army Command and Staff Course-qualified, who had attended Div I or Div II at the Royal Military College of Science, because his name appears in the Army List with *psc* and a dagger against it.)

Death Star MPA   The Mount Pleasant Airfield accommodation complex on the Falklands. The most hated posting in the British Army.

Desertspeak   Gulf jargon.

Dhobi   laundry or washing. A relic from Indian Army days.

Dhobi dust   washing powder.

Dicker   an IRA informant watching movements of British troops for a vulnerable moment and a spotter for a control-wire or remote-control explosion. Also used as a verb.

Diffy   deficient, lacking kit, as in 'I've gone diffy on my KFS' (I've lost my knife, fork and spoon).

Dinky Toys   armoured reconnaissance vehicles.

Dixie-bashing washing dishes. See also *Pan-diving*.

Dockyard confetti nuts and bolts used as shrapnel in home-made terrorist bombs.

Donkey-walloper a cavalry officer.

Dotted lines an 'organigram' or 'wiring diagram' showing chains of command has unbroken lines to denote reporting to a direct superior, and dotted lines to other departments or directorates to denote liaison or consultation.

Double-hatted to wear two hats is to perform two jobs or two roles. For example, the British four-star general who commands the Rhine Army also commands the Northern Army Group NORTHAG.

Driving a desk a regimental officer posted to the staff. (RAF equivalent is flying a desk and Navy is sailing a desk.)

Dropshort a member of the Royal Artillery.

Egyptian PT sleep achieved during the day.

Fastball a demand for a rapid response to incidents in Northern Ireland.

Fat Albert C 130 Hercules. Otherwise called a Herc.

FILF Falklands Island Laundry Facility.

FINCO Field Intelligence NCO. Both an agent-handler and one who operates undercover himself.

Fish-and-chip outfit a worthless regiment with low standards.

Fispeak Joint Service Falkland Islands jargon.

Flash to bang time Officially, the time taken for the arrival of the sound after the flash of a nuclear explosion for calculating the distance of its 'ground zero', but used more often in a ribald context.

Flatties, the or, more fully, 'our flat-buttoned friends'. Gunner officers who have not been in the Royal Horse Artillery. A reference to the fact that they do not have the ball buttons of the RHA on their mess kit waistcoat, a privilege which former members of the RHA are allowed to keep for good (RHA officers).

Flexiplan no plan whatsoever. To play it off the cuff.

Fragging the practice of disenchanted soldiers in Vietnam of chucking a fragmentation grenade into the quarters of a particularly hated officer or senior NCO.

Franging a pastime, occasionally a competitive sport, in which each contestant rolls a condom down over the top half of his head as far as the upper lip and then inflates it with his nostrils. The largest inflation wins, but explosions can be painful. Especially popular in Germany, where exotic varieties including Walt Disney characters are on sale. The word comes from the Australian slang for a condom – a franger.

Friendly fire fire from own forces or allies. Casualties from friendly fire are the result of a *Blue-on-blue*.

Fudge factor the margin by which statistics are manipulated.

Gat gun, especially rifle when used in a personal sense.

Gimpy a GPMG – general-purpose machine-gun.

Gobbling rods cutlery.

Going to the stars an officer on his way to getting a general's stars.

Gold-plating the setting of unnecessarily sophisticated requirements for equipment.

Gold tops phosphorus grenades. Used to devastating effect in Falklands conflict.

Gonk to sleep.

Gopping disgusting.

Gozome 'Goes home', as in *gozome party* or farewell bash, or *gozome chart* to tick off days to do, or *great big gozome bird*, the RAF Transport Tri-Star.

Gravel belly marksman obsessed with competition shooting who loves spending his time flat on his stomach on the range.

Greasy a last fried breakfast before departure.

Green army the uniformed army in Northern Ireland

as opposed to those operating in plain clothes and the euphemistically entitled 'other agencies'.

Grunt   an infantryman (from US Army).

HDC   honest decent crime as opposed to terrorist offences.

Hackpack   group of journalists accompanied by a conducting press officer.

Half colonel   a lieutenant colonel as opposed to a full colonel.

Happy snaps   photographs soldiers take of each other on exercise or operation, especially in Northern Ireland. Also to send home, they take snaps of 'traced terrorists' they pass in the street but are not allowed to arrest. Sometimes called *warries*, but depends on unit.

Hanging the brick   a custom in most of the Household Division sergeants' messes when a brick is mock-ceremonially suspended to open celebrations and signify that the bar will stay open so long as the brick remains aloft.

Hard target, to   to run from cover to cover on patrol in Northern Ireland to avoid presenting an easy target. Sense extended to keeping a low profile in general and avoiding senior officers.

Hatman   a Guards officer, from their practice of wearing hats in the mess, particularly at breakfast.

Haver-bag   haversack ration, or packed lunch, also known as a *horror-bag*.

Heavy army   the armoured division of the Central Region as opposed to the *light army* of out-of-area operations personified by Paras and Gurkhas. Also applies to generals who have 'gone the heavy army route'.

Helmets   Royal Military Police personnel doing a conventional uniformed job as opposed to plain-clothes work such as SIB and close protection (RMP).

Her with the handbag   Mrs Thatcher (senior officers).

Hooker   member of a helicopter support unit attaching underslung loads.

Hotbedding   when soldiers on a continual round of duties or patrol in outposts like in Northern Ireland have to use the same bed on rotation.

Injection, to get a 7.62 to be hit by a bullet.

Inner ring-knockers Graduates of School of Advanced Military Studies at Fort Leavenworth. Another name for *Jedi knights*. Ring-knockers are West Point graduates who draw attention to their fraternity rings by knocking them on the table to make a point (US).

Irishman's pay rise when a pay rise is accompanied by increased food and accommodation charges which wipe out any advantage.

Isodets Isolated detachments. Small groups far from any parent unit such as close-protection teams in embassies.

Jedi knights Graduates of the senior division Command and General Staff College at Fort Leavenworth and apostles of Operational Art sent out two by two to carry the message to US headquarters everywhere (US and British initiates).

Jimmy's St James's Palace (Guards).

Jock private soldier in a Scottish infantry regiment, the Scottish version of a *Tom*.

Jointery the application of a Joint-Service approach.

Jungly warlike, off the beaten track.

Lemoned, to be to be given a job. Alternatively, to be *Jiffed*.

Lift to arrest a suspect in Northern Ireland.

Liney a Royal Signals linesman.

Live freight a soldier's perception of his treatment on RAF transport.

Loamshires a notional infantry regiment. *Blankshires* are used as an alternative.

Loggies members of logistic corps such as RCT, RAOC and REME.

Loose change shrapnel.

Lose your name to have your name taken from subsequent punishment.

Lumpies women soldiers, because of 'gender-specific' bulges under their uniforms.

Lurker a coward or skiver.

Lurk a hide or concealed sub-unit base in countryside such as south Armagh.

Maggot or **green maggot** an army issue sleeping-bag.

Mark I Boot on your feet with no other equipment or skill.

Mark I Eyeball naked eyesight, especially at night without night vision equipment.

Master-race RAF and Royal Navy terms for those officers who go to the top via the operational route, as opposed to technical or support elements within the Service.

Mattress-back man who spends his spare time in bed.

Meals Rejected by Ethiopians unenjoyable US Army rations known as MREs, or Meals Ready to Eat (Gulf).

Micks Irish Guards.

Milling a military version of boxing which owes little to Queensberry rules. Used in training for the Paras to develop aggressive instincts.

Minjo Man In Need of Jolly Outing (Joint Service Falklands).

Mod plod Ministry of Defence constabulary.

Mojo member of civil labour organization in BAOR.

Monkey a Military Policeman.

Music sheet a joint-operational air-tasking order (Gulf).

Nerdles a game for two teams which can only be compared to a coconut shy with defenders. Each side fixes a shovel or spade in the ground with a small tin of compo ration balanced on the handle. Turns are taken to hurl a heavy hammer at the opposing team's tin. The defenders must try to catch the tin before it touches the ground. Four points are awarded for a tin hitting the ground and one point for hitting the shovel handle. First team to reach twenty-one points wins.

Neutralize   to kill. See also *Slot*, *Take-out* and *Zap*.

Next fixture   the Third World War.

Niff-naff   petty paperwork and administrative queries.

Number three haircut   standard haircut, as opposed to a Number one, which is shearing 'right down to the wood'.

Nut strangler   member of Royal Electrical and Mechanical Engineers.

Off-net, to be   to miss the point.

Open prison   Mount Pleasant Airfield complex on the Falkland Islands.

Opsi   Operator in Special Intelligence. Intelligence Corps specialist trade.

Orbat   Order of Battle. Used to mean the official organization of the field army.

Out-of-area   outside the Nato area of responsibilities, in land terms therefore outside the sweep from Northern Norway to Eastern Turkey. The Falklands, Belize and Hong Kong are clear examples of out-of-area bases. Out-of-area operations tend to be of the *come-as-you-are-war* variety. In the Ministry of Defence OOA comes under the heading of ROW – Rest of World.

Own goal   terrorist bomb which kills only the terrorists making it or trying to plant it.

Packing   transferring good team sports players within trickle-posted organizations such as gunners, sappers or signals to help their regiments win army championships.

Pads   The unit's families or married soldiers, as opposed to *singlies*. Shortened form of 'married pad'.

Paddybashing   service in Northern Ireland.

Paddy factor   the allowance to be made for gross human error in any plan.

Pan-diving   cookhouse fatigue washing dixies.

Peanut time or **zoo time**   an official visit, when officers and soldiers have to put on a demonstration of 'normal working'.

Pinball wizards   light air defence groups armed with Javelin anti-aircraft missiles (Gulf from US Army).

Pink list   the annual list of majors designated for promotion to lieutenant colonel.

Pit   bed.

Plank   a gunner, from First World War when the bodies of fallen guncrew were put under the wheels to stop the gun from sinking into the mud.

Player   identified IRA terrorist. *Top player*: leading terrorist.

Plays for the other side   homosexual.

Pongoes   soldiers (Royal Navy and RAF). See also *Brown jobs*.

Ponti   a Person of No Tactical Importance.

Purple   joint-service as opposed to single-service. It is a reference to the colour which supposedly would be achieved by mixing the colour of all three uniforms. A *purple* appointment is usually one which rotates in turn between the three services, as opposed to one which is *tied* to a single service. See also *jointery*.

Pushing out the zeds   sleeping.

Retread   disobliging term sometimes used by subalterns from Sandhurst about older late-entry commission officers (not quartermasters) who have come up through the ranks.

Reverse press-gang   civilian employers going round pubs in areas of acute labour shortage in southern England and offering to buy soldiers out of the Army.

Ring-knockers   West Point graduates, from the practice of knocking their fraternity ring on the table to draw attention to it when making a point (US).

Rodney   a Royal Navy officer.

Rotor head   helicopter pilot.

Rupert   disobliging term for a young officer, used mainly by sergeants. Implies that he is something of a prat. Some sergeants' messes have an informal Rupert of the Year Award.

Sangar originally a defensive position made up with rocks when digging in was difficult. Now refers to almost any small constructed defensive position. In Northern Ireland can be mounted on observation towers and on top of buildings like the Divis flats. A *super-sangar* is constructed with a sandwich of concrete and steel.

Scaley-backs members of the Royal Corps of Signals. From the supposed effects of carrying radio sets on back.

Schoolies Officers of the Royal Army Educational Corps.

Schrank syndrome the compulsion of soldiers and their wives to buy a large and expensive cabinet and wall unit system (*ein Schrank*) on credit to replace the Army-issue furniture in their quarter.

Scoff to eat, but also used for a senior NCO 'sorting somebody out'.

Scran: food. Also *Scoff*.

Scratch pad all the unprintable information on an officer's personal manning card on the computer of the Military Secretary's Department.

Scratcher a soldier's bed.

Shining parades period between tea and bedtime or at weekends when recruits work on their kit under the supervision of NCOs.

Shiny arse a clerk.

Shreddies underpants.

Shufti, to take a to take a look.

Singlies unmarried soldiers.

Skipping Chickens the 14th/20th Hussars, a reference to their capbadge which consists of a rather undernourished eagle with its legs out sideways.

Skive shirk, escape, or an excuse from duty. A great skive can also mean a good swan.

Sky-pilot   the padre, also known as 'the only man on a one day week'.

Slab   a case of beer.

Slop jockey   cook, usually from the Army Catering Corps.

Slot, to   to slot someone, is to shoot him (particularly Northern Ireland).

Smoker   a communal drinking session, held round a fire when in the field, but otherwise in the squadron or company bar.

Sneaky-beaky   covert intelligence operations.

Son of Black Hole   The shortage of middle-ranking officers caused by the second wave of captains and senior subalterns leaving from around 1988.

Stabs   members of the Territorial Army.

Stag   period on sentry duty.

Stonk   mortar bombardment, originally from artillery term 'Standard Regimental Concentration'.

Tab   army version of *yomping*.

Take out   to kill.

Talk and chalk   classroom instruction with blackboard.

Talking baggage   the observer in a helicopter (Army Air Corps).

Tango Sierra   Tough shit, as in tough luck.

Teeny Weeny Airways (TWA)   the Army Air Corps.

Throw your teddy in the corner   leave the Army in a huff (officer, mainly Royal Artillery).

Ticks   'getting the right ticks' for an officer means clocking up the right appointments and experience so that you are perfectly qualified when your name comes up for consideration by the Promotion Board.

Timmy   The RAF Transport Tri-Star from Brize Norton via Ascension to Mount Pleasant Airfield (Joint Service Falklands).

Tom   an English infantryman, an abbreviation of Tommy Atkins. Thomas Atkins was a soldier in the 33rd Foot (later the Duke of Wellington's Regiment) who had served under the Iron Duke. Wellington later chose his name to represent the average British soldier.

Towel head   An Arab.

Track-bashing   routine maintenance work on armoured vehicles.

Tread head   an armoured corps soldier.

Trick-cyclist   Psychiatrist.

Trickle-post   the system of moving personnel individually between regiments, as opposed to a block move. All arms except infantry, cavalry and gunners trickle-post as standard practice.

Trogs   members of the Royal Corps of Transport.

Tube, the   the communication zone (the Com Z) to BAOR which stretches from Ostend and Antwerp right up to the rear combat zone around Dortmund.

Ulu, the   open country miles from anywhere, from Malay for up-river.

Viet Taff   Originally the Free Wales Army in the late 1960s, still applied to other militant Welsh Nationalists.

Wagon   Warrior infantry fighting vehicle.

Walk-on-water-merchant   a technocratic high-flyer on the weapons staff.

War Box, the   an archaic term, still used in the Guards at least, for the Ministry of Defence.

Wedgehead   a Royal Engineer.

Whenwees   officers and their wives who continually reminisce about previous postings, beginning conversations: 'When we were in Cyprus . . .'

Whitehall warrior   a staff officer working in the Ministry of Defence.

Wilco   enthusiastic, as in 'a very Wilco sort of chap'. From radio abbreviation of 'will comply'.

Wokka   a Chinook helicopter.

Woodentop   Guardsman or Guards officer.

Woofers Worcestershire and Sherwood Foresters Regiment.

Wormspeak Arabic calligraphy.

Wriggly tin corrugated iron – CGI in sapper-speak.

Yellow handbag a pack of Herford Bier, much carried by soldiers in BAOR.

Yomp a heavy slog with kit across country (Marine). See *Tab*.

Zulu warrior A soldier 'doing the Zulu warrior' in drunken exuberance strips off to music while other soldiers chant and egg him on. Some help to keep him cool by pouring beer over him.

Notes

Foreword
1   *Independent*, 5 March 1991.

PART ONE: GOING FOR A SOLDIER

1   Joining Up
1   Text provided by MoD.
2   Text provided by MoD.
3   Statistics provided by MoD.
4   Statistics provided by MoD.

3   The Life of a Single Soldier
1   *Daily Telegraph*, 30 July 1988.
2   *Journal of the Royal Artillery*, September 1989, p. 102.
3   Conversation with Sir James Spooner, 26 August 1988.

4   Of Stripes and Crowns and the Sergeants' Mess
1   In answer of the question: 'Do you like your normal work in your present posting?' 10 per cent of privates 'like it very much', 18 per cent of corporals, 24 per cent of sergeants and 36.5 per cent of warrant officers. Statistics provided by MoD.

5   Married to the Army
1   *Neighbours* (The Federation of Army Wives magazine), December 1988.
2   *British Medical Journal*, 10 September 1988.
3   Taking the years 1983 to 1987 inclusive, the divorce figures for officers and soldiers combined averaged

14.94 per thousand couples (statistics provided by PS4 (A) Ministry of Defence) against an average of 12.62 for England and Wales over the same five-year period. Total UK figures are not available (*Social Trends*, 19, 1989, p. 43).

At 31 December 1988 no less than 72 per cent of the officer corps were married (11,183 out of a total of 15,494), as opposed to only 51.5 per cent of soldiers and NCOs (65,336 out of 126,832). ('Analysis of Changes in Marital Status', statistics provided by the MoD.)

PART TWO: TO BE AN OFFICER

6 Officer Selection
1 For a comparison of commissioning practices with other armies, see Richard Simpkin, *Race to the Swift*, 1985, pp. 247–9.

7 Sandhurst
1 *Encounter*, June 1959, quoted in Dixon, *On the Psychology of Military Incompetence*, 1976, p. 234.
2 Simpkin, op. cit. p. 248.

8 Young Officers
1 Text provided by MoD.
2 See Peter Hennessy, *Whitehall*, 1988, p. 623.

9 Onwards and Upwards
1 *British Army Review*, No. 91, April 1989, p. 94.
2 The 1987 officer attitude study was based on those attending the junior division of the Staff College. Aged about twenty-eight, just under half of those on the course had degrees. By this stage of their career two-thirds were married, and most of them had already invested in a house, although only a fifth were able to live in them. While the 'variety' and 'challenge' of Army life still appealed to them, over half did not

think the Army was fun any more, 64.2 per cent no longer considered the Army style of life attractive, and over half were dissatisfied with the resources and opportunities for training. These proportions will almost certainly have risen considerably in the meantime. Another widespread complaint was the lack of career advice they received. Nearly half thought their job satisfaction would deteriorate if they stayed in the Army. Those results which concerned married life were even more striking: 62 per cent of the married officers were dissatisfied with the long-term career prospects for their wife. 'March in/March out' procedures with married quarters were particularly disliked, but the sorest subject of all was the lack of assistance with house purchase: 94.6 per cent were dissatisfied. Statistics provided by MoD.

10 Staff College

1 *Design for Military Operations – The British Military Doctrine*, 1989.

11 Commanding the Regiment

1 Evelyn Waugh, *Officers and Gentlemen*, Penguin, 1964, p. 46.
2 Lt Col M. J. Nicholson, *Royal Artillery Journal*, spring 1989.
3 Text provided by MoD.

12 Going for the Stars

1 Introduction by General Sir John Chapple, *Design for Military Operations*, p. vii.
2 See Roger Graef, *Talking Blues*, 1989, pp. 57 and 80.
3 The point has been made that, contrary to received opinion, British military disasters could seldom be attributed to stupidity, but to the psychological blocks of the generals concerned. Dixon, op. cit. Chapters 14 and 18.

4   Major I. Foxley, Royal Signals, 'The Politics of Gener-
     alship', the *British Army Review*, No. 91, April 1989.
5   See John Keegan's article 'Too many Generals?', *Daily
     Telegraph*, 16 May 1989.

PART THREE: COMMAND AND CONTROL

13 Whitehall Warriors: The Ministry of Defence

1   Michael Carver, **Out of Step**, 1989, p. 451.
2   Conversation with the author, 18 July 1989.
3   Conversation with the author, 19 July 1989.
4   Michael Heseltine's sketch is reproduced in his book
     Where There's a Will, 1987, p. 29.
5   Hennessy, *Whitehall*, p. 416.
6   General Sir Peter Inge, *RUSI Journal*, winter 1989.
7   Hennessy, op. cit., p. 414.
8   Carter, op. cit., p. 436.

14 BAOR: 'The Next Fixture' Indefinitely Postponed

1   See National Audit Office Report, April 1989, p. 14.
2   Spencer Report, p. 3.
3   WO 1 Clive Elliott, RA, *Soldier*, 24 July, 1989.

15 'The Next Fixture' Transferred to the Gulf

1   See Mark Urban, *Independent on Sunday*, 3 March
     1991.
2   *Sun*, 6 February 1991.
3   BBC Nine O'Clock News, 23 February 1991.
4   *Daily Record*, 11 February 1991.
5   *Independent*, 20 February 1991.
6   BBC Nine O'Clock News, 23 February 1991.
7   *Soldier*, 1 April 1991.
8   *Soldier*, 18 March 1991.
9   ibid.
10   *Soldier*, 1 April 1991.
11   *Sunday Telegraph*, 3 March 1991.
12   Tom King to House of Commons Defence Select
     Committee on 6 March 1991.

13 *Evening Standard*, 28 February 1991.
14 *Sunday Mirror*, 3 March 1991.
15 *Soldier*, 18 March 1991.

16 Home and Away: United Kingdom Land Forces and Out-of-Area Operations
1   *Design for Military Operations*, p. 12.
2   NAO Report, para 5.14, p. 26.

17 Northern Ireland: The Long War
1   *Independent*, 13 April 1989.
2   *Independent*, 7 March 1991.
3   For a further account of undercover work in Northern Ireland, see Mark Urban, *Independent*, 16 January 1990.
4   Chris Ryder, *The RUC: A Force Under Fire*, 1989, p. 20.
5   *Independent*, 3 August 1988.
6   See Ryder, op. cit., pp. 140–2.
7   ibid., p. 157.
8   *Independent*, 22 October 1988. This rate compares with an average for the province of 1 per 7,518 adult males and a world-wide army average in 1988 of around 1 per 5,100. 'Thirty-one of the 33 police suicides since 1978' were carried out with the constable's personal firearm.
9   *Soldier*, 27 November 1989.
10 *Independent*, 31 August 1989.
11 *Independent*, 7 February 1991.
12 See *British Medical Journal*, 14 January 1989. His account was confirmed in a letter from the regimental medical officer in a subsequent issue.
13 See Graef, op. cit., Chapter 2.
14 *Soldier*, 23 January 1989.

18 Overseas: Sunshine and Other Postings.
1   Denis Healey, *The Time of My Life*, 1989, p. 278.
2   *Soldier*, 24 July 1989 and 7 August 1989.

3   *Sunday Telegraph Magazine*, 23 April 1989.

PART FOUR: ARMS AND THE CORPS

19   The Regiment's Tribal System
1   Interview in *Soldier*, 11 December 1989.
2   Carver, op. cit., p. 396.
3   Interview in *Soldier*, 11 December 1989.

20   Queen and Army
1   Text provided by MoD. See also the *British Military Doctrine*, p. 12.
2   In addition to all the regiments of the Household Division, the Queen is colonel-in-chief of SCOTS DG, 16/5L, RTR, RE, RWF, QLR, A and SH, RGJ, RAOC, RMP, and Captain-General of the RA.
The Queen Mother: QDG, QOH, 9/12L, KINGS, R ANGLIAN, LI, BW, RAMC and Commandant-in-Chief WRAC.
The Duke of Edinburgh: QRIH, DERR, QO HLDRS, REME, INT CORPS and Captain-General of the Royal Marines.
The Prince of Wales: 5 INNIS DG, CHESHIRE, RRW, GORDONS, PARA, 2GR.
The Princess of Wales: 13/18H, R HAMPS.
The Duke of York: STAFFORDS.
The Princess Royal: 14/20H, R SIGNALS, RS, WFR.
Princess Margaret: 15/19H, RHF, QARANC and Deputy Colonel-in-Chief R ANGLIAN.
Princess Alice, Duchess of Gloucester: RH, KOSB, RCT and Deputy Colonel-in-Chief R ANGLIAN.
The Duke of Gloucester: GLOSTERS, RPC.
The Duchess of Gloucester: R IRISH, RAEC.
The Duke of Kent: RRF, D and D.
The Duchess of Kent: 4/7DG, PWO, ACC.
Princess Alexandra: 17/21L, KINGS OWN BORDER.
3   *Soldier*, 23 February 1987.

21 Infantry at the Double

1   *Daily Record*, 11 February 1991.

22 Land/Air Battles: The Royal Armoured Corps and the Army Air Corps

1   Conversation with the author, 18 July 1989.
2   See also Michael Willcocks, *The British Army and the Operational Level of War*, 1987. Brigadier Willcocks, a gunner, was Assistant Chief of Staff on the operations side at HQ UK Land Forces when this was published. Wing Commander G. A. Woolley in the spring 1989 number of the *RUSI Journal* gave a justification of continuing RAF control of support helicopters. For the last four years, helicopters and air mobility have formed the most intense subject of debate in military journals.
3   *RUSI Journal*, autumn 1988, p. 67.
4   General Sir Peter Inge, *RUSI Journal*, winter 1989.

23 Rival Siblings and Adam's Rib: Gunners, Sappers and Signallers

1   Lt Col M. J. Nicholson, *RA Journal*, spring 1989, p. 48.

24 Special Intelligence and Special Forces

1   Martin Van Creveld, *Command in War*, 1985, p. 247.

25 The Three Qs and Other Corps

1   Brigadier A. H. Fernyhough, *A Short History of the RAOC*, 1965.
2   NAO Report, April 1989, para 5.22.
3   Allen Nacheman of Agence France Presse, 16 March 1991.
4   NAO Report, para 3.18.

27 'Female Manpower'

1   Terry, op. cit., p. 217.
2   Geraghty, op. cit., p. 181.

3 *The Times*, 26 September 1989.
4 *Daily Telegraph*, 3 January 1990.
5 *Independent*, 7 March 1991.
6 *Guardian*, 14 October 1982.
7 Terry, op. cit., p. 226.
8 *Sunday Telegraph*, 3 August 1988.
9 *Soldier*, 20 February 1989.

28 The Other Army: The Territorials
1 *Soldier*, 10 July 1989.
2 *Soldier*, 10 July 1989.
3 NAO, para 5.13, p. 26.
4 *Design for Military Operations – The British Military Doctrine*, p. 16.

PART FIVE: CONCLUSION

29 Public Perception and Political Masters
1 Alexis de Tocqueville, *Democracy in America*, translation 1900, p. 280.
2 Dixon, op. cit., p. 204.
3 Van Creveld, op. cit., p. 260.
4 *Independent*, 5 March 1991.
5 Quoted in *Soldier*, 7 August 1989.
6 *Time*, 5 September 1988.
7 General Sir Michael Gow, *Trooping the Colour*, 1988, p. 74.

30 Setting Suns and the Future
1 Conversation with the author, 18 July 1989.
2 idem.
3 *Design for Military Operations*, p. 32.
4 Paul Kennedy, *The Rise and Fall of the Great Powers*, 1988, p. 482.
5 G. M. Dillon, *Defence Policy Making*, 1988, p. 5.

Bibliography

Arthur, Max, *Above All Courage* (1985)

Blaxland, Gregory, *The Regiments Depart* (1971)

Broadbent, Sir Ewen, *The Military and Government: From Macmillan to Heseltine* (1987)

Carver, Michael, *Out of Step* (1989)

Dixon, Norman, *The Psychology of Military Incompetence* (1976)

Dillon, G. M. (ed), *Defence Policy Making: A Comparative Analysis* (Leicester, 1988)

Edmunds, Martin (ed), *The Defence Equation: British Military Systems, Policy Planning and Performance* (1987)

Enloe, Cynthia, *Does Khaki Become You? The Militarization of Women's Lives* (1988)

Esmonds, Martin, *Armed Services and Society* (Leicester, 1988)

Fernyhough, Brigadier A. H., *A Short History of the Royal Army Ordnance Corps* (1965)

Geraghty, Tony, *The Bullet-Catchers* (1988)

Gow, General Sir Michael, *Trooping the Colour* (1988)

Graef, Roger, *Talking Blues* (1989)

Healey, Denis, *The Time of My Life* (1989)

Hennessy, Peter, *Whitehall* (1989)

Heseltine, Michael, *Where There's a Will* (1987)

Hockey, John, *Squaddies: Portrait of a Subculture* (Exeter, 1986)

Holmes, Richard, *Firing Line* (1985)

Jolly, Ruth, *Military Man, Family Man, Crown Property?* (1987)

Kennedy, Paul, *The Rise and Fall of the Great Powers* (1988)

Kitson, Frank, *Low Intensity Operations* (1972)
   Directing Operations (1989)

Morton, Peter, *Emergency Tour* (1989)

Parker, Tony, *Soldier, Soldier* (1987)

Rose, Clive, *Campaigns against Western Defence* (1988)

Ryder, Chris, *The RUC – A Force Under Fire* (1989)

Simpkin, Richard, *Race to the Swift* (1985)

Strawson, John, *Gentlemen in Khaki* (1989)

Terry, Roy, *Women in Khaki* (1988)

Van Creveld, Martin, *Command in War* (Harvard, 1985)

(All editions London unless otherwise marked)

Index

For detailed listings of regiments, organization, ranks and terms see pp xxvi–xli. For individual regiments see under Regiments *and* Corps *in this index; for brigades and divisions see* Formations.

522